pages. V&A Museum. Paperbound
845779 NELLIE MELBA: A Contempor
notes and discography by William R. Moran. A rich and multi-faceted
portrait of one of opera's greatest divas, including reviews, interviews, memoirs of her greatest performances, Melba's own advice
on the art of singing, and more. No jacket. 22 illus. 491 pages. Greenwood. Pub. at $45.00   **$5.95**

Nellie Melba.

Melba as Juliette. Miniature portrait painted in 1902 by Ada Whiting of 198 Collins St., Melbourne, from photo by E. W. Histed, Baker St., London, ca. 1890.

NELLIE MELBA
A CONTEMPORARY REVIEW

Compiled with notes and
discography by
William R. Moran

Contributions to the Study of Music and Dance, Number 5

Opera Biographies

GREENWOOD PRESS
Westport, Connecticut • London, England

Library of Congress Cataloging in Publication Data

Main entry under title:

Nellie Melba, a contemporary review.

  (Contributions to the study of music and dance,
ISSN 0193-9041 ; no. 5) (Opera biographies)
  Bibliography: p.
  Discography: p.
  Includes index.
  1. Melba, Nellie, Dame, 1861-1931. 2. Singers—
Australia—Biography. I. Moran, William R. II. Title.
III. Series. IV. Series: Opera biographies (Westport,
Conn.)
ML420.M35N44 1985   782.1'092'4 [B]   83-26444
ISBN 0-313-23893-6 (lib. bdg.)

Library of Congress Catalog Card Number: 83-26444
ISBN: 0-313-23893-6
ISSN: 0193-9041

First published in 1985

Greenwood Press
A division of Congressional Information Service, Inc.
88 Post Road West, Westport, Connecticut 06881

Printed in the United States of America

10 9 8 7 6 5 4 3 2 1

To the Memory of E.V.M.

CONTENTS

ILLUSTRATIONS

ACKNOWLEDGMENTS

This book has been a long time in the making. Although I never heard Melba in person, I became fascinated by the Melba voice on recordings at an early age and determined to gather a complete collection of the singer's records. With the records came the desire to know more about their maker, to the extent that every scrap of printed matter about the singer has been eagerly sought. In compiling this work, the problem has been mainly one of selection and elimination. While working in Australia in 1959-1960, I met and talked with many people who had known Melba, and I remember with special pleasure the kindness of the singer's son and daughter-in-law, Mr. and Mrs. George Armstrong, who invited me to spend a day at Coombe Cottage, Melba's home at Coldstream, near Lilydale, Victoria.

Many people have provided help and encouragement: the late doctors Barbara and Findlay Mackenzie shared much of the fruits of the research for their book *Singers of Australia*. Peter Burgis, sound archivist of the National Library of Australia, Canberra, was most helpful in searching newspaper files for Melba articles, and it was he who introduced me to Catherine Santamaria, director of Australian studies at the National Library, who was especially helpful in tracking down Australian authors and publishers for permission to use quotations from copyrighted works. Mrs. Richard Bonelli kindly made available for reproduction the programs from some of Melba's early concerts (when she appeared as Mrs. Armstrong); the singer Carlo Modini, who is also listed on these programs, was Mrs. Bonelli's father. Jack Alpen Richards of Hawthorne, Victoria, was most helpful. Thanks are also extended to Gordon C. Simpson of Johannesburg.

In the preparation of the Discography which is found at the end of this volume, the cooperation of officials of the Gramophone Company, Ltd.

(now EMI Ltd.) is acknowledged. Data on the Victor recordings was compiled from the files of RCA Records (successors to the Victor Talking Machine Company) and it is a pleasure to acknowledge the assistance of the author's colleague, Ted Fagan, indefatigable researcher and coauthor of *The Encyclopedic Discography of Victor Recordings*. Thanks are extended to Desmond Shawe-Taylor, Howard C. Sanner, Jr., and the late Stephen B. Fassett for their help in critically reviewing the Discography and notes. The author, however, must assume full responsibility for the ofttimes controversial assignment of playing speeds for the individual recordings. Andrew Farkas, director of libraries for the University of North Florida, deserves special thanks for reviewing the entire manuscript.

COPYRIGHT ACKNOWLEDGMENTS

The author and publisher are grateful for permission to reprint from the following works.

William Armstrong, *The Romantic World of Music*. Copyright 1922 by E. P. Dutton & Co., New York.

Ailwyn Best, "How I Sang with Melba," *Opera* 21, no. 12 (December 1970).

John Brownlee, "Melba and I," *Saturday Review* (December 25, 1954). © 1954 Saturday Review Magazine Co. Reprinted by permission.

Maie Casey, *Melba Revisited*. Melbourne, privately printed, 1975. Reprinted by permission of her family and estate trustees.

J. Daniel Chamier, *Percy Pitt of Covent Garden and the B.B.C.* London: Edward Arnold (Publishers) Ltd., 1938.

John F. Cone, *Oscar Hammerstein's Manhattan Opera Company*. Norman: University of Oklahoma Press, 1966.

Olin Downes, "Melba's Art of Song," *New York Times*, March 1, 1931.

John Alan Haughton, "Melba's Career a Long Succession of Triumphs," *Musical America* (March 1931). All Rights Reserved.

John Hetherington, *Melba: A Biography*. Melbourne: F. W. Cheshire, 1967; and New York: Farrar, Straus & Giroux, 1968.

Herman Klein, *Great Woman Singers of My Time*. London: George Routledge & Sons, Ltd., 1931. Reprinted by permission of Routledge & Kegan Paul Ltd.

John Lemmoné, "The Merry Pipes of Pan," *The Herald* (Melbourne), June 7, 1924. Reprinted by permission of The Herald and Weekly Times Ltd.

Barbara Mackenzie and Findlay Mackenzie, *Singers of Australia, from Melba to Sutherland*. Melbourne: Lansdowne Press Pty. Ltd., 1967. Reprinted by permission of Peter Burgis, Literary Executor for the authors.

Claude McKay, *This Is the Life: An Autobiography of a Newspaperman*. Sydney: Angus & Robertson Publishers, 1961.

Nellie Melba, "Melba on Life after Death: 'The True, Eternal Me,' " *The Herald* (Melbourne), October 26, 1925. Reprinted by permission of The Herald and Weekly Times Ltd.

Nellie Melba, "Melba's Indictment: 'Our Musical Reputation a Myth,' " *The Herald* (Melbourne), September 5, 1927. Reprinted by permission of The Herald and Weekly Times Ltd.

Nellie Melba, "Where Is Happiness? Is It in Fame?" *the Herald* (Melbourne), September 10, 1927. Reprinted by permission of The Herald and Weekly Times Ltd.

"Melba's Voice" (Editorial), *New York Times*, March 1, 1931.

William R. Moran, "Melba's Farewell Concert," *High Fidelity* (July 1977). All Rights Reserved.

Ivor Newton, *At the Piano—Ivor Newton: The World of an Accompanist*. London: Hamish Hamilton, 1966.

Beverley Nichols, *All I Could Never Be*. London: Jonathan Cape, 1949.

Beverley Nichols, *Are They the Same at Home?; Being a Series of Boquets Diffidently Distributed by Beverley Nichols*. London: Jonathan Cape, 1927.

Beverley Nichols, *25; Being a Young Man's Candid Recollections of His Elders and Betters*. London: Jonathan Cape, 1926.

Cyril Pearl, *Wild Men of Sydney*. London: W. H. Allen & Co., 1958.

Andrew Porter, "Melba: The London Recordings," *High Fidelity* (January 1978). All Rights Reserved.

Francis Robinson, Introduction to *Melba: A Biography*, by John Hetherington. New York: Farrar, Straus & Giroux, 1968.

Landon Ronald, *Myself and Others: Written Lest I Forget*. London: Samson Low, Marston & Co., Ltd., 1931. Reprinted by permission of Purnell Books.

Donna Shinn Russell, "The Meanest Woman in the World," *Opera News* 28, no. 9 (January 11, 1964). Reprinted courtesy of *Opera News*.

Frank A. Russell, "Melba Looks Back on Magic Moments in Her Great Career," *The Herald* (Melbourne), October 13, 1924. Reprinted by permission of The Herald and Weekly Times Ltd.

Henry Russell, *The Passing Show*. London: Thornton Butterworth, 1926. Reprinted by permission of Methuen London Ltd.

Percy A. Scholes, *The Mirror of Music, 1844-1944*. Kent: Novello & Co., and London: Oxford University Press, 1947.

Bernard Shaw, *Music in London, 1890-94*. London: Constable and Co.,

1932. Reprinted by permission of The Society of Authors on behalf of the Bernard Shaw Estate.

John Thompson, *On the Lips of Living Men*. Melbourne: Lansdowne Press, 1962.

Charles L. Wagner, *Seeing Stars*. New York: G. P. Putnam's Sons, 1940. Copyright 1940 by Charles L. Wagner. Reprinted by permission of The Putnam Publishing Group.

Unless otherwise noted, the photographs are from the author's collection.

Every reasonable effort has been made to trace the owners of copyright materials used in this book, but in some instances this has proven impossible. The publisher will be glad to receive information leading to more complete acknowledgments in subsequent printings of this book and in the meantime extends its apologies for any omissions.

INTRODUCTION

Mrs. Charles Nesbitt Frederick Armstrong, *née* Helen Porter Mitchell and known to the world as Nellie Melba, never suffered from obscurity during a life span of nearly seventy years, nor has she been forgotten since her death on February 23, 1931. As one of the greatest (many would say *the* greatest) female singers of her time, she had a personality that automatically created news no matter where she was or what the circumstance. She has been the subject of two full-length biographies published during her lifetime, and three since her death. Throughout her meteoric career, she generated not only reams of copy in the musical press of the world, but a like amount in other fields. Melba was news during the latter part of the Victorian era, throughout the Edwardian period, and well into the post-World War I epoch, with the locale beginning in Europe, eventually shifting in part to the United States and toward the end to her native Australia. As her orbit touched the famous in many countries and in many walks of life, usually generating incidents of the kind that are remembered, stories about Melba are found in hundreds of memoirs, be they recollections of opera singers, impresarios, politicians, dilettantes, or businessmen. It seems that her clipping file will never be closed: Each year sees new additions, but it is getting to the point where stories are being repeated, each time with new variations and added embroidery, so that anecdotes that were initially apocryphal are now stated as fact. The overall picture is becoming blurred. Perhaps it is time to reexamine some of the source material and see where at least some of the yarns came from.

First, let's examine the biographies. The first, titled simply *Melba: A Biography*, was written by Agnes G. Murphy and published in London and New York in 1909. The most important fact about this book, and one that seems to have escaped most writers who quote extensively from it, is that its author was Melba's personal secretary. Thus the biography is not only what is usually termed "authorized," it is a ghost-written autobiography, with the ghost masquerading as an independent author. Melba apparently used this method of getting into print those facts about her personal and professional life that she felt needed to be told, but of course told as she wished them to be presented. Viewed from this aspect, it is revealing for what was included and likewise what was omitted from the "official" story. While her birthdate is never given, the exact date of her marriage to Charles Armstrong is stated, as well as the date of her departure for Europe, "accompanied by her husband and baby," which puts to rest the stories that Melba left her husband in Queensland to pursue her career. Not only is credit given by name to her piano and organ teachers, there are numerous references to her Melbourne singing teacher, Pietro Cecchi, about whom I will have more to say in the following pages. C. Haddon Chambers, who was so influential in helping Melba with her dramatic development, is shown in a photograph but never mentioned in the text, presumably because it would have been difficult to bring up his name without involving that of Louis Philippe, Duc d'Orléans, and thus reopening a painful chapter of her life that the singer felt already had had too much public scrutiny. Agnes Murphy's book is factual and informative, if incomplete because of omissions and its publication date, when read with an understanding of its source.

The second book about the singer, published during her lifetime, was her official autobiography, *Melodies and Memories*, first serialized in *Liberty Magazine* in the United States in 1925, reaching publication in book form in London in the same year and in New York in 1926. A translation in Swedish made its appearance in Stockholm in 1927, and the U.S. edition has been reprinted twice (in 1970 and 1971) in the United States, with a completely reset edition with added notes issued in Melbourne and London in 1980. It was ghost-written, with no textual credit, by the young Beverley Nichols and is discussed in some detail in a later part of this work. Suffice it to say here that the book has the objectivity one would expect, and while very readable, it is certainly not an example of a definitive biography.

The year after Melba's death, Percy Colson produced his *Melba: An Unconventional Biography*. Colson was a sometime critic, sometime newspaper man who loitered around the fringes of the world of music and wrote gossipy articles and books dropping the names of the famous in an authoritative fashion. The book was obviously rushed into print, with little more research than that required for a hasty regurgitation of previously published material, liberally sprinkled with a few new but mostly old anecdotes. He devotes a couple of pages to Melba's affair with the Duc d'Orléans before breezing off to other matters. The book is particularly deficient in recounting the singer's activities in Australia and, in sum, makes little in the way of contribution to its subject.

Red Plush and Black Velvet: The Story of Dame Nellie Melba and Her Times is a book by Joseph Wechsberg, published in Boston in 1961 and London in 1962. The book is noted here for the sake of the record: It draws almost entirely on the abovementioned works, nearly always with unjustified embellishment. There are so many errors of fact, confidently stated, that the author loses all semblance of credibility.

By far the most nearly definitive biography of Nellie Melba published to date is that by Australian John Hetherington, titled simply *Melba*. It was first published in Melbourne in 1967, the same year in London, and one year later in New York (with an introduction by Francis Robinson of the Metropolitan Opera). Here, for the first time, we have the Australian side of the story, well researched and presented: The singer's husband, Charles Armstrong, is not merely dismissed. His part in the story is filled in, and something is told of his activities, life, and character. Working from previous publications as a base, the author has filled in many gaps that needed filling. While strong on the Australian end, he has not added much that is new to the facts of Melba's early career in Europe. Hetherington was not a musician, nor does he appear to have been very familiar with things operatic or vocal. The reader is constantly aware of this, although the slippage is minor. Unfortunately there is no discography, and Melba's legacy of recordings is barely touched upon. Since Melba's voice was recorded commercially from 1904 to the end of 1926 at fairly regular intervals, a study of her records is most illuminating and deserving of analysis. Throughout Hetherington's book, however, Melba as a person comes through well.

So why a new book on Melba? Actually, the content of this book is for the most part not new, but it is composed of materials brought together for the first time. I have tried to cover a broad range of sources: interviews, reviews, newspaper and magazine articles, and specific chapters from books of memoirs, all of a contemporary nature. These have been brought together more or less in chronological order, up to the time of Melba's death. There follows a sampling of obituary notices in which her career is reviewed by some who knew her work well. Following articles generated by her death is a selection of material culled from many books by people who knew and worked with the singer and whose contributions have been scattered by publication through the years in various parts of the world. The two concluding sections of the book are composed of advice on singing and discussion of singing technique taken from the words of the artist herself, and, finally, a brief discussion of Melba's recording career, the historical setting in which some of the recordings were made, and a complete list of her known recordings.

No one will agree on the choice of selections, and some are obviously more important and valid than others. A few smack of the publicity release but have been included as useful in establishing a feeling for the times. Not all are complimentary. There has been no conscious attempt at whitewash; rather an effort has been made to see Nellie Melba through the eyes of many people in many places and at many times. The reader is thus allowed to form a mental picture from a wide base of materials. The editor has tried to be as unobtrusive as practical, merely setting the scene for the individual actors, allowing each to speak in his or her own words.

AN OVERVIEW

NELLIE MELBA

BARBARA MACKENZIE AND FINDLAY MACKENZIE

For forty years the pure and silvery voice of Nellie Melba made her an undisputed Queen of Song during the "Golden Age of Opera". After her voice was stilled on February 23, 1931, she lived on as a legend in operatic circles throughout the world and in her native Australia as a warm human being.

In order to understand the person behind "The Voice", as she often referred to herself, it is necessary to see her as the child of an enterprising Scottish pioneer in Australia and as a native daughter who loved the freedom of the life there during the second half of the nineteenth century. As Marie Narelle, one of her contemporaries, said in an interview in which she spoke of her own early childhood experiences, "I have recalled them because I think that the pre-eminence of Australian voices is not the outcome so much of climate or any exterior influence, but of our character. It is the Australian personality that has made the Australian voice. We are a natural people . . . free in all we do and say and think and it is that freedom, I believe, that makes us good singers".[1]

Melba's maiden name, Helen Porter Mitchell, conveys some of the strength of the woman who was said by her contemporaries to have had such high intelligence and acumen that she could have been successful in

This chapter is reprinted from *Singers of Australia, from Melba to Sutherland,* by Barbara Mackenzie and Findlay Mackenzie. It was as a result of a favorable review of this work that the authors and the present compiler became close friends. Unfortunately, neither author has lived to see this volume in print. It would have pleased them to have their chapter on Melba selected as a relatively brief but comprehensive biographical sketch to form a general background for the material to follow.

whatever field she chose. Having chosen music she needed all her other gifts of mind and courage to bring to fruition the native talent that her early life had fostered. Her capacity for hard work, her imagination, courage, perseverance and concentration, all were placed at the service of the amazing gift with which she had been born.

But Melba had far more than a voice, even though it was a voice which for quality, flexibility, purity and sheer lasting power will probably never be excelled. She had a personality which carried across the footlights of the biggest opera houses in the world and, as a young woman, an austere type of beauty which compelled the admiration, when it did not excite the affection, of audiences.

John Thompson, of the Australian Broadcasting Commission, said at the time of her centenary:

It would be a poor compliment to a great personality to pretend that Melba had no failings. She was ambitious, proud, domineering and she was sometimes ruthless. She was capable, too, of great kindness and generosity . . . an indefatigable worker . . . a woman of great intelligence. . . . she had all the unconventionality and all the authority of a genius, who knew she was a genius. She succeeded, unlike most creative artists, in leaving her mark on the musical life of her native land where she is still a living force, thanks to the teachers she taught and the performers she helped and trained.[2]

Another view came from her accompanist, John Lemmoné, who described her as

. . . dynamic, forceful, compelling—but a woman, human and sympathetic. Fiery temperament she had, but it was the fire of a woman with a big mind, big ideas and a personality seldom found more than once in an age. [She was] a strange mixture of human woman and dynamic personality. She always had her way, and always she seemed right. Dame Nellie was a woman of an age; it took a man to understand her.[3]

Helen Porter Mitchell was born on May 19, 1861, in Richmond, then a semi-rural suburb adjoining the infant city of Melbourne. The daughter of a Scottish pioneer, she spent her formative years in a primitive country where society was still in a state of flux after the greatest gold rush in history.

Migrating from Forfar, Scotland, in 1852, her father, David Mitchell, arrived in Australia during a momentous period. In less than two years the immense gold discoveries of 1851 transformed Melbourne from a raw settlement serving as entrepot for the pastoral district of Port Phillip into the capital of the new colony of Victoria.

In 1834 Melbourne consisted of a single house. When Mitchell first saw it eighteen years later, Hobson's Bay was crowded with ships abandoned by crews who were digging for gold. Like most new arrivals, Mitchell joined the gold seekers, but he soon tired of washing for colours along the bush creeks. Returning to Melbourne, he became a building contractor—a well-timed move when a fourth of the population was living under canvas.

Time and place were made for a man of his energy and enterprise. Moreover, he built to last. The quarries and cement works he established are still in operation, while bricks made in his works form parts of buildings standing today. In addition to his other enterprises he became a large landowner. Before his death on March 25, 1916, he saw Melbourne grow from a mining port into a substantial modern city with a population of more than half a million.

His daughter Helen was the eldest of four girls in a family of seven. The tide of immigration still ran strong while she was a child but as the first effervescence of the gold discoveries subsided, the Victorian mining camps either disappeared altogether or evolved into regular towns.

Music flourished, both as public entertainment and private hobby. The "musical evening" became standard home entertainment, and the ability to play an instrument, usually piano or violin or flute, was a passport to social success. One of the first questions asked about newcomers to a district was "Are they 'musical'?" Musically, the Mitchells were well abreast of their contemporaries. David Mitchell's rugged exterior concealed an excellent bass voice, while the ramifications of his business did not prevent his playing the violin and harmonium. It would not be easy to find a modern magnate so accomplished.

His wife played the piano, violin and harp, while two of her sisters who were regular guests at "Doonside" had excellent voices and possessed musical knowledge "quite exceptional for amateurs". Thus Nellie grew up in a musical atmosphere. Among her earliest memories were crawling under the piano to listen while her mother played, and sitting on her father's knee on a Sunday afternoon while he amused himself at an old harmonium. Later an organ was installed in the drawing room and there were many opportunities to hear well-known visiting musicians, among them the pianist Mme. Arabella Goddard who made an outstanding impression on the girl.

Nellie loved to sing and had a habit of going about the house humming to herself. When she was only six years old she appeared at a public concert singing two ballads in the authentic Scottish dialect taught to her by her grandmother. She was a high-spirited child, not at all interested in dolls and picture books, and indifferent to any studies except music. She was sent to a boarding school for several years with the hope that she would receive the discipline her family thought she needed. Later she attended the Presbyterian Ladies' College in Melbourne which was only a short ride from home in one of the four-horse omnibuses for which the city was becoming noted. Here she was a day pupil and studied with Mme. Ellen Christian, an English contralto who had been a student of the renowned teacher Manuel Garcia, brother of the famous Mme. Malibran. In an interview many years later Mme. Christian said:

At that time her youthful voice boasted a sweetness in the lower register by which it resembled the violin tone of Kubelik in legato passages, a fact revealed to me years later while listening to a phonograph record. As "Melba" she lost the timbre in question under the training necessary to acquire the top notes characteristic of the coloratura repertoire.[4]

Nellie's friends remembered her as an expert in the art of whistling popular tunes, an activity sometimes credited with having helped to develop the exceptionally fine breath control for which she was famous at the height of her career. During the lunch hour at the college, while her classmates gathered for sociability, Nellie spent her time practising on the organ, an instrument to which she was much attracted throughout her lifetime.[5] Dr. A. E. Floyd, the English organist who came to St. Paul's Cathedral in Melbourne in 1911, recalled in an interview fifty years later that on numerous occasions when she was home on a visit Melba would come to the big church and ask him to play for her.

Exactly when Nellie Mitchell determined to adopt music as a career is uncertain. Obviously her father gave her no encouragement. No doubt he was very proud of her accomplishments as singer and pianist, of the invitations she received to appear at private parties and musicales and of her position as organist at Scots Church. Mitchell himself had built this big church as the headquarters of Presbyterianism in Victoria. However, the thought of his eldest daughter becoming a public entertainer was quite another matter.

Evidently Nellie had a musical career in mind when about 1880 she began taking lessons from Pietro Cecchi, a former member of one of Lyster's opera companies who had established himself as a teacher in Melbourne. Had her father been in favour of this step, he would probably have paid for the lessons. As it was, Cecchi apparently agreed to wait for his money until she could afford to pay for them out of her earnings. Before that could happen, however, the death of her mother and a younger sister started a train of events which turned the Helen Porter Mitchell of 1881 into the Dame Nellie Melba of history and legend.

So intense was the girl's grief at her mother's death that she ceased to be her gay and out-going self and her father began to worry about her health. Since he was scheduled to take a business trip to Queensland, 1,500 miles away, he suggested that Nellie and her sister Annie accompany him in the hope that the steamer trip and a change of scene and climate would benefit them. He was financially interested in a property in the Mackay district of North Queensland where in the 1870's the importation of labourers from the islands north of Australia had lifted the sugar industry into a state of prosperity.

Mackay sprawled along the estuary of the Pioneer River. At first glimpse, the town which was to have so decisive an influence on her life must have seemed peculiarly romantic to the girl from Melbourne—tropic skies, mild winter days, the off-shore islands with their palms, coral reefs and white beaches, the dark-skinned Kanakas working in the canefields, the sugar schooners in the river, the exotic birds, flowers and insects, and the general air of leisure which reminded American visitors of life in the old South.

The sugar growers had developed a social life mainly centered on the School of Arts, where Nellie Mitchell found her services much in demand as singer and pianist. On October 15, 1882, she wrote to Cecchi, naively informing him of her success at two concerts: "The ladies up here are all jealous of me. I was encored twice for each song and they hurrahed me and threw me no end of bouquets". [6]

Some of the younger women may have had an even stronger reason for their jealousy. In December Nellie left Mackay for Brisbane to marry Charles Nesbitt Frederick Armstrong, twenty-three-year-old son of an Irish baronet and manager of the Mirani sugar plantation. The marriage took place in the manse of the Ann Street Presbyterian Church, on December 22, 1882. The wedding party which rattled up from the wharf in a four-wheeled cab consisted of David Mitchell, Annie Mitchell and the best man, Arthur Herman Feez, afterwards a well-known Queensland barrister.

Described as a tall, handsome, young Irish gentleman, Armstrong was known in Mackay as "Kangaroo Charlie". Whatever the implications of this nickname may have been, he was certainly very unlucky to marry a girl so utterly unsuited for life on a North Queensland sugar plantation. If the pair had any common interests, they did not extend beyond social activities, sex attraction, youth and horses. Temperamentally, they seem to have been far apart. Normally, Nellie Mitchell was high-spirited, impulsively generous, and filled with the joy of life. Armstrong appears to have been quick-tempered and moody.

Once they were married the riding, driving, yachting and dancing came to an end, and the social life of the remote little port disintegrated in the steamy heat of the rainy season. Existence became a battle against humidity, insects, snakes and boredom. The situation was made more difficult when Nellie became pregnant almost immediately, and Armstrong proved to be chronically hard-up. By the time her son was born on October 16, 1883, Nellie Armstrong had decided to return to Melbourne. She wrote to Cecchi that she would like to study for opera but that she would have to earn money at the same time, adding, "There is nothing to detain me now that Mr. Armstrong is agreeable". [7]

She had studied both singing and piano but it was as an instrumentalist that Nellie Armstrong was most frequently invited to appear at private gatherings. Soon after her return to Melbourne she played at a reception given by the Marquis of Normanby, then Governor of Victoria. Between piano solos she sang to her own accompaniment and must have felt greatly encouraged when the cosmopolitan Lady Normanby said, "Child, you play brilliantly but you sing better. Some day you will give up the piano for singing and then you will become famous".[8]

Appearances at concerts in Sydney and Melbourne during the next two years led to the growth of her reputation as a singer. Of her performance at a benefit for Herr Elsasser, the former conductor of the Melbourne Lieder-tafel, on May 17, 1884, the critic of the *Australasian* wrote, "She sings like one out of ten thousand". Two days later the Melbourne *Argus* reported:

Mrs Armstrong (née Mitchell) was the only non-professional singer present, but we are glad to think that she was moved to give of talent, as well as good-will toward the object aimed at, because she both surprised and delighted her hearers. She chose the elaborate cavatina, "Ah fors e Lui", from the second [*sic*] act of the opera *La Traviata*. She commenced with something like hesitancy of manner, but as she proceeded this evidence of nervousness wore away and she developed such a high, clear and flexible soprano voice, and such well-trained method as a vocalist, that all hearers who remember the best performances of the opera in this city were caught in the charm that belongs only to good singing, so the kindly and accomplished singer, when she came to the end of her song, instead of receiving only that modified approval that greets the best of amateur effort, was awarded, with good reason, the enthusiastic reward of the accomplished artist. This performance was quite an unexpected treat. It is right to mention here Signor Cecchi was Miss Mitchell's teacher.

This occasion was notable also for the fact that it marked the first appearance on the same programme of Nellie Melba and John Lemmoné, the flautist[9] who was to become her life-long associate and general manager.

In 1885 the theatre manager George Musgrove paid Nellie her first professional fee, a modest £20, for singing at a series of concerts. Then for a time she was soloist at the Roman Catholic Church of St. Francis, and made a concert tour with the Australian violinist Johannes Kruse. The next year David Mitchell was appointed a commissioner to the Indian and Colonial Exhibition in London and decided to take his daughter and grandson with him. It is said that he hoped that this trip would serve to rid his daughter of the ambition to become a great singer and that if she were not well received in London she would be content to return to Australia and settle down to domesticity.

Before they left home an incident occurred which disturbed Nellie deeply. When it was announced that she was to go abroad her teacher, Signor Cecchi, submitted a bill for about £90 to cover twenty months of tuition and threatened to have her luggage impounded if it were not paid immediately. She raised the money by giving a concert that netted £60 and borrowed the rest from friends. Subsequently, she never mentioned any artistic indebtedness she might have felt towards Cecchi although Thorold Waters described him in his book as "the very man to locate the glowing, pearly rarity of Melba's voice and to make the most of it". Five years later, in 1891, Fanny Simonsen wrote in the Italian publication *Il Mondo Artistico* of her surprise at Melba's failure to express a word of appreciation of the man who she declared had laid the foundation for the diva's career. Whether Melba's silence would have continued if Cecchi had not died the next year is a matter of conjecture. We do know, however, that Melba held no grudge against him because she wrote him a friendly letter a few months after her arrival in London telling of the artists she had heard and of an occasion on which she sang. She gave him her London address and signed herself, "Your old pupil, Nellie Armstrong".

When she set out for London she took with her letters of introduction to several influential people in the musical world but she received little encouragement. Sir Arthur Sullivan advised her, as he did all young singers, to study for a year and then return with the hope of receiving a small part in one of his operas. Brinsmead, the manufacturer of fine pianos, noted that the timbre of her voice was almost as pure as that of one of his instruments but he made no overture to help her. The society teacher, Alberto Randegger, was not the least interested in an unknown singer from a remote part of the world known only for its wool, wheat, minerals and cricket players.

Despite her lack of success in securing the assistance of those in a position to help launch a career the young Mrs. Armstrong's early weeks in London were not wasted. By June she had heard not only the singers Adelina Patti, Christine Nilsson, Emma Albani, Zelia Trebelli, Charles Santley and Edward Lloyd, but also the violinists Sarasate and Hallé, and the pianist Vladimir de Pachmann whose wife, Marguerite, was New South Wales-born Maggie Oakey, one of Australia's first piano virtuosi. Apparently the only individuals to recognize her great gift were Vert, the concert agent, who tried hard to secure engagements for her, and Wilhelm Ganz, the German pianist and song writer. Having heard her sing "Ah, fors' è lui" in a manner which he thought could not have been bettered, Ganz arranged for her to appear at a dinner for the Royal Theatrical Fund, presided over by Augustus Harris. Known in the world of the theatre as "Augustus Druriolanus", Harris was soon to take over the direction of the Royal Opera House, Covent Garden, and loom large in the subsequent career of Nellie Melba.

At the dinner, her singing of "Ave Maria" made so deep an impression that Ganz arranged an audition with Carl Rosa, but he forgot the appointment. Nellie thereupon picked up her son and left for Paris armed with a letter to the redoubtable Mathilde Marchesi, who she hoped would undertake her training.[10] The success of their first meeting has become history. Having heard her sing, Marchesi dashed out to call to her husband, *"Salvatore, enfin j'ai trouve une etoile!"* Madame was right. She had found a star of such magnitude that the years have not dimmed the memory of its brilliance.

It is evident that Nellie Melba always considered that Marchesi had laid the foundation for her success, and treated her with deep affection all her life. Subsequently Madame herself stated that her chief contribution to her celebrated pupil's vocal progress was in teaching her to sing pianissimo. Cornelius Reed, while discussing the art of the bel canto, wrote:

> Marchesi, who claimed the celebrated Melba as her pupil, never "built" that great voice, or provided it with the flawless technique for which the prima donna was so justly renowned, simply because the nine months of study Melba had with her prior to making a sensational debut was too short a time to do more than polish the technique.[11]

Discussing Melba's probable reasons for seeking out Marchesi, Bernard Shaw referred to the "advice as to style, habits, phrasing and pronunciation, stage business and tradition, which make eminent professors of singing so useful to pupils who already know how to sing".[12] He failed, however, to mention another essential service Marchesi was able to render. Her influence in the international world of music was so great that any student of hers could be sure of being heard by influential people and under favourable conditions.

On the last day of December, 1886, Nellie Mitchell-Armstrong disappeared from the record, and Mademoiselle—soon Madame—Melba appeared in her place. The transformation occurred at one of Marchesi's "matinees musicales" held at her home in the Rue Jouffroy. According to Melba, the name originated with Marchesi who felt that to sing as Mrs. Armstrong would be a handicap. Among the guests in the Rue Jouffroy that afternoon was Maurice Strakosch, the Hungarian pianist, conductor and impresario. As the husband and manager of Carlotta Patti and one of the teachers of her sister Adelina, Strakosch was an authority on sopranos. Having heard Melba sing "Caro nome" he took her aside and persuaded her to sign a ten-year contract which virtually gave him control of her actions for the next decade. Doubtless Melba was delighted to think that her vocal career had begun at last, but she soon realized that the contract was much more to Strakosch's advantage than to hers. If it guaranteed her against poverty until the year 1896, it likewise prevented her from taking advantage of better opportunities that might present themselves in the future. One of these opportunities occurred a few months later when Joseph Dupont, principal conductor, and Lapissida, a director, of the Théâtre de la Monnaie, Brussels, called on Marchesi in search of a soprano. They auditioned several of her students and then asked, "Where is the Australian?" After hearing Melba sing they immediately offered to engage her for the forthcoming season, their terms being three times Strakosch's figure. Melba's heart sank when she realized that the contract she had signed precluded her acceptance of their offer, but Marchesi felt sure that Strakosch would understand how much the chance in Brussels meant to her and be generous enough to release her.

Strakosch, however, did not intend to let himself be talked out of his legal rights by Marchesi. Loudly denouncing what he called Melba's ingratitude, he assured her that he would not permit her to appear at the Monnaie or anywhere else except under his management. That he meant what he said was apparent when she reached Brussels only to find that he had taken out an injunction to prevent her entering the theatre. Dismayed, she returned to her hotel, flung herself on her bed and lay there all day wondering what she could do.

Her release came in a manner thoroughly operatic. Evening brought Lapissida bounding up the stars calling, "Strakosch est mort!" Death, breaker of all contracts, had come to Strakosch that afternoon. It was October 9, 1887.

Four days later, Melba made her operatic debut at the Monnaie as Gilda in *Rigoletto*.

Although the operas of the time were lavishly staged and costumed, so little importance attached to the histrionic side that apart from a brief and chilly audition at the Paris Opera, Melba had never been on the stage of a theatre until the hurried rehearsals for her debut at the Monnaie. But if her acting displayed shortcomings, her looks at the age of twenty-six delighted the most captious, while her singing of the role of Gilda made the night memorable in the history of the Brussels opera house.

This performance was followed by equally fine appearances as Violetta and Lucia. The enthusiasm of her audiences increased with each production until it touched something like frenzy when she sang the title role in Delibes' *Lakme* on March 8, 1888, and a month later Ophelie in the *Hamlet* of Ambroise Thomas. Leo Delibes felt that her interpretations were invested with a magic and poetry far loftier than the ordinary "triumph" of vocalization. He told her, "In a sort of reverie I heard your ideal voice interpreting my work with a superhuman purity. It gave me the keenest and most delicious impression I have ever known in hearing anything I have written".

Brussels critics acclaimed her as "a new and brilliant star" and described her voice as "a revelation, unique in quality, with a remarkable trill and perfect technique". Melba's trill was subsequently remarked on wherever she sang. She once wrote, "I was born with a natural trill",[13] and her American accompanist, Samuel Harwell, said it was the most beautifully executed ornament he had ever heard.

Melba's trill . . . her marvellous crescendo in the Mad Scene in *Lucia*, remains a vocal feat. It began pianissimo. It grew steadily stronger and stronger, more and more intense and at last . . . that vast auditorium which is the Metropolitan Opera House of New York, just vibrated with its wonderful fortissimo of crystalline purity. What a thing to have heard![14]

The trill remained with her always. In the late 1890's, Anton Seidl wrote:

The trill in her case is of quite fabulous sostenuto; for instance, she has at her command a long powerful crescendo on the highest notes that is without parallel, and yet performed with a clearness and certainty which simply excite astonishment and are at the same time soft, clinging and cajoling.[15]

Many years later Beverley Nichols persuaded Melba to meet Professor A. M. Low, inventor of the audiometer, an apparatus for photographing sound with which Low made a photographic record of her famous trill. This was reported to be so uniform that it might have been drawn by a geometrician.

During Melba's first Brussels season, the inadvisability of tying herself up to Strakosch for an entire decade was clearly shown when she was asked to appear at Covent Garden, now under the direction of Augustus Harris. In his "Golden Age of Opera",[16] Herman Klein records that Harris had no burning desire to engage Melba, and did so only after considerable persuasion on the part of some of the wealthy and socially powerful ladies connected with the Covent Garden Syndicate. From Melba's point of view, the most important was the immensely influential Lady de Grey, who became her patron and remained her friend for life.

Despite her Brussels success, Melba's Covent Garden debut on May 24, 1888, was not a triumph. The audience was enthusiastic but small and critics referred more to her powers of acting than to the unique quality of her song. One of them did state that her voice was the best to have been heard since Patti's, but the *Athenaeum* reviewer, after acknowledging her fine performance, added, "But we do not for a moment imagine that Mme Melba will ever hold the highest position in her profession".[17] With the applause of Brussels still ringing in her ears Melba, after three performances at Covent Garden, asked to be released from her contract. Augustus Harris reluctantly agreed to do so adding, "In a little time they will clamour for Melba above all others and, by gad, they will pay for her, too".[18]

After another season at Le Théâtre de La Monnaie, Melba made her debut at The Paris Opera on May 8, 1889, in the role of Ophelie in Thomas' *Hamlet*. This was a great success despite a number of mishaps at the opera house which made it necessary for her to appear with a Hamlet she had never seen before and without having had a single rehearsal with the orchestra. August Vitu, critic of *Le Figaro*, spoke of her success in the early part of the performance and of "a triumph after the Mad Scene which literally moved the listeners to frenzy". He referred to her as the most delicious Ophelie since Christine Nilsson, and added

. . . Madame Melba has a marvellous soprano voice, equal, pure, brilliant, and mellow, remarkably resonant in the middle register, and rising with a perfect pastosita up to the acute regions of that fairylike major third. That which ravished us was not alone the virtuosity, the exceptional quality of that sweetly timbred voice, the exceptional facility of executing at random diatonic and chromatic scales and trills of the nightingale, it was also that profound and touching simplicity and the justness of accent which caused a thrill to pass through the audience with those simple notes of the middle voice, "je suis Ophelie".[19]

Echoes of this great occasion soon reached the other side of the world. "Now that we are basking in the reflected glory of Mrs Armstrong", wrote a correspondent to Melbourne *Punch* in June, 1889, "you will be specially interested in hearing further of the Australian diva. I was fortunate in hearing Madame Melba on her first appearance in Paris as Ophelia. After her scene with Hamlet and the Queen, the curtain had to be raised three times, but her greatest triumph was achieved in the Flower Scene when, amidst the enthusiastic cheering of a critical Parisian audience, the curtain had to be raised again and again, even the ladies joining in the rapturous clamour".[20]

Melba's Paris season produced offers from Madrid and Berlin as well as a letter from Lady de Grey urging her to give Covent Garden another chance. Fully aware now of her own powers, Melba saw to it that nothing was left undone to assure her success this time. She appeared as Juliette, singing Gounod's opera in French with the great tenor Jean de Reszke as Romeo and his bass brother, Edouard, as Friar Lawrence. When the curtain rose on June 15, 1889, the big opera house was full and in the audience were Edward, Prince of Wales, and the Princess Alexandra.

An additional reason for this being an important occasion for Melba was that it marked the fulfilment of a long-cherished ambition to sing with Jean de Reszke whom she had first heard when a student, in a performance in Paris with Adelina Patti. It also marked the beginning of a long association with the two brothers which continued for the rest of their lives and made their performances together so noteworthy during the "Golden Age".

After subsequent performances as Juliette and as Marguerite the London public recognized that Melba was indeed the British Queen of Song and this she remained until her last performance at Covent Garden on June 6, 1926. Every night she sang was a "Melba Night" and tickets were at a premium. All over Europe people were clamouring to hear her. The Czar of Russia invited her to make a series of appearances with the de Reszkes at the Imperial Opera in St. Petersburg in February, 1891. She accepted and was acclaimed whenever she sang; on the night of the farewell performance, a group of Russian youths spread their coats on the snow for her to walk on. Czar Alexander the Third added to her already mounting collection of jewels a diamond necklace which was insured for the equivalent of one hundred thousand American dollars when it was exhibited at a benefit in Melbourne in 1963.

After a noteworthy debut in *La Traviata* at Palermo, Italy, in the spring of 1892, Melba appeared at Covent Garden on July 5 with Jean de Reszke in the opera *Elaine* which had been dedicated to them by its composer, Hermann Bemberg. . . .

In the autumn of 1892 Melba appeared in *Aida* for the first time. Although critics noted that she displayed great energy as an actress and faultless diction she felt that the role was not suited to her voice and subsequently dropped it from her repertoire. Her initial experience with *Otello* at about the same time was quite different and the role of Desdemona became one of her favourites. The following spring, at the request of the composer, she created the role of Nedda in Leoncavello's *I Pagliacci*, with Fernando de Lucia singing the title role.[21] The opera was received so enthusiastically that it was presented thirteen times in two months. Sir Henry Wood, who played for her rehearsals, recalled that her scale and arpeggio technique were perfect. "Her notes were like a string of pearls, touching, yet separate, strung on a continuous vocal line of tone that was never marred nor distorted".[22]

One of the most vividly remembered events in Melba's career was her first appearance at La Scala in March, 1893, in the role of Lucia. Italian audiences seldom welcomed foreigners and Melba had a hostile reception in Milan, where anonymous letters threatened her with dire consequences should she have the temerity to appear. Halfway through the Mad Scene, however, the audience realized that they were hearing a singer who could rival even the beloved Adelina Patti and at the end of it they greeted her with an ovation seldom equalled in the annals of this historic opera house. The Italian press next day commented on "the marvellous felicity of her production, the seduction of *timbre*, the finished art and the pureness of intonation". Her position in Italy was established and she went on to appear in Turin, Genoa, Florence and Rome.

Melba first appeared at the Metropolitan Opera House in New York in 1893, in the distinguished company of Emma Calvé, Emma Eames, Lillian Nordica, Sophia Scalchi, the de Reszke brothers, Fernando de Lucia and Pol Plançon. Although she had been singing for only five years Melba's technique and tone production were noted as being unusually natural. Of her debut as Lucia on December 4 the critic H. E. Krehbiel wrote in the *New York Tribune:* "She moved with the greatest of ease in regions which her rivals carefully avoided". . . .

Two nights after the performance of *Lucia* Melba appeared as Ophelie in Thomas' *Hamlet* and a week later, on December 11, as Nedda in the Metropolitan's first performance of *I Pagliacci*. These were roles that had brought her great acclaim in Europe. On January 12, 1894, she sang the incredibly difficult part of the Queen in *Semiramide*, one of the unusual operas presented by Joan Sutherland during her Australian tour in 1965. *Tannhauser* and *Romeo and Juliette*, both sung in French, completed her repertoire during the first year in New York. Her appearances at the Metropolitan's Sunday evening concerts infused new life into them.

Writing of that season's Metropolitan Opera Company tour of major cities of the United States, Quaintance Eaton[23] refers to Melba's triumph in Chicago, singing Marguerite in *Faust*, as being "as complete and instantaneous as was Sembrich's in 1884". An article in the periodical *Interocean* at about this time speaks of her as "gifted by nature with a graceful personality, queenly figure, expressive eyes", and after noting the phenomenal purity of her voice adds, "we have a new goddess of song".

Melba proved herself to be a great showman as well as a great singer when she appeared as Rosina in *The Barber of Seville* in San Francisco on the eve of the Spanish Civil War. The sinking of the battleship *Maine* had aroused antagonism to all things Spanish and the diva sensed this feeling in the audience. Taking advantage of her privilege to utilize an aria of her own choosing in the "Music Lesson" scene, Melba sang "The Star Spangled Banner" and brought an electrified audience to its feet.

After appearing with the de Reszke brothers in two triumphant opening nights at the Metropolitan—*Romeo and Juliette* on November 16, 1894, and *Hamlet* on November 19, 1896—Melba launched forth on what Oscar Thompson later referred to as "a celebrated if somewhat disastrous excursion . . . when forsaking the velvet of her coloratura she attempted the declamation of Brunnhilde".[24] Melba sang this role in the opera *Siegfried* against her own better judgement and the advice of Mme. Marchesi.

Despite the fine support she received from her friends the de Reszkes and other members of the cast, she disappointed the audience and critics alike and afterwards was forced to rest her voice for three months.[25] The morning after the performance H. E. Krehbiel, in a review in the *New York Tribune*, quoted from the Psalms, "there is one glory of the sun, another of the moon and another of the stars; one may not have all three. Mme Melba should have been content with her own particularly glory". Another critic addressing the singer herself wrote, "Your voice is like a piece of Dresden china. Please do not smash it". Melba's own comment was characteristically frank, "I've been a fool. I'll never attempt that again".

The composers Delibes, Gounod, Massenet, Thomas and Verdi all helped Melba prepare roles in their operas. Thomas called her the "Ophelie of my dreams"; to both Massenet and Joachim, the violin virtuoso, she was "Madame Stradivarius"; and Saint-Saëns named his opera *Hélène* for her. The reputations of these composers had all been made before Melba appeared on the scene; Puccini, on the other hand, was somewhat of a controversial figure, musically speaking, when she went to Lucca in 1898 to study *La Bohème* with him. At the time considerable prejudice existed against him in the higher musical circles; even in Italy many regarded him as a purveyor of cheap sentiment. Melba, however, expressed the belief that he was the coming composer and it is scarcely an exaggeration to say that it was she who established *La Bohème* in the standard repertoire. After singing the role of Mimi in Philadelphia she persuaded the Covent Garden Syndicate to mount the opera. It received its first London performance on May 19, 1899, with the diva as Mimi, Fernando de Lucia as Rudolfo and the sprightly Zelie de Lussan as Musetta. Six months later it was presented at the Metropolitan Opera House in New York and has never lost its world popularity.

Few singers have become as closely associated with a role as Melba did with Mimi. Many people thought Puccini wrote *La Bohème* for her, yet she did not appear in it until she had passed her thirty-seventh birthday and was by no means physically ideal for the role of the consumptive young model of the Montmartre tenement. Nor did the gifted Caruso, with whom she sang it for the first time at Monte Carlo in 1902, remotely resemble a starving poet of 1830 vintage. None the less, the famous pair became symbols of grand opera as no others have before or since. Many people have testified to the eerie effect of her singing in the duet at the end of the first act. As Mary Garden described it, "The note came floating over the auditorium of Covent Garden. It was Melba's throat, it left Melba's body, it left everything and came like a star and passed us in our box and went out into the infinite . . .".[26] How greatly Melba's singing of Mimi aided the popularity of *La Bohème* is a matter of history. Many people, however—some of them her greatest admirers—regretted that she clung to the role for nearly thirty years.

Some commentators have asserted that Melba never encouraged anyone who might be able to challenge her supremacy and made sure that she was never adequately supported by a first-rate Musetta. Whether or not this is completely true she found a summary way of dealing with the Austrian soprano Fritzi Scheff who was endowed with unusual histrionic ability. Percy Colson, who was present at a performance of *La Bohème* at Covent Garden early in 1903, recounted that during the second act while Fraulein Scheff was singing the "Waltz Song" and preparing to take the high "B natural" at the end, "a clear angelic voice in the wings landed on it with effortless ease and sang the rest of the phrase with her". The audience whispered "Melba" and after the curtain fell Neil Forsyth, the manager, announced that due to an indisposition, Fraulein Scheff would not be able to continue with her role but that Madame Melba had kindly consented to complete the evening by singing the Mad Scene from *Lucia di Lammermoor*. Fraulein Scheff was described as expressing "the extremity of displeasure" and the following day was on her way back to Vienna.

Melba frankly admitted to Hermann Bemberg that she could not bear any other artist on the same programme to get as much applause as she. It must have disturbed her, then, even to share the honours of the evening with Emma Calvé, when, in 1895, the Metropolitan first linked *Cavalleria*

Rusticana to *I Pagliacci* and created the famous double bill. Calvé sang Santuzza while Melba followed with Nedda making a marvellous evening for the audience but not necessarily for the two stars. Fortunately their orbits, though coming dangerously close, bisected each other only when "as a special courtesy to the management" Melba sang Micaëla to Calvé's Carmen.

Fritzi Scheff did not emerge from her encounter with Melba as well as did the celebrated Italian baritone, Titta Ruffo, who went to England in 1901 to sing at Covent Garden. He was billed to substitute for Antonio Scotti who was too ill to sing Rigoletto to Melba's Gilda. To Ruffo's astonishment the diva refused to appear with him, on the ground that, at twenty-four, he was too young to be cast as her father. Ruffo, however, had good cause to believe that the real reason was the ovation he had received from the orchestra and chorus at the dress rehearsal at which Melba had refused to sing. Giving full rein to his Tuscan temperament, the infuriated Ruffo told Higgins, the director, what he thought of Covent Garden and, presumably, of Melba. So pungent were his remarks that Higgins threatened legal action, whereupon Ruffo fled to Italy. Years later, when he was one of the leading baritones of the world, Melba stopped in Naples on her way back to Australia. Having heard him in *L'Africaine* and *Hamlet* she offered to appear with him at the San Carlo. This was Ruffo's opportunity, and he made the most of it by requesting the director to give Madame Melba his compliments and to inform her that she was now too old to sing with him.

In 1902 she returned to her native land for the first time since leaving it sixteen years before. Great changes had taken place. The Federation of the six colonies had transformed Australia from a geographical abstraction into a new nation of which Melba, now an assured woman of forty-one, was the best-known representative. She had arranged with George Musgrove to organize a concert tour for her, and his former partner, J. C. Williamson, suggested that she should appear afterwards in *La Bohème* with a small Italian opera company he was then recruiting. If anyone in Australia had any doubt about the heights to which David Mitchell's daughter had risen, they became fully aware of where she stood when Williamson announced that he could not meet the diva's terms, which, among other stipulations, called for £400 a performance, the engagement of the costly tenor Albert Saléza and French pitch in the orchestra.

Reaching Australia by way of Canada, Melba began her first Australian concert tour in Brisbane on September 14, 1902. Everywhere she received the kind of welcome which up to that time had been reserved for the rare visits of royalty. When she sang at the Melbourne Town Hall, traffic in Collins and Swanston streets was practically suspended and police had to fight all evening to get the cable trams across the intersection and the carriages to and from the hall. Musgrove, who had paid Nellie Armstrong

£20 for a series of concerts seventeen years before, handed Nellie Melba a cheque for £2,350, her share of the proceeds for a single night's performance.

After the concert tour, Melba gave Australians a glimpse of what Williamson had deprived them of, when she appeared at the Princess Theatre, Melbourne, and the Theatre Royal, Sydney, in scenes from *Faust*, *La Traviata* and *Rigoletto*. In these excerpts, which were complete with costumes and scenery, she had the assistance of several members of George Musgrove's Opera Company, including Louis Ahrens, the tenor, Lempriere Pringle, the Tasmanian basso, and Madame Slapoffski, the soprano, whose husband, Gustav, conducted the orchestra. She left Australia to the plaintive strains of "Wull ye no come back again?" and with the knowledge that her absence had made her not less but more an Australian than she had ever been.

In 1907 and 1908 Melba did some of the finest singing of her career during the two seasons she appeared at Oscar Hammerstein's new Manhattan opera house in New York. The previous autumn Hammerstein had spent much time and effort trying to persuade her to become a member of a new company he was forming but she had steadfastly declined his many offers. On one of these occasions after Melba had withdrawn from an interview Hammerstein scattered £4,000 in bank notes on her living-room floor before leaving. Melba, still uncommitted, banked the money in Hammerstein's name but later, impressed by what she called his "pluck" in attempting this operatic venture, she accepted a very favourable contract with him.[27]

Her first appearance at the Manhattan was in *La Traviata* on January 2, 1907. The house was sold out and Hammerstein was so delighted that he met Melba at the stage door and had her stand on the stage behind the huge curtain to listen to the dull roar of conversation in the crowded house. As the curtain rose Melba was greeted with thunderous applause, quite contrary to the custom of this period. As soon as her voice rang out with its famous bell-like clarity Melba knew that she and Hammerstein had won at least temporarily the battle to establish a second opera centre in New York City.[28] Reviewing the performance in the *New York Times* Richard Aldrich wrote: "Her vocalism has its old time lusciousness and purity, its exquisite smoothness and fullness; Mme Melba's singing of Violetta was a delight from beginning to end". Of her performance on January 11, in *Rigoletto*, with Bonci and Renaud—a costly and delicate casting of three famous artists—John Pitts Sanborn, another well-known music critic, wrote: "The voice of Madame Melba is sculptural; it has the qualities of physical form. The voluptuous large body of her voice takes shape in the air. . . . she can lay out a note as a painter lays colour on his canvas, so that it stays there . . . as if it had and would always exist".

The mutual interest which Melba and Hammerstein shared in presenting *La Bohème*, notwithstanding the many attempts of the management of the

Metropolitan to prevent it, is an interesting story but cannot be recounted here. On the morning after the performance of this opera—March 2, 1907—the *New York Times* reported, "She [Melba] sang the music more beautifully than she had anything else this season in New York". This was the opera in which she also gave her last performance of the season and after which, as an encore, she sang the Mad Scene from *Lucia*. Melba had originally agreed to sing at ten performances but had extended the number to fifteen and had declined all offers to appear elsewhere in New York City. A farewell statement was issued to the press the day before she left for Europe, which stated in part: "I have never enjoyed any season in America as much as the one now closing. . . . I am proud to have been associated with Mr Hammerstein in his launching of New York's new opera house. . . . His pluck appealed to me from the first, and I leave, as I came, his loyal friend and admirer".[29]

Melba had filled the theatre every time she sang, and had helped to rescue the reckless Hammerstein from bankruptcy; but all her efforts could not establish his opera house permanently. After what his son Arthur called "four years of torture", he sold out to the Metropolitan, one of the conditions being that he was not to produce opera again in New York for ten years. This condition, alone, speaks for the strength of the competition Hammerstein's venture had offered to the older establishment on Broadway.

Between her two seasons with Hammerstein and after her last performance at the Manhattan Opera House, Melba made short trips to Australia, one of them to be with her father on his eightieth birthday. She returned to London, however, in time to celebrate her twentieth year at Covent Garden at a charity matinee on June 24, 1908, at which she and Emmy Destinn raised £2,000 for the London Hospital. She sang the first act of *La Traviata* and Destinn the first act of *Madame Butterfly*.

From 1906 to 1908 Melba had divided her time between the United States and Australia and had taken no part in the Covent Garden seasons. She was vacationing on the Riviera in the autumn of 1907 when Tetrazzini made her sensational debut there. However, by 1909 when audiences began to clamour for her return she agreed to appear for single performances of operas in her repertoire for her usual fee of 500 guineas. This was also the amount she was receiving at the height of her career for private appearances at the homes of wealthy patrons in London and New York. Hostesses sometimes invited her to their parties hoping that she would sing without a fee. But as one Australian writer pointed out, "No one ever bustled David Mitchell's daughter out of her due". When a hostess approached her saying, "Surely, Madame, it is no trouble to sing a little song", she would reply: "No more trouble than to write a little cheque".

It was also in 1909 that Melba was able to fulfil a long-held wish to sing to her countrymen in the remote areas of the Outback. Incidents frequently occurred on this tour which revealed how much her appearances meant to people in isolated areas. One evening Melba was seated in the ante-room of a hall in a small town when she felt a draft from a window that John Lemmoné, her manager, had closed a few minutes earlier. Looking out she saw two urchins crouching in the rain hoping to hear at least part of the concert. She invited them inside and after the performance said to them in jest, "Now boys you owe me a guinea each". The younger one came forward with a smile and said, "Madame, we owe you much more than that".

A similar sense of indebtedness had been expressed during Melba's first visit in 1902 by Professor Marshall-Hall. In a welcoming address he said:

You represent to us all the possibility, the promise, the glamour of that rich imaginary world which each one secretly in his heart of hearts dreams attainable . . . you represent more than a particular person . . . you represent an idea. . . . Your living presence has compelled this immature, partially cultured, somewhat unintellectual city to dimly feel for a moment the presence of art, the supreme manifestation of joyous strength.[30]

After Melba's return to London in 1909 the plan to take her own opera company to Australia began to take shape. With representatives of J. C. Williamson and Company she visited the musical centres of Europe to select outstanding artists.[31] When John Lemmoné returned to make final arrangements for the season in 1911 he asserted that at fifty years of age Melba's voice was as fresh as ever. He quoted Dr. Milson Rees, the eminent Harley Street specialist who had peered down nearly every musical throat in Europe, as saying that Melba's vocal cords were the most elastic he had ever seen and that her voice would never grow old. Melba had hoped that Caruso would be a member of the company but he declined because of the long journey and in his stead came the twenty-six-year-old Irish tenor John McCormack, who was promised a concert tour after the opera season in order to make the trip worthwhile financially. The company opened at Her Majesty's Theatre, Sydney, on Saturday, September 23, 1911, with *La Traviata*. The demand for tickets was enormous. Scalpers, who bought up places in the Gallery at seventy-five cents, were able to unload them at a profit of anything up to 1,000 per cent.

At that time, the Gallery had not been dignified by any such title as Upper Circle and reserved seats were not issued for that elevated region. Patrons of "the gods"—originally so called because they were perched beside the mythological deities usually frescoed on theatre ceilings—sat on hard backless benches, their feet wedged between the people in front. Expert packers jammed them together in a solid mass, not an inch of space being wasted. Uncomfortable though this was, it developed a feeling of unity which helped to detonate the explosions of enthusiasm which were a feature of live theatre in its greatest days.

The premiere of the first Melba-Williamson opera company was a series of such demonstrations, culminating in an immense ovation at the finale, when the diva was left standing alone on a stage knee-deep in flowers. Those who had heard Melba before agreed that her marvellous voice had not deteriorated, despite her fifty years. Oddly, J. C. Williamson himself did not witness her triumph. While she was on her way to Australia, he left for Europe, their ships crossing in the Indian Ocean, so that the task of keeping the opera season running smoothly devolved on George Tallis and Hugh J. Ward. At the time, it was said that although Williamson had steeled himself against losing money on the season, his heart quailed at the thought of facing Melba if it failed.

It did not fail, although Melbourne did not respond as Sydney had done. The original plan had been to play eight weeks in each of the capital cities, but although tickets for the Melba nights in the Victorian capital were always sold out, attendance at other performances fell off to such an extent that the diva cancelled the last eleven nights of the Melbourne season and moved the company back to Sydney. This was the only time many Australians had an opportunity to hear the diva in the roles for which she had become celebrated—Mimi, Gilda, Marguerite, Juliette, Desdemona and Violetta. When she had sung Desdemona in *Otello* during the previous season of the Boston Opera Company Melba was said to have "triumphed by the sheer perfection of her singing and the unearthly quality of her voice. At the completion of the 'Ave Maria' the audience rose in a body to applaud".[32]

The 1911 Melba-Williamson season of grand opera was considered enormously successful. Despite production costs of £4,000 a week the partners were reported to have split a profit of £30,000, an enormous sum in light of the purchasing power of money at that time. Cynics who suggested that the diva had been interested primarily in the prospect of large financial returns ignored the fact that at this time she was one of the world's wealthiest artists. If making money had been her principal objective she could have made it more easily from a concert tour without any of the worries of an opera season. She had told a reporter for the Melbourne *Argus* on February 16, 1910, "It is my greatest ambition to be able to present grand opera in Australia on the same line as it is presented in the great opera houses of the world. . . . When I have appeared in grand opera here my highest ambition will have been realized". To this end she wished to appear in her best roles supported by other artists of high calibre. Before leaving for London she gave a concert in March, 1912, to raise money to erect the concert hall which bears her name at the Melbourne University Conservatorium. One of the titles she valued most highly was earned during this period when she sold a flag for £2,100 at a concert for Belgian Relief and was called "The Empress of Pickpockets".

On May 22, 1913, John McCormack appeared with Melba in a special performance of *La Bohème* to which he referred later as "the memorable occasion when she celebrated the quarter of a century of professional life at Covent Garden", adding, "it must always be reckoned amongst the great events of my life. I had the honour of being Rudolpho. I never witnessed such a demonstration. It was a splendid tribute to a marvellous woman and incomparable artist. I believe—in fact, I know—that I sing better with Melba than with any other soprano. . . . It is an inspiration".

That same season Melba also appeared in *La Bohème* with Caruso when he returned to Covent Garden for the first time after an absence of seven years. Of this performance a review next day stated: "They sang as if truly inspired". Early in 1914 she appeared in Paris with the Boston Opera Company and later toured the United States and Canada with Jan Kubelik, the violinist returning to London for the closing of the opera season at Covent Garden.

The outbreak of war in August, 1914, was a great blow to Melba, who had closer contacts with Europe than any other Australian had ever had. Returning to Coombe Cottage, her home at Lilydale near Melbourne, she turned it into a headquarters from which she organized concerts in aid of the Red Cross, travelling all over Australia to make personal appearances. She extended her activities to New Zealand, Canada and the United States, and according to the *Sydney Morning Herald* of February 24, 1931, she raised more than £100,000 for patriotic purposes.

During this period Melba also devoted much time and attention to training voice students at the Melbourne Conservatorium in Albert Street.[33] She had become interested in this institution because operas were being produced there regularly and the singing was of high quality. One day she sent for the director and inquired abruptly, "Fritz Hart, what would you do if I offered to come to the Conservatorium and teach singing?"[34] Of course Hart was delighted and the students had many memorable experiences, some of which are described in an article in the student magazine.[35] On one of these occasions, after a student had sung the aria from *Herodias*, "Dame Nellie, who had been pacing the broad middle aisle during the performance, swung round suddenly and said 'Sing it this way: Il est doux, il est bon'. A thrill went through us all as she painted those two short phrases with just the lovely tone colour she desired. They will remain in the memory of all those who heard them".[36]

Melba's work with individual pupils was described in 1965 by Miss Ethel Walker, librarian for J. C. Williamson's in Sydney. She recalled that

Melba had the most dynamic personality and, great as she was, found time to impart to us Australians much of her wonderful knowledge. . . . She would hear me sing and give me advice and, believe me, Melba could teach you more in ten minutes than many could in six months (or ever). . . . When I met her later in New York where I was playing and showed her the good notices I had received for my part as Teresa in *The Maid of the Mountains* she said she was proud of me. Melba liked people to stand on their own feet and fight for themselves.

The diva's method of teaching was an extension of that of the renowned Garcia which she had learned from his pupils Mme. Ellen Christian and Mme. Mathilde Marchesi. Melba was said to have been "an indefatigable worker who tired out everyone in the studio but herself. She left fresher than she came although she appeared habitually at an early hour and expected students to report on the dot for their lessons". Shortly after her death, John Lemmoné wrote:

On her frequent returns from abroad, Melba's first visit was always to the Conservatorium. I have known her to arrive in Melbourne in the morning—after two years' absence!—and be at the Conservatorium in the afternoon. She frequently spent from 9 a.m. until lunch, giving gratuitous lessons. Had you seen her there, with her enthusiasm, her kindly encouragement, you would have forgotten your Melba of the theatre in your love of Melba the helper.[37]

The important role she played in recognising and encouraging the development of talent wherever she found it is illustrated by the story of her encounter with Lauri Kennedy, the cellist. He says,

I shall never forget Melba. Indeed it is to her that I owe my career and whatever success and position I have achieved. In 1919 I was playing, with several others, at a little concert arranged by Fritz Hart at the Albert Street Conservatorium in Melbourne at which Melba was present and I little dreamed that this day was to be the turning point in my life. I cannot remember the details of the concert which pursued the even tenor of its course, but I sat down to play in all modesty. When I had finished, bedlam broke loose. I dimly remember Melba standing up in the middle of the people, shouting, "Bravo! Bravo! Encore! He must play an encore". Still in a daze, I was confronted with the great lady. She said: "What are you doing here! You have a great talent and a career before you. You must go abroad!"

These words had a great impact on the young artist:

When I got home that day, I sat down to think things out. I had, up to that time played quite naturally, taking it for granted, and never thinking there was anything remarkable in what I could do.[38] Melba had now, however, started new thoughts in my head. If such a great artist thought I had talent, and made such a fuss, I reasoned, perhaps I could become a great player and make my name in the world.[39]

Melba was in the United States continuing her Red Cross concerts after the Armistice, when she was called to London to take part in the peace celebrations. In 1918 she was made Dame Commander of the newly established Order of the British Empire, the equivalent of a knighthood. Later she made a tour of the English provinces and opened and closed the 1920 opera season at Covent Garden, in *Romeo and Juliette*. After the war Melba's appearances in Australia became more frequent.[40] In 1923 she was back in London singing at a benefit performance for Mme. Albani and in *La*

Bohème with the British National Opera at Covent Garden as a gesture of support for the many Australians who were singing with this company.

Roland Foster relates an interesting incident concerning a visit Melba made to the New South Wales Conservatorium. As was his custom, the Director, Henri Verbruggen, took charge of the Diploma class on Monday afternoons and gave strict instructions that under no circumstances was he to be disturbed. An insistent demand by Melba sent a messenger up to announce her but the diva had to wait. When Verbruggen finally appeared she said jokingly, "Henri, this is a nice way to treat the Queen of Song", to which he replied with a smile, "But I am King of the Conservatorium and the King can do no wrong".

Melba's immense personal popularity was partly due to her high regard for her public, no matter what they paid at the box office. Gallery patrons long remembered her admiration for their fortitude in waiting hours for theatre doors to open and then sitting on hard benches until the performance started.

More than once during the 1911 season she arranged with a nearby caterer to have afternoon tea sent up to the early comers while at the final performance she ascended in person to the "gods" and thanked them so warmly for their appreciation that the packed multitudes felt they had made a real contribution to the success of the occasion. During her visit in 1921 Melba announced in December that owing to the disappointment expressed by many who had been unable to afford the minimum price of a guinea a seat required at her earlier concerts she had decided to give a series at which no seat would cost more than five shillings and sixpence. When she heard that speculators had bought up tickets for the first concert of the series and sold them at higher prices, she stationed herself outside the box office when bookings opened for the later ones and saw that no one bought more than enough for his own personal use. History records many instances of artists hoping wistfully for a rush on the box office, but Melba provides the sole example of a star trying to restrict the sale of tickets. In the end she check-mated the scalpers by increasing the number of concerts until more than 70,000 people in Melbourne and Sydney had heard the diva at phenomenally low cost.

In 1924 Melba brought another opera company to Australia in conjunction with J. C. Williamson Ltd. The post-war absence of German, Australian and Russian artists was compensated for by a strong contingent of Italians, including the celebrated soprano Toti dal Monte, who became immensely popular, as did Apollo Granforte and Dino Borgioli.[41] Once more Melba was heard in *La Bohème* and proved that her voice, unimpaired at sixty-three, was still capable of filling the theatre with the famous floating high C.

The Melbourne season closed with another performance of *La Bohème* for the benefit of the Limbless Soldiers' Association. By auctioning boxes and seats total proceeds reached £18,000. That performance also marked the inauguration of broadcasting in Victoria; the complete opera was transmitted from station 3AR giving the few hundred radio owners of Victoria a share in the historic occasion.

Melba spent most of 1925 in England completing her recollections which were published under the title *Melodies and Memories*.[42] Then, in anticipation of giving a farewell concert at Covent Garden, she made a last tour of other English cities. The official farewell took place on June 8, 1926, and was a brilliant event. The programme opened with Melba singing Act II of *Romeo and Juliette* under the baton of Sir Percy Pitt; Vincenzo Bellezza conducted the rest of the programme which included Act IV of *Othello*, and Acts III and IV of *La Bohème* in which three other Australian singers, John Brownlee, Fred Collier and Browning Mummery, appeared with her. The greater part of this performance, including Melba's farewell speech after the final curtain, was recorded by H.M.V. Of this occasion John Brownlee wrote:

How can one describe such a night, when the whole of England, from the Royal family down, had come to pay homage to another kind of queen? The atmosphere was charged almost beyond endurance, and at the end of it all the ovation, with all its overtones of love, affection and adoration, as only the cold English can bestow them upon those whom they worship.[43]

On December 7 of the same year Melba gave a final performance of *La Bohème* at the Old Vic to augment the funds being raised by Lilian Baylis to establish opera at the Sadler's Wells theatre. The Musetta of the occasion was the Australian soprano Gertrude Johnson, who later was to train so many young Australians for roles with the Sadler's Wells company.

Eventually the sands of farewell tours and last appearances ran out. In 1928 Dame Nellie brought her third opera company to Australia. It was long remembered for introducing *Turandot* and *The Love of Three Kings* to Australian audiences, and for the magnificent presentations of *Aïda* with Anna Surana in the name part and John Brownlee as King of the Ethiopians. The diva herself said farewell to the operatic stage in Sydney in August, 1928, forty-two years after her debut in Brussels. In November she made her last Australian appearance in a concert in Geelong. After this she returned to London.

On her final visit to Covent Garden, the scene of many triumphs, she seemed to have a premonition of her death because she is said to have shivered suddenly and said, "I can see ghosts here. There are Caruso, Forsyth and others of the past". Then she broke down and wept inconsolably and said she would never return. At about this time her splendid health began to fail. Returning to Australia by ship she was taken gravely ill in Cairo and on reaching Sydney was taken to St. Vincent's hospital where she died on February 23, 1931, in her seventieth year.

After a funeral service at the Scots Church, Melbourne, long associated with the Mitchell family, Melba was buried in the Lilydale cemetery near her beloved Coombe Cottage and in sight of the beautiful Dandenongs. At the end of the burial service the Melbourne Liedertafel sang "The Long Day Closes" and after a brief silence a chorus of Australian song birds rose from the nearby gum trees. They sang a fitting requiem to the passing of a great Australian.[44]

Melba's centenary in 1961 was celebrated in many ways in different parts of the world. An Homage to Melba Committee in Melbourne organized a memorial exhibition; Australia issued a special commemorative postage stamp, and Angel Records of London released a Melba disc in their "Great Recordings of the Century" series. On November 22, 1962, a stained glass window designed by Brian Thomas was installed in the Musicians' Memorial Chapel in St. Sepulchre's Church, London, portraying a medallion of Melba with full-length figures depicting her favourite roles on either side.

Roland Gelatt, reviewing Joseph Wechsberg's book *Red Plush and Black Velvet*[45] in 1961, provided an excellent picture of Melba as a prima donna. He wrote:

She began with an incomparable voice. For this we have the testimony not only of ear witnesses who heard her in person, but also of the recorded legacy she left us.[46] . . . most notably two actual-performance recordings, one made from the stage of the Metropolitan Opera House on primitive cylinder equipment in 1901, the other made from the stage of Covent Garden with benefit of microphones at Melba's farewell in 1926. It is hard to say which is more incredible, the recklessly brilliant coloratura on the early cylinder or the serene purity of tone and magical legato of the 65-year-old veteran. Certainly you will not hear her like today.

Melba's voice was not the only element that gave her stature as a prima donna. She was good looking; she had the air and bearing of a great personage, and she was given to saying and doing exactly as she pleased. Her forthright tongue and her penchant for young men were the talk of Europe. She was also rich . . . and Melba did not boggle at spending as lavishly as she earned.

Melba, a film produced in Hollywood in 1952, although considered entertaining by a large segment of the American public, seemed far from an acceptable picture to those familiar with the facts of her life. Evan Senior, the Australian-born editor of *Music and Musicians*, ended a review with the statement, "No, I do not have to wonder what Melba would have to say about *Melba*. Her command of blistering invective far outshone anything I could summon up for the purpose. She would have blasted the whole film from its wide screen".[47] A far better portrayal was the radio serial *The Melba Story*, first broadcast over a nationwide hook-up in Australia in 1946 with Glenda Raymond, a leading Melbourne soprano, playing the title role and singing many of the operatic arias associated with the diva's career.

The best portraits, however, probably are those that lie embedded in the living memories of those who knew her well. Freda Barrymore, a Tasmanian journalist, wrote: "Had I met Melba against any other background than Coombe Cottage, Lilydale, I doubt that she would have appeared to be the same person. When I saw her later in London, Paris and America it always seemed to me that only in her Australian home was she the real woman as well as the artist. She was much happier there and less sophisticated, more interested in simple things".[48]

John Brownlee, Melba's most illustrious vocal protégé, recalls: "She could be graciously warm or uncompromisingly frigid; tolerant to novitiates, she liked to queen it over her equals. Outwardly austere, Melba never wore her heart where it could be seen. She went out of her way to make contacts for her protégés. She was almost fanatical in her attempts to foster young talent and was never happier than when surrounded by a group of young ambitious singers, who were sincere in their attempts to strive for a professional career".

Melba was the first of a distinguished line of singers whose fine voices and strong personalities have brought Australia to the attention of the world as a cradle of musical talent.

NOTES

1. *British Australasian*, April 19, 1906.

2. Thompson, J., *On Lips of Living Men* (Melbourne: Lansdowne Press, 1961).

3. The *Sun*, Sydney, January 24, 1932.

4. *Sydney Morning Herald*, 1927.

5. Reid, M., *And the Ladies Came to Stay* (Melbourne: Presbyterian Ladies' College, 1961).

6. Waters, T., *Much besides Music* (Melbourne: Georgian House, 1951).

7. Ibid.

8. Murphy, A. G., *Melba* (London: Chatto and Windus, 1909).

9. John Lemmoné was considered one of the greatest flute virtuosi of his time but he was closely associated with Melba for so long a period that his achievements as an artist in his own right were often overlooked.

He was born in 1861 at Ballarat, Victoria. When he was a child his father bought a penny whistle and offered to give a fife to the first of his three young sons who learned to play a tune on it. John won the contest but practised so persistently that the family forced him out of the house and on to the common to play. One day, when passing a pawnbroker's shop, he spied a flute in the window and determined to have it. Not possessing the required 12/6 he dredged a small quantity of gold from the creek that flowed through the town and became the proud owner of his first flute. Years later he said, "I have since had special instruments made for me by the best makers of flutes in the world but somehow none has equalled this in my regard. It was my whole world. It moulded my destiny and the walk in life that I would sincerely follow again".

10. In her memoirs Marchesi wrote: "The wife of the Austrian Consul in Melbourne gave her a letter to me. This lady was Mme Elise Pinschoff (née Wiedermann) one of my former pupils and for several years a distinguished opera comique singer"—Marchesi, M., *Memoirs* (London: Harper Bros., 1897).

11. Reed, C. L., *Bel Canto—Principles and Practice* (New York: Coleman & Ross, 1950).

12. Shaw, G. B., *Music in London, 1890-1894*, Vol. 2 (London: Constable & Co., 1932).

13. *New York Herald Tribune* magazine, May 28, 1961.

14. Duval, J. H., *Svengali's Secrets and Memoirs of The Golden Age* (New York: Robert Speller and Sons, 1965).

15. Murphy, op. cit.

16. Klein, H., *Golden Age of Opera* (London: Routledge, 1933).

17. *Sydney Morning Herald*, February 24, 1931.

18. Murphy, op. cit.

19. Ibid.

20. Some of the French papers with hostile inclination made themselves ridiculous in the eyes of cultured citizens of that city by writing that they did not want "Aborigines" in the classic music halls of Paris. Continental journalists were always rather baffled by Australians. If not aborigines, what were they? Twenty-five years before, Sydney-born Lucy Chambers had been referred to as a "creole" by the newspapers of Florence.

21. Melba created the role of Nedda for Covent Garden on May 19, 1893 and for the Metropolitan on December 22, 1893. She did not take part in the first performance of the opera, which was held at the Teatro dal Verme in Milan on May 21, 1892. Fernando de Lucia was the Canio in all three of these performances.

22. Wood, H., *My Life of Music* (London: Gollancz, 1946).

23. Eaton, Q., *Opera Caravan* (New York: Farrar, Straus, Cudahy, 1957).

24. Thompson, O., *The American Singer* (New York: Dial Press, 1927).

25. Why Melba ever essayed a role so patently unsuited to her voice and temperament was not clear. Perhaps she wished to prove that she could equal any other singer in versatility as well as surpassing most in vocal quality.

26. Garden, M., and Biancolli, L., *The Mary Garden Story* (New York: Simon and Schuster, 1951).

27. Sheehan, V., *Oscar Hammerstein I* (New York: Simon and Schuster, 1956).

28. Ibid.

29. Ibid.

30. Murphy, op. cit.

31. Among these were Mme. Jeanne Wayda, the Countess Eleanora de Cisneros and Rosina Buckman. The men included the tenors Ciccolini and Juesnel, bass baritones Edmund Burke, Alfred Kaufman and Andreas Scandiani. The principal conductor was Angelini and the producer Frank Rigo.

32. Eaton, Q., *The Boston Opera Company, Its History* (New York: Appleton Century, 1965).

33. This was later to be renamed in her honour and to have £8000 bequeathed to it by her for a scholarship to be used "in the search for a successor".

34. Hart, F., "Words from Honolulu", *Melba Conservatorium* magazine, no. 5, 1938.

35. Sutton, V., and Tregear, W., "Those Were the Days", *Melba Conservatorium* magazine, no. 12, 1945.

36. Editorial, *Melba Conservatorium* magazine, no. 10, 1943.

37. The *Sun*, Sydney, January 24, 1932.

38. This is an attitude encountered among many Australian artists. When it was mentioned to Sir William McKie in his study at Westminster Abbey he considered for a moment and then commented, "That is a very interesting observation; I had never thought there was anything extraordinary in what I had done before I came to England".

39. Kennedy had never received any instruction on the cello. He had learned to play by studying each evening by candlelight under the stage where the Kennedy Concert Company had performed earlier and while the others packed in preparation for moving on to the next town the following day.

40. In 1919 she gave a concert with the Australian violinist Leila Doubleday and others at the Sydney Conservatorium and when John Lemmoné became ill she quickly arranged a benefit performance for him which raised more than £2,500. In 1921, after an extensive tour of the United States, she gave another series of concerts in Australia with Lemmoné as flautist and Una Bourne as pianist; several concerts were also given in conjunction with the New South Wales State Orchestra under the direction of Henri Verbruggen who later became conductor of the Minneapolis Symphony Orchestra.

41. Sixteen operas were presented, among them *Andrea Chenier* for the first time. The Australian singers were Vera Bedford, Doris McInnes, Rita Miller, Rosa Pinkerton, Anita Roma, Strella Wilson, Vida Sutton, Roy Dunn and Alfred O'Shea (brought back from Europe by Melba). Later in the season Eileen Castles joined the company. Frank St. Leger, one of the conductors, had been Melba's accompanist, the later became an administrator of prima donnas and legers at the Metropolitan Opera House.

42. London: Thornton, Butterworth, 1925.

43. *Saturday Review* (New York), December 25, 1954.

44. *Walkabout*, Vol. 27, no. 5, May 1961.

45. *New York Times Book Review*, December 17, 1961.

46. Between the years 1904 and 1926 Melba made over 150 recordings, more than a third of which, it is said, were never released. Of the royalties on these records which were sold for a guinea each (which at the time was roughly equivalent to five American dollars) half went to the singer. Referring to this income Peter Dawson once remarked in a radio interview, "Imagine how the wool grew while she slept".

47. *Music and Musicians*, London, September, 1953.

48. "The Great Melba", *Women's Weekly*, Sydney, May 6, 13, 20, 27, 1957.

MELBA'S AUTOBIOGRAPHICAL SKETCH OF 1898

NELLIE MELBA

It was Oscar Wilde who said that a woman should never be quite accurate about her age, as it looks so calculating. Perhaps nowhere is a woman's age such a sensitive subject as in the world of opera. Melba had a late start, and was not especially anxious to dwell on her experience in Australia prior to her study with Marchesi and her debut in Brussels on October 13, 1887, and the matter of her exact birthdate seemed to have been a fairly well-kept secret throughout her life. Olin Downes, in his obituary in the *New York Times* in 1931, begins, "No one knows for a certainty the year of her birth. . . ." In an article on the care of the voice (reproduced later in this volume) which was presumably reviewed by the singer, her birth year is given as 1865. For years reference books disagreed, many listing 1859 (including Colson in his 1932 biography). In the autobiographical sketch which follows, published in 1898, she states that she came to London with her father in 1887; we are told in the 1909 Murphy biography that she set sail from Melbourne on March 11, 1886, and that she heard Albani in London on May 4, 1886. In the 1898 sketch, she states that she was married at the age of seventeen. Since her marriage took place on December 22, 1882, this would have fixed her birth year as 1865. Actually, Melba was born in 1861, so she was twenty-one at the time of her marriage. To set the matter straight once and for all was a fairly simple matter, which the editor took care of as long ago as 1959 (see figure 2).

From: *The Musical Age* (New York), August 25, 1898.

STATE OF VICTORIA

"EXTRACT" OF ENTRY   N⁰   36038·&

ED

Office of the Government Statist,

Melbourne, ...7th April, 1959._

Re Application Fol.   94864
MEMO.

According   to   the   Registers   in   this   Office,

Helen Porter MITCHELL

was born at Richmond

on 19th May, 1861.

The   Official   Number   of   the   entry   is....... **12520/61**

V. H. ARNOLD,

Government Statist

N.B.—The Fee for an Uncertified Extract or a search over any period of five years or part thereof is 5/-. A Certificate of above entry will be supplied for an additional fee of 5/-. In all correspondence bearing on the entry, the "Application Folio No. and the Official Number" must be quoted.

N.482/7.57—1694

2. Official Certificate of Melba's Birth Date

Mme. Nellie Melba has written for T. P. O'Connor's London periodical the history of her life. It really is not a history; it is rather a recital of the things in her life which she likes to tell and thinks her friend, the public, would care to hear.

I suppose "the days of my youth" began with my birth, and so, although I fail to see how it will interest anybody, I may tell you that I was born at "Doonside," a dear old rambling house, with a large garden, at Richmond, which is still my father's town residence in Melbourne, Australia.

But the wealth of my childhood's memories always rushes to Steel's Flat, Lilydale, one of my father's country places in Victoria, which he sold some years ago to Mr. David Syme, the wealthy proprietor of the "Age" newspaper, to whose generosity the visit of the Victorian military contingent in Jubilee year was mainly due.

In this charming country place, free from the restraint of Melbourne school life, it was my delight to spend hours galloping barebacked across the plains and through the winding bridle-tracks of the bush. I am sure my wanderings were only limited by my pony's endurance, and not by any sense of satisfaction or fatigue on my part.

Although unusually high-spirited, I loved to be alone, and have often spent five or six hours on the edge of a creek, fishing with bait that rarely brought me a good return. But I was quite happy. The silent plains, the vast ranges of eucalyptus forest, the sunny skies and the native wild birds were all one glorious harmony, and the time seemed all too short as I rode or fished, singing, singing all the time. I was never at the homestead, nor, indeed, anywhere else, when I should have been, and the question "Where is Miss Nellie?" grew to be a first-class conundrum.

HER FIRST CRITIC

At six years of age I was, by some strange freak of parental favor or childish despotism, allowed to appear at a concert, and my singing of "Shells of the Ocean" was so kindly received that I had to give an encore, my extra number being no other than "Coming through the Rye." The next day I was playing about with a little girl who lived opposite, and, elated with my concert success, I waited eagerly for some comment. The minutes passed—years, I thought them—but my child chum continued to ignore what was to me the chiefest thing in the world.

Unable to curb my eagerness any further, I at last blurted out: "Well, the concert—you know I sang at the concert?" She inclined her face toward mine, and, lowering her voice to a significant pitch, answered: 'Nellie Mitchell, I saw your drawers!" I have never forgotten the spontaneous malice in the criticism of my little playmate. Since then I have had many occasions to be amused in recalling the malicious innuendo of my first critic.

My willfulness and aggravating contrariness on all occasions eventually led to my being sent to a boarding-school, where it was hoped some sense of docility might enter into my rebellious head. But it was no use. It seemed impossible to teach me anything except music. I was always at the bottom of the class, and generally in disgrace. From the balcony of the school I could see the turret of "Doonside," and my father, who rode past each day, considered it wisest not to acknowledge in any way so fractious a pupil. This was perhaps the bitterest experience of my younger days. To be in sight of my home and unable to go there, to see my father and not be noticed by him, so filled me with sorrow that I was constantly in floods of tears. During this time of banishment the most marked kindness from those in charge of the school failed to bring me any comfort, and when I was allowed to return home my delight was unbounded.

3. An Early Photograph of Nellie Melba

HER FIRST CONCERT

One day, when driving around the town of Sorrento, I noticed that the fence of the local cemetery was in a deplorably dilapidated condition, and I determined on getting up a concert to provide funds for a new railing.

I had very flaring posters printed, and as a solution of one question of "ways and means" I took charge of them myself, and with paste and brush set out to stick them in the best positions, a task which I successfully accomplished. I raised £20 by this exploit, and later on, when I saw a nice new fence round the cemetery, I felt it was more due to my tact as a bill-sticker than to any attractions my concert had to offer.

Not very long afterward I decided to give a sort of drawing-room concert in my native city of Melbourne, from which I take my name, and I wrote to all my friends asking their presence. My father heard of the scheme, and determined to thwart the desire for a public career which was even then faintly manifesting itself. He wrote to them all, too, and as a personal favor begged them not to attend. All unconscious of this parental strategy, I repaired to the scene of the concert, and when I stepped out on the platform I was greeted by an audience of two! All the same I went through with my program, and sang as well as I knew how for the loyal duo—and ever since I have had larger audiences.

HER MARRIAGE

At seventeen I was married to Mr. Charles Armstrong, youngest son of the late Sir Andrew Armstrong, Bart., of King's County, Ireland. My husband was not musical, and as I soon found that domestic life did not fill the entire range of my girlish fancies the old love for music returned with renewed force, and I sang whenever I could. I may mention, too, that I was the first lady to perform on the grand organ of the Melbourne Town Hall, my appearance being at a charity concert.

Free from the opposition which I had always encountered at home, my appearances became very frequent, and I won considerable success as an amateur, and, later, gave a few concerts on ordinary businesslike lines. In 1887 my father was appointed by the government of Victoria a commissioner to the Indian and Colonial Exhibition in London, and I accompanied him home. I had a letter of introduction to Mme. Marchesi, and I lost no time in going to Paris. She heard me sing and from the first gave me the most generous encouragement. After my second song she rushed excitedly out of the drawing-room, and, calling to her husband, she said: "Salvatore, j'ai enfin une étoile!"

MARCHESI'S PUPIL

When I had finished singing she asked me gravely: "Mrs. Armstrong, are you serious? Have you patience?" "Yes," I answered. "Then, if you can stay with me for one year I will make something extraordinary of you," and she divided the long word in quite a curious staccato way. To Mme. Marchesi I owe more than I can say, and the great teacher who encouraged me so warmly remains my cherished friend.

When I look back on the nine years of my professional life many memories crowd upon each other, and in the tangled jumble it is not always easy to recall any particular event.

Personally, I think I have been most impressed by my first appearances at La Scala, Milan, where I sang "Lucia," and at the Grand Opera, where "Hamlet" was the opera.

HONORED BY A KING

Both occasions were trying ordeals for a singer of very little experience, but in each case I received generous inducement to push ahead; in fact, the people were more than kind.

Once, during a brief season in Stockholm, it happened that all dates on which I sang were evenings on which the King could not possibly be present. When his Majesty returned to town I received a royal message asking if I could by any chance give an extra performance, so that he and the members of the Court might attend.

Circumstances permitted me to do so, and my desire to please so popular a sovereign gave tremendous delight to the people. The theatre was packed to the suffocation point, and the enthusiasm of the audience, in their excessive kindness, was really overwhelming. After my chief scene the King rose in his box, and, facing me where I stood on the stage, bowed very low. This act of courtesy his Majesty repeated several times, everyone in the house having risen meanwhile, and their cheers were almost too much for me.

THE KING'S KISS

On the morning following I was summoned to the palace to receive the personal congratulations of the King and Queen and a decoration from the hands of his Majesty. A pin was necessary to fasten the ribbon, and as none had been provided I offered one to the King. "Oh! I must not take a pin from you," he said, smiling; "it might mar our friendship."

Then, after a moment's hesitation, he added, as he took the pin: "I will break the evil spell, though, with a kiss, and we will be friends always."

When I was leaving the city, a little later, I had further evidence of the people's good will. The way from my hotel to the railway was so crowded that traffic was completely stopped, and at the station itself there were over five thousand people, who did everything possible to enhance the memory of a really delightful visit.

So much for past days! As to the future, I think my warmest wishes centre themselves round a visit to my sunny southern home. I have a great dislike to sea traveling, or probably I should have taken that long trip already. That visit will be more a matter of sentiment than business, and I look forward to it with the very keenest pleasure. I intend to take out with me a complete, but small, opera company of the very best artists. I shall take my own orchestra, chorus and scenery, and I'll sing with all my heart for dear old Australia.

MELBA BEFORE MARCHESI

In the early days of her career, Melba stated flatly that she had come to the *École Marchesi* in 1886 with no prior training (see her article on "Voice Culture" published in 1895 and reprinted in this book). As we can see from the following, the question had been raised in the press at least as early as 1891. By 1909 (in Murphy) Melba was persuaded to give some acknowledgment to her lessons with Signor Pietro Cecchi of Melbourne, which had apparently begun sometime in late 1879 or early 1880. We are informed that

on Saturday, May 17, 1884, as a pupil of Signor Cecchi, she made her first public appearance as a singer . . . and during the latter part of that year and throughout 1885 she regularly sang at concerts . . . at Sydney, Ballarat, Bendigo, Hamilton and other places. In Melbourne, too, her concert appearances were many, if not very lucrative. Under these circumstances, Signor Cecchi had said he would make no charge for these intermittent lessons, but that, if she ever made the success which he believed she would make, she could then pay him. . . . All this time her heart was set on seeking fame in Europe—an ambition which Signor Cecchi constantly encouraged. . . . [When ready to depart for Europe] Signor Cecchi, acting on foolish advice, or for some other reason, applied for immediate payment at full rates for the lessons he had given her during the preceding twenty months. . . . She finally found a friend willing to lend her the money for the satisfaction of the teacher's account [which] she paid to the last penny. . . . Then she drove the circumstance from her memory—or at least appeared to do so; for the name of Signor Cecchi never again escaped her lips, and if she has been resolutely silent as to his share in her early vocal training, her lips have also been as resolute in the still more characteristic silence that refused to link his name with one word of blame.

The story seems fairly straightforward, but it should have been left alone by Beverley Nichols in *Melodies and Memories*. In 1951 some of Melba's letters to Cecchi were published for the first time in a book which probably did not receive much in the way of world-wide circulation, so it seems worthwhile that they be preserved here. There follows a brief biographical note on Signor Cecchi, resurrected from an 1889 Melbourne paper.

WHO WAS THE REAL TEACHER OF MELBA?

THOROLD WATERS

Judging from the instances I have known, the longevity of men's voices seems to be greater than women's. Sims Reeves, Santley, and Battistini are names which occur at once, and who could sing Handel's supremely difficult "Waft Her, Angels" with more exquisite phrasing than Ben Davies when in his sixties, or stride befeathered and moccasined through the Albert Hall arena with such gusto of mien and voice as I heard from that veteran at the age of seventy-two in the pageant of *Hiawatha*?

Dame Nellie Melba's voice remained with her when she was within months of seventy, but she wisely kept within the legato bounds of Desdemona's and Mimi's arias—and who could do those to such perfection? By this time, however, Melba found it essential to give out some little extra which replaced with a rather more ordinary gold the special sheen of voice reminding me of Debussy's "girl with the flaxen hair" that hitherto had been hers. Having heard Adelina Patti only in the last farewell concert of her career, in 1911 with Sarasate, I cannot say what had been special in her voice behind the diamond coruscations it still retained. Perhaps Melba was a happy chance, the chaste gold coming into her tones in variance with the governing laws of "wide" production that in other singers usually induce those shallow sounds known to the French as "voix blanche." I hear that sort too often in Australia, robbed of anything auriferous.

And now enters the delicate question, who (besides God) was responsible for what may best be termed the rare and inimitable complexion of the Melba vocal sounds? Of course, we all know the legend of Mathilde

From: Thorold Waters, *Much Besides Music* (1951).

Marchesi's excited announcement, "Salvatore, I have found a star!" A parcel of letters which came into my hands some time ago does not allow dismissal of the subject just like that. Those letters were sent by Melba, as Nellie Mitchell, and later as Nellie Armstrong, to her original vocal teacher in Melbourne, Pietro Cecchi, with whom she studied over seven years. They certainly impress one towards a decision that he had more to do with the fashioning of a very great singer than the Parisian finder of stars (including Calve, Etelka Gerster, Emma Eames, and Ilma di Murska) was able to achieve in the less than a year's tutelage of the Australian "find" before her historic Brussells debut. Something went amiss in the loyalty due to Cecchi, and it would appear that the something was financial, so that in the end Cecchi's name was kept well in the background, and that influential personage Marchesi "found" and was resplendently reillumined by another star.

The letters were handed to me to peruse, and at discretion to use, while Melba still lived, and it seemed to me that sometime they should be revealed, but not in her lifetime. The earlier ones indicate that the record in biographical dictionaries of her having made her first public appearance as an adult singer at a *Messiah* performance in Sydney in December of 1885 is at least three years out. Her studies with Signor Cecchi had been brought by 1882 up to a stage when mentor and pupil considered her fit to undertake some concerts in Queensland. The first missive came from Port Mackay, North Queensland, Friday, Sept. 15, 1882.

My dear Signor Cecchi,

I suppose you will be astonished to hear from me, but I want to tell you that although I am nearly 2,000 miles from Melbourne I am not forgetting my practising, for I manage to get a little every day. I am going to sing at two concerts, one on Monday [September 18] and the other on Saturday [September 23]. I hope I shall be successful.

Will you please send me six or seven nice *English* songs up, as the people here do not understand Italian. I daresay you will be able to find some pretty ones; send them as soon as possible.

I shall not be home for two or three months yet. I intend taking a long holiday, as I am enjoying myself so well. I go out either riding, driving or yachting every day. Will you kindly remember me to Mr. Nobili, also to Mr. Bracchi, if he is in Town?

Hoping you are quite well,

Believe me,
Your affectionate pupil,
Nellie Mitchell.

Presumably the "Mr. Bracchi" referred to in this letter and a postscript to the one that follows was Signor Baracchi, a distinguished Italian who had been brought out to fill an important Public Service position.

Port Mackay,
N. Queensland,
Oct. 15th/82.

My dear Signor Cecchi,

I was indeed delighted to get your nice letter, and with it the songs. They are all very pretty, but three of them I have had before. Next time you write to me, write in French, as I can understand it. I am sure it must be very difficult for you to write in English. I had *great success* at the two concerts I sang at, so much so that all the ladies up here are jealous of me. I was encored *twice* for each song, and they hurrahed me and threw me no end of bouquets. Everyone asks me who my master is, and when I say Signor Cecchi, they all say "When I go to Melbourne he shall be my master, too."

Has my sister commenced singing with you yet? If she has not, you insist on her going to you, as I want her to learn very much. I am still enjoying myself very much, and I shall not be home until January. If you come across any other pretty songs, you can send them to me, please. I shall now stop, hoping that you are quite well and that you have lots of pupils,

Believe me,
Your affectionate pupil,
Nellie Mitchell.

Remember me to Mr. Nobili and Mr. Bracchi.

By the next letter she had become Mrs. Armstrong (on December 22, 1882), and Captain Armstrong had in view a career in the Queensland sugarlands:

Rushcutters' Bay,
Sydney, N.S.W.,
April 12th/83.

My dear Signor Cecchi,

I might have stayed a week or two longer in dear old Melbourne, for when I arrived here I found that my husband could not meet me for some time, and I have been quite miserable here, just thinking how many lessons I have missed.

I start for Port Mackay and I expect to arrive there on Monday week, so I shall soon be in the tropical regions again. I met a German gentleman here that you know. His name is Mr. Ampt. He thought a great deal of my singing, as indeed everyone does, for they all call me the "Australian Nightingale." I have had four musical parties given me since I have been in Sydney. I was asked to sing at a Liedertafel concert, but of course I had not time; I have promised to sing for them next time I am here.

I hear Mrs. Kemmis leaves Melbourne today [probably wife of Canon Kemmis, of fashionable St. Mark's, Darling Point]. She has not had much time for her singing lessons; she is a regular grand. I am staying with Mrs. Bagge, who has been most kind and nice to me. The Italian opera season commences here tonight. I hope they will have more success here than they had in Melbourne. I intend going to hear them on Monday night. I wish Alice Rees were going to sing, for I would like to hear her so much.

I shall now stop, hoping to hear from you soon. With kindest regards to Mr. Nobili.

Believe me,
Always your affectionate pupil,
Nellie Armstrong.

This Alice Rees, wife of the distinguished pianist and composer Max Vogrich, who seems to have been on the rise to distinction, was a pupil of my old teacher William Parkinson. She and Vogrich settled subsequently in New York. Melba's next letter was once more from Mackay, and was dated May 11, 1883:

My dear Signor Cecchi,

I am once more in Mackay and 2,000 miles away from dear Melbourne and all my dear friends there. I arrived here last Tuesday week after a most dreadful trip, for I was seasick the whole way. It has been raining in torrents ever since I have been here. I have just come in nicely for the end of the wet season, and it is really most dreary and miserable. We are not in our own house yet. We do not expect to get into it for six weeks. The Montague-Turner Company are expected to arrive here in a week or two. I sincerely hope they will do well, for they have been very unfortunate lately.
[Note: Headed by the prima donna Annis Montague, this company was still touring in *Maritana, Bohemian Girl*, and some of the old Italian operas ten years later.—T.W.]
How is my sister getting along with her singing? I hope she goes regularly and practises well. Will you kindly send me up the low copy of a song called 'Ehren on the Rhine'?
I hope to be able to get down to Melbourne early next year, so it will not be so very long before I see you all again. I shall now stop, as there is no news to tell you, except that my voice is in very good order, and I practise every day. My husband wishes to be kindly remembered to you.

Hoping you are well,
Believe me, your affect. pupil,
Nellie Armstrong.

Again from Mackay, on July 4, 1883:

My dear Signor Cecchi,

I received your welcome letter yesterday, and with it the songs. Thanks very much for sending them. I had "The trysting tree" before, but that does not matter, as it is always useful to have two copies. I do not care very much for the Neapolitan song, as I do not think I pronounce the words properly. Is it the same pronunciation as Italian? I hope you will send me some more songs when they come out, as it gets very monotonous singing the same songs over and over again.
The Montague-Turner Company are up here just now. I called on Mrs. Turner and like her very much indeed. This afternoon Mr. Armstrong and I are going to take them for a drive and show them some of the sugar plantations. They are having

very good houses, I am happy to say, and I think will do a very good business. They charge six shillings for dress-circle seats, and it is well filled every night, so they ought to be satisfied.

I have quite recovered from my small illness, and feel very jolly and happy. My voice, I think, is better than ever, although I am afraid I do not practise as I ought. Mackay is very gay just now. Any amount of dances and balls. I am glad to hear Annie is improving in her singing; it would please me so much if I thought she would ever be able to sing well. You never told me how Alice Rees got on in opera. There was a gentleman here from Melbourne the other day, and he said she was simply perfection—lost all her stiffness, and was altogether charming. Is that true? I hope we shall be able to get to Melbourne in January. Of course I shall go on with my singing when we do come. I wrote to Mr. Nobili the other day asking him to get me a comic song that my husband is very anxious to get. I hope he did not think me very rude for asking him, but I knew he was the most likely person to be able to procure it for me.

We are having the most lovely weather. Very cold mornings and evenings and warm in the middle of the day. Very like Spring in Melbourne. We have not had any fires yet. I suppose you have them burning all day long in Melbourne. I have exhausted my small stock of news, so I shall stop.

Believe me, Your affect. pupil,
Nellie Armstrong

Now comes the letter which definitely turned Melba into a singing career-ist, her husband having presumably sickened of sugar planting by then:

The Hollow,
c.o. Mrs. Rawson,
Port Mackay,
N. Queensland

My dear Signor Cecchi,

I suppose you have heard from my sister that we have arrived safely in Mackay, after a rather tedious journey. My baby [George Armstrong was born on October 16, 1883] is very well, and stood the journey better than I expected. It is very hot up here, and I feel it very much.

Now to business. My husband is quite agreeable for me to adopt *music* as a profession. I do not mind telling you that times are very bad here, and we are as *poor* as it is possible for anyone to be. We have both come to the conclusion that it is no use letting my voice go to waste up here, for the pianos here are all so bad it is impossible to sing in tune to them. Not only that, the heat is so intense that I feel my voice is getting weaker every day. So you will understand that I am anxious to leave Queensland as soon as possible. *I must make some money.* Could you not form a small company and let us go touring through the Colonies, for of course I should like to study for the Opera, but would have to be earning money at the same time. My husband will accompany me, and my baby will be quite big enough to leave in Melbourne with my sisters. Madame Elmblad would join us, I am sure. Do you think we could make money? I shall wait anxiously for a letter from you, for I am very unhappy, here where there is no music, no nothing. We spoke of August next year; let it be much earlier than that if you can possibly arrange it, for I believe I should be

4. Grand Concert Programme, April 17, 1885. Courtesy of Mrs. Richard Bonelli.

PROGRAMME.

PART I.

1. PART SONG ... ... "The Warrior's Song" ... ... HATTON
   LIEDERTAFEL.

2. SONG ... ... "Steering for Home" ... ... REYLOFF
   MR. A. C. CARNEGIE.

3. SONG ... ... "In Olden Days" ... ... ANDREWS
   MRS. CARTER.
   VIOLIN OBLIGATO BY MR. A. HOLLANDER.

4. SOLO (with humming accompaniment) "The Drowsy Woods" ... STORCH
   LIEDERTAFEL.
   SOLO BY MR. V. WOOLCOCK.

5. GRAND SCENA—*Dinorah* ... "Ombra Leggiera" ... ... MEYERBEER
   MRS. ARMSTRONG (of the Metropolitan Concerts).

6. SONG ... ... "My Queen" ... ... BLUMENTHAL
   SIGNOR MODINI.

7. QUARTET ... "Tho' the World with Transport Bless Thee" ... WALLACE
   MRS. ARMSTRONG, MRS. CARTER, MESSRS. A. & J. L. HOLLANDER.

8. VOCAL WALTZ (with full band accompaniment) "The Star of Love" ... SIEDE
   LIEDERTAFEL.

Interval of 15 Minutes,

During which the Band will play "The Rip Van Winkle Lancers," by D'Albert, and the "Grand Mogul Waltzes," by Metra.

PART II.

1. PART SONG ... ... "The Long Day Closes" ... ... SULLIVAN
   LIEDERTAFEL.

2. SONG (with full band accompaniment) "The Children's Home" ... ... COWEN
   MRS. CARTER.

3. GRAND ARIA ... ... "Ah Crudele"
   (Specially written for Signor Modini by CHEVALIER FITTIPALDI)
   SIGNOR MODINI

4. SOLO (with vocal accompaniment) "O World ! Thou Art Wond'rous Fair" F. HILLER
   LIEDERTAFEL.
   SOLO BY MRS. ARMSTRONG.

5. SONG ... ... "My Queen of Hearts" ... ... HARPER
   MR. A. C. CARNEGIE.

6. SONG ... ... "When the Heart is Young" ... ... BUCK
   MRS. ARMSTRONG

7. VOCAL WALTZ ... ... "Haste to the Dance" ... ... VOGEL
   LIEDERTAFEL.

GOD SAVE THE QUEEN.

47

dead by then. I shall be advised by what you say in this. I hope what I say will be agreeable to you. I hope you will answer this letter as soon as you receive it, so as to let me know what ought to be done. Remember, whenever you are ready for me I can come at once, for there is nothing to detain me now that Mr. Armstrong is agreeable. I want you to keep this quite a secret from my sisters and friends. Do not mention it to anyone until everything is settled.

Will you give Miss Dawson my dearest love and tell her I received the Polish Dances quite safely. And now I shall say Goodbye, with deepest affection, hoping to hear something very favorable soon.

> Believe me,
> Your affect. pupil,
> Nellie Armstrong.

"In response to this letter Signor Cecchi sent a telegram saying to come to Melbourne at once," my informant related. "He arranged for her debut and took all responsibility. She made £750 the first year after her appearance." The career had begun in earnest, and the next letter reveals that Mrs. Armstrong was singing at concerts in Sydney well in advance of that "first public appearance" (anywhere as an adult) in December, 1885, in that city:

> Metropolitan Hotel, Sydney,
> June 7th, 1885.

My dear Signor Cecchi,

Although I have had great success as regards public taste, my critique in the *Sydney Morning Herald*, although not bad, was not good. Mrs. Fisher writes for that paper, and as she is a great friend of Alice Rees, I can understand why she is afraid to praise me too much. In one of the evening papers, it said that I was the best singer that had ever visited Sydney. We have all been run down, even Kruse in two papers yesterday, and we all wish we were back again in Melbourne. I cannot think what the people want here.

I feel too disgusted to write any more. I shall send you the papers. With love to Miss Dawson,

> Believe me,
> Your affect. pupil,
> Nellie Armstrong.

The Kruse she mentions was, of course, Johannes Kruse, most celebrated violinist Australia has yet produced, later not only a member of the historic Joachim String Quartet, but also founder of a distinguished similar ensemble in London, and leader of the Berlin Philharmonic Orchestra. It must have been on this tour that Melba found an audience of three in Bathurst, two reporters and one man who paid, and sang a bit of her concert to them. There was just one more letter, and one telegram, from Nellie Armstrong to Signor Cecchi thereafter, the letter coming from England in the following year. The telegram, from Sydney under the date January 23, 1886, preceded her departure for England, and ran:

ALFRED HALL.

Friday Evening, August 21st, 1885.

Kowalski Grand Concert,

— ARTISTES —

MRS. ARMSTRONG,   **MISS ADA WILLETTS,**

MR. GEORGE DAWSON COLEMAN,   **SIGNOR MODINI,**

MR. GEORGE HERBERT, R.A.M.,

M. HENRI KOWALSKI,

THE BALLARAT LIEDERTAFEL,

Mr. JOHN ROBSON, ... CONDUCTOR.

✳ PROGRAMME⁝⁝PART I. ✳

1. ⎰ a. "When Evening's Twilight" ... ... ⎱ b. "Tar's Song"	}	Hatton.
THE LIEDERTAFEL.		
2. VOCAL WALTZ—		Bucalossi.
SIGNOR CARLO MODINI.		
3. PARAPHRASE ON MARTHA—		Kowalski.
M. HENRI KOWALSKI.		
4. CAVATINA—"Lucia di Lamermoor"		Donizetti.
MRS. ARMSTRONG.		
5. "Tambour Battant" (Marche)		Kowalski.
MISS ADA WILLETTS AND M. HENRI KOWALSKI.		
(Expressly written for two Pianos for this occasion.)		
6. "Comrades in Arms"		Adam.
THE LIEDERTAFEL.		

✳ INTERVAL OF FIVE MINUTES—PART II. ✳

7. "Drowsy Woods"		Storch.
THE LIEDERTAFEL.		
8. "L'addio" *(Expressly written for Mr. Modini)*		Lamperti.
SIGNOR CARLO MODINI.		
9. SCHERZO IN B FLAT MINOR—		Chopin.
M. HENRI KOWALSKI.		
10. "The Angel at the Window"		Tours.
MRS. ARMSTRONG.		
11. "Marche—Hongroise"		Kowalski.
PLAYED AT THREE PIANOS BY		
MISS ADA WILLETTS, MR. GEORGE DAWSON COLEMAN, AND M. HENRI KOWALSKI.		
12. DUET—"Dimmi che m'ami"		Campana.
MRS. ARMSTRONG AND SIGNOR CARLO MODINI.		
13. "Hark the Merry Drum"		Krugh.
THE LIEDERTAFEL.		

MR. GEORGE HERBERT, R.A.M., ACCOMPANIST.

The three Pianos used on this occasion are kindly lent by Messrs. Harrison, Sutton, and Birtchnell.

Prices of Admission, 3s., 2s., and One Shilling.

Chairs taken in advance at Harrison's and Sutton's Music Warehouses. ' Carriages may be ordered quarter past ten (10.15).

5. Kowalski Grand Concert Programme, August 21, 1885. Courtesy of Mrs. Richard Bonelli.

Benefit great success. Presented with medal. Introduced to Lord and Lady Carrington. Sending papers. Nellie Armstrong.

Lord Carrington, later raised to be Marquis of Lincolnshire, was Governor of New South Wales, and subsequently became an important figure in the English Liberal Party. A note appended by the owner of these letters to the one from England reads: "Before going to London, owing to a coolness which had arisen over her nonpayment for lessons which she had daily for seven years except when away, and her unwilling payment of £90, they parted not good friends. She apparently was sorry and wrote one letter (herewith) which he did not answer—hence her future conduct." And here is the letter:

Burley House,
Belgrave,
Leicester,
27th June/86.

My dear Signor Cecchi,

It is already more than two months since we arrived in London. I have commenced writing to you two or three times, but I have never been able to finish them. I am charmed with London, and think it is a beautiful city. I have heard all the great singers, viz.: Patti, who is divine, Albani, Nilsson (*I do not like*), Madame Patey, Trebelli, Mr. Lloyd, Santley, Foli. I have been to hear Sims Reeves four times, but he has never sung once. Is it not disappointing? He was to have sung at Patti's concert on Wednesday, but of course did not appear, so Nicolini sang instead. I have also heard Rubinstein, Halle, and de Pachmann. The latter is a wonderful pianist. Sarasate and Carrodus are wonderful violinists. It is really wonderful the beautiful music one can hear in London.

You will be pleased to hear that I have already sung twice in London, and had the greatest success, splendid critiques, and everyone predicts a great future for me. Herr Ganz, the man who wrote "Sing, Sweet Bird," has taken a wonderful fancy to me, and declares my voice is more like Patti's than any voice he has ever heard. Vert, the concert agent, is working hard for me, so I am sure to get on. Antoinette Sterling was singing at one concert where I sang, and she was in a fearful rage because I got a bigger reception than she did. The first concert I sang at I had the biggest orchestra in London to sing to. I sang, "Ah! fors e lui" and "Sing, Sweet Bird." Ganz conducted both.

You will be sorry to hear that my Father has been very ill in Scotland. He is not at all well yet. The other day I jumped out of a train in motion (it was the wrong train), and landed on my head. I was knocked quite senseless, and felt very ill for two or three days afterwards. I have also had bad toothache, so I have been in the wars altogether.

I am very pleased to hear you have had *success* with another pupil. Will you give her my congratulations? I suppose it is the young lady I heard before I left. My husband has gone into the Army, so as his regiment will be stationed in Ireland for the next month I am going over there next Tuesday. I shall stay with my brother-in-law. Little "Jackie" has grown so big and fat, and talks so well. I hope you will write sometimes to me. My address will be c.o. Lady Armstrong, Seconfield House, Little-

6. Soirée Musicale, October 27, 1885. Courtesy of Mrs. Richard Bonelli.

PROGRAMME.

Part I.

1. QUARTETT—In E flat - - - - - - *Mozart.*
   Allegro ma non troppo—Andante con moto.

   Mr. WESTON, Mr. CURTIS, Mr. ZERBINI, and Mr. HART.

2. SONG - - - "Alone on the Raft" - - *P. Rodney.*

   Mr. T. BERGIN.

3. SONG - - - "Vocal Waltz" - - - *Buccalossi.*

   SIGNOR MODINI.

4. PIANO SOLO *a.* "Elegie et Idylle," Etude, op. 41 *Taubert.*

   b. Valse de Concert, op. 64 - - *Hause.*

   Mr. CYRIL DE VALMENCY.

5. CAVATINA - - "Regnava nel Silenzio" - - *Donizetti.*

   Mrs. ARMSTRONG.

   (Pupil of Signor Cecchi.)

6. VIOLIN SOLO - - Aria in C - - - *J. S. Bach.*

   Mr. WESTON.

Conductors - - - { *SIGNOR ALBERTO ZELMAN.*
                   { *Mr. ZERBINI.*

52

Part II.

1. QUARTETT—In E flat - - - - - - *Mozart.*
Menuetto—Allegro vivace.

Mr. WESTON, Mr. CURTIS, Mr. ZERBINI, and Mr. HART.

2. SONG - - - - "L'Addio" - - - *Lamperti.*
SIGNOR MODINI.

3. SONG - - "The Bird that came in Spring" - *Benedict.*
Mrs. ARMSTRONG.

4. PIANO SOLO - *a.* Nocturne, in F sharp, op. 15 - *Chopin.*
b. Air—"Hongroise," in A minor - *Liszt.*
(By Request.)
Mr. CYRIL DE VALMENCY.

5. SONG - - - - "Severed" - - *Sir W. Robinson.*
Mr. T. BERGIN.

6. VOCAL DUET - "Dimmi che M'ami" - - *Campana.*
Mrs. ARMSTRONG and SIGNOR MODINI.

Conductors - - - - { *SIGNOR ALBERTO ZELMAN.*
{ *Mr. ZERBINI.*

The Piano to be used on this occasion is the Full Concert Aliquot
Grand, by Julius Bluthner.

hampton, Sussex. Give Miss Dawson my best love and tell her I expect a long letter from her. I shall write to her as soon as possible. And now I shall cease. With love to all enquiring friends,

Believe me,
Your old pupil,
Nellie Armstrong

Baker's Biographical Dictionary of Musicians relates one of these appearances: "Her first concert in London (June 1st, 1886) convinced her of the necessity of further study, and she went to Madame Marchesi in Paris." Biographical details of the sort are of course supplied by the subject or a secretary. Naturally Melba would need more intensive study for an operatic career in Europe than she could possibly obtain in Australia, then as now. She had also been discouraged by mightier folk in London than fussy little Wilhelm Ganz, whom I met many years later when he had lost much of his old ground as accompanist to Patti and such. Sir Arthur Sullivan was one of them. He didn't think she could ever qualify for the Savoy comic operas. The powerful singing teacher Alberto Randegger was another. He declined her as a pupil. The *Times* critic, bumptious man, heard her in one of those concerts. He intimated bluntly that she was not much of a singer, as he had told that Paderewski was not much of a pianist. Yet there is no doubt whatever that Nellie Armstrong's career was founded on the security of Cecchi's teaching. Otherwise, nine months of Paris and Mathilde Marchesi would not have done it.

Those Melba letters, and the shade drawn over Pietro Cecchi and his seven (too interrupted) years of guidance, do seem to tell a story. Long before I saw them I wrote in an article, "Melba Abdicates," in the then *Evening Sun*, Melbourne, of which I was music critic as well as of the morning *Sun-Pictorial*, these paragraphs which possess a bearing on the story:

She was of the sort who see their star from the first, and follow it with magnificent confidence. When others were dubious and even obstructive, Melba pushed on. She must become a wee bit grim, I should imagine, when memory drifts back to those early days when she was struggling to win the plaudits of her grudging compatriots. Not for her the lightning leap to favor with which one or two of her song-sisters have since been blessed. She sang in Melbourne many times, but did not storm it. She went afield and failed.

Does she recall the night in Bathurst, over in New South Wales, when three people went to the hall to listen to her; only one of whom had paid to go in? She gave her audience his money back, and then sang him a song.

Some have declared to me that in those days Melba's voice was huge and hard. Frankly, I don't believe it. Cecchi, who was Melba's teacher then, has not been given much of his share of the laurels, but he was no exponent of hugeness or hardness, and indeed he was the very man to locate the glowing pearly rarity of Melba's voice and make the most of it.

I wrote that in the knowledge of what Cecchi had done for the tenor Walter Kirby.

By outstanding musical people in Australia it was felt within a few years of Melba's triumphal disclosure of her quality in Brussels, Covent Garden, and Paris, that she was rendering scant justice to her old teacher. An extract from the Italian journal *Mondo Artistico* runs:

MASTER OF MELBA

Signora Fanny Simonsen, the distinguished celebrated soprano operatic singer, who follows up her profession with great success in Melbourne, from where she has lately come to Italy to form an Italian Opera Company for Australia, before departing forwarded to us the following letter,

Milano, 22nd June, 1891.

Dear Signor Fano,

I have been for more than two months in Italy and have naturally read with interest all the critiques, biographies, etc., which have appeared in Italian papers, referring to our Australian singer Madame Melba (Nellie Mitchell Armstrong). To my great surprise, I have not seen a single mention of the name of Signor Pietro Cecchi. As, when building a house, the principal thing is to have good foundations, so in singing the teacher who gives the first lessons lays the good or bad foundations of the artistic career of a pupil. For four or five years, Signora Melba had the good fortune to have almost daily lessons from Signor Pietro Cecchi, my friend and colleague in Melbourne. Signora Melba has since had lessons from celebrated professors in Europe, but her whole attention has been devoted to the artistic qualities of her already beautiful voice, and it seems to me that she should have directed that in the first place should be named Signor Pietro Cecchi, a tenor of the highest rank, settled in Melbourne for eighteen or twenty years.

I hope you will join with me in rendering justice to an absent one, by publishing the enclosed letter. Greeting you, etc., Yours,

Fanny Simonsen.

Madame Fanny Simonsen was, of course, head of an opera company of signal service to Australia in its time, like Lyster's and others.

Thirst for essentials of fact, allied with comprehension that in all strong characters there are vulnerable points, do not detract an iota from this opening to my tribute to Dame Nellie Melba on her death:

Song conquers history more powerfully than statecraft, more beautifully than war. Among all those born of Australia who have shone effulgently in their spheres there is perhaps but one of whom it can be said that centuries will make her legendary. Three others born of the marrow of our continent, Alfred Deakin, Edmund Barton, "Australia's noblest son," and Monash the warrior, stand forth in our minds as great personalities accomplishing their ends, but their touch was more national than world-inspiring, and beyond the confines of Australia who will seek them out for more than passing curiosity, as part of the technique of nation-building or of conflict, half a century from now? Who beyond the delvers making books will trouble their souls as to what manner of men those were?

But Melba is no more, and all the lands of earth are concerned. This is not alone because she won their ears with the uncommon textures of her voice, that perfect filagree of gold, but also because she sustained her supremacy in the art of song with a strength of personality, an inveterate purpose, which applied to any other art or occupation must have thrown her into strong relief against the escarpment of fame. It has been said of her somewhere, and with little real exaggeration when one analyses the admiring phrases, that "If she had not been a great singer, the greatest of her age, she would have been a great painter, or a great organiser, or a great architect; in short, nature dowered her with a supreme quality of brain by which she could have won fame in any one of a dozen directions." That is it! Brain—and she applied it to the governance of song and queenship over peoples.

SIGNOR PIETRO CECCHI

Among the most popular of all the Italian residents who have made Melbourne permanently their home, Signor Pietro Cecchi takes a prominent place, both on account of the assured position he formerly held on the operatic stage, and the excellent work he is doing now, as an instructor of the vocal art. Born in Rome in the midst of all the powerful musical influences which have made Italy famous as a land of song, Signor Cecchi was not allowed to follow his natural bent. No notice was taken of his passionate longing towards an operatic career, but seeing that the lad possessed a considerable amount of skill in designing and drawing, his father caused him to become an architect, at which profession he continued for some years, honestly giving it close study.

But he gave closer study to music, and worked so hard that at the age of twenty-one, he made his debut at the famous Academy of Music, Rome, an institution that has been four centuries in existence, and from which he holds a diploma. Romani, who was his master, was so satisfied with Signor Cecchi's first effort as an operatic vocalist that he prophesied a most successful career for him. For five seasons Signor Cecchi remained in Rome, appearing in all the first tenor roles, after which he passed on to all the great theatres of Italy. A tour in Russia was succeeded by a tour in Spain, and finally by a tour in America.

In 1871 Signor Cecchi came to Australia as the first tenor of the States Company, which included Signore Susini and Orlandini with Giorza as conductor. The troupe were further strengthened in Melbourne by the

From *Table Talk* (Melbourne), December 6, 1889.

engagement of Madame Lucy Chambers as the contralto, and it can easily be imagined that this "group of talent" were received with great enthusiasm throughout the season. The late Mr. W. S. Lyster—than whom Australia has never seen a more enterprising theatrical entrepreneur, nor a more generous manager—had the honor of presenting this company to Melbourne at the old Princess Theatre when his spirited venture was rewarded with emphatic success. Signor Cecchi travelled for two years throughout Australia, and then settled down as a teacher of the vocal art, in which he has been eminently successful.

Signor Cecchi has introduced many pupils to the public, but it is only necessary to allude to the one great example of his skill—Madame Melba— or as she is more familiarly known in Melbourne—Mrs. Armstrong—who has just made such a brilliant European success. Mrs. Armstrong was a continuous pupil of Signor Cecchi from 1879 to 1886, seven years, and was an excellent musician before even she thought of having her voice cultivated. Consequently her success was assured. Young ladies whose heads are turned by the dazzling ambition to become *prime donne* would do just as well to remember the valuable aids Mrs. Armstrong brought to bear upon her vocal studies. Seven years of patient work supplemented by a musical knowledge, almost professional in its completeness, qualified the now-celebrated Australian singer to attain a leading position, and paved the way for her European success.

The majority of aspirants for operatic honors give themselves twelve months study, with little or nothing in the way of previous musical knowledge to help them, and then they consider themselves finished artists. All the greater honor then to Madame Melba, whose seven years' study of the vocal art alone under Signor Cecchi's judicious guidance have resulted in such phenomenal success. Her two years [sic] additional study under Madame Marchesi have added finish to her vocalism, but the credit rests with Signor Cecchi for his excellent groundwork.

This program, for a soirée presented at the École Marchesi on April 10, 1887, gives evidence of the earliest known date when Mrs. Charles Armstrong used her new stage name, "Melba." The hand-written notes were made by Marchesi pupil Louise Natali (born Belle Barnes in Bloomington, Ill.; 1856-1943), who had a successful singing and teaching career in the United States. Emma Eames (1865-1952) was another American soprano who had a distinguished career in Europe and the United States (Paris Opéra, Monte Carlo, Covent Garden, Metropolitan Opera, for example). In her autobiography (1927) Eames tells of hearing Louis Diémer, who was professor of piano at the Conservatoire, play "with impeccable technique. His interpretations, however, were so shallow and meaningless that I marveled at the ovation he received. . . ." Marie Gabriele Krauss (1842-1906) had been a pupil of Marchesi in Vienna. She was considered one of the great singing actresses and was a star of the Paris Opéra for many years. Her debut was in Vienna in 1867; she retired from opera in 1887 and taught singing in Paris. Melba had become a pupil at the École Marchesi in December 1886 and was to make her debut in Brussels only six months after this concert. It is evident that Marchesi considered her one of her star pupils at this time. Louise Natali's notes read: (1) "Chorus led by *Joncières himself*"; (5) "the favourite pianist of the day"; (8) "accompanied by *Gounod*"; and (12) "sang this so that I *chill* yet in remembrance of it. Great voice & *great artiste*."

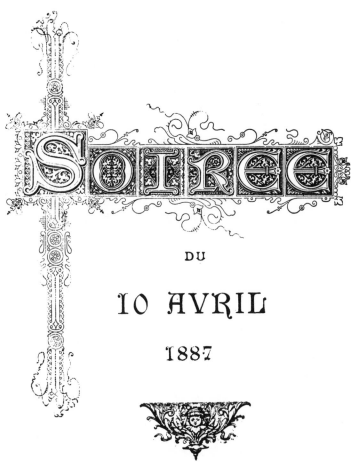

SOIREE

DU

10 AVRIL

1887

7. Soirée at the École Marchesi, April 10, 1887

PROGR

Chome lia by Joncières himself.

X 1. Scène du « *Chevalier Jean* » (Chœurs
et Chanson Sarazine). . . . JONCIÈRES
   Mlles HORWITZ, EAMES et HIBBARD.

2. *a* « *Chanson du Printemps* » . . . MENDELSOHN
   b « *Tarantelle* ». . . . . . . ROSSINI
   M. TAFFANEL.

3. *a* « *Au Temps jadis* » . . . . . BEMBERG
   b « *L'Inquiétude* ». . . . . . DIÈMER
   Mme KRAUSS.

4. *Air de* « *Lucie* ». . . . . . DONIZETTI
   Mme MELBA.

5. *a Quatrième Orientale* . . . . . DIÈMER
   b Polonaise d'Oneguine. . . . . TSCHAIKOWSHY-LISZT
   M. DIÈMER. *the favorite pianist of the*

6. *Air d'*« *Alceste* ». . . . . . GLUCK *day*
   Mme KRAUSS.

———————

Le Piano sera tenu par MM.

60

ᛘᛘᛘᛖ

7. *a « Mélodie ».* . . . . Th. Dubois
   b « Le Tambourin . . . . . . Rameau
   M. FISCHER.

8. *Cantilène de « Sapho »* (avec chœurs) Gounod
   Mme KRAUSS. *accompanied by Gounod* —

9, *Air des « Noces de Jeannette »,* avec
   accompagnement de flûte . . . Massé
   Mlle HORWITZ et M. TAFFANEL.

10. *Air de « Rigoletto ».* . . . . . . Verdi
    Mme MELBA.

11. *Nocturne.* . . . . Chopin
    M. TAFFANEL.

12. *« Le Roi des Aulnes »* . . . . . Schubert
    Mme KRAUSS. *sang this so that I shall*
    yet in remembrance of it.

    MANGIN & BOSONI *Great voice & great*
    artist

8. Nellie Melba, Paris, 1887

9. Melba and Her Son, George Armstrong, Paris, 1887

MELBA AFTER MARCHESI

WORDS FROM
BERNARD SHAW

BERNARD SHAW

Melba's progress following her debut has been well documented by
Klein (1903, 1931, 1933), Rosenthal (1958), Seltsam (1947), and
many others. The best-detailed review of her progress, the new
rôles she assumed, and her travels is found in Murphy (1909),
which also contains excerpts from reviews, even if they are possibly
carefully selected ones. Two press comments are given here, from
the pen of Bernard Shaw who, as many do not realize, began his
literary career as a music critic. From 1876 through the fall season
of 1894, his usually witty and often penetrating comments on the
London musical scene could be found first in *The Star*, later in the
Pall Mall Gazette, and still later in *The World*. Shaw's crusading
zeal often resulted in ruthless reviews. He knew his music and his
singing, and to win his praise was considered an accomplishment.

3 August 1892

A long string of mishaps prevented me from hearing Mr. Bemberg's Elaine
until last Saturday week, when the second act somehow got omitted. The
oversight passed unnoticed, however; and I cannot say that I was greatly
disappointed: indeed, I should not have mentioned the circumstance if it did
not form a practical criticism of the opera as distinct from its presentation,

From: Bernard Shaw, *Music in London, 1890-94*. London: Constable and Co., 1932.
Reprinted by permission of The Society of Authors on behalf of the Bernard Shaw Estate.

with which I shall, by your leave, not concern myself. Mr. Bemberg is no English composer, but rather a music-weaver who, having served an apprenticeship to Gounod, and mastered his method of working, now sets up in business for himself. In Elaine we have the well-known Gounod fabric turned out in lengths like the best sort of imitation Persian carpet, the potential supply being practically unlimited.

There is one ballad, "L'Amour chaste comme la flamme," which would probably never have been written if Gounod had not supplied the pattern in Mireille, but which is certainly a charming elaboration of the master's suggestions. Mind, I do not hurl Mr. Bemberg's want of originality at him as a reproach. One of the greatest artists the world has ever seen began in this very way. Raphael mastered Perugino's style before he developed his own. Mr. Bemberg may yet leave Gounod as far behind as Raphael left Perugino. But there are no signs of his doing so yet. . . .

I am obliged to Elaine for one thing in particular: it reconciled me to Madame Melba, who is to all intents and purposes a new artist this year. I do not mind confessing now that I used not to like her. Whilst recognizing the perfection of her merely musical faculty, I thought her hard, shallow, self-sufficient, and altogether unsympathetic. Further, she embarrassed me as a critic; since, though I was utterly dissatisfied with her performances, I had nothing to allege against them; for you really cannot take exception to an artist merely because her temperament does not happen to be sympathetic with yours.

This year, however, I find Madame Melba transfigured, awakened, no longer to be identified by the old descriptions—in sum, with her heart, which before acted only on her circulation, now acting on her singing and giving it a charm which it never had before. The change has completely altered her position: from being merely a brilliant singer, she has become a dramatic soprano of whom the best class of work may be expected. . . .

6 June 1894

On Saturday last we had Faust, with Melba as Margaret. De Lucia accosted her in the second act in Italian; she snubbed him in French; Bauermeister kept her in countenance by conversing with her in French in the garden; and Mephistopheles, at home in all countries, tempted Faust in Italian and Marta in French. And, to give the devil his due, his French was the best in the collection: Margaret's, in particular, being occasionally rather like mine. De Lucia's dramatic instinct helped him well through a part in which he seemed likely to be overweighted. Several times in the garden scene he found the right musical treatment with exceptional success.

Ancona's Valentine is the best we have had for a long time. His "Dio Possente," sung in the original key with great expression and with a magnificent high G, was one of the features of the representation. But he should go over the part with the book some morning; for he has forgotten the exact notation of one or two passages. I am not, of course, alluding to his intentional taking of the first line of the *reprise* in Dio Possente right up the scale to the high E flat. Melba, with her unspoiled, beautiful voice, and, above all, her perfect intonation—you never realize how wide a gap there is between the ordinary singer who simply avoids the fault of singing obviously out of tune and the singer who sings really and truly in tune, except when Melba is singing—received boundless welcome, and, with the usual mysterious luck of American and colonial prima donnas, received flowers across the footlights in those large baskets which English ladies and gentlemen invariably carry with them in the theatre, and which they present to singers in moments of uncontrollable admiration. Melba has commanded Sir Augustus to put on that favorite Donizettian *chef-d'œuvre* Lucia di Lammermoor, for the better display of her roulades; and Sir Augustus has gallantly consented. Having heard the work rather frequently in the course of my early career, I do not look forward to the occasion with much curiosity.

10. Nellie Melba, ca. 1890

11. Nellie Melba, Milan, 1893

AÏDA? BRÜNNHILDE? HOW BIG WAS THE MELBA VOICE?

WILLIAM R. MORAN

To those of us who think we know the Melba voice from commercial phonograph records (the first of which was made in 1904, to be sure), it has always been difficult to understand how she could have had any success in the role of Aïda. She first sang the part at Covent Garden on November 4, 1892, "displaying greater energy as an actress than ever before, and displaying faultless vocalization" (Rosenthal 1958). Hurst (1958) states that as Aïda "her performance was so fine as to excite the highest admiration, for she threw aside her usual reserve to sing with passionate emotion, and easily dominated the great *ensemble* in the second act without apparent effort or loss of quality." The London *Daily Telegraph* said, "It is needless to say she sang well, for that she always does, but the feeling she threw into her work—feeling which sometimes reached abandonment to the passion of the minute—was a revelation of power not generally suspected. Both her singing and acting in the scene which ends with the arrest of Radames were fully equal to the demands of the music and the situation." On the other hand, a little more than five years later, Henderson thought her Aïda of January 24, 1898, at the Metropolitan was "alien to her voice, her style, and her temperament." Kolodin (1953) notes that he thought the clue to the "unfathomable mystery of Melba's abuse of one of the most precious gifts that heaven ever put in a human throat was a desperate quest for new rôles." From Murphy (1909) we learn that Melba had coached her acting for Aïda with Sarah Bernhardt, and actually studied the role with Verdi! But it was Henderson, again, in writing of Melba's first Metropolitan Elizabeth in *Tannhäuser* (January 29, 1894), who said "Melba's treatment of the scene with Tannhäuser in the second act was so beautiful in the finish of its declamation, and so just in its intent, that it amazed the soprano's friends, and put her enemies, if she ever had any, to confusion." Of the same performance, the *New York Tribune* noted "Melba made superb use of the wealth of voice with which Nature has endowed her. Its powerful and ringing timbre, together with the perfect utterance which is hers, made her Elizabeth singularly effective. Of her Elsa in *Lohengrin,* the *New York Herald* critic wrote, "Incomparably the most attractive thing she has done since her advent. . . ." The year before, her Elsa had been acclaimed with extravagant reviews in Stockholm. But Klein, writing in 1931, said: "The ambition to sing heavier rôles led her now and again to essay tasks that lay physically beyond her. She should never, for instance, have attempted Wagner. . . . on the whole her voice was naturally too light for Elsa; she was unable to cope with its declamatory needs."

Of Melba's attempt to add the role of the *Siegfried* Brünnhilde to her repertory, much has been written. Murphy (1909) states that "she gave nearly two years' earnest study to the music, the drama and the language," for it was her first role on any stage in German, Elsa and Elizabeth having been sung in French and Italian. Of the single performance, on December 30, 1896, the *New York Herald* said: "Mme. Melba's Brünnhilde, all things considered, was surprisingly good. . . . With perfect ease she surmounted all the vocal difficulties of the score, and towards the end, as she gained more confidence, she sang with much greater freedom, and in the final duet her voice had the ring of true passion." W. J. Henderson, writing in the *New York Times,* was more blunt: "It is undeniable . . . that the quality of her voice and her style of singing are not suited to a complete embodiment of Brünnhilde, and she can be praised now only for her conscientious effort and for her ambition, which was more potent than wise. . . ." Henry Krehbiel, of the *New York Herald Tribune,* warned:

The sincerity of [Mme. Melba's] effort was admirable. . . . To the loveliness of her devotion and the loftiness of her ambition honest tribute must be paid. But the music of the part does not lie well in her voice, and if she continues to sing it, it is much to be feared there will soon be an end to the charm which her voice discloses when employed in its legitimate sphere. The world can ill afford to loose a Melba, even if it should gain a Brünnhilde. But it will not gain a Brünnhilde. . . ."

But Nellie Melba needed no warning from others. After the performance she sent for her manager. "Tell the critics that I'm never going to do that again. It is beyond me. I have been a fool!" It was also Henderson who likened her voice to a piece of Dresden china, not to be smashed. Thus it gives considerable pause for thought when this same critic, some thirty years later, was reminded of Melba when reviewing the Brünnhilde of Kirsten Flagstad: "No other singer, except Melba," he wrote, "ever equalled her in liberation of voice, in the utter freedom from all constraint of production and articulation."

The music critic Pitts Sanborn (as quoted in Lahee 1912), in writing about Luisa Tetrazzini, had a good deal to say about Melba:

Of course, when Tetrazzini came here, she provoked comparison at once with her seniors, Sembrich and Melba, the two great coloratura sopranos that have given the generation of New Yorkers that knew not Patti its standards. . . . Melba had the evenest soprano voice throughout its liberal range that has been heard here in our time. Her singing has always been called cold and with reason. The voice itself was full and rich, its flexibility extraordinary, her vocal utterance incomparably spontaneous and easy. And there is reason to suppose that Melba has not lacked temperament, but she never related it to her singing. That was a business which she discharged in a workmanlike manner, without enthusiasm, at the least cost to herself. At her best, there was a certain insolence in the easy way she spun her cantilena, a disdain as she tossed off fioriture, but she never sang them as if they meant anything to her or had anything in particular to do with musical expression. Her phenomenal trill was just a trill, her scale of matched pearls just a scale. In their way they were perfectly beautiful, but it was the beauty of faultless machine work.

The singing never fell below a high level, but it never rose from the astonishing to the transporting. There was a lack of completeness in Melba's singing—crudity is hardly the word for anything in a way so finished; she made little use of her great vocal means. She could sing in a wonderful full voice and in a wonderful half voice, but who ever heard her pass from one to the other with the exquisite swelling or diminishing of tone that carries you away when Tetrazzini sings? One might stretch a point and say in her famous crescendo trill, but nowhere else. Her use of portamento was so sparing that her phrases generally seemed cut in lengths, not deliciously rounded and poised as by Sembrich and Tetrazzini. Any one who recalls her treatment of the word "Salce" in the "Willow Song" in Verdi's *Otello* knows just where she fell short. She had the technique for great Italian singing, but never quite the style, quite the feeling. How cold her "Caro Nome" left the audience that was worked up to cheers by Tetrazzini's!

Melba sang accurately and with the dignity of good workmanship. Her singing was stereotyped, without excitement of the unexpected, the suddenly improvised, the heat and joy of song. Sometimes, as Tetrazzini's harshest critics insist, that soprano injures the music by the variation she introduces; oftener she lifts it beyond the clouds. This sort of thing was inherent in the great Italian style as in the Italian temperament. Melba had neither. Melba's style was rather mid-century French, the style of *Faust* and *Roméo et Juliette*, than that of the older Italian rôles, though in many respects she sang those rôles so well and so delightfully.

The singing teacher J. H. Duval (1958), writing many years later, also recalls Melba's "crescendo trill":

Galli-Curci had some splendid vocal effects, as had Sembrich, but when we think of Melba's trill . . . whoever has heard her marvelous crescendo on the trill in the mad scene from *Lucia* will remain unmoved by any vocal feat that has been performed since. It began pianissimo. It grew steadily stronger and stronger, more and more intense, and at last . . . that vast auditorium which is the Metropolitan Opera House of New York, just vibrated with its wonderful fortissimo of crystalline purity. What a thing to have heard!

Henry C. Lahee (1898) said: "Of the numerous successors of Patti, Madame Melba seems to have more fully met the requirements than any other. In many respects she has exceeded them, for her voice is fuller and more powerful than Patti's ever was, but she has the same easy vocalization and marvellous spontaneity that constituted the great charm of Patti's singing."

Emilio de Gogorza (1937) told of a 1907 recording session at which he officiated:

Madame Melba was perfectly at ease before the horn. One morning in 1905 [*sic*] . . . she stepped off the train, came to the laboratory, and made several records. "La Serenata" by Paolo Tosti struck me particularly, its ending written especially for her by the composer. Her voice was in prime condition, and her execution, while not too rapid, was impeccable in its clarity and accent: another God-given voice, but hardly a pure coloratura. She had volume, and could have sung heavier rôles had she possessed a warmer temperament; her medium voice, however, was white in quality, therefore it would have hampered her, and she remained a light soprano although she seldom sang higher than D above the staff.

Those who knew the Melba voice firsthand never thought her records did her justice. Edmund Burke (1876-1970), the Canadian bass-baritone who sang with Melba at Covent Garden, in Australia as a member of her 1911 opera company, and on several extended concert tours, had some difficulty in recognizing her voice on recordings. He knew immediately the voices of such singers as Louise Edvina, Paul Franz, Edmond Clement, Louise Kirkby-Lunn, Charles Dalmorès, and Pol Plançon, singers he recognized by the quality of their voices as preserved on recordings. He only recognized Melba by her technique and sometimes by some of her low notes, never strictly from the sound of the voice itself. "It sounds too small . . . too thin. Melba had a big voice," he said.

Some years ago in Sydney I was discussing the Melba voice with a musician who had heard her many times.

The records show some of the technique, but what they completely lack was a quality almost uniquely Melba's: a sort of ability to project the voice in three dimensions. I once heard her sing the Rossini *Inflammatus* with full orchestra, organ and chorus in the gigantic Sydney Town Hall, and I will never forget the way that voice was a thing apart from all other sound, clean, clear and distinct, soaring above all the tumult like something from a different world.

But Melba knew her limitations. Years later (1914) she wrote, "I have never continued rôles that proved unsuited to me." How she found *La Bohème*, how she studied it with the composer, and how she promoted the opera with the public and made the rôle of Mimi almost her exclusive property for many years has been told elsewhere (Moran 1982).

MELBA.

13 AND 15 WEST 24TH ST. N.Y.
·MADISON SQUARE·

12. Melba as Juliette, New York, 1895

13. Melba as Marguerite, New York, 1896

14. Melba as Massenet's Manon, New York, 1896

LA CALUNNIA

WILLIAM R. MORAN

In Rossini's *Il Barbiere di Siviglia* Don Basilio gives us a classic description of slander. "Calumny," he says,

is like a sigh of the gentlest zephyrs breathing by . . . so soft that sighing 'mid the bowers, it scarcely fans the drooping flowers . . . then passing on, from tongue to tongue, it gains new strength, it sweeps along and gains fresh vigor in its race, till, like the sounds of tempests deep . . . it shakes the trembling soul with fear. At length the fury of the storm assumes its wildest, fiercest form, in one loud crash of thunder roars, and like the earthquake, rocks the shores. . . . Thus calumny, a simple breath, engenders rain, wreck, and death; and sinks the wretched man forlorn beneath the lash of slander torn, the victim of the public scorn.

When Melba paid her first visit to Australia in sixteen years, from September 1902 until March 1903, she must have thought that she had found the inventor of slander in her countryman, John Norton. Among other things, Norton was the publisher of a so-called newspaper named, of all things, *Truth*. Author Cyril Pearl, in his book *Wild Men of Sydney* (1958), tells us:

When he came to Australia in 1884, Norton was an indomitable alcoholic; in 1916, a few months before he died, he was described by Mr. Justice Pring of the New South Wales Supreme Court, as "an habitual drunkard of the worst type". He was treated over and over again for drunkenness in Sydney, Brisbane, Melbourne, London, and at sea. He was arrested for drunkenness almost as often, and at times was locked up on the liner on which he was travelling. . . .

So fierce was Norton's craving for alcohol that it had to be given to him even when he was under treatment in private hospitals and sanatoriums. Sometimes his drinking bouts lasted for months. He drank everything, usually beginning with beer, stout and sherry, and working up, after about a week, to brandy. A chauffeur who described a session that lasted six weeks said Norton drank about a dozen bottles of brandy and "Chartreuse wine" every two days. In the early stages of a debauch, Norton was dangerously violent, obscene, and uncontrollable. This intransigent period was followed by a condition when, in his wife's words, he was like "a big helpless baby".

From a clinical point of view, Norton's alcoholism is less interesting than the fact that he expended great quantities of energy, ink, and newsprint in excoriating other people for drunkenness. In his fervid denunciations of well-known citizens for drinking, often delivered when he himself was submerged in alcohol, Norton perversely allied himself with his eternal enemy, the execrated wowser. Among the subjects of these extraordinary outbursts were the poet Victor Daley, the singer Nellie Melba, and the politician, Edmund Barton. . . .

Norton's attack on Melba's drinking habits was launched from Melbourne, only a few weeks before he was dragged, roaring, struggling, and protesting, into Dr. O'Hara's hospital in Collins Street, to be treated once more for alcoholism.

Norton did not begin by starting his attacks as a gentle breeze and allowing them to grow "from tongue to tongue". He was much less subtle, and began with the loud crash of thunder. He also had another technique which, in the days of travel by steamship, made his position in Melbourne almost invulnerable. He would wait until his prey had embarked for distant shores to release his unbelievable invective so that by the time his victim heard about it, the story was weeks old, and he could only be attacked from afar. In Melba's case, John Hetherington (1967) comments:

If she had sued him for libel, she would undoubtedly have won a judgement against him with substantial damages but no sum a court could give would have compensated her for going back to Australia, then staying for months to fight the case. She also knew that Norton would have defended himself by dragging into evidence every scrap of unsavoury gossip about her, both the true and the apocryphal; he would have rejoiced in the chance to have her cross-examined, on the pretext of testing her character and credibility, about the Duke of Orleans, Haddon Chambers, and other men whose names had been linked with hers, then headlining her answers in *Truth*. Her counsel could have retaliated by questioning Norton about his alcoholic exploits, his career as a blackmailer and a seducer, and his brutality to his wife, but this was old stuff, familiar to every Australian. And since Norton had no reputation to lose he did not mind mud; on the contrary, he revelled in it.

Here is a sample, then, of John Norton's work, published in Melbourne on March 28, 1903, just after Melba had sailed for Europe.

An Open Letter to Madame Melba concerning Her Champagne Capers, Breaches of Public Faith, Outrages against Good Manners, and Insults to Australian Citizens!

Madame,—Marvellous Melba, Mellifluous Melba, Supreme Singer, Crowned Cantatrice, and Monarch of Matchless Music though you be, your public and private conduct during your short six months' sojourn in Australasia makes it compulsory that you should be told the truth. Genius is mostly eccentric; the eccentricities of genius are generally pardoned—up to a certain point. You have great genius, which is only excelled by your eccentricity. The public have heard too little of the first and a great deal too much of the last. The turpitude of a talented termagant can be forgiven ten times ten, but there is a limit of license which cannot be condoned. You have so often transgressed that limit that the public has at last become tired of your truculent tricks, and vicious vagaries. Public patience is exhausted; public opinion exasperated; and in that style of language to which you have shown that you are not a stranger, you have to be told, on behalf of an abused and outraged community, that "it's time you took a pull," or were "pulled up with a round turn." Your scandalous breaches of public faith, and private propriety are no longer to be borne without protest. That protest I now make; and if you resent it, I invite you vindicate yourself by civil or criminal process in a Court of Law.

You are not the first, though you undoubtedly are the greatest, prima donna who has brought the blush of shame to the fair cheek of Australia, your native land. During the last thirty years there have been dozens of dubious donnas perambulating Australia upon professional pilgrimages, and among them have been one or two real daisies in their eccentric ebullitions. It is somehow the tendency of genius to break out in picturesque fireworks. Histrionic history is full of instances, and the world will never be free of the entertainment afforded by their pranks, whether they be done for advertisement or are just the irrepressible coruscations of volcanic exuberance. Patti for years kept the public excited by her sensational freaks in the way of castles, counts, and costly escapades; Bernhardt too, with her coffins, quarrels, 'possum shooting, amours, and autocratic antics; Emily Melville astonished and amused Australia with her knickerbocker suit, her sprees; and there have been countless others, Lily Langtry, Lola Montes—names out of number—who have revelled in scandals, sensations and insanities, which have delighted the middle class millions. The leading lady or prima donna who does not shake up, shock, or scandalise humanity with a series of audacious antics does not do her duty to that prurient portion of the people who love to be shocked by a clever or pretty woman. You built up a record in this line in Europe, and you've added to it since your return to Australia. I am not going to dig up the squalid scandal of your married life, or of your grass-widowhood, nor to resuscitate the sordid story of your alleged intrigue with that French royal router, the Duc d'Orleans, nor to revive the details of the celebrated action for *crim. con.* brought against you and him. The matter may well be left to lie covered up in the mantel of mystery, under which it was hidden when the proceedings were quashed. I want to confine myself entirely to your conduct here in Australia; and in doing that I shall be doing all that my duty as a publicist demands.

You began your career in Australia by a gross breach of faith to the people of Melbourne and Victoria, by postponing your first announced series of concerts in Town Hall. This meant a loss of time and money to thousands who could ill afford to lose either. It meant extra expense, and loss of time to many country residents, who, in addition to paying the extravagant prices for your tickets, and the heavy cost of railway and other travelling expenses to and fro, and hotel tariffs, had been put to special expense for new toilettes, in which their wives and daughters might do due honor to Marvellous Melba, the diva, whom they delighted to honor. Yet, without any reasonable, or at any rate reliable, explanation, the dates of your first series of five concerts were altered, and thousands of the public disappointed and greatly inconvenienced. Sims Reeves, in England, used to be allowed to do this sort of thing with impunity until it was discovered that his repeated non-appearances were due to drunkenness, when the public began to "drop him"—as, indeed, they'll drop you if you don't have a care. If this first breach of faith had been attributable to serious and unavoidable indisposition, it could well have been overlooked, as, in fact, it was, especially as your non-appearance was attributed at the time to the sudden illness of your father. That may or may not have been the true cause, Though I believe it was Not, but that you yourself were the cause, and that you were really "indispoged," as Sairy Gamp would say; and that your own conduct was the cause of the "indisposition," especially as stories were current in Melbourne, and believed by those "in the know," of your gay goings-on at sumptuous suppers at or about [here the statement of location is rendered illegible in the original archival copy of the newspaper held by the State Library of Victoria, Australia] when you should, according to public engagement, have been singing to thousands of your enthusiastic admirers in the Town Hall. What has since come to light concerning your champagne capers on the "Continong," in gay "Paree," in the "Rue de Revelry," and elsewhere: in London, at the Hotel Cecil; in 'Frisco, Sydney, and Launceston, and last, but not least, at Menzies' Hotel in Melbourne, lends color to the suspicion that your first and subsequent breaches of faith with the Australian people was as much, if not more, due to champagne as to real pain. Moët and Chandon have a lot of misery and chagrin to answer for, especially among prima donnas.

You are pretty plain and free of speech yourself towards others, whom you think you can bully and bounce; permit me, therefore, to exercise the same privilege towards you by expressing the opinion that you indulge in intoxicants a great deal more than is good for you and your divine voice. You are in the heyday of your cultured, ripened powers, at the zenith of your fame; and occupying, of right, the position of proud pre-eminence formerly filled by the peerless Patti. Your powers are ripe; your reputation is made; all the world asks of you is the privilege of paying to hear you, and applauding you. What more could woman wish or desire? What woman with a heart or soul would rashly risk such rich gifts and golden opportunities as yours by wantoning in wine? The careers of great divas—some of whom have died drunk and destitute—who have caressed the cup and drowned their songs in strong drink, should cause you to look upon champagne with a shudder, and to shun it with a shiver so long as God shall give you leave to sing. Your voice will not last for ever; it should be cherished like chastity, and not submitted to the risk of ruin that banquets and drinking bouts entail. Divas as divine and delightful as yourself have been dethroned and damned by Drink before to-day. That you can escape their fate, if you follow in their footsteps, is not in the Providence of God, who gave you your great gift of song, in trust, for the gratification of the highest instincts of your generation.

I'm not posing as a moralist, nor pretending to be a teetotaller, or even a temperance man. I'm neither one nor the other, but I daresay that my morals are quite as good as Melba's, and I am quite certain that so far as "langwidge" goes, I'm just as modest and moderate as she; while I'm certain I'm more temperate than she, simply because she could drink with impunity what would make me doubly drunk. But "no scandal about Queen Elizabeth, please," who, by the way, was, like yourself, a woman of strong and sometimes not very savoury words, and could swear like a trooper, and love like a Lesbian. She, too, like you, was a terror of a termagant, swearing, slapping, and scratching all who came near her in her tantrums. Blunt old Bill Cobbett calls her "Redheaded, rampageous, redhot, ripping-up Betsy." But, after all, "good Queen Bess," even if she had as many lovers as those imputed to her, was decorous and discreet in her alleged amours, which, from her very temperament, she was not likely to have been had she indulged in strong drink, which she didn't. This is probably why she maintained her dignity amid all the dangers of dalliance, and why she never shocked her subjects with the scandal of her liaisons. She was the subject of spicy stories, but in deference to her discretion and decency she was always spoken of more in admiration than derision, as the Virgin Queen, although most of her faithful and trusted courtiers must many a time have laughed in their sleeves at their royal mistress' lingering longing to be loved long after she had passed that period of life when love in woman becomes ludicrous, if not lecherous. Like the great Elizabeth, so, too, has the great Melba been made the subject of spicy stories. But tell me, Melba, can it be possible that the whole or any part of the following lurid description could be truthfully applied to you:

> She has been a constant affliction to maddened managers; a harrowing handful to harassed hotelkeepers; a real strike-a-light startler to staggered stagehands, a terrorising termagant to trembling time-servers; and a whole sackful of surprises to slanderous scandal-mongers. From the day of her arrival in Australia she has scattered consternation in her wake. She has cancelled contracts, upset arrangements, flouted conventions, kicked up her heels at propriety, and altogether swept the Commonwealth in a wild and wooly whirl, like a whiskied willy-willy on a jim-jam junketing jackeroo's jamboree. Hotelkeepers have opened their hostelries to her feeling honored, and banged the door behind her feeling horrified.

While awaiting your reply, in whatsoever form you see fit to send it, permit me to place before you a pen picture of you and your capers which comes closer to the truth than most caricatures. It is written by the same scribe who had the honor of describing for *Truth* your first appearance and enthusiastic reception in the Melbourne Town Hall, and of wiring to Sydney the most accurate and enthusiastic account of your wonderful performance on that memorable Saturday night. Compare this with his description of your triumphant appearance in the aria from the Scena in *Lucia*, and see what a sad difference there is between Melba on and off the stage:

> Every place she has visited has experienced her imperious pretensions, combined with her peevish proclivities, so much so that Society, with a big S, has been compelled to drop her as "really not nice." Notwithstanding this, however, she has had one lordling so continuously in tow that he has been labelled as part of her baggage. Some say she intends to marry him, but as there is "just cause and impediment," unless it has really, as rumored, been removed by an American divorce, the surmise is very likely of only shimmery substance. Throughout, this Prima Donna's progress has been characterised by a paling of her social lustre. "She is not a lady," is the verdict of the "very naicest." "She's a dysy, a real lydy," with no a's and two y's, is the summing up of the vulgar. One night she was due at a theatre. She arrived an hour late, and dropped droopingly into the dress circle, too nervous to risk a grand tour around to the manager's box. That haven might have involved a too stormy and disastrous passage. The way to it is strewn with steps, at any of which the star might have fallen. Fancy so august a personage coming a champagne cropper in a public place! So she wisely stuck where she sat first, which was at the nearest seat handy. There she stayed a sorry spectacle, "pale and palsied," known of all, yet knowing none. There might have been sympathy displayed towards this weak woman did but amiability accompany her human frailties. But she has done everything to estrange solicitude. She has bossed, bounced, bullied, bluffed and buncoed to right and left of her. Many a stage star has shot an erratic course before, but none has done it with such vicious vulgarity, such bourgeois bumtiousness, and such indiscriminative cruelty. But it doesn't matter much to anybody but herself, and the few who temporarily suffer from her pranks. Australians will simply be diversely astonished, amused, and ashamed that such a series of sensations should have been sprung so suddenly upon them. After all, it is only a passing epidemic, which an ocean liner will some day transport to another hemisphere, probably for ever. Meanwhile, the whole scandal can be patiently submitted to with a smile and a shrug of the shoulders.

You'll probably say that none of this is true, and that even if it were all true, I've no right to thus publicly arraign your conduct. A court of law is the proper place to challenge the truth of the charge, and dispute my claim to publish it. Meanwhile I base my right to call you to account on personal as well as public grounds. I have in a manner been "buncoed" by you as thousands of others have been by being put to great expense and enormous inconvenience through your failures to keep faith with the public. At considerable trouble and cost I succeeded in obtaining two seats in the second front row for your first series of five concerts, and travelled specially from Sydney with a friend to hear you, only on arrival to find that the concerts were postponed because Madame was "indisposed." You broke faith with me and the public a second time in Tasmania, where I was on a holiday tour. I purchased two tickets for your announced concert at Launceston, and curtailed my stay at the Southern end of the island by at least ten days in order to attend. As a matter of fact I drove over from Hobart to Launceston in hot haste in order to be in time and arrived on the afternoon of the day fixed for the concert, only to be told "Melba will not sing tonight," which was part of the chorus of a comic song sung about you in a Launceston music hall that very night with the refrain, "Melba, she's not tight tonight," this last line being sung with sarcastic emphasis and a sly significant sidewink at the audience, who loudly applauded, and hooted the mention of your name. There was a very bitter feeling of resentment engendered against you throughout Tasmania, but more particularly in Launceston, at your public professional breach of faith, and your private conduct and conversation at the Brisbane Hotel. The feeling was well justified. You had been cordially invited by the citizens to sing; an enterprising citizen guaranteed to pay you £1000 for a single concert, which sum was duly lodged in a local bank. You accepted the engagement and the fact was announced weeks before hand throughout Tasmania. Your advent was awaited with intense interest. The Government advertised "Melba Excursion" trains between Launceston and Hobart specially for the occasion. Hundreds flocked to Launceston from the Hobart and remoter parts of the island to hear you. Scores of men and women travelled many weary miles by road to hear you, only to be disappointed at the eleventh hour. The special train conveying the Governor, Sir Henry Havelock and his lady and suite to Launceston was stopped half-way at Paratta, and the travellers told to return to Hobart as "Melba would not sing that night," or any other night in Launceston. But why wouldn't you sing? Couldn't you sing? Of course you couldn't without you could, could you? But if you couldn't, why couldn't you? There must have been some serious reason to induce Melba, notorious for her Caledonian caution, not to say Scotch stinginess in money matters, to voluntarily forfeit a cool thousand pounds, and to remunerate the local entrepreneur for his expense in organising and advertising the concert. What was the reason? The one given on your behalf was not accepted by the irate Launcestonians as the real and true one.

On your behalf a belated medical bulletin was issued to the effect that you could not sing in consequence of a "strain." This was looked upon as a deliberately concocted canard, intended to gull the Tasmanians who, having, in a sense, been "taken down," looked upon this "strain" tarradiddle as adding insult to injury. I myself regarded it as such, and expressed my opinion of it in the following telegram which I sent to Melbourne *Truth* the next day:

MELLIFLUOUS MELBA.

Hoodwinks Hobart.

Leaves Launceston in the Lurch.

Curious Caprices of a Cantatrice.

(By Special Wire)   Launceston, Friday

Melba made another mess of it here yesterday by again breaking her engagement with the public. She landed after a rough passage per the *S.S. Coogee* in a bad temper, and complained of the weather, the ship, and the voyage. Melba declared that the whole affair was horrible. She was welcomed on the wharf by a large crowd, but her recognition of this reception was curt, not to say contemptuous.

Melba was officially received in the most courteous manner by Mayor Storrer, a leading local undertaker, and his wife, and was driven to the Brisbane Hotel, where she had bespoken rooms for herself and suite at a cost of £100. A cold collation had been provided by the hostess, and Melba picked a row with her because the spread was not hot. The pampered favorite ordered a beefsteak, but refused to eat it when served, and shut herself in her room. She declined to be serenaded by the Town Band, sending her manager on to the hotel balcony to inform the vulgar mob who wished to do her honor that she was ill.

Later she sent for a local doctor, who issued a bulletin stating that Melba was suffering from a strain and could not sing. The doctor's name is Hogg, but Hogg's bulletin does not say what sort of strain Melba was suffering from, or what part of her frame she had strained—throat, chest, or stomach, and gave no indication to even encourage a modest conjecture. There is no doubt of one thing that Melba has strained, and that is public opinion here, which is much incensed, and adjudges Melba as ill-bred.

Hobart considers her a badly behaved shemale whatever she may be as a singer. The cause of her refusal to sing is said to be what she considered her paltry reception. The real reason *Truth* will give later on.

Meanwhile Melba went off to Hobart by express yesterday, and was hooted and groaned at by a large crowd at the station. Governor Havelock, on his way from Hobart by yesterday's express to hear Melba, was stopped by wire at Paratta, and returned to Hobart by the same train as the cantatrice was travelling in.

Melba leaves Hobart to-day for her New Zealand tour. She promises to return to Tasmania to fulfil her broken engagement, but she won't have a chance, as Tasmania won't take her again at any price.

No wonder you were hooted and hissed on the railway platform, and such was the feeling against you that had you not suddenly scooted away from Launceston by the first train, I am sure that you would either have been accorded a tin-kettle serenade outside your hotel, or escorted to the railway station by the town rabble yelling the vulgar chorus:

Champagne Nellie is her name,
Who sings a very sad and secret "strain";
She came last night, looking none too bright,
And is off again at daylight in the morning.

Your conduct at the Brisbane Hotel was not of a character to cause the public to condone your breach of faith. Poor old Storrer, the Mayor of Launceston, turned up to officially welcome you with his "Old Dutch" in a brand new sailor-hat and blouse and shining sateen skirt. Yet you are said to have treated them both with cruel contempt. Did you take umbrage at Mayor Storrer's profession as an undertaker, or at his principles, as a teetotaller? Were you offended because he declined to enter the hotel with you? Why should you be? It's not true that he came to meet you in one of his mourning coaches, or that the mayoral procession from the steamer *Coogee* was closed by a hearse with black plumes and two dreary death mutes stalking on either side. Nothing of the kind; the simple old planter of "stiff 'uns" politely escorted you to your hotel and left you there. Judging by what occurred there he was wise to hurry away. You stormed, scolded, and sneered like a drunken drab. Finding only a cold collation awaiting you, instead of a hot dinner, you "kicked up hell's delight." You couldn't leave the poor waitress alone. Here's a cameo cut out of a chunk of your choice conduct:

> Narked Nellie: Where's your cap?
> Terrified Waitress: We don't wear caps, madame.
> Narked Nellie (yelling fortissimo): Get out, and go get one at once.

Here's another:

> Melba (studying menu in disgust): Is this a sixpenny restaurant or a common hash-house? Order me a steak and be quick about it!

When the steak's brought Melba is too mad to munch, but rails and raves at everything and everybody, and tears off to her room in a towering tantrum, where she remains, after her manner on such occasions, giving ground for the impression that she is either half mad or wholly drunk. Is it any wonder the curly-headed Quigley, the beatified "boots" boss of the Brisbane Hotel, should have torn his hair and cursed the luck that ever sent Melba along to Launceston, or that Quigley should have danced a quadrille "all on his own" next day when he saw you take yourself off to the train for Hobart? Not at all; the only wonder is that Quigley didn't compel you to quit before you did.

It is this sort of conduct that has made you a terror to hotelkeepers. Termagant tenants are not conducive to a good class of trade or to the safety of the chamber crockery, which at times is said to suffer sadly at your hands. But it is not because you can afford to pay the piper that such things are to be permitted or passed over in silence. Your conduct towards those who are in any way dependent upon you is not always amiable or attractive. You tried to "take down" Tait, tour organiser, and he had to take you to court to make you part up. Then there's poor Miss Gill; what about her? Well, she's left you. Why? That's your and her business which you can settle with her when she takes that action for damages which she has been advised to bring against you in London. Then what about Miss Donaldson, who came out with you from London as companion to you? Why and under what circumstances was this young lady compelled to leave you? Then there's Bensaude the baritone, what of him? In order to accompany you to Australia he relinquished a 40,000 francs London season engagement, on the understanding that he was to accompany you all through your Australian tour. What have you been and gone and done to Bensaud that the Melbourne lawyers should advise him, too, to sue you in London for breach of contract? Griffiths, your flautist, has publicly stated that you used to swear and curse at him and others in the coarsest terms. But, perhaps, Griffy deserved it, as to my certain knowledge, Griffy could at times cut a lively champagne caper himself. Parsimonious and cantankerous conduct of this kind would ill-become any prima donna at any time under any circumstances; but in Madame Melba, in her native land, where she has been literally raking in the shekels by charging prices probably higher than she could ever obtain or average in London or on the Continent of Europe, yet breaking her public engagements with impudent impunity, such conduct does indeed seem doubly mean and contemptible. Surely you have made enough money out of your offended and outraged countrymen and countrywomen, and given so little out of your easily gotten superfluity to the deserving charities of your native land, to enable you to deal not only fairly but liberally with the few second-rate artistes who accompany you, and with two such responsible and deserving attendants as your private secretary and your personal companion. It is altogether too bad to add to the truculence of the termagant, the vagaries of the virago, and the proclivities of the poculent pocharde those of a miserable miser, who, while revelling in wealth and swigging champagne, balances and buncoes dependents who have kept better faith with her than she has kept with the public who have paid her so liberally, and generously forgiven her so much.

Madame, I've done with you for the meantime. Perhaps now that I've done with you you'll think about time to begin with me. Be it so, but be sure you count the cost before commencing; and consider well who will gain most by a public investigation by way of cross-examination in the courts—you or your legal advisers. I tell you frankly that I court such a contest, and feel confident that if it is commenced that I shall come off more than conqueror. Maintenant il faut que je vous fasse mes adieux, en chantant to the classic air of "Dolly Gray."

> Good-bye, Nellie, I must leave you;
> Give up swigging dry champagne;
> Else your friends will surely leave you
> In disgust and poignant pain.

I remain, Madame,
Your admiring admonitor,
JOHN NORTON.

Melbourne, March 27, 1903.
From: *Truth* (Melbourne), March 28, 1903.

Marcus Antonius was right: "The evil that men do lives after them." To this day, more than fifty years after her death, many Australians, to whom the name Nellie Melba is a kind of ill-defined legend, will ask, "But wasn't the old girl a real boozer?" Those who knew her well, those who worked with her, those who lived in her home—even Beverley Nichols, who displayed no compunction about defiling her memory after her death—said "ridiculous!" An occasional glass of sherry or a sip of champagne, yes, but excessive use of alcohol, which she was convinced would damage the vocal chords, no—and yet Norton's invective of some eighty years ago has become part of the legend!

Melba's reputation for being blunt, outspoken, and not overly sensitive to the feelings of others was certainly well deserved, and has often been documented. Many stories are undoubtedly apocryphal, but none-the-less characteristic. The manager, Charles Wagner (1940), tells one of these:

For many years, Melba, Nordica and Eames held the operatic reins in the days of Abbey and Grau. A good story, illustrative of their differing natures, is told about the time Nordica was planning her second marriage. Eames, her friend, asked the bride-to-be: "Have you told him everything, Lillian, about your former marriage and former sweethearts?" "Certainly," replied the frank and lovely Nordica, "I have nothing to conceal." "Oh, what courage!" sighed the innocent Eames. "What a memory!" interposed Melba, who had overheard the conversation as she passed into her dressing room.

Emma Eames (1865-1952), the American soprano, had every reason to be jealous of her Australian contemporary. She was already a pupil at the *École Marchesi* when Melba made her sensational entry as a student and quickly became Madame Marchesi's favorite. Note the program for the *soirée* of April 10, 1887, where Eames appears only as one of three soloists with a chorus, while Melba is given two solos. In her autobiography (1927), Eames does not mention Melba by name, but her identification is thinly veiled: She claims that Melba prevented her from making her *début* in Brussels, and refers to "this singer whom I have mentioned previously as my life-long instructress in operatic intrigue. . . ." Marchesi's partiality to Melba was not disguised: Writing in 1897 she says:

Of my pupils, those most successful were Miss Emma Eames, Mademoiselle Jane Horwitz, Mrs. Julia Wyman, and Nellie Melba. . . . I may add that these four pupils finished their studies in the same class at *École Marchesi*, and all of them have since become famous artists, indeed, I may properly state that one of these, Madame Melba, is to-day without a rival on the lyric stage. As a vocalist, she more resembles a bird than a human creature, and it is impossible to conceive anything more musical or more flexible than her marvellous voice, which is always clear as a silver bell. I am only repeating what the critics of every country, in Europe and America, have written, when I say that unquestionably, as regards taste, style, and vocalization, this pupil of mine is superior to any living singer.

Small wonder that Melba remained fiercely loyal to her old teacher, and took it as a personal affront if anyone criticized Marchesi or her methods, as Eames later did. Eames became a mainstay at Covent Garden and at the Metropolitan. Her voice was heavier than Melba's, and her principal roles were Tosca, Eva, Sieglinde, Santuzza, Aïda, Elsa, Iris, Elizabeth (in *Tannhäuser*), the Countess (in *Le Nozze di Figaro*), Amelia, Donna Anna, Donna Elvira, Leonora (in *Il Trovatore*), Desdemona, and the Juliette and Marguerite of Gounod. Of these roles, only five were in Melba's regular repertoire during the period when the two ladies were singing with the same companies, both having studied Juliette and Marguerite with the composer. Eames retired from the Metropolitan in 1909, and from the stage completely in 1911, while Melba went on singing for another seventeen years. She lived in New York, where she did some teaching and much talking, as she was frequently sought out by opera buffs and record collectors and asked to express her opinions. Like Melba, Eames was exceedingly outspoken, and towards the end of her life she apparently became almost paranoid on the subject of her Australian rival. Many of her less caustic remarks have found their way into print, while many more of her stories have been passed around "from tongue to tongue" and have lost all reference to their origin, to become part of the "hate Melba" syndrome.

Another of Melba's detractors who was quite vocal in expressing her opinions was Blanche Marchesi, daughter of Mathilde, Melba's teacher. A singer of great intelligence, she was, unfortunately, not blessed with either the voice or the good looks of a number of her mother's pupils. After a brief experiment with opera in Prague and London, she had a distinguished career as a concert artist, followed by a long career as a much respected singing teacher. She somehow blamed Melba for her lack of an outstanding success as an opera singer, and was even responsible for the story that Melba, through her power with the Gramophone Company, had prevented the circulation of her recordings made for that company. This is patently false, as Blanche's recordings were produced and sold; the fact that they were not popular and sold few copies had nothing to do with Melba!

Surely, if Melba had wanted to exercise any power that she might have had with the Gramophone Company with respect to rival artists, she would have done so in connection with the recordings of Tetrazzini, Eames, Galli-Curci, and others who recorded exclusively for the Gramophone/Victor combine when Melba was also an exclusive artist for those companies. But most of Blanche Marchesi's unkind remarks about Melba were reserved for personal comments to her pupils. In her autobiography (1923), she chastises Eames for her lack of loyalty to her mother, but seems to be more appreciative of Melba:

From [the day of her debut] Emma Eames went her way, never turning her head back, never remembering her student years nor her master, and erasing from her memory everything that had been the making of her career. Not so Melba. Melba remained a student for many years after her career had started, and she rarely sang anything that she had not first worked at with my mother in Paris, even when she was at the height of her success. . . . The most striking voice and finest quality of a light soprano that my mother ever brought out was Melba. . . . she was an ardent student, and also stepped straight from the class-room to the stage of the Brussels Royal Opera, keeping for my mother lifelong feelings of deepest respect and loving gratitude. Melba's friendship for my mother was one of her great joys; it made up for the forgetful hearts of many others. Needless to say that the success of Melba created much jealousy among the students of the school, for unfortunately, pupils often believe that success depends entirely on the teacher's managing powers, and that some are pushed and some are neglected. The truth is that those who follow their work with steadfast seriousness must surely get ahead of those who work in an indifferent fashion, and those whose ambitions are limited. . . .

Gabriele Krauss, first dramatic soprano for twenty-five years at the Paris Grand Opera, was, in my eyes, the greatest dramatic singer of my epoch, although her voice was of second order and had to be constructed. Etelka Gerster, the favourite of America who successfully competed with Patti, was partially naturally gifted, partially constructed. Emma Nevada and Nellie Melba were naturally prepared and had only to be taught the right line. Emma Eames and Emma Calvé—the first spoilt, the second a nearly ruined voice—had to be reconstructed and saved. They would never have made career and name without my mother's art. . . .

Mary Garden (1951) tells of her first meeting with Melba when they both sang at a "command" performance at Windsor Castle, the same performance described by Ernest de Weerth (1961), after which Melba behaved in a rude manner with a cutting remark about the younger singer. The two of them rode back to London together in a special train, and, Garden says, became fast friends. Melba consulted Garden about acting and costuming Tosca.

Well, I told Nellie Melba everything I could about Tosca, about costuming her and so forth, but I knew it was perfectly useless because she never could sing Tosca—and never did. She just wasn't made for Tosca. I found Melba a cold person, but she could be charming when you knew her, You see, she grew to like me because I wasn't a coloratura like herself. . . . She could be quite funny . . . and wherever she went she always had people laughing. In the evening she would often sit at the piano and play and sing for me—just small English songs, but she turned them into little things of heavenly beauty. . . . When you knew her, you couldn't help liking her. When you didn't know her, you thought her frightfully rude. . . .

I have no hesitation in declaring that Melba had the most phenomenal effect on me of any singer I ever heard. I once went to Covent Garden to hear her do Mimi in *La Bohème*. Of course Melba didn't look any more like Mimi than Schumann-Heink did. I never saw such a fat Mimi in my life. Melba didn't impersonate the rôle at all—she never did that—but, my God how she sang it! You know the last note of the first act of *La Bohème* . . . is a high C, and Mimi sings it when she walks out of the door with Rodolfo. . . . The way Melba sang that high C was the strangest and weirdest thing I have ever experienced in my life. The note came floating over the auditorium of Covent Garden: it left Melba's throat, it left Melba's body, it left everything, and came over like a star and passed us in our box, and went out into the infinite. I never heard anything like it in my life, not from any other singer, ever. It just rolled over the hall of Covent Garden. My God how beautiful it was! . . . That note of Melba's was just like a ball of light. It wasn't attached to anything at all—it was *out* of everything.

A good collection of Melba stories is found in Quaintance Eaton's well-indexed book, *The Miracle of the Met* (1968), a number of them passed on from her *protégé* Frank St. Leger, who was for some years her accompanist, and later an assistant manager at the Metropolitan. Vincent Sheean (1956) sums it up very well:

She was, as a personality, one of the most arguable of all prima donnas. The Melba stories, both in her favor and against her, are almost without number. . . . Her particular kind of fame, so pervasive and unlocalized, transcended opera and even the theater itself, becoming a part of the general consciousness. She was, as they say, a household word, and more literally than could be said of almost anybody else in her time.

Even today, especially in Australia, Melba's name is still a household word. Since she died over fifty years ago, there are few still around who knew her personally, but the Sunday supplements still have columns that must be filled with articles which need headlines which will sell papers. "The Dame Was No Lady: The Naughty Nellie Melba" and "Our Dame Nellie—Peaches with Very Sour Cream" are recent examples which perpetuate her name to the modern generation. Yes, the evil that men speak lives after them, and like Slander's Whisper, grows from a zephyr to a storm with the passing years!

MME. MELBA'S CONCERT AT CARNEGIE HALL, DECEMBER 18, 1903

RICHARD ALDRICH

The Brilliant Soprano Sings at Carnegie Hall with the Philadelphia Orchestra

Mme. Melba gave a concert last evening at Carnegie Hall that was attended by a large audience eager in its desire to hear and applaud the brilliant singer, who has been so little heard in New York this season. The concert was of the sort usually provided by prima donnas on such occasions, very miscellaneous in its character and requiring the services of a number of other singers and of instrumentalists to fill up the intervals between her three appearances. More significant was the cooperation of the Philadelphia Orchestra, under the direction of Mr. Fritz Scheel, which had not appeared in New York for a year, and was brought up from its home city for the occasion on a special train. Its function in the concert, however, was very limited, extending no further than playing two overtures and providing the accompaniments.

Mme. Melba gave the two "mad scenes" that are especially set apart for the display of coloratura sopranos' voices—those from *Lucia di Lammermoor*, with flute obbligato, and Ambroise Thomas' *Hamlet*—and the waltz song from the first act of *Romeo and Juliet*. She sang the florid music brilliantly, with great fluency and clarity. Her runs, trills, and

From: the *New York Times*, December 19, 1903.

staccato notes glittered and scintillated, and especially in the aria from *Lucia* compelled a new admiration for the marvelous vocal mechanism over which she has such absolute command, and which has not its superior at the present day. Yet admirable as this singing was, in neither of the two mad scenes did she equal the extraordinary exhibition she made the other day with the air from Handel's *L'Allegro, il Penseroso ed il moderato*, in which she so electrified her hearers in the concert of the Boston Symphony Orchestra.

The power and purity of her voice, at its best, are a delight to the lovers of such singing as she exemplifies in its highest estate. Warmth, emotional expressiveness, are not hers to give, and never have been, and she is wise enough to avoid in general the music that depends for its proper effectiveness upon such qualities. In their way Mme. Melba's natural talent and acquired skill are of the most perfect, but she can compass but a limited range in the whole art of music.

In the more sustained passages of her music, Mme. Melba seemed to show that neither her voice nor her mood was most favorable. In such passages the purity of her voice was at times affected by an unpleasant open quality that detracted from its sensuous charm and smoothness. She sang with a certain carelessness, and more than once her intonation was imperfect. But nothing stood in the way of the unbounded admiration of her hearers, and she was rapturously applauded and many times recalled.

The orchestra made a creditable showing in Beethoven's third "Leonore" overture, though the quality of its tone seemed somewhat rough, but it played with much vigor, and Mr. Scheel showed himself, as he has before, to be a skillful and accomplished conductor. The company of assisting artists included Mr. Gilibert, the admired French baritone of last season's opera at the Metropolitan, whose singing is a standing example of what art and intelligence can do with a voice not naturally beautiful; Mr. Ellison Van Hoose, tenor, who sang the prize song from *Die Meistersinger* in excellent style, and Signorina Sassoli, harpist, whose principal number was a set of variations with orchestra accompaniment by Widor—a piece with several charming moments, but falling into monotony before the end was reached.

15. Nellie Melba, 1903

OSCAR HAMMERSTEIN AND HIS WAR WITH THE METROPOLITAN OPERA

JOHN F. CONE

The story of how impresario Oscar Hammerstein challenged the
Metropolitan Opera Company of New York with his own Manhattan Opera Company from 1906 to 1910 has been told time and time
again. Hermann Klein, distinguished British music critic and singing
teacher, was a resident of New York at the time and knew most of
the protagonists personally. In a book published in the midst of the
fray (*Unmusical New York*, 1910), he describes some of the problems that had beset Heinrich Conried, manager of the Metropolitan
from 1903 until his death in 1909. He wrote:

. . . Had Mr. Conried never lived to be director of the Metropolitan Opera
House, I do not think we should have ever seen aught of the so-called
"Operawar" which started in New York at about midway of his *régime*
[that is to say, in the autumn of 1906], and is now in active progress.

  I do not think we should have ever beheld another manager so "exceed-
ing bold" as to start a second opera house at full grand opera prices,
without the pledged support of society, without the Metropolitan "Horse-
shoe" of tiaras and diamonds representing millions of dollars; and above
all, at a new theater situated in an inferior part of the town. But there was
a man in New York with aspirations in this direction. . . .

From: John F. Cone, *Oscar Hammerstein's Manhattan Opera Company*. Norman:
University of Oklahoma Press, 1966.

Vincent Sheean, in his *Oscar Hammerstein I: The Life and Exploits of an Impresario* (1956), helps us understand that man, and his place in operatic history. Hammerstein won his fight in a sense: Representatives of the Metropolitan bought him out in April 1910. That he could never have gotten through the first season without the help of Nellie Melba is a fact acknowledged by all historians. The story of Melba's part in the affair is best told by John F. Cone in his excellent and detailed history, *Oscar Hammerstein's Manhattan Opera Company* (1966), from which the following excerpts are taken.

Second to None

With his son Arthur in charge of the final stages of the construction of the opera house, Hammerstein set out for Europe on March 6, 1906, to recruit his company. Although there were many artists available to him, it soon became apparent that his task was more difficult than he had anticipated. When he tried to negotiate with music agents in Paris, he found these gentlemen cold to his offers. At first they had received him graciously, but in a few days' time he found them unwilling to be of assistance. Hammerstein did not hesitate to explain why: " 'Their demeanor reminded me of December icicles as they told me one by one that anything they might do in my interest would endanger their relations with the Metropolitan Grand Opera Company and that they could not afford to risk losing Mr. Conried's good will by entering into business relations with me.' "[1]

Hammerstein always maintained that the adversities he experienced in assembling his company were due to the machinations of Conried, who apparently was determined to quash the upstart. . . . Conried certainly had wasted no time in securing the production rights to Puccini's operas. Moses, his official biographer, said: "When the latter [Conried] heard of Hammerstein's entrance into the operatic field, he hastened to secure exclusive rights to all of Puccini's scores for America."[2]

His greatest good fortune at this time was the engagement of Cleofonte Campanini, a marvelously gifted conductor, who had just resigned from La Scala, dissatisfied with conditions at that opera house. He was not entirely unknown to the United States, having been an assistant conductor at the Metropolitan in the first season of 1883-84. . . . Since then he had devoted his efforts to seasons of opera in the great European music centers, as well as in South America, constantly gaining authority and artistic stature. He had become a celebrated Italian maestro, one of the master conductors of the day.

Having Campanini as the leading conductor promised much for the artistic quality of the new venture. Still lacking, however, was the pre-eminent star, an artist to be a counterattraction to the best the Metropolitan had to offer. There was but one, and Hammerstein resolved that he must have this luminary: Nellie Melba, the greatest singer in the world. With this purpose in mind, he returned to Paris, determined that if he could not secure her as a member of his company, he would give up the entire undertaking. How he persuaded her to be his leading prima donna is now a part of operatic legend. Both Hammerstein and Melba had their versions.

His has hitherto been ignored or unknown:

I got back to the Grand Hotel in Paris on a Sunday afternoon almost disheartened. . . . I had travelled to all the musical centres of Europe, hearing voices, visiting artists and negotiating with agencies.Everywhere I had gone I found that hostile cablegrams had preceded me and an icy reception was awaiting me. But one by one I had gathered together artists who more than fulfilled my desires.

I say I had gathered them in, but technically I hadn't. In every contract was a punitive clause by which, with the payment of a forfeit, I could withdraw. I had made up my mind that if I couldn't get Mme. Melba I would be obliged to drop the whole grand opera undertaking.

It was make or break with me, and I decided there was no time like the present. So I got into fresh linen, brushed my travel-stained clothes, called a cab and at 6 in the evening headed for Mme. Melba's home in the Boulevard Malesherbes. I [sic] was a big project that I had on my hands, and I had reached the point where I had to trust to luck.

The house loomed up in the dusk big and beautiful. In answer to the bell a maid came to the door. She could not speak English and I didn't know much French, but I finally made her understand that I wanted to talk with Mme. Melba on a matter of business.

"Madame is entertaining at dinner to-night and I do not think she will be disturbed, but I will see," the maid replied as she left me standing in the dark, with my hat in my hand.

Three minutes later I heard a great rustling on the stairs and in came Mme. Melba with a great sweep and flourish.

"You are Mr. Hammerstein of New York—yes, I have heard of you—you want to give grand opera there—so New York is to have two companies?" she said in a quick, single sentence.

"And I have come to ask you to be my leading prima donna," I answered. "I—"

"It is impossible to talk of such a thing now. Why, I have guests at dinner. Come around to-morrow. Perhaps I will have an hour to talk with you then," Mme. Melba interrupted.

But I had made up my mind it must be now or never. "Tomorrow is impossible," I replied, "for I am going to Berlin. I have a great list of artists, but my contracts are punitive and I have made up my mind that without you I must give the whole thing up."

"Ah, that would be unfortunate indeed," she cried. "You must not do that."

"Then give me ten minutes and hear what I have to say," I answered.

Melba hesitated a moment and said, "But only ten minutes, for my guests are waiting. I will excuse myself and return directly."

Mme. Melba disappeared with another prodigious rattling of skirts and a majestic sweep. I put down my hat and got ready for the struggle of my life. Almost instantly she was back again.

"Now," said she determinedly, "what do you want?"

I named the other singers I had engaged and gave a quick outline of my plan. She quickly interrupted me with a gesture and the remark, "I know all about that. See here."

Then she crossed the room to a desk and grabbed up a big bundle of telegrams and cablegrams. "I have been annoyed to death with despatches [sic]," she exclaimed. "My time is open next season, and perhaps I would just as soon sing under your management as any one else's, and so end the whole matter."

I almost gasped, but caught myself in time. "And your terms?" I asked.

She named the figures and conditions in a snappy, business way.

"I am well-to-do," she concluded. "I need not sing unless I want to—therefore I come high."

She certainly did come high! "Is this your final stipulation?" I asked.

"It is," replied Mme. Melba with a fidget and a look toward the stairway whence the sound of her guests could be heard.

"Will you give me ten minutes to consider?" I asked.

"To-morrow morning will do," she answered.

"No, it must be to-night," I retorted, with determination.

"Very well," said she. "Take your own time."

It has always been my practice, when about to close an important deal, to take a walk around the block. So I bowed myself out into the Paris street. You can believe that before I had travelled half way around that big block my mind was made up. So I headed back toward Melba's house.

She came down again in a very few moments with a pleasant bow and stood waiting for me to speak.

"I accept," said I.

"Very good," said she, "and now I want to help you all I can to make this thing a great big success. Call on me for anything you wish, but come in to-morrow morning and we will sign the contracts."

It had all taken place quicker than I can tell it. But I had made up my mind to seal my bargain instanter.

"Take another minute and write me a line stating your acceptance," I pleaded.

Mme. Melba opened a little desk and scribbled a few words on a slip of paper. . . .

As she dropped the pen I picked it up and wrote her a reply in a couple of dozen words.

"That's settled," said I, and I still wonder if she noticed the exultant ring in my words.

"Not quite," she replied, dryly. "You know, Mr. Hammerstein," she went on, "I always require a guarantee, no matter for whom I sing—whether for Conried or Covent Garden, or—"

"Certainly," I answered. "How much must it be?"

"Twenty thousand dollars deposited wherever you desire—preferably in the Credit Lyonnaise," said she, without a quiver.

"Why not deposit it with you and avoid all the red tape of recording it?"

"That's asking too much," she exclaimed, with a surprised look, "but let it go until to-morrow. I must be getting back to my guests."

Two minutes later, less than half an hour after I had first driven to Mme. Melba's house, I was back in my cab and on my way to the Grand Hotel. The prospects of the Manhattan grand opera project had brightened into clear day in that brief time. For every disappointment and rebuff of the preceding six weeks I had been repaid a hundred fold.

Bright and early next morning I started for the bank, and had $20,000 changed into new, crisp thousand franc gold certificates. Then I drove back to Mme. Melba's house.

"You're early, Mr. Hammerstein!" she exclaimed, as she greeted me. "I thought you were starting for Berlin."

"Ah, I had more important business in Paris," I said. Then I laid on her desk twenty of those big scraps of paper that go for money in Paris.

She brushed the pile into a drawer of her desk without even counting it and turned the key.

"And now," said she, "we must work together, and I shall do all in my power for you. Last night you told me you could not get Renaud. You must get him, for he is the greatest baritone in France. Yes, you must—we must—get Renaud. I will get him for you. In three days you will receive word at your hotel to meet him and sign the contracts." . . .

Three days later, as Melba had promised, word came from Renaud that he had arrived in Paris, prepared to reopen the negotiations. A day before a note from Mme. Melba had informed me that we had secured him. How she contrived to do so I do not know.[3]

Hammerstein related his initial experience with the prima donna approximately a month after the event; Melba told her version years later in her autobiography *Melodies and Memories,* published in 1925. Apparently the soprano had decided that she would sing less during the season of 1906-1907, that she needed time for quiet and contemplation. At any event, Melba was in no mood to consider Hammerstein's proposal.

The diva wrote:

One day, when I was in my flat in Paris, thinking what fun I was going to have in my coming season, Mr. Hammerstein called. I had an idea of what he wanted, and I wouldn't see him.

Hammerstein went straight off to Mr. Maurice Grau, who, sad to say, was very ill at the time, and persuaded him to give him a letter to me. In view of the letter, I felt obliged to give him an appointment. But I kept on saying to myself: "I'm not going to America. I'm not going to America."

When Hammerstein arrived, my first impression was of a determined man of Jewish persuasion, shortish, thin and dark, with piercing black eyes. He carried a top hat with a very wide brim in his hand, and he addressed me in a strong American accent.

Hammerstein: "I'm out to do the big thing in opera. I am building the biggest and finest opera house in the world. And I can't do without you."

Myself: "In what way do you want me to help you?"

Hammerstein: "I want you to come and sing."

Myself: "I'm very sorry, but I have no intention of going to New York next year."

Hammerstein: "I can't do without you."

Myself: "That's a great pity, because I'm not going."

Hammerstein: "I shall give you fifteen hundred dollars a night."

Myself: "Please don't discuss terms, Mr. Hammerstein, because I assure you that is useless."

Hammerstein: "Oh, you'll come all right. (A pause.) What do you say to two thousand?"

Myself: "If you offer me twenty thousand I shall still say the same thing."

Hammerstein: "It'll be the biggest thing you have done yet. Oscar Hammerstein says so."

Myself: "And Nellie Melba says 'No.' I have no intention of going. Good-morning, Mr. Hammerstein."

Had anyone else been so importunate, I should probably have been very angry. But there was a naïve determination about Mr. Hammerstein which appealed to my own character. He knew what he wanted, and did not hesitate to say so. We therefore parted good friends, and I regarded the matter as closed.

Not so Mr. Hammerstein. At intervals of six days during the next month he either called, wrote notes or telephoned, always prefacing his remarks by "Now that you have decided to come to America. . . ." I merely sat tight and set my lips. On one occasion, I remember, he obtained an entry into my rooms while I was in my bath. Not in the least deterred he came and battered at the door.

Hammerstein: "Are you coming to America?"

Myself (between splashes): "No!"

Hammerstein: "I'll give you two thousand five hundred a night."

Myself: "Not for ten times the money."

Hammerstein: "And you can sing as many nights as you like."

Myself: "Go away."

Shortly after that, Mr. Hammerstein decided on his Napoleonic *coup*. I had just breakfasted and was sitting down, reading *Le Figaro*, when he burst into my rooms in a great hurry.

Hammerstein: "It's all settled. You're to have three thousand dollars a night."

Myself: "But I've told you a hundred times—"

Hammerstein (interrupting): "Never mind about that. Three thousand dollars a night, and you open in *Traviata*."

Here, to my astonishment, he drew from his pocket a bundle of thousand-franc notes and began scattering them over the floor like cards, until the carpet was littered with them. I was so surprised that I could say or do nothing, and before I could call him back, he had swept out of the room like a whirlwind, crying that he had to catch his train, and had no time to wait.

I picked up the notes, smiling quietly, and found that in all he had strewn my carpet with one hundred thousand francs. To-day it may not sound such a very vast sum, but then it meant four thousand pounds. And even nowadays one does not go strewing thousands of pounds on people's carpets.

I took the notes at the earliest possible opportunity to the Rothschild Bank, telling them that they were not mine, and that they must be kept safely until Mr. Hammerstein called for them.

However, he did not call for them. Instead, he called once again for me, in the early morning.

Hammerstein: "Well, and so you've made up your mind at last. Didn't Oscar Hammerstein say you would?"

Myself: "He did, and Oscar Hammerstein was wrong. As I've told you before, I am *not* going to America."

Hammerstein: "Oh yes, you are. You've got all my money."

Myself: "The money is in the bank. It has nothing to do with me."

Hammerstein: "Was there ever such a woman? Still, you'll come. Mark my words."[4]

It is difficult to say why Melba decided to appear at the Manhattan. Of course, Hammerstein had made the whole arrangement attractive financially, since she was to receive $3,000 a performance (an extraordinary sum in those days) as well as her traveling expenses. In addition, he had permitted her to arrange concerts outside New York whenever she was not singing at the Manhattan.[5] Still, money was not the sole inducement. . . . Melba was a proud lady who loved the sense of power. The most persuasive factor, perhaps, was that at the Manhattan she knew she would be the prima donna *assoluta*, with all the attendant glory and authority that title bestowed. Melba herself said:

If I had been one of the regular staff of the Metropolitan, I should have had to sing when and where they wanted. My rôles would have been dictated for me. I should have been at their beck and call. No artist gives her best under those conditions. I said to myself: "I am Melba. I shall sing when and where I like, and I shall sing in my own way." It may sound arrogant, but arrogance of that sort is not a bad way to get things done.[6]

The Divine Diva

The new year began auspiciously, as it was now time for the long-awaited appearance of Madame Melba. Hammerstein announced that she would make her debut with the company on January 2, 1907. For months there had been rumors (Hammerstein claimed they had been inspired by Conried) that the diva would not appear at the Manhattan Opera House, that she had lost her voice, or that her health had been seriously impaired. From London, Melba denied these allegations and said that she would fulfill her promise to Hammerstein. She informed an American representative of the press that she actually was in *splendid* (!) vocal form.[7]

Melba's comments on the excellent condition of her voice were more than borne out by the criticisms of her appearances at Covent Garden during the fall season. In the opening night performance of *Rigoletto* (October 5), the London *Times* said that she was in "exquisite voice."[8] More praise followed; and when she appeared as Violetta in *La Traviata* (October 31, 1906), she triumphed "with even more than her usual success. Her singing in the brilliant music of the earlier scene was as faultless as was her delivery of the whole scene in the last act."[9] The tenor of the London reviews certainly did not indicate any diminution of Melba's powers.

Her return to New York was anticipated with the keenest pleasure, as the metropolis had not heard her in opera since December 16, 1904, when she appeared only once (as Mimi in *La Bohème*) at the Metropolitan. Although she was to have sung in opera four times that season, illness had forced her to cancel her engagements. Before that one appearance, she had been absent from the New York operatic scene for almost four years. It was greatly to be regretted that the city had been denied the pleasure of Melba's singing for what amounted to almost six years.

On December 19, 1906, the diva cabled Hammerstein that she would appear first as Violetta. She had wanted her initial performance to be in *La Bohème*; but since the dispute concerning the rights to Puccini's opera had not been settled, Melba had no further recourse than to select another role: Verdi's lady of the camellias. Anticipation was kept at fever pitch. It was widely reported that her costuming in the opera would be an innovation, that she would wear $2,500,000 worth of jewelry, and that among the magnificent gems was a five-strand necklace formerly in the collection of Marie Antoinette. Every word concerning the celebrated soprano was now so newsworthy that even a nondescript cable to Hammerstein, which she sent en route to New York, found its way into the papers: "Splendid passage. Feeling very well. Hope for season's success."[10]

At last divinity came to earth the morning of Sunday, December 30, 1906. Melba was in New York! Waiting to greet her were friends, admirers, the press, and Hammerstein. She set about at once to dispel the malicious rumors that had been circulated concerning her voice: " 'I have had a very pleasant trip. . . . My voice is said to be better than it has been for years. I expect that the season will be a great success. I have been singing at Covent Garden, and I come here not only in good voice, but in the best of health.' "[11] When photographers asked her to pose for pictures, she would not permit any to be taken, but after Hammerstein whispered some soothing words, she willingly consented. The interview over, Melba and her entourage went to her hotel, followed by the two detectives Hammerstein had provided to guard her person as well as her jewels and costumes. She granted other interviews soon after her arrival at the St. Regis. To a representative of *The New York Herald* she said: " 'I was tremendously struck with Mr. Hammerstein's pluck in organizing an opera company, when one was already playing in an established house here. . . . As a result I have entered into his plans most enthusiastically and have aided him gladly both with advice and with personal effort and persuasion in getting his company together.' "[12]

The following day Melba went to the Manhattan for the first time. In her autobiography *Melodies and Memories*, she records that when she arrived there, she found the opera house in the greatest ferment of excitement. She and others in the cast had to rehearse to the accompaniment of hammering, since extra chairs were being installed for the overflow audience at her initial appearance.[13] The Manhattan was anticipating a rousing, royal welcome for the acknowledged Queen of Song.

In the short time before her first appearance, the prima donna was to have little solitude. Her friends in the United States had warned her not to associate herself with the Manhattan, which they believed was a failure; now they visited her at her hotel, telling her that "society was talking of nothing else but the coming war"[14] and that the "first night promised to be one of the most remarkable in the whole history of the American stage."[15] No doubt Melba suffered some qualms; she admits that she wondered whether she would actually be able to carry off a great triumph that would redound to her glory as well as to the Manhattan's. She claimed that her accommodations at the St. Regis were not altogether pleasing. Was this nerves? The ringing of the telephone and the doorbell annoyed her to such an extent that she told her maid to remove the one from the receiver and to cover the other with padding. The very day of the performance, still not her usual composed self, Melba tried to take a nap in the afternoon, but not being able to relax, she went for a long drive along the Hudson. Returning to the St. Regis, she felt ready for the ensuing fray, determined to sing gloriously.

An hour before the opera, people were being turned away from the packed lobby. There had not been such a crowd since opening night. Many members of society, pillars of the Metropolitan, were there, lured to the Manhattan by the siren sound of Melba's voice. When the diva arrived at the 35th Street entrance, Hammerstein was waiting for her and, according to the prima donna, "trembling with emotion."[16] He led her to the stage to hear the voices emanating from the full auditorium. Melba confessed that she, too, trembled, although she was not sure whether from excitement or fright. Hammerstein, she said, was convinced that he was going to triumph; and, Melba, like-minded, made a vow to herself that she would "sing as . . . never . . . before."[17]

At its best, the Melba voice, with its seamless scale, was of unparalleled beauty. The tones were equalized throughout the enormous range, extending from the lowest tone of B flat below the staff to F above high C.[18] Henderson, recalling the soprano's very first season in New York (1893-94), wrote that even then it was a voice "unique, impeccable, translucent, glittering. . . . There was nowhere a change in quality. And it had such astonishing power and brilliancy."[19] The word "silvery" was often used to describe it, but at this period of her career, critics had begun noting dramatic qualities and a warmth that had not been associated with her earlier singing. Her trill was phenomenal; her attack of a tone, miraculous; she gave the impression of singing with ease and restraint.[20] *Grove's Dictionary of Music and Musicians* notes that she used "her tone within rather than beyond its true limit of resonant power."[21] Possessed with such technique, the diva was able to sing with ravishing beauty of voice for many years. Brilliant and musical staccati, mellifluent cantilena, impeccable phrasing, superb musicianship—all were facets of the divine Melba's singing and artistry. Before such perfection, criticism bends the knee.

The house burst into applause when Campanini entered the pit. From the wings, Melba saw familiar faces from the Metropolitan. At last came the moment for her entrance. When she appeared on stage, many in the audience did not recognize her in her blond wig; but in a moment the applause was tumultuous. Then there was silence. Melba began to sing, spinning one glorious tone after another; and she related that, though it may have been vanity on her part, in thirty seconds she "knew that [she] had won."[22] The *Herald* reported the next day that "the first few notes Mme. Melba sang more than confirmed recent London reports as to her particularly brilliant singing during the past season at Covent Garden, and the scene's succeeding numbers, the 'Ah for se [*sic*] lui' especially, which she sang seated . . . made it clear that she has never been in finer voice."[23]

At the end of the first act the house went wild and recalled Melba eleven times.[24] Twice she towed Hammerstein before the footlights to share in her overwhelming reception. Going to her dressing room, she was jubilant and said: " 'I am delighted, and as happy as a king.' "[25] The rest of the performance was just as exciting and electrifying; all of the singers "sang as if their very reputations were at stake, and Campanini led the orchestra as though his greatness was still in doubt—so much fervor marked the work of everyone."[26] When the opera was over, the audience remained, vociferously applauding and cheering Melba, her vis-à-vis, and Campanini. Then when the diva appeared with Hammerstein, "the enthusiasm of the audience passed all bounds, and for some minutes there was a deafening uproar, during which hundreds of people waved their handkerchiefs, and the younger members of the audience threw their floral buttonholes at her feet."[27] The next morning the *Tribune* posed a provocative question: "Does the great success of the evening mark a turning point in local operatic history?"[28]

Critics were lavish in their praise of the performance. The *Press* called it the "most satisfying representation of Verdi's work heard and seen here in years."[29] Of Melba's voice, Richard Aldrich, of the *Times*, said that it had "its old-time lusciousness and purity, its exquisite smoothness and fullness; it is poured out with all spontaneity and freedom, and in cantilena and in coloratura passages alike it is perfectly at her command. Such a voice is a gift such as is vouchsafed but rarely in a generation, and her art is so assisted by nature, by the perfect adjustment of all the organs concerned in the voice that, like Patti's, it seems almost as much a gift as the voice itself."[30] Her acting had improved, though she relied on her voice for most of her dramatic effects. Renaud, the elder Germont, was also a revelation to the critics. He actually made the role sympathetic, dignified, sincere, transforming "a character so often represented in a manner at once sickly and artificial. It was the achievement of a remarkable artist."[31] Bassi (Alfredo) received mixed reviews. Campanini was superb, artistic to the smallest details, infusing everything with his enthusiasm.

The costuming also received much favorable comment. Melba had been anxious to do the opera in the style of the time in which it belonged: 1848. Usually it was presented in seventeenth-century décor, an anomaly that the diva did not countenance. At Covent Garden that fall season she had worn gowns of the correct period when she appeared in the opera. She brought them with her, and Mme. Freisinger made all the other costumes for the production in one week. Richard Aldrich, in the Times, commented: "The old operagoer must have been somewhat startled; the young one views it with composure; and here is a straw, not very important in itself, that shows which way the wind blows now for dramatic verisimilitude, and how it has changed in the last half century."[32]

Melba's presence gave a lustre to the company that it had not had before. Society, which had been very slow to attend performances at the new opera house, now flocked there. Town Topics noted that the "Manhattan is fast becoming a rendezvous of fashion, and it is to be regretted that the house does not possess more boxes"[33] and that whenever "Mme. Melba lets loose her golden notes, the Manhattan audience is sprinkled with social topliners and although carriage facilities are even more trying than at the [Metropolitan], these disadvantages are overlooked."[34] As the prima donna assoluta, she put the whole company on its mettle, with the result that performances, as a whole, seemed better than ever before. Melba, to be sure, was aware of what her presence meant at the opera house. She was especially cognizant of the inspiration she gave to the young American women in the chorus, many of whom had been eager to sing at the Manhattan simply because they would have the opportunity to observe firsthand the vocal method of the great diva. Melba said: " 'I have never known young women of the chorus to be more ladylike, more honest, more sincere, or more ambitious than the girls here at the Manhattan. It is a pleasure to feel their appreciation silently bestowed, and when, while singing, I glance toward the wings and see their attentive faces and realize that my every note

is a guide to them in their musical path, you may be sure I sing my best.' "[35]
No doubt many of the principals also benefited from her example; for, of
course, they, too, could learn from her, the greatest living exponent of *bel
canto*.

After the initial performance in *Traviata*, Melba appeared four more
times in January: another *La Traviata* on the nineteenth; *Rigoletto* on the
eleventh and thirty-first; *Lucia di Lammermoor* on the twenty-eighth. The
performance of *Rigoletto* (January 11) had a superlative cast; joining Melba
were Bonci and Renaud, a combination that was second to no parallel trio
at the Metropolitan. Again the house was sold out; the box office had been
closed long before the curtain went up and speculators were reaping profits.
Outside, crowds of people stood about watching the opera-goers; inside
every available space was occupied. Hammerstein had to call the police to
control the crush. Society was in force, faithfully in attendance for a Melba
night. As for the performance, the *Times* said that it was "without question
one of the best productions of *Rigoletto* that has been given in New York for
many years."[36] Melba was peerless; Bonci amazed by adding "a volume of
luscious tone which surprised his warmest admirers"[37] and Renaud "sang
and acted with a power that carried all before him."[38] As for *Lucia*, both
Melba and Bonci outdid themselves, the auditorium reverberating with
their incomparable voices. The diva never spared herself in an effort to save
her vocal resources for the difficulties of the mad scene, but "sang every
note of the part with her full power."[39] It seemed as if the cascades of limpid
tones were poured forth from an inexhaustible source.

The Repertory Grows

[The following] month Melba appeared five times: *Faust* (February 8),
Rigoletto (February 14 and 25), *Lucia* (February 16), and *La Traviata*
(February 23). The performance of *Faust* on the eighth was the only
occasion she appeared in this opera during her engagement. Krehbiel said
that the audience "revelled in the outpouring of scintillant notes in the jewel
song and were stirred to rapture by [her] invocation at the window."[40] The
comment in the *Times*, though it praised her singing, was not entirely kind:
"Her impersonation has not at the present time attributes of girlishness nor
of ingenuous pathos, for the years have told upon Mme. Melba's presence,
as they have not been able to tell upon her voice."[41] Apparently before the
performance Melba had been temperamental and imperious. Hammerstein,
needless to say, was equal to any rebuff or demand, inured to the turmoils
of the opera house. Walter Prichard Eaton, who interviewed him this evening, asked why he preferred to be an opera director rather than a captain

of industry, a manufacturer of cigars. The answer was characteristic of the impresario. Eaton said:

[Hammerstein] smiled, and his eyes squinted as they do when he doesn't wish you to know whether he's ironic or not, and he said, "Ah, but the tobacco business is prose, this is poetry—you know? It's more fun to make Melba sing than it is to make a cigar. Tonight, now, first she tells me it's too hot in her dressing-room; then it's too cold; then she wants me to ring up at eight, when there are only two people in the house, and I have to set my watch back and show her it's only seven-thirty—you know? You must handle these singers just so—it's an art—or else they'll go out on the stage and phrase like the devil. If you let 'em do that you'd have to admit people to your house on transfers—you know?"

The scene was set by now, there was a sudden awareness of the people out front as the curtain hissed up its wires, a muscular chord from the orchestra, a "Sssh" for silence from the stage manager. Oscar spread out his palms. "You see, in my own house, too, they won't let me speak!" Presently Melba, prayer-book in hand, stole along behind the canvas frame that to the audience was a garden wall, paused for her music cue, and entered the gate. Then we heard her voice, luscious, perfectly phrased, and once more he spread out his palms, this time with another inflection. He tiptoed up to the window of Marguerite's house . . . and peeped out upon the stage. He patted the scenery affectionately as he did so. He was smiling to himself when he came back to his chair, his hands behind him, his head down. . . .[42]

This performance and the other Melba nights were gala affairs; always there were tremendous crowds, excitement, and enthusiasm with society out in force—the Vanderbilts, Goelets, Belmonts. Hammerstein had cause to rejoice for, in the words of *Town Topics*, the "gold poured no more lavishly from her throat than it piled up in the box-office."[43]

Cause *La Bohème*

The production announced for March 1 received the greatest fanfare of any presentation in the Manhattan repertory this opening season. At one time, it had seemed well nigh impossible for Hammerstein to give the opera at all, for it was none other than Puccini's *La Bohème*. After all the fuss, Ricordi and Company had not been awarded an injunction to prevent the production.

The whole matter was long and involved. In an affidavit Hammerstein declared that before he went to Europe in March, 1906, he had had a verbal agreement with George Maxwell, the American representative of Ricordi, and that it had been agreed he might produce any Puccini opera except *Madama Butterfly* for $150 a performance, the same fee Conried paid.

Hammerstein said that he had conferred with Tito Ricordi in Milan regarding the production of the Puccini operas and had sought his advice concerning the artists for them. He then had gone ahead to invest many thousands of dollars for scenery and costumes. It was not until July 25, 1906, that he received a letter from Maxwell reminding him of the copyright. The letter did not mention that the Metropolitan had been granted an exclusive contract for the Puccini operas. Maxwell, on the other hand, denied that there had been any verbal contract. He said that he had seen Hammerstein the first time on March 5, 1906, the evening before the impresario went to Europe to recruit his company, and that when Hammerstein asked for a contract, he replied that he could not grant one until he knew precisely who was to sing in the operas. He declared that this was a policy of Ricordi and Company. Hammerstein promised that ten days after arriving in Europe, he would advise him of the artists he intended to engage. Maxwell then stated that after this initial meeting he had not received a word from Hammerstein. In May he granted Conried the exclusive license and, upon hearing that Hammerstein intended to produce Puccini's operas, sent the letter of July 25. Since Hammerstein, however, had persisted in his efforts, Ricordi and Company filed the injunction, on October 19, to enjoin him from producing La Bohème.

Several months later, on January 3, 1907, Judge Townsend refused to grant the injunction. It was his opinion that " 'most of the assertions and counter assertions may be so harmonized as to show that even if said agreement was not originally made, Maxwell and Tito Ricordi, by their conversation and conduct led or permitted Hammerstein to make said contracts, and incur said expenses upon the faith of an understanding that a license would be given him to produce La Bohème, provided the usual conditions were complied with.' "[44] Furthermore, the Judge asserted that if Ricordi and Company wanted to grant Conried an exclusive contract, Hammerstein should have been notified of this action and in good time. He continued: " 'But although Maxwell states that he made the exclusive license to Conried in May he did not notify Hammerstein of that fact even so late as July 25, and the letter then written might fairly be interpreted merely as a notice of the complainants' copyrights.' "[45] For these reasons the court refused to grant the injunction " 'in view of the great hardship which would be imposed thereby on Hammerstein in view of the contracts made and expenses incurred on the faith of the situation produced or permitted by Maxwell and Ricordi as established by their own statements.' "[46]

On the following day, January 4, 1907, Ricordi and Company appealed the decision. Hammerstein, of course, was pleased by the court's ruling and said he had expected it in his favor all during the controversy. The Metropolitan, however, persisted in its prosecution and after Melba had appeared four times in the opera, Hammerstein consented to the injunction on April 15, 1907. By then Ricordi's victory (or was it Conried's?) meant nothing.

Hammerstein had successfully produced *La Bohème*, much to the delight of many opera-goers and Mme. Melba. . . .

During his American sojourn (January 18-February 26), Puccini refused to make any comments concerning the Metropolitan-Hammerstein dispute over *La Bohème*; and yet it was during this precise period that the wrangling was at the highest pitch. A man of discretion, he remained silent; even if he had wanted to voice his opinion on the affair, to do so would have placed him in an awkward position. He ws the guest of the Metropolitan and the Ricordis' friend; he also would not want to offend Mme. Melba and Campanini, artists whom he admired. As far as the public was concerned, however, his sympathies were entirely with the older house. At the time, Puccini and the Metropolitan seemed indissolubly linked. Perhaps this was the effect which Conried desired.

Although Hammerstein had the legal right to present the opera, he possessed no score; for the work had never been published. The Ricordis saw to it that he would not be able to obtain any of the manuscript copies, which were numbered and accounted for all over the world. Ultimately, however, Hammerstein did succeed in finding one: a copy that the Ricordis had considered too mutilated for use again. Agnes Murphy maintains that it had been used in the United States by the Del Conti Opera Company, a touring group from England.[47] The *New York Times* of March 2, 1907, said that Hammerstein had obtained a score that Clementine de Vere had used when she was touring the United States some years before. Campanini knew the opera so well that he was able to write in the missing parts. He refused, however, to conduct any of the public performances, apparently fearful of the Ricordis' ire. As the time approached for the first presentation of the work, some maintained that his refusal was due to a difference with Melba concerning her interpretation of the role of Mimi. He denied this and wanted it understood that he held the highest admiration for the prima donna both as a person and as an artist. In a letter to the editor of *The Evening Telegram*, he gave his ostensible reason for not conducting the opera: "The true reason why I am not directing *Bohème* is because I am very tired and am greatly occupied in directing rehearsals and performances, as you can see for yourself."[48] Fernando Tanara, one of his deputies, had the honor of leading the public performances, though Campanini had rehearsed the opera *in segreto*.

The night before the *première* of *La Bohème* at the Manhattan, the Metropolitan offered the same opera with Caruso, Cavalieri, Alten, Stracciari, and Journet in the authorized version. The older house hoped, no doubt, that the comparison would be in its favor. On the very afternoon of the performance, Maxwell issued the following statement: "Mr. Hammerstein's presentation of the opera *La Bohème* is without the authority and consent of the composer, Giacomo Puccini, or ourselves as owners of the copyright. It will be given with an unauthorized orchestration, and we would request all who attend the performance not to hold Signor Puccini as composer or ourselves responsible for it."[49] The natural reaction was that many thought Hammerstein's production would be inadequate. Even up to curtain time, the opposition was intense; for the lobby of the Manhattan was filled with detractors who harassed those going into the auditorium.[50]

In spite of the dire predictions, the evening was a triumph. Years later Melba recalled that it was "one of the best performances"[51] of this opera in which she had appeared during her entire career. No doubt keyed up by the occasion, she never spared herself, singing "with positive recklessness. At times her voice fairly flooded the auditorium."[52] According to the *Times*, she sang "more beautifully than she [had] done anything else this season in New York."[53] Her impersonation of the frail seamstress was touching, although her appearance hardly suggested a Latin Quarter grisette. Bonci surprised his most ardent admirers by the plenitude and fervor of his singing. Trentini, as Musetta, was a revelation. Earlier in the season she had appeared in such various secondary roles as Siébel in *Faust*, Berta in *Il Barbiere di Siviglia*, Frasquita in *Carmen* without any special distinction; but as the dashing vixen in Puccini's opera, she was a sensation. It was "a piece of work that [raised] this young person perceptibly in the estimation of the frequenters of the Manhattan. It [was] her most important contribution to the operatic history of that institution: a most vivacious and mirthful character sketch, full of the highest spirits and boisterous mischief, yet very intelligent and very well sung."[54] John McCormack considered her the ideal Musetta.[55] Sammarco (Marcello), Gilibert (Schaunard), and Arimondi (Colline) were entirely satisfactory. Gianoli-Galletti and Tecchi, who was Bonci's brother, rounded out the cast. The only adverse criticism was that the orchestra was frequently too loud, obliterating some of the singing of the principals.[56] All in all, it was a red-letter night for the Manhattan and a victory for Melba and Hammerstein.

The Final Weeks of the Season

On March 25, Melba made her farewell performance for the season in the fourth presentation of *La Bohème*. As on each previous occasion when this opera was performed (March 1, 6, 11), she was again the Mimi. This gala marked her fifteenth appearance with the company. Although originally having contracted to sing only ten performances, she had twice extended her stay so that she could be in additional presentations at the Manhattan, concertize in various cities, and make some recordings. Seats for her farewell were at a premium; it was reported that some orchestra stalls had gone for $30 each, or even more.[57] At the end of the opera, which had been a spirited performance, Melba sang the mad scene from *Lucia*. The audience responded by giving her perhaps the greatest ovation of the season. It remained cheering and applauding for some forty minutes as the beloved diva came before the footlights twenty-three times.[58] After a while Melba had the stagehands push a piano onto the stage, where, accompanying herself, she sang the air "Mattinata," apparently not considering this song anti-climactic to the mad scene. When she finished, the house was pandemonium all over again. Finally the lights were dimmed, and those still in the auditorium made their way outside, glorying in an unforgettable operatic evening.

Meantime caterers on stage were busily preparing for a supper party to be given in honor of the departing star. To join in the festivities, Hammerstein had invited all the principals and their husbands or wives, as well as some of Melba's friends. Thirty-five musicians entertained the guests as they dined with "Memories of the Manhattan Opera Season," composed by the impresario himself. The menu was apropos, for it included *suprême de volaille Hammerstein* and *pêche Melba*. In an expansive mood, Hammerstein extolled his guest of honor as a person and as a singer. And well he might! He had every reason to be proud of what she had accomplished and of what his company now meant to New York. No doubt he contemplated that the concluding weeks of the season should be highly successful, since he had been able to engage another great star to add lustre to the Manhattan: the inimitable Emma Calvé. His opera house would not lack a prima donna. It is likely that he was sorry she had not come to the supper party, even though she had been invited. Perhaps Calvé realized it was best that the impresario not share his attentions with his two *prime donne*.[59] Even for a man of his known fortitude, such a combination might have been a hazardous undertaking.

Melba's final word about Hammerstein and her experiences with the company was made known on the eve of her departure for Europe:

I have never enjoyed any season in America so much as the one now closing. All through I have been in splendid health and spirits, and I shall never forget the kindness with which I have been received. The demands on my time have been so exacting that many courtesies must remain without direct acknowledgment.

I am proud to have been associated with Mr. Hammerstein in his launching of New York's new opera house. What courage Mr. Hammerstein has shown and what wonders he has done! I think there must be something in the conditions of American life to encourage him, for I know of no manager in any city of the world who, single-handed and under circumstances of such difficulty and competition, would have risked his fortune on opera.

His pluck appealed to me from the first, and I leave as I came, his loyal friend and admirer.[60]

A New Opera Season

Since we are concerned here with the work of Nellie Melba in the Hammerstein company, we will omit discussion of the 1907-1908 season in which she had no part. Suffice it to say that Hammerstein did not lack for stars, as his list of artists included the names of Calvé, Nordica, both Luisa and Eva Tetrazzini, Gerville-Réache, Schumann-Heink and Mary Garden. Melba was back for the 1908-1909 season, however.

Not content with upsetting the operatic balance in New York, Hammerstein also had plans for Philadelphia, where the New York Metropolitan also provided performances. In March 1908, Hammerstein's New York company presented two performances at the Philadelphia Academy of Music. So well were they received that the impresario announced on March 26 that he intended to build a new house in that city also, and that it would be ready for the opening performance the following November. And so it was! Hammerstein's third season in New York opened November 9, and his first in Philadelphia November 17.

Again, we quote from John Cone's history.

Melba's return had been eagerly anticipated. She reappeared on Monday, December 14, 1908, in *La Bohème*, with a superlative cast that included Zenatello, Trentini, Gilibert, De Segurola, Sammarco, Gianoli-Galletti, a group of singers perhaps impossible to duplicate in any other opera company in the world. When the beloved soprano first appeared on stage, the house, filled to capacity, burst into wild applause, at once leaving no doubt whatsoever of the esteem and affection which the Manhattan opera-goers held for her. After the tumult subsided, she began to sing somewhat tentatively, apparently overexcited or nervous; but as the performance continued, Melba was her magical self, the perfect artist and vocalist, glorifying Puccini's music with her phenomenal voice. Always singing without a trace of effort, she sustained tones that were sumptuous, velvety, smooth. It was still a voice of ineluctable loveliness, although perhaps not quite so crystalline as in the past. Whatever it may have lost, however, was compensated for by a more profound eloquence in her singing, a deeper artistry, and more attention to the dramatic requirements of the role. Henderson observed that "what it has lost in silver it has gained in gold. It is still youthful and a warmer, more winning, more touching voice to-day than it ever was before; and better than all, it is backed by a more beautiful sincerity and a more rounded musicianship."[61] Of course, the diva did not look the part, as she had gained in weight and in years; but the exquisite voice and flawless musicianship carried all before her. The others in the cast, inspired by her presence, gave a rousing performance, wholeheartedly entering into the spirit of the occasion.

Several days later, on December 17, Hammerstein presented *Bohème* in Philadelphia with virtually the same cast. What made Melba's return particularly significant was that she was appearing as Mimi, a part which she had first essayed on a stage in Philadelphia. That had occurred almost ten years before, December 30, 1898.[62] Her last appearance in opera there had been in 1904. For these reasons, Philadelphians were eager to pay homage to the long-absent diva; Melba, in turn, was anxious to sing for them and to appear in the new opera house. Before the opening of the season, she had written a brief message, printed in the November 17, 1908, issue of *The North American*:

Mr. Hammerstein is a wonderful genius in opera. He has done so much for opera, and against such odds to begin with, that it makes me believe that impresarios, like singers, are born and not made. I am glad to be one who will assist in the inauguration of his great enterprise in Philadelphia, for I am certain that it will prove a most important factor in the making of the history of music in America.[63]

The evening was a triumph. The entire house was sold out. It was reported that there were more carriages in line than at any other time since the opening. The *Press* observed that the performance was the signal "for a gathering of 'everyone in town,' the like of which is usually known only on 'opening nights.' With the possible exception of the stupendous 'first night' last month, the opera last evening was beyond question the most brilliant social event of the Winter season."[64] On stage there was tremendous excitement, Melba having a glamour and prestige unrivaled in the opera world. For a time, however, there were some doubts whether or not she would sing, since she had been suffering from a slight throat ailment. Ordinarily, under these circumstances, she would not have appeared; but, as she said, " 'That wizard [Hammerstein] can make me do almost anything.' "[65] She had no reason to regret her decision to go on with the performance, for she was in perfect voice. Melba also seems to have been in excellent spirits. Coming offstage at the end of the first act, she said to Hammerstein, sitting in his usual place, with the ubiquitous cigar in his mouth: " 'I have never sung in such a house. It is simply delightful. All one has to do is to open one's mouth, and the house does the rest. You are a wonder. But how dare you smoke in my presence, you beast?' " Hammerstein, understanding the soprano very well, assumed an air of abject humility, which achieved its desired effect. Bursting into laughter, Melba said: " 'Oh, smoke away, you old fraud!' "[66] . . .

The only new role in which Melba appeared was as Desdemona in Verdi's *Otello*, first presented at the Manhattan Opera House on Friday, December

25, 1908. The opera had not been given at the Metropolitan for six years, the artists at that time being Eames, Alvarez and Scotti. Hammerstein's production of this masterpiece was superb. According to De Koven, there was "a fervid sweep of passionate intensity that fairly whirled one along in a rush of varied emotions and made the atmosphere seem even overcharged with a vibrant force that was electrical."[67] Although Melba's impersonation was attractive and artistic, her singing was somewhat disappointing; for in her efforts to make her voice more dramatic, she lost some quality in her tones. However, in the last act her singing of the "Salce! Salce!" and "Ave Maria" was ravishing to the ears.[68] Zenatello, as the Moor, found the role congenial to his robust style; in fact, he had never appeared to greater advantage and scored a triumph with his passionate singing, emotional feeling, and dramatic ardor. As Iago, Sammarco was vocally magnificent, but he left something to be desired histrionically. Even so, what an evening this must have been! Zenatello's thrilling "Esultate!," Sammarco's intense singing of the "Credo," Zenatello's impassioned outburst of "Ora e per sempre addio," the two men's voices blending in the duet at the end of the second act, and Melba's angelic singing in the last act—all were treasured, ineffable moments in an overwhelming performance. . . .

Too soon came the time for Melba to say farewell. Her final appearance in Philadelphia was at the Saturday matinee of January 9 in *La Traviata*. She had been heard there but two other times with the company, both being in *La Bohème*. Since the patrons who held subscriptions for Saturday evenings had not had an opportunity to hear her, Hammerstein invited them to attend the afternoon performance as his guests. Any lingering doubts as to the condition of her voice were set at rest. She sang more brilliantly than at her other appearances in the house, which was filled to its capacity. The music critic of the *Press* said: "From her very first utterance there was evidence of her splendid form, and all through the performance she not only sang with remarkable volume, but with all her old purity of tone in the whole range of her voice and with great brilliancy. Moreover, as if in an effort to give her audience more than it might naturally demand of the greatest florid singer of her time, Tetrazzini not excepted, a number of the arias were sung in a diminished tone, pure gold drawn to the finest thread, with a pathetic delicacy of shading that gave the sentiment of the words a double meaning."[69] At all times her singing demonstrated that she remained the prima donna *assoluta* whose star was still fixed in the firmament.

On January 11 Melba bid adieu to New York in *Rigoletto*, with an all-star cast: Renaud, Constantino, Gilibert, and Arimondi. It was the largest house of the season. Again the soprano was in excellent voice, "her tones having all their old-time lusciousness, rounded beauty, and freshness."[70] The audience seemed reluctant to let the singers go; and at the end the tributes to Melba were for her not only as an artist but also as a woman. Flowers, numerous recalls, cheers, her Australian countrymen's cries of the bushmen's "Coo-e-e!"—all must have lingered long in her memory. In the four weeks Melba was with the company she appeared in ten performances. In New York she sang in three *Bohèmes*, three *Otellos* and one *Rigoletto*, while in Philadelphia she was seen in *La Bohème* two times and in *La Traviata* once. . . .

Grave Problems, but Ultimate Victory

As might have been expected, Hammerstein had overextended himself financially. After some well-publicized fights with his financial backers, described in some detail in Mr. Cone's account, he announced that the last performance in the new Philadelphia house would be January 23.

Among those who publicly expressed the desire to see him remain was his devoted friend Nellie Melba. At her farewell performance in Philadelphia, which occurred the day after Hammerstein announced his withdrawal from the city, the diva invited reporters to come to her dressing room at the end of the matinee, Saturday, January 9, 1909, as she desired to make a statement. Surrounded by friends and admirers, Melba took the initiative in the interview. She said to the representatives of the press:

Now, boys—for we are all boys and girls today—I must interview you. Tell me what I can say that will help to save this glorious place to Philadelphia? Oh, it would be such a disgrace to have it closed, such a disgrace, not only to Philadelphia and to America, but to the whole world. It would seem like a death-blow to opera to me. It must not be, it must not be. . . .

Mr. Hammerstein is such an operatic genius, the greatest world ever had. You mustn't let him get away from you. He will prove the glory of the city yet, if you only will not let him leave it. Oh, but it would be such a disgrace! I am so happy over the way you have shown that you liked me this afternoon that almost nothing could make me feel sad; but I would feel very, very sad if I thought that I would never sing in this superb house again."[71]

Addressing one of the members of the Box Committee, she urged him not to be annoyed by Hammerstein's eccentricities but to remember only his fine qualities. The gallant gentleman responded that his utmost desire was that the season would continue, promising the diva he would do everything possible for that result. Again appealing to the reporters to do all they could via the press, Melba hoped that before she left for Europe in four days' time, the issue would be settled and the season saved. Mrs. John Reyburn, the mayor's wife, assured Melba that a way would be found. The diva's final word was a peremptory command:

. . . Tell the people of Philadelphia that Melba says it would be a disgrace for them to sit idly by and see the splendid opera house closed. Tell them that I expect greater things of them, individually and collectively. . . .[72]

. . . On January 13 Hammerstein obtained his loan from Edward T. Stotesbury, who personally took the $400,000 mortgage with only the Philadelphia Opera House as security. . . .[73]

Perhaps Melba also played a part. Apparently she and Stotesbury had been friends for years, enjoying a pleasant camaraderie. One anecdote will suffice. Months before, she had bet him a new hat that Hammerstein would have the opera house ready by November 17, 1908. When the season began on time, he had to pay the diva $200.[74] After her seasonal farewell performance in Philadelphia and her interview with the press (January 9), she went to the Stotesburys' home for a supper party. Some of the conversation may have concerned the fate of the opera house. At any event, before leaving for Europe, Melba may have heard that the loan had been effected. Providentially, she left on the same day Hammerstein received his $400,000.

Vincent Sheean (1956) sums it up rather nicely:

Whether (Melba) was really as imperious, demanding, grandiose, and unreasonable as some of the stories would indicate can hardly be ascertained now. There are stories to prove that she was, certainly, but there are just as many to prove that she was not. She was extremely kind when her heart was moved, and the available evidence is that Hammerstein had in some way moved her heart. She had no other reason for revisiting New York: she could have made just as much or more money in any of the great opera houses of Europe, and her American fame was already well established. We are led to the conclusion that she liked and admired what he was doing (his "pluck," as she called it) and actually wanted to help him. She would not do so, of course, without a whacking big fee, for she was an excellent businesswoman; but, after all, fees had presented no problem to Melba for some years past.

NOTES

1. "Monsieur Hammerstein Tells in Nobody's Words but His Own How He Engaged Songbird Melba," The [New York] *World Theatre Section*, May 6, 1906, p. 2.

2. Montrose J. Moses, *The Life of Heinrich Conried* (New York: Thomas Y. Crowell Company, 1916).

3. "Monsieur Hammerstein Tells . . . How He Engaged Songbird Melba," *The* [New York] *World Theatre Section*, May 6, 1906, p. 2.

4. Nellie Melba, *Melodies and Memories* (London: Thornton Butterworth, 1925; New York: George H. Doran, 1926), 236-39.

5. Agnes G. Murphy, *Melba: A Biography* (London: Chatto and Windus, 1909; New York: Doubleday, Page & Co., 1909), 255-56.

6. *Melodies and Memories*, 243-44.

7. News item in *The* [New York] *Morning Telegraph*, July 21, 1906.

8. *The* [London] *Times*, October 6, 1906.

9. Ibid., November 3, 1906.

10. News item in *The New York Times*, December 29, 1906.

11. Ibid., December 31, 1906.

12. News item in *The New York Herald*, December 31, 1906.

13. Nellie Melba, *Melodies and Memories*, 242.

14. Ibid.

15. Ibid.

16. Ibid.

17. Ibid., 243.

18. Eric Blom (ed.), *Grove's Dictionary of Music and Musicians* (fifth ed.), Vol. 5, 660.

19. W. J. Henderson, "A Dream of Two Singers," *The* [New York] *Sun Theatre Section*, January 6, 1907, p. 6.

20. W. J. Henderson, *The Art of Singing*, 421.

21. Blom (ed.), *Grove's Dictionary*.

22. Melba, *Melodies and Memories*, 243.

23. *The New York Herald*, January 3, 1907.

24. *The* [New York] *World*, January 3, 1907.

25. Murphy, *Melba: A Biography*, 258.

26. *The* [New York] *World*, January 3, 1907.

27. Murphy, *Melba: A Biography*, 258.

28. *New-York Daily Tribune*, January 3, 1907.

29. *The New York Press*, January 3, 1907.

30. *The New York Times*, January 3, 1907.

31. Ibid.

32. Richard Aldrich, "*Traviata* at Last Properly Costumed," *The New York Times Theatre Section*, January 6, 1907, p. 5.

33. Vol. 57 (January 17, 1907), 5.

34. Ibid., February 14, 1907, 5.

35. "Serious Students of Music in Manhattan Opera Chorus," *Musical America*, Vol. 5 (April 6, 1907), 14.

36. *The New York Times*, January 12, 1907.

37. Ibid.

38. Ibid.

39. *New York American*, January 29, 1907.

40. *New-York Daily Tribune*, February 9, 1907.

41. *The New York Times*, February 9, 1907.

42. "Oscar Hammerstein A Boy Who Never Grew Up," *The American Magazine*, Vol. 64 (May 1907), 32-34.

43. Vol. 57 (January 24, 1907), 16.

44. "*Bohème* for Hammerstein," *Musical Courier*, Vol. 54 (January 9, 1907), 24.

45. Ibid.

46. Ibid., 23-24.

47. *Melba: A Biography*, 269.

48. Letter dated February 28, 1907, p. 8.

49. News item in *The* [New York] *Sun*, March 2, 1907.

50. Murphy, *Melba: A Biography*, 269-70.

51. Melba, *Melodies and Memories*, 245.

52. *The* [New York] *Evening World*, March 2, 1907.

53. *The New York Times*, March 2, 1907.

54. Ibid., March 7, 1907.

55. L.A.G. Strong, *John McCormack*, 138.

56. *The* [New York] *Sun*, March 2, 1907.

57. Murphy, *Melba: A Biography*, 272.

58. Ibid., 274.

59. News item in *The* [New York] *Evening Telegram*, March 26, 1907.

60. News item in *The New York Times*, April 1, 1907.

61. *The* [New York] *Sun*, December 15, 1908.

62. *The* [Philadelphia] *Press*, December 18, 1908.

63. Nellie Melba, "Singers Born, Not Made, Says Melba," *The* [Philadelphia] *North American Grand Opera Edition*, November 17, 1908, p. 1.

64. News item in *The* [Philadelphia] *Press*, December 18, 1908.

65. "Oscar Inspects Operas from His Seat in Wings," *The* [Philadelphia] *North American Theatre Section*, December 20, 1908, p. 8.

66. Ibid.

67. *The* [New York] *World*, December 26, 1908.

68. *The* [New York] *Globe and Commercial Advertiser*, December 26, 1908.

69. *The* [Philadelphia] *Press*, January 10, 1909.

70. *The* [New York] *Evening Post*, January 12, 1909.

71. News item in *The* [Philadelphia] *North American*, January 10, 1909.

72. News item in *The Philadelphia Inquirer*, January 10, 1909.

73. Ibid., January 14, 1909.

74. Horace Mather Lippincott, "Edward T. Stotesbury" (paper read at the Old York Road Historical Association, Jenkintown, Pennsylvania, November 19, 1941), p. 23.

LA BOHÈME AT
THE MANHATTAN
OPERA HOUSE

RICHARD ALDRICH

Last night was one of the red letter nights of the season at the Manhattan Opera House. It was marked by the reappearance there of Mme. Nellie Melba, who was one of the mainstays of Mr. Hammerstein's first season but who did not return last year. She made her reappearance as Mimi in Puccini's opera, *La Bohème,* and the large audience that filled the house let her remain in no doubt as to the place she holds in the admiration of the New York operatic public. Her welcome was most enthusiastic.

La Bohème had not been heard at the Manhattan Opera House since Mr. Hammerstein's first season, when the performance was under serious suspicion of not being strictly in accordance with the letter of the composer's score and was dependent, so far as the orchestration was concerned, upon the memory and conjecture of those who took part in it. Last evening's performance was of a different sort and was in due accordance with all the composer's intentions. It was an uncommonly spirited performance, full of humor, sparkle, bristling gayety and pathos that are by turns uppermost. There was an admirable effect of ensemble throughout it, and the several members of the cast played into each other's hands with skill and understanding. And once more the value of the added vividness and comprehensibility, the greater intimacy and convincing power of such an opera when given in the Manhattan Opera House was made manifest. Much of the enjoyment of the performance was in the close relation of the audience with the proceedings on the stage.

From: the *New York Times*, December 16, 1908.

Mme. Melba has had an especial fondness for the part of Mimi in *La Bohème* ever since she first introduced it upon the stage of the Metropolitan Opera House, now near a decade ago. Yet it may be doubted whether it is so well adapted to her powers, either in voice or in action, as some of the others with which she is identified in the public mind. This is naturally more and more the case as she advances in maturity of figure and face. Her Mimi cannot today suggest all of the girlish freshness and sprightliness that belong to it. But it was a renewal of delight, of cherished memories, to hear the marvelous voice, the delightful clarity and luscious quality, the ease and spontaneity of its production, the purity of its intonation, the finish of its phrasing, the equality in all its ranges, that are so well remembered in Mme. Melba's singing.

She returns with all these things scarcely touched by the tooth of time. It seemed in the first act that she was not giving her voice out in all its volume and that it showed a certain fatigue, but she later gave it in abundance. Such singing as hers is a lesson and a rebuke to some of the pretentious and half-finished attempts that are much exploited in these latter days as phenomenal and wonderful artistry and that dazzle and bewilder the public for a time. She is not a great dramatic artist in the highest sense, but the voice and singing of Mme. Melba are an inestimable boon.

The rest of the cast of this performance was an uncommonly fine one. Miss Trentini has most of the qualifications to make an ideal representative of Musetta—archness, vivacity and a very good voice, which she seemed particularly anxious last evening to let forth with much power. Her performance was one of the cleverest that she has presented since she has been a member of Mr. Hammerstein's company. The quartet of Bohemians was likewise excellent. Messrs. Zenatello, Sammarco, Segurola and Gilibert were the Rudolph, Marcel, Colline and Schaunard, respectively. Mr. Gilibert's inimitably humorous and unctuous performance is well remembered from older days at the Metropolitan.

Mr. Campanini carried the performance through with an intense dramatic life and color. Some of his tempis were more rapid than have been usual, but they stimulated the effects of the comedy. The chorus acquitted itself, as it usually does at the Manhattan, commendably.

THE MELBA REPERTOIRE

WILLIAM R. MORAN

The repertoire of most opera singers who have had to work their way up the ladder, beginning with any small parts that were offered to them, is often quite extensive; as these singers reached stardom, they could usually be more selective and pick rôles with which they felt they had a particular affinity. The amazing Lilli Lehmann (1848-1929), who made her début as the First Boy in *Die Zauberflöte* and whose list of parts ranged from the Shepherd Boy in *Tannhäuser* to all three Brünnhildes, perhaps had the record for any principal singer: some 170 rôles! Schumann-Heink's list was close to one hundred, although she sang only eighteen of them at the Metropolitan. Jenny Lind, who had a relatively short career in opera, sang thirty parts; Patti and Nordica each listed forty-two, and Caruso's repertoire is given as fifty-nine rôles, although some of them he, like Melba, sang only once. The list of operas in which Melba sang totals twenty-five, a number of them sung at relatively few performances. Two of these operas (Bemberg's *Elaine* and Saint-Saëns' *Hélène*) were written especially for her, although neither was particularly successful. Marcella Sembrich, Melba's principal rival at the Metropolitan, sang twenty-six roles in that house, Emma Eames twenty-one, and Melba eighteen. Melba's complete repertoire was as follows:

Bemberg	*Elaine*
Bizet	*Carmen* (Micaëla)
Berlioz	*La Damnation de Faust*
Delibes	*Lakmé*
Donizetti	*Lucia di Lammermoor*
Goring Thomas	*Esmeralda*

Gounod	*Faust*
	Roméo et Juliette
Leoncavallo	*I Pagliacci*
Mascagni	*I Rantzau*
Massenet	*Le Cid* (L'Infante)
	Manon
Meyerbeer	*Les Huguenots* (Marguerite de Valois)
Puccini	*La Bohème*
Rossini	*Il Barbiere di Siviglia*
	Semiramide
Saint-Saëns	*Hélène*
Thomas	*Hamlet*
Verdi	*Aïda*
	Otello
	Rigoletto
	La Traviata
Wagner	*Lohengrin*
	Siegfried (Brünnhilde)
	Tannhäuser

Melba is known to have sung "The Voice of the Forest Bird" in *Siegfried* at a private performance. On April 21, 1921, she sang the Countess in Act III of *Le Nozze di Figaro* at the Théâtre Royal de la Monnaie, the scene of her début in 1887, in a benefit performance which also included the Garden Scene from *Faust*. She studied *Mireille* with Gounod, but apparently never sang it on the stage. Other rôles that she prepared but never sang in public were Martha (Flotow), Tosca (Puccini), and Senta in Wagner's *Der Fliegende Holländer*.

VIEWS ON MELBA
BY HER
CONTEMPORARIES

NELLIE MELBA

HENRY T. FINCK

The British Isles have given to the world some of the greatest tenors and baritones, but no prima donnas of the highest rank. The British colony, Australia, has, however, come to the rescue with Nellie Melba, whose success as a lyric and colorature singer has been as great as that of Marcella Sembrich.

Her maiden name was Nellie Mitchell; her husband's, Charles Armstrong; but to the world she is known by the name she assumed by way of suggesting Melbourne, near which city she was born in 1859 [sic]. She was a lively girl, fond of riding bareback across the Australian plains or fishing all day in a creek. Both her parents were musical. Her father was Scotch. Her mother, who was of Spanish descent, and from whom, as Gustav Kobbé suggests, Melba inherits her handsome looks, was a good pianist; when she played, little Nellie would sometimes hide under the piano listening intently. Like Sembrich, she learned as a child to play the piano and the violin; and she also played the organ in a church frequently. When not busy at school, she was always humming, and even in those days she attracted attention by that trill which subsequently alone would have sufficed to make her famous—a trill that became so pure, so easy, so even, so subtly graded in the increase or decrease of loudness, that it has been the model and despair of her greatest rivals, including Selma Kurz.

Her vocal organs were, like Patti's, seemingly built so that it was almost impossible for her to sing otherwise than beautifully. As Mabel Wagnalls

From: Henry T. Finck, *Success in Music and How It Is Won* (1909).

says: "All things came easy to her, because her voice never had to be *placed*; her tones were jewels already set." Yet that did not absolve her from the necessity of working hard to acquire the necessary fluency and brilliancy of execution. Her parents were wealthy, and her desire to go on the stage was discouraged by them, so that it was not till after her marriage that she had an opportunity to do as she pleased. The marriage was not a happy one, and after the birth of a son Nellie returned to her father's house. She accompanied him to London, and there she was heard and admired at an entertainment. Among those present was the wife of the Austrian consul at Melbourne, who urged her to study with Mme. Marchesi in Paris, and gave her a letter of introduction.

Marchesi had hardly heard her when she excitedly called to her husband: "Salvatore, at last I have a star!" She then asked the singer: "Are you serious? Have you patience?" And when the young woman answered "Yes," Marchesi added: "Then if you will stay with me one year I will make of you something extraordinary."

The eminent German teacher kept her word to the Australian, who, in Marchesi's own words, "soon became one of my most industrious, pliant, and talented scholars." At a musical in Marchesi's house she sang the mad scene from *Hamlet* in such a way as to win the most flattering praise of its composer, Ambroise Thomas, who was among the guests. This was in 1886; in the following year she made her operatic début at Brussels—the beginning of a brilliant career, during which she has distinguished herself particularly as Lucia, Gilda, Ophelia, Marguerite, Juliet, Nedda, Mimi, Micaela, and Desdemona.

It has always been great fun, for those who like that sort of sport, to watch Melba and the flute player, in the mad scene from *Lucia*, run a steeplechase across a scaly country full of dangerous staccato stubble and wide leaps, or—to change the figure—to watch the dazzling explosion of runs, trills, and staccato rockets. What her voice chiefly lacks is warmth and variety of coloring, but these qualities the lovers of florid song do not care for so much as brilliant execution. Nor do they consider it a serious flaw if a prima donna enunciates indistinctly, sacrificing words to tones. Like Schopenhauer, they rather like the "contemptuous indifference" with which Rossini, Donizetti, and their singers often treat the text; and if the indifference extends to the action, as it does sometimes in Melba's case, they forgive, and applaud no less violently.[1]

Concerning her appearance in *La Traviata* in 1896, I wrote: "The audience saw a healthy, vigorous Australian prima donna, looking as fresh as a rose and singing like a skylark. There was not a single tuberculous microbe in this Violetta; she was simply an elegantly dressed young woman who seemed to be happy at first and more or less distressed afterward by two men, and then she suddenly expired, for no visible reason. It was neither sad nor particularly entertaining, and it showed that there was, after all, an advantage in the old indifference of operatic audiences to plots, which is most vividly illustrated by the story of the man in the gallery, in an Italian opera-house, who shouted: 'Great Heavens! the tenor is murdering the soprano!' But Mme. Melba's singing atoned for everything." There are many ways of winning great success—fortunately.

This success, however, in Nellie Melba's case, did not come at once, so far as New York is concerned. In the same criticism from which I have just quoted I stated that "the sidewalk speculators were offering tickets at greatly reduced rates, and in the house itself there were rows of empty seats." This prima donna had to win her way slowly in America, in striking contrast to Tetrazzini, a decade and a half later. The reasons therefor are given succinctly in that invaluable storehouse of information, Mr. Krehbiel's *Chapters of Opera*: Mme. Melba "did not make all of her operas effective in her first season [1893], partly because a large portion of the public had been weaned away from the purely lyric style of composition and song, in which she excelled, partly because the dramatic methods and fascinating personality of Mme. Calvé had created a fad which soon grew to proportions that scouted at reason; partly because Miss (not Mme.) Eames had become a great popular favorite, and the people of society, who doted on her, on Jean de Reszke, his brother Edouard, and on Lassalle, found all the artistic bliss of which they were capable in listening to their combined voices in *Faust*. So popular had Gounod's opera become at this time with the patrons of the Metropolitan Opera House, that my witty colleague, Mr. W. J. Henderson, sarcastically dubbed it 'das Faustspielhaus,' in parody of the popular title of the theatre on the hill in the Wagnerian Mecca."

Subsequently Mme. Melba became so popular that she could dictate her own terms and monopolize whatever rôles she wanted. In one case, however, this proved a disadvantage. Mme. Sembrich attributes the preservation of her vocal powers during a career of nearly three decades to the fact that she always knew what rôles and songs were suited to her voice, and avoided the others. Mme. Melba did not always do this, and for her mistake on one occasion she suffered serious, but luckily not permanent, injury to her voice.

It was at the time when the De Reszkes were in New York and Wagner was all the rage, so that even Melba longed to appear in one of these rôles that brought their interpreters so much glory, while Calvé likewise talked as if she was in similar mood. The Frenchwoman refrained, but the Australian succumbed. One day Jean de Reszke suggested to her, half jocularly, maybe, that she should try Brünnhilde, in *Siegfried*. She promptly made up her mind to do so, and had a clause inserted in her contract securing that part for herself. To sing that rôle, one must have a voice pliant and strong as a Damascus blade. Melba's was pliant, but not of steel, and it broke in its contest with the Wagnerian orchestra; she had to retire for the season and make it whole again.

There were not wanting critics who asserted that Wagner was to blame. If that was the case, were Puccini and Verdi to blame for the impairment of Caruso's voice toward the close of the season of 1908-9?

Melba's triumphs at the Metropolitan Opera House were even surpassed by those she won at Oscar Hammerstein's Manhattan Opera House, which her presence helped to make a fashionable resort. What pleased the more critical of her admirers particularly was that her biggest success was won in the season 1908-9, in a part which her matured art as singer and actress now enabled her to assume with most satisfactory results—the part of Desdemona, in Verdi's *Otello*, an opera which she actually succeeded in making popular.

Nellie Melba is one of the few lucky singers whose vocal gifts came to her naturally. Yet, as already intimated, she was from her girlhood a hard worker, practising on several instruments besides training her voice. To Mabel Wagnalls she once said: "I didn't *sing* much when a child; I only *hummed*. And, by the way, a child's voice should be carefully guarded. I consider the ensemble singing in schools as ruinous to good voices. Each one tries to outdo the other, and the tender vocal cords are strained and tired. I, personally, did not seriously study singing until after my marriage at seventeen [*sic*] years of age."

NOTE

1. Mme. Melba knows her audiences, and she does not resent criticism or banter. I once asked her if she remembered that when she first came to America I referred to her as the kangaroo prima donna. "Oh," she laughed, "that did not worry me. My husband used to be known as Kangaroo Charlie."

16. Nellie Melba, ca. 1910

MELBA AND BEHIND THE SCENES WITH MELBA

HARRY BURGESS

The author [Burgess] wishes to express his indebtedness to Madame Melba for her kindness in correcting the proofs of this chapter, and in supplying certain data. The dates of Madame Melba's first English and Continental appearances vary with different biographers, but those given in this chapter are authentic.

Melba

"Singers come and singers go, but Melba lives in our hearts for ever" were the words of a telegram handed to Melba just before she made her entrance as "Mimi" in Puccini's *La Bohème* at the commencement of the Covent Garden season of 1911. Melba was very touched at the sentiment expressed, and the ovations at the close of each act must have proved beyond doubt that time cannot lessen the hold this great artist has upon the affections of metropolitan music-lovers.

The opera house was over full. Celebrities of every walk of life were in evidence, and from the first words, heard from behind the closed door of the attic-studio, it was evident that the vast audience had assembled to do homage not to Puccini's masterpiece, but to the genius of Melba.

From "Mi chiamano Mimi" to the last note of the dying struggle, Melba was in finer voice than I have ever heard her before. That wonderful pene-

From: Harry Burgess, *My Musical Pilgrimage* (1911).

trating quality, that gift of artistry which renders the softest whisper audible even at the back of the far distant gallery of this great opera house, seemed more remarkable than ever, and in the "big" passages, in the "O soave fanciulla," the volume of melody poured out in harmony with that of John McCormack without the slightest trace of effort. It was the consummation of art, founded upon the most superb technique, and the most glorious of natural gifts.

A celebrated critic has told us that "Melba sings first and acts afterwards," but on this occasion, her personation of the fickle Mimi was instinct with dramatic grace. We almost forgot Melba and the opera house, as we sat and pitied the wilful little milliner in her struggles against the inexorable hand of fate. The picture was complete: our eyes, our ears and our hearts in unison called out sympathy for the sorrows of the little band.

The greatest of prime donne are, at times, almost unable to prevent some of the situations of operatic tradition from being ludicrous, but Melba was so truly the "Mimi" of Murger that the "picture" was complete. It is (to me at any rate) the height of absurdity that Rudolfo should add, between acts one and four, the dainty little bed to the meagre accoutrements of his studio, and the necessity for Mimi to climb into the said bed to die picturesquely, also provokes a smile.

But Melba handled the matter so gracefully, so naturally, that I saw nothing but the tragedy of the girl's dying moments. The whole work was a beautifully enacted drama, not a selection of melodies strung upon the attenuated frame of a highly improbable story, as is so frequently the case.

Melba's voice is very difficult to describe, because I know of no other of similar tone colour with which to compare it. Its clarity is amazing, as is the ease with which it is produced. In all the brilliant roulades of Verdi and Rossini, dangerous flights from the lowest to the highest notes of her range, and dazzling shakes of almost interminable length, there is never the slightest trace of effort or harshness. There is never that pose, that "Prepare! Be alert! I am about to startle you," that so many prime donne affect, and the beautiful, round, luscious melody is as rich and pure on the E in alt as it is upon the middle notes.

Massenet once called Melba "Madame Stradivarius," and the conceit is pleasing, for the voice resembles no instrument so closely as a violin. I remember another critic describing Melba's notes as a string of perfectly matched pearls. Every pearl a gem, and no one of greater beauty than its neighbour. Every note round, clear, and perfect, alike to the connoisseur and the uncultured.

In the early days of Melba's married life, the ambition to be a great lyric singer came to her, and after a course of study, she sought out several impresarios, with results disastrous to their perspicacity. Sir Arthur Sullivan could find no place for her in the Savoy chorus, Alberto Randegger could not see his way to accept her as a pupil, and other musical caterers were sufficiently blind to their own interests as to completely overlook what might have been a gold mine to them.

So the disappointed aspirant decided to seek the advice of one who was probably the greatest authority upon the voice then living, the renowned Mathilde Marchesi. Crossing over to Paris, Melba presented herself at the Marchesi studio, and the audition commenced. At the conclusion of the song, Marchesi rose from the piano and walked from the room without a word! The rebuffs had been so frequent, the disappointments so bitter, that this last slight of all broke down Melba's fortitude, and sinking on a divan, she buried her face in her hands. But the flow of bitter tears was arrested by the voice of Marchesi calling to her husband upon another floor of the house, "Salvatore, Salvatore, come quickly, I have found a star."

Returning with her husband, Marchesi took Melba's hands in hers, saying, "Mrs. Armstrong, if you are serious and will study, I will make of you something wonderful," and Marchesi's prophecy, thanks to the natural gifts of her pupil, was fulfilled in a few months.

Melba found many ready to assist her. She possesses that charm of manner which makes it easy for men and women to give her their friendship and help, and she has repaid what she has received with unparalleled generosity. I do not want to make this chapter a catalogue of names, but I could mention a great number of aspirants to musical honours who have had the way made easy by Melba's kindness and forethought. Some years ago, when collecting data for my lectures, I approached Melba with fear and trembling, asking certain favours which seemed to verge almost on the unwarrantable, and the charming manner in which my wishes were met, and the kindness I received on that occasion and many times since, are not lightly esteemed nor easily forgotten.

A further proof of Melba's generosity is one that will be a lasting testimony to her, and a perennial benefit to the study of English vocal art. Melba is founding, in connection with the Guildhall School of Music, a "Melba Scholarship," which is to provide the winning student with a course of training for the operatic stage. What a lasting monument this will prove.

Melba's first appearance in opera was at the Théâtre Monnaie, Brussels, in "Rigoletto," on October 13, 1887, and her first appearance in opera in England was at Covent Garden, under Augustus Harris, in 1888, the opera being *Lucia di Lammermoor*. She has a repertoire of some twenty-five operas, including such widely divergent works as *Faust*, *Roméo et Juliette*, *Esmeralda*, *Mignon*, *Lakmé*, *Il Barbiere di Siviglia*, *Traviata*, *Otello*, *Manon Lescaut*, *La Bohème*, *I Pagliacci*, *Tannhäuser*, and *Lohengrin*, while, as I write, the lurid *Tosca* is being rehearsed. "Mimi" is considered by many critics to be her greatest achievement, and while others have told us that "Elsa" is her favourite rôle, I have Melba's authority for saying that she has no favourite part, as she never sings in an opera that she does not like.

I would strongly recommend my readers to take the first opportunity of hearing Melba upon the concert platform. If you would have the supreme pleasure of hearing the diva in our own tongue, coupled with an exhibition of her art that the operatic stage does not wholly demonstrate, you must hear her in Tosti's "Goodbye," with its poignant grief; in Bishop's "Lo, here the gentle lark," and "Bid me discourse" (the latter showing you the wonderful and delicious Melba trill *in excelsis*), and in similar ballads and songs. Her gramophone records of these compositions have made her art familiar with thousands of persons who have never heard Melba *viva voce*, and they have proved the finest and most valuable advance-agents a star singer ever had.

In summing up the qualities that have made Melba a Queen of Song in both hemispheres, I would put down absolute tone purity, amazing technique, and intense personality. And the last is not least. Melba would have been a great artist with her natural vocal gifts only, but she is a great-souled woman too, and the combination has proved irresistible. Among those who know her intimately, Melba, the woman, is as great as Melba, the artist.

Behind the Scenes with Melba

In my lecture on "Marvels of Sound Reproduction, or the Romance of Sound" nothing seems to delight my audiences more than a description of a recording séance, in which I am assisted by the lantern and gramophone. This peep behind the scenes seems to have a peculiar fascination for all and sundry, and it is only my limited power of graphic description that makes it less interesting and romantic than the reality.

Come with me and I will take you into the *sanctum sanctorum*, the musical holy of holies. To-day there shall be no strict rule against the presence of any unconnected with the séance, and I will endeavour to give you some moments that will live in your memory.

We step into the lift that takes us to the entrance to the "Hall of Song," but, in an antechamber, we are confronted with a Dragon in the path, who challenges our right to enter. I utter the "Open Sesame," and lo, the Dragon is transformed into a good fairy who ushers us in, and who may even be persuaded to regale us with anecdotes and experiences of the celebrities it is her duty to receive. We glance around at the walls covered with volumes of music, comprising every conceivable composition, from Comic Opera to Gregorian Mass, and from instrumental solo to the polyphonic phantasmagoria of the Strauss school, for "stars" are sometimes forgetful, and arrive without their scores, so a full library is maintained. And if we have time to spare, the good fairy of the reception room will let us peep into her autograph book, which contains the signatures of every musical celebrity one is likely to think of, and a great many that one is not. I do not know that cupidity is one of my vices, but I confess I have cast longing eyes upon this valuable volume, and perhaps it is as well that I cannot reach its restingplace in the absence of its owner!

We pass into the recording room, which comes as a surprise to some of us. It is simply a square chamber, unfurnished. One of the walls is a screen of frosted glass and pitch pine, through which projects the mouth of a narrow recording trumpet. A piano, a pipe organ, and seats for an orchestra are almost the sole contents of the room, but some chairs are brought in for our comfort. The well-known cellist, Mr. W. H. Squire, is tuning his instrument, while the recording experts are engaged in conversation with Mr. Landon Ronald, the brilliant composer and conductor who is to be the accompanist. Suddenly, a telephone bell rings, and we are told that Melba has arrived. All is electrical at once. The door of the lift swings open and in another second Melba is shaking hands and making the plain, dull room brilliant with her personality.

A few words of murmured conversation, and Melba announces that she will sing the Bach-Gounod "Ave Maria." Before the actual recording commences, a "time" trial is made. One of the experts times the rendering with his stop watch, and then the recording apparatus is put into working order. Behind the frosted screen, shadowy forms are seen at work, for here it is that the great secrets of gramophonic perfection are enshrined. None of the officials commercially engaged in the building are ever allowed to peep here, the *artistes* are rigidly excluded; none but a little band of men devoted to the recorder's art have entry to this shrine of wonder. We see the mouth of the trumpet, but what is taking place at its invisible end we can only guess.

Melba moves into position, Squire and Landon Ronald are at their instruments, a voice gently gives the signal, the accompaniment throbs out into the room, and Melba's voice rises in gentle appeal, soon to be joined by the rich tones of the cello obbligato. Suddenly the singer stops, and turning to the company, expresses her regret that she will have to begin again, as she is not quite in touch with the spirit of the work. A few minutes interval, and the song is recommenced, but after a few bars Melba turns to us, saying, "It is no use, I cannot sing it. I feel *cold*," and she tells us that the absence of an audience and the sight of only the recording horn frequently neutralizes that state of spiritual exaltation which is necessary for the accomplishment of the *artist's* best work.

Landon Ronald is told that the séance must be postponed, but, large in faith in the power of the great master passion of music, he allows his hands to stray with seeming carelessness over the keys, and out of a murmur of rising and falling tones, there steals into our senses a wild, weird melody that sets the blood coursing. Our feet ache to hurry into movement, our bodies long to break into action, for the wonder-worker at the piano is elevating us into a state of excited animation by a melody that has magic in its notes. It is with Melba as with us. Suddenly she cries "Stop, I am ready now," and standing before the trumpet, she pours into it such a burst of melody that the recording-room vanishes, and we seem to stand in some great temple wherein a soul is revealing its inmost depths to its Maker. We have lost all consciousness of Melba and of ourselves; we know nothing, hear nothing, but that one passionate supplication, and, as the voice rises and falls, and then dies away in the soft syllables of the archangel's salutation, we feel the tears rising to our eyes. We are lost in an ecstacy of melody, and it is only the conclusion of the song that brings us to earth again.

Thanks are uttered, farewells are exchanged, and Melba hurries away, leaving behind her, not the bare room we knew before, but a chamber which has heard things unspeakable, a chamber that must always be to us as the shrine of a great experience.

Some days later, the record is placed in our hands, and we hasten to try it over. And the Vision, do we see it again? That is the test. We do not speak. We close our eyes and the spirit of music works within us. The record ends—no word is spoken. But—again these tears. Do not *they* give the answer?

MME. MELBA SINGS IN CARNEGIE HALL, OCTOBER 21, 1913

RICHARD ALDRICH

A Great Audience Hears Her Concert in Carnegie Hall

Mme. Nellie Melba, after just three years' absence, made her reappearance in New York yesterday afternoon, and delighted a great audience that completely filled Carnegie Hall. In November, 1910, she sang here with the Boston Symphony Orchestra, and she also made two appearances then at the Metropolitan Opera House, in *Rigoletto* and in *La Traviata*. A third projected appearance there had to be abandoned because of her illness. Her visits to New York are so rare in these later years as to be of notable importance; for Mme. Melba is still—and her singing yesterday afternoon again attested it—one of the greatest singers of a school that seems almost inevitably destined to neglect and extinction; the school that cultivates the highest beauty of pure vocalism, of pure vocal style, of completely mastered vocal technique. It is well, therefore, that her reappearance on the New York concert stage should be recognized as an occurrence of great significance, and that it should be acclaimed by such an audience as greeted her yesterday.

The New York Symphony Orchestra assisted her, playing several numbers, and she sang to its accompaniment the "mad scene" of Ophelia from Thomas' opera of *Hamlet*, the "Ave Maria" from Verdi's *Otello*, and the

From: the *New York Times*, October 22, 1913.

"Voi che Sapete" from Mozart's *Marriage of Figaro*. She added to these the song of Mimi from the third act of *La Bohème* and then Arditi's brilliant waltz song, "Se Saran Rose." With accompaniment of piano she sang two beautiful songs by Henri Duparc, "Phidyle," "Chanson Triste," a setting of "John Anderson," and Tosti's "Good-Bye, Summer," at the end.

Mme. Melba is still in the plenitude of her voice. It has not perceptibly lost anything of its most beautiful quality. Its lusciousness, its spontaneity of utterance. In the middle range it still has that greater richness that was heard at her last visits here. It would be idle to maintain, that the dazzling brilliancy of her earlier years is wholly unimpaired. Her upper tones are not quite what they were in power and freedom; some of the lower ones seem to have gained. Nor can it be said that everything in her colorature has the flawless perfection that was hers. Certain ornamental figures yesterday were produced with some effort. On the other hand, her scales and arpeggios came limpidly and fluently from her lips, and trills upon her most advantageous tones were brilliant and even. Her legato was beautiful, her phrasing of delightful finish.

Mme. Melba did nothing finer, in some ways, than the two songs by Duparc, in which her delivery of the sustained melodies had poignant eloquence and a true nobility of style. Mme. Melba could not always have sung them so well. She touched, too, much of the profound beauty of Desdemona's "Ave Maria." There was much brilliancy and élan in her singing of Ophelia's air—and this, perhaps, she could once do better than she can now. Finally, the lovers of Mozart could rejoice to hear such a performance of the "Voi che Sapete," such purity of style and finish of phrasing. And in all Mme. Melba's singing, in whatever tongue, French, Italian, or English, it was good to hear the clearness of her diction and enunciation which then was seen to be an essential part of the finest and most artistic singing, and not an ornamental adjunct to it.

17. Nellie Melba at Coombe Cottage, Her Home at Coldstream, near Lilydale, Victoria, ca. 1915

18. Nellie Melba, London, June 1920

19. Nellie Melba, London, June 1920

20. Melba Singing into the "Wireless Phone," Chelmsford, England, July 13, 1920. It was said that she was heard in Madrid.

ABOUT MELBA AND MORE ABOUT MELBA

LANDON RONALD

Landon Ronald Russell (he used his two given names only throughout his professional life) was born in London in 1873. He made his début as a pianist in 1891, and had had some experience as a comic opera conductor before his meeting with Melba. The prestige he gained as her personal accompanist gave him his entrée into social and musical circles. By 1900 he had played for many of the great singers of the day, and was in demand at state concerts at Buckingham, Windsor, and Balmoral. He was conducting at the Lyric Theater in London in 1900 when he was engaged as "Musical Advisor" to the Gramophone and Typewriter Company (later His Master's Voice) at a time when this company was struggling with the commercialization of the first disc records. His specific assignment was to try to induce prominent artists to record for the scratchy little machine which was considered little more than a toy and not taken seriously by musicians. He was directly responsible for the first recordings of the voices of Calvé, Plançon, Scotti, Ancona, Renaud, and Santley as well as instrumentalists such as Backhaus, Elman, De Greef, de Pachmann and more. It was because of his association with the company that records were obtained of Adelina Patti, Melba, and many others, as he did much to gain recognition for the gramophone as an instrument of musical culture. In later years he was known principally as a symphonic

From: Landon Ronald, *Variations on a Personal Theme* (1922).

conductor and composer of ballet, symphonic music, and over 200 songs, many of which were used by Melba in her concerts and some of which she recorded. Ronald was especially effective in his lifelong sponsorship of Sir Edward Elgar.

The two selections presented here from his autobiography *Variations on a Personal Theme* (1922) are chapters relating to his work with Melba. They are disappointing, and rather lightweight. Other portions of the book dealing with experiences making recordings with Patti and others are highly interesting. With respect to Melba, his remarks written after her death in his second book, *Myself and Others* (London, 1931) are more revealing and are quoted later in this book. Ronald died in London in 1938.

About Melba

My friendship with this great singer dates back many, many years, and I can scarcely think of one milestone in my career without the name of Melba being in some way identified with it. As a matter of fact, my first meeting with her was actually on Covent Garden stage, when, as I have narrated elsewhere, I was a boy of nineteen, doing all the dirty (musical) work there was to do! Why she ever took the slightest notice of me, or troubled to ask my name of Arthur Collins, will ever remain a mystery to me. She has so often told the tale herself in her own inimitable manner, that I repeat it here with the greatest hesitation. I have already said how much Arthur Collins favoured me in allowing me to stand—vocal score in hand—in what is called the "prompt corner" of the stage, so that I might see and hear everything. And thus it came about that one memorable night I was in my usual place during a performance of "Faust," when in walked Madame (as she was then) Melba, about five or ten minutes before Mephistopheles shows Faust the apparition of Marguerite. She sat on a wooden bench, looked about her, saw me, glanced quickly at me, turned her head, then looked me up and down, and asked in a very direct fashion, "And who on earth are you?" I went hot and cold, red and white, tried to stammer out that I was a sort of maid-of-all-work but a humble worshipper of hers, when Arthur Collins bounced in, gave some direction to the limelight man above, and turning to Melba said in his quiet way, "This is the young fellow I spoke to you about, Madame. I want you to give him a chance." In telling the story she always declares that from that moment her every movement on the stage was followed by my "two great brown eyes." I think it most likely, because her singing was so far removed from everything I had ever heard in my life, that she completely hypnotised me. A night or two afterwards, Collins asked me if I knew Massenet's opera *Manon*. I told him I never had heard a note of it. He seemed much perturbed and disappointed. I asked him the reason. "Oh, it's just bad luck," he said. "Melba wants to be coached in it, and I have told her I would send you to the Savoy to-morrow morning at eleven instead of old X. As it is, I suppose I must send him in place of you." I had no intention of allowing such an opportunity to slip, so I begged him to get me a copy of the opera, and promised him that I would be note perfect in the morning. He slapped me on the back, saying, "That's the right spirit, young fellow. You'll do!"

At 11:30 that night off I walked with a copy of *Manon* under my arm, to the bed sitting-room I occupied in Cambridge Circus, determined to sit up all night rather than fail to justify whatever Collins had told Melba regarding my powers. I think I finished my studies about 5:30 in the morning; and then I was so excited that I couldn't sleep; I just dozed and kept on waking up with a start, convinced that I had overslept. I was very nervous when I was eventually ushered into Melba's sitting-room and found her waiting for me. She was quite amiable and nice, but lost no time in superfluous conversation. She seemed to take it for granted that I knew the opera I had come to play, but explained that she was singing it the following week, and wished to refresh her memory by going over her particular part. And go over it she did with a vengeance! She would repeat one passage or recitative a dozen times until it satisfied her. I have heard people talk about what a marvellous thing it must be to be born with a gift such as Melba has, but how little they know the work that is necessary before that gift reaches the state of perfection which makes it unique! There is no new Patti or Melba to-day; and I fear the reason is not so much that there are no great voices, as because the young people will never have the patience to practise roulades, scales, trills, month in and month out as their great predecessors did. They want to get to arias and songs before they are in any sense prepared—to run before they can walk. At the end of the practice, Melba asked me a few questions about myself, and paid me some charming compliments about my touch on the piano and the patience I had shown. I told her that my ambition was to become a great conductor and accompanist, and she took me seriously and encouraged me. Suddenly it occurred to her to ask me to play one or two of her famous arias for her. I knew them all and was at my ease by that time, and played them really well. She became enthusiastic, and went into minute details as to what she wanted here and what she wished there, seating herself at the pianoforte and actually showing me. She told her maid to bring her a big pile of songs, and made me play Tosti, Bemberg, Hahn, Gounod, Lalo, and many of the songs of that period, with the result that, as I left her, she uttered a single sentence, which probably meant little enough to her, but everything to me in the world: "Remember, that for the future you are Melba's sole accompanist."

And for something like fourteen consecutive years she kept to her word and had no one else to play for her. It was only when my work became so heavy that it was impossible for me to travel with her, that she reluctantly got someone in my place. But during those fourteen years, what fun we had, whether it was in America, or on tour in England, or in London itself! One tour in particular stands out in my memory, and that was under the aegis of the late Percy Harrison of Birmingham, the best-known concert-impressario of his time. Huge crowds, thunderous applause, lots of polite officials, policemen, and hotel servants, hundreds of autograph hunters, heaps of motoring, plenty of fun, very little time or inclination to work— these are a few impressions left after a Melba concert tour. To those who are not in the habit of travelling with Royalty, a short tour with a famous prima donna is strongly recommended as the next best thing! Perhaps I should qualify this by saying a famous prima donna with Melba's temperament. From the moment she rises till bed-time comes, always full of fun, laughing incessantly, telling one joke after another, recounting all sorts of experiences with much humour, and for ever brimming over with mirth and merriment. It is contagious; we laugh with and at her. A hard-worked man like myself must perforce forget all the worries and troubles of life and make merry too, or feel out of it. But here's the motor just arrived to take Dame Nellie to the concert hall. Of course she leaves half an hour before she need; she always does that for trains and concerts, with the result that she has never been known to be late in her life. There is a crowd waiting in the hotel hall downstairs, and a much larger one outside with three or four policemen keeping order. "Oh, ain't she beautiful?" is heard on one side. "Look at her real *diaminds!*" shouts an excited voice from the top of a lamp-post. At the stage door another large crowd to pass through, and on reaching the artists' room piles of autograph books and letters. One little girl hasn't bought sweets for a month, so as to be present to-night; another little boy confides that he has a great longing to kiss a great singer like Melba. (A wag promptly remarks that he knows plenty of "little boys" suffering from the same trouble.)

About this time Melba suddenly discovers she has no voice. This may disconcert the uninitiated until the first solo is over, but those who are "in the know" are prepared for the statement and sympathise with a twinkle in their eye. Then the interval comes and the artists' room is bombarded by people hoping to get in by some means or other. All their efforts are in vain. A London policeman couldn't be more polite but more resolute than Mr. Percy Harrison in his refusal to allow anyone to pass that sacred portal.

"But I am a friend of Madame Melba,and"—"And so am I," is the rejoinder, "and that's why I cannot let you pass."

The concert is over; crowds rush round to see the diva leave, amusing themselves until she comes by making remarks about her Rolls-Royce and her chauffeur, who never takes the slightest notice. Here she is! Shouts of "Bravo!" and "Oorah!" burst forth; a mounted policeman keeps the road clear, and off we go back to the hotel to enjoy a quiet little super, perhaps the hour that all artists enjoy the most in their lives.

Next morning it is decided to motor over to Liverpool. It is only forty miles, and she should do it easily in a couple of hours. We leave in the most brilliant weather, and everything goes well until the chauffeur discovers that something has gone wrong. I never notice it, but he does, which I, in my blissful ignorance, consider very wonderful. The "something wrong" being duly righted, off we go again, spinning merrily along at a very legal rate, when without the slightest warning a most awful explosion occurs and the motor is brought to a standstill. I feel myself all over to see if any bits of me are missing, and finding myself whole, I learn that nothing worse than the bursting of a tyre has occurred. The optimistic French chauffeur assures us that he can put a new tyre on in a *petit quart d'heure*, so Melba suggests that we should stroll on and let him overtake us. We accordingly begin to stroll, and it seems that we are strolling through lonely country lanes for the longest quarter of an hour on record. Eventualy we find that we have "strolled" about four miles, and that it has taken us nearly an hour and a half. I admired a sweet old eighteenth-century house, and got barked at by a vicious dog for doing it! Most horrible burglar-looking tramps were liberally tipped, partly out of sympathy, but mostly out of fear. But here comes the car, and without further adventure I find myself landed at the Adelphi Hotel, Liverpool. At night another concert, with similar scenes of enthusiasm, similar crowds, similar—but wait! One little episode varies the order of things somewhat. Many of my readers may remember a phenomenal little violinist, who made his début as a boy of ten, called Franz von Vecsey. This was just previous to the advent of Mischa Elman, who practically killed Franz von Vecsey's success. There is no denying the fact, however, that von Vecsey had genius, and Melba got to know the little boy well and was most enthusiastic in her admiration for him. The little chap on this occasion was among the audience, and in the interval rushed round to kiss his "liege tante Melba." More jokes, more fun, heaps of chaff. "Franz cannot play a violin; all he can do is to eat chocolates." With mock humility and a low bow, Melba handed a violin (belonging to a violinist of the party) to young Franz, and suggested that he at once disprove such a statement. The challenge is accepted, and without a moment's hesitation the little fellow leans against the pianoforte and, facing his small audience, plays an unaccompanied prelude of Bach. Immediately there fell over us all a feeling of awe and wonderment, and we listened spellbound to the remarkable phrasing, the beautiful tone, and the astounding execution of this little wizard. A few moments elapsed before we all regained our usual spirits. Melba was affected as much as, if not more than, any of us. Franz gets kissed by everybody, and I couldn't help thinking of the different effect I produced when I used to play the violin. Certain it is I never got kissed afterwards! Franz obviously liked it, and would have played another piece on the same terms, but the interval was over and we had to get back to work. With an affectionate leave-taking and a parting kiss for "Tante Melba," the little chap was taken back to his seat in the hall.

On to Edinburgh, Glasgow, Newcastle, Sheffield, Bradford, and then back to dear old London which we all love so well. One concert differed but slightly from another, the enthusiasm being identical in almost every town. Touring under such conditions is great fun, excepting for the inconvenience of having to live in one's trunk!

I have been on many tours, orchestral and otherwise, with all kinds of artists, but I have never found a more delightful travelling companion or a kinder, merrier chum. Yes, that is what Melba is on tour—just a dear good chum.

More about Melba

One of Melba's most marked characteristics is her bluntness. She says what she means and means what she says. I remember her plain speaking causing a little scene at Paddington Station which tickled my sense of humour. It was at the time she had a house at Marlow. After singing at the opera, or indeed almost under any other pretext, she would always have a special train. But on this particular Saturday afternoon she chose to travel by the ordinary train, accompanied by her maid, a foreign violinist of repute who was on a visit to this country, and to whom she wished to pay some attention (and whose name once again I forget), and myself. It was in the height of summer, and the train was packed. Just as we were about to depart (having found seats in a carriage where soon afterwards at least five people were standing), a regular English dude, with an eyeglass in his eye and a drawl, sauntered up to our carriage and addressing Madame Melba, who was nearest the window, said in a very affected voice, "Is there any room he-ear?" "Can't you see?" was the prompt reply, "we are more than full up, unless you wish to sit on the floor." The young man stared at her for a second and drawled, "Oh, no! I should prefer to sit on your lap," and moved away. A minute's awful silence reigned, but immediately the train was well on the move, our gallant foreign fiddler friend got up from his seat in great excitement, and shouted at the top of his voice out of the window, "You plackguard! You scountrel! If you kom here, I gif you one ponch in ze nose." The wrath of this chivalrous defender of the fair sex only subsided when the train was well away from the young man, left behind on the platform, roaring with laughter, and shouting, "Come on, froggy, I'll knock you out in the first round."

A few days afterwards I received an invitation to spend Sunday at Marlow, as Joachim was staying with the prima donna. I must admit they made a funny couple together. The heavy, ponderous, learned Hungarian fiddler, used to being listened to with awe and bated breath; and the vivacious, chaffing, light-hearted prima donna, throwing all seriousness to the wind, and heartily disliking hero-worship in her own home. They were in very truth the two extremes meeting, and yet Joachim's fascination and admiration for Melba were very real and very sincere. As far as I remember there was only one other person present, Mr. Arthur Davis, a Stock Exchange magnate, a well-known "first nighter" and patron of concerts and opera. After dinner some informal music began. Joachim played with me several of the Brahms-Joachim Hungarian dances, and played them wonderfully. Then Melba sang a Mozart aria with violin obbligato, and eventually Joachim and I played the Kreutzer Sonata of Beethoven. Just as we were about to begin the last movement, I discovered to my dismay that we had missed the last train back to town. Davis and I had to get back, so what was to be done? There was only one way—a special train! The local station-master placed every possible obstacle in the way, but eventually, on being persuaded that the matter was of vital importance to the State, the special train was duly obtained. It was composed of one saloon carriage and an engine, and when Davis was called upon to pay for it I remember him remarking that it was the greatest and cheapest concert he had ever been to in his life.

For several years I conducted Sunday concerts at the Winter Gardens, Blackpool, in the summer, and Melba on many occasions came and opened the season for us by appearing at the first concert. It was on one of these annual visits that an incident occurred quite worth relating. The great diva had sung innumerable encores, and could not make up her mind what to choose for another. Just as she was going on to bow her acknowledgments once again, she said to me, "Come and play 'A Little Winding Road' for me"—that being a song of mine which she sang a good deal at that time. Oddly enough, it was originally written for a contralto—Clara Butt, to be precise; but owing to certain difficulties with publishers which it is unnecessary to go into here, it was never sung by her. It is a song (one of a cycle called "Four Songs of the Hill") which has been a great selling success, and the artist who first sang the complete cycle was that exquisite singer (who has now retired) Miss Muriel Foster. As it was very much in vogue at the time, I happened to have been playing it in the contralto key a great deal. It was fairly natural, therefore, that on the sudden demand of Melba to play it for her, I should strike up the original key—two or three tones lower than the soprano key. The diva had not sung a bar before she also realised it, and in the most natural manner imaginable, stopped and said in her very carrying speaking voice, "Landon, you are playing it in the wrong key." I laughed, played a few chords of transposition, and began again. She caught my eye and we both burst out laughing, with the result that the whole audience took it up, and that it was *the* success of the evening.

A year or two after I became principal of the Guildhall School of Music, I was most anxious to get so great a singer and so dear a friend to come and give the students the benefit of her advice and great experience. After very much persuasion, I got her to promise to read them a paper "On Singing," written by herself. It is very curious that at that time she could neither read nor speak well to a public. During and since the war I have heard her make admirable little speeches without fear or hesitation, but at the particular period to which I am referring, her nerves, as a rule, completely prevented her doing herself justice. Realising all this, she asked permission to come to the school a day or two previously and rehearse her essay on singing in the theatre where she would have to read it. This impressed me very much, because it showed how serious she was about everything she undertook. I duly sat in front with one other friend of hers, and she went on the stage and began reading. Continually she stopped and assured me she could never do it, and continually I assured her that she was doing splendidly. She went away very "fussed" and unhappy, but promised that she would not disappoint me by keeping away altogether, as I rather feared. We had made great preparations to give her a royal reception. The chairman and committee, all dressed in their mazarine gowns, were there to receive her; hundreds of girls had donned their white dresses with red sashes; and an address of welcome and a small souvenir of the occasion was to be presented to her by the chairman. Her entry into the theatre was the sign for an enormous outburst of cheering, such as even Melba could have seldom experienced. The chairman having duly performed his part, it was my turn to say a few words about the great artist whom we were entertaining. This done, she got up with the manuscript in hand to reply. But the cheering and applause were deafening, and at least two minutes must have elapsed before she was allowed to begin. She was cruelly nervous, and this overwhelming reception unnerved her the more. I was sitting next her on the platform, and felt, after her few opening phrases, that she would never get through. I was but too right! Another heroic attempt to master her nerves failed, and, with a pathetic smile and a gesture of regret, she turned to the audience and said, "I'm awfully sorry, but I cannot go on." The students did not know whether to applaud or keep silent. But I at once got on my feet, took the manuscript from Melba's hands, and announced that I had arranged with her to read it on her behalf. It was a difficult thing for me to do, because I had never read it and had only heard part of it at the private rehearsal to which I have alluded. I believe I got through all right, but it was a job I should not care to have to repeat. It is the only time during the many long years of our friendship that I have known Melba break down before a public, and I believe it was a unique experience on her part.

The great singer has not had many "narrow escapes" during her travels, but one that occurred at Chicago when I was with her is worth relating. She was announced to give a concert, and the newspapers, in true American fashion, had written columns about "the great musical treat in store," but dwelling more on the fact that "the great singer has with her all her most priceless jewels, and will wear them the night of the concert." Melba had been in the habit of occupying the same suite of rooms in the Auditorium Hotel (they were called "the Melba Suite"), and it caused her great annoyance when she was informed that on this particular occasion they were already occupied by a lady and her husband. As after-events proved, this was fortunate for the prima donna. On the day of the concert two well-dressed men entered the hotel, walked upstairs to the "Melba Suite," and ringing the bell, were admitted by the lady in question. Promptly closing the door behind them, one of the ruffians, producing a pistol, said, "If you scream, I'll shoot! Show me where you keep your jewels." The poor lady had the presence of mind to answer, "My husband's inside, and if you don't leave, I'll call him." This happened to be untrue, but in any case it made no impression on the men, as they believed they were speaking to Melba, whom they knew was not married. Accordingly they proceeded with their work, one keeping the pistol pointed at his victim's head, whilst the other ransacked the rooms. Finding nothing of any particular value and afraid to prolong their stay, they cleared out a wardrobe, taking several coats and trousers, and escaped. The unfortunate lady completely collapsed. When the story leaked out, Melba was most sympathetic and kind, and did everything she could to help. Since that fortunate escape she has ceased to travel with many jewels, at any rate any of great value.

NELLIE MELBA

WILLIAM ARMSTRONG

William Armstrong was an American music critic, born in Frederick County, Maryland. He studied in Stuttgart and Vienna, and from 1893 to 1898 he was music critic for the Chicago *Tribune*. He was closely associated with Lillian Nordica and prepared her *Hints to Singers* for publication after her death. The selection presented here is the chapter on Nellie Melba from his *The Romantic World of Music* (New York, 1922), which has similar chapters on Patti, Nordica, Garden, Paderewski, Caruso, Galli-Curci, and others. The "romance" theme is unfortunate—perhaps something foisted on him by his publisher—and Mr. Armstrong is not known for his accuracy (for example, Nordica was shipwrecked when her ship struck Bramble Cay near Thursday Island *after* she had left Australia), but his contribution is thought worthy of preservation here.

Madame Melba's romance as the most acclaimed singer of the British Empire was long and glorious. In return she has given a splendid loyalty; her American tour during the World War, when she devoted every penny she received to her country's cause, was one proof of this. I have seen her in creations from the Rue de la Paix, her corsage encrusted with diamonds, but she appeared to me handsomer in those days of self-sacrifice, wearing her old gowns on the stage that she might have the price of new ones to add to her soldiers' fund.

From: William Armstrong, *The Romantic World of Music*. Copyright 1922 by E. P. Dutton & Co., New York.

The war itself meant to Madame Melba a very near and harrowing thing. Early in it she wrote to me from Australia, saying: "I have lost so many dear ones and so many friends in this cruel war—the world can never be the same again to me." Of her circle this was sadly true, for in England, as in all countries, the flower of the aristocracy had been the first to enlist and to fall.

During recent years much of the singer's time has been spent in Australia, where she has practically and nobly encouraged music. In her zenith Madame Melba's London home was a palace in Great Cumberland Place near the Marble Arch. Her admirers ranged from King Edward and Queen Alexandra to the crowds in waiting outside the gallery entrance at Covent Garden on nights when she sang there.

With vast means, for her earnings were doubled through skillful investments by the Rothschilds, she set out to plan a home. During her days of study in Paris with Madame Marchesi, the great Palace of Versailles had struck Melba's fancy. Buying the Great Cumberland Place house, she had its interior remodelled along Versailles lines. A small army of workmen, brought over from France, required two years to complete its wall decorations done in Cupids, garlands, and panels to hold paintings.

Furniture in keeping she selected personally, piece by piece: gilded chairs and sofas of the Louis periods; Aubosson carpets, pale blue and white, garlanded with faint pink roses; crystal chandeliers hung with pear-shaped pendants. The task in its elaborateness took her spare time for long.

Quarry Wood Cottage on the Thames near Maidenhead was then her summer home. It was a simple, charming place, overrun with cascades of *gloire de Dijon* roses. In the London social season, lasting from May until late July, she sang at Covent Garden, travelling up to town and back again after the performance.

Chauncey Depew came one day to Quarry Wood. Delighted with its roses, its clustering shade trees, its close-clipped lawn running to the river, he expressed a wish to stay.

"Then do," said Madame Melba.

"But I brought nothing with me," he retorted.

"Never mind that, we'll go shopping," suggested the diva. And they did, over at Maidenhead, the Senator returning with a night-shirt and tooth-brush as baggage.

There was always something very straightforward, very frank, very big-hearted about Madame Melba. Her Australian birth and rearing had left its unconventional impress. What she had to say she said directly and to the point. Her astounding frankness at our first meeting was, indeed, almost startling. "What family of Armstrongs do you belong to?" she asked bluntly. "My husband was an Armstrong and I abominated him."

Her motto was "Live and let live." She sustained it. Madame Melba had a broad way of overlooking irritating happenings even when they affected her stage success. Vignas, a Spanish tenor of the Grau régime, sang

Tannhäuser to her Elisabeth the first and only time, I think, that she essayed the part. At that juncture the great success of Madame Nordica and Jean de Reszke in Wagner had set the other prima donnas aflame to sing his music. Even Madame Calvé announced that she would sing Isolde, later, though she could never get the time right in certain ensembles of Berlioz's *Faust*.

In the circumstances Madame Melba had fixed high hopes on her Elisabeth. Vignas with the influenza risked singing Tannhäuser and wrecked the performance. Only as far as Wolfram's "Evening Star" did it get, and then the curtain had to be rung down. Mr. Grau made a little speech, saying that Madame Melba to extend the program would sing Lucia's Mad Scene. Which she did, in the costume of Elisabeth, crown and all. Every other artist in the cast looked on Vignas' foolhardy risk and consequent defection as a personal affront. Madame Melba, the most seriously affected of any, alone came vigorously to his defence.

Madame Melba did not always attain to the angelic. Then she was amusing. Massenet's *Werther* had its American première at Chicago. Madame Eames was the Charlotte. Neither Melba nor Calvé just then loved her. Wonderfully gowned the pair sat in a lower box. Before them on its upholstered rail rested a score of *Werther*, upside down. But that the public did not know. Neither did Eames.

Every little while, first Calvé then Melba would shoot out a disapproving forefinger at some spot on the score and raise her eyebrows. Being much observed, a vastly interested public began to watch for mistakes too. That Madame Eames knew what was going on, no doubt remained. Her increasing stiffness and angularity proclaimed it. But not being on speaking terms with the two ladies, she could not tell them later what she thought.

No prima donna escapes her evil quarters of an hour. A most trying episode came to Madame Melba, herself, in that same Chicago where she was accustomed to wild enthusiasm. The committee of a sectarian hospital had engaged her to give a benefit concert for their institution. The program was of operatic selections. Many tickets had been sold to people of the congregation, who had, perhaps, never heard an opera. And thriftily they used their tickets to get their money's worth.

The solemn frigidity of that audience could scarcely have been greater; rigid and unbending it sat in silence. Not until the Mad Scene came was it prodded into enthusiasm. Seizing the moment, I went behind the scenes to ask after Madame Melba's health.

Coincident with my arrival there was rolled into her dressing room a big, upright clothes basket, of the kind that holds bushels. From its top spouted a quantity of American Beauty Roses. "What is that damned thing?" called Madame Melba, just as the leading nose of the Hospital Committee, which had contributed this floral offering, appeared in the doorway.

To prima donna subtleties Madame Melba was a stranger. When she said a thing, nothing was left to her hearer's imagination. Shortly after Madame

Nordica's death, I went to London to say good-bye to Melba, who was sailing for Australia. Her first words were regarding the great American's sad end.

Shipwreck in the Gulf of Papua on her way to Australia had put Nordica in no condition to sing, especially before strange audiences. Her reception on arriving in that country had been icy. This Melba resented, feeling that Nordica's great art alone deserved their hearty recognition. "They murdered her in Australia," cried Melba passionately, her eyes full of tears, "and I shall tell them so when I get back!" Doubtless she did.

At one time there had been estrangement between the prima donnas. But that was completely blotted from Melba's mind; her one thought was of her dead colleague's greatness. Madame Melba was splendidly fearless. She hesitated as little to tell a nation as she did an individual what she felt to be the truth.

None could travel about the globe as did this diva without meeting exciting adventures on the way. By chance, I experienced one of these with her. It came at the California Theatre at San Francisco, and during her first concert tour of the Pacific coast. There were ill omens that night as prelude to the final climax. During an act from *Rigoletto*, pipes burst under the stage, sending up a cloud of steam that made the place look like a scene from *Walküre*. The curtain was rung down immediately and repairs started.

Finally, when all was supposed rectified, up the curtain went again on the exact spot that *Rigoletto* had left off. The program was long, and so they were economical. Being like all plumbers, the men had left something undone. So great hammering under the stage mingled with the singing on it. Madame Melba came off furious and nervous, vowing she would go home. The house was packed. After great persuasion she decided to remain; going to her dressing-room, she changed Gilda's costume for that of Lucia, whose Mad Scene was to follow.

Presently, when Melba took her place behind the scenes, increasing nervousness set in. Twice she exclaimed, "I am going to faint!" Leaving me alone with her, Miss Bennet, her companion, went for a glass of water. While she was gone a great outcry started in the audience. People began climbing over the footlights, pushing aside the curtain, which was down, and running across the stage on that side next an exit. By flashes, the swinging curtain disclosed a glare of fire in the auditorium. Madame Melba, in her Lucia costume, her hair about her shoulders, and nearly fainting, gave in that moment a pretty fine example of British pluck. Not knowing the real cause of trouble, she started staggering through the wings; she knew that something had happened in the audience, and her one idea was to go out and quiet it.

By that time Miss Bennet had returned. Each with an arm about the diva we were leading her back, when Charles Ellis, her manager, and Rigo, the stage director, grabbed her from us and made toward the stage entrance.

Someone rolled up the curtain. With that a mob came struggling across the footlights onto the stage: Orchestra players, their instruments hugged in their arms; ladies in torn evening gowns; men, helping and helped.

From the orchestra pit rose a frantic cry, "My hat and my harp! My hat and my harp!" It came from a woman harpist in whose mind these treasures remained uppermost. The aide-de-camp of Prince Albert, now King of Belgium, and who had remained behind the scenes during the concert, gallantly rushed to her rescue, dragging lady, harp, and hat over the footlights. Next morning an enterprising newspaper carried in its columns a sketch of the incident. It showed two heroic workmen saving a lady in distress.

Subjects for more authentic sketches were not lacking. The tenor, Salignac, later of the Paris Opéra Comique, and dressed as Faust for the Garden Scene, was sent home in a cab; Leon Rains, subsequently long at the Berlin Royal Opera, started off afoot to his hotel wearing over his Mephisto costume a mackintosh reaching only to his knees.

Another proof that I recall of Madame Melba's courage came at the Chicago Auditorium on the night when a madman sprang upon the stage. The curtain had just risen on the Balcony Scene in *Romeo and Juliet*. Melba was the Juliet; Jean de Reszke was singing Romeo. Running swiftly down a side aisle, and reaching the stage by way of a little stairway leading from the great organ, the lunatic was behind the footlights almost before any saw him. In a few minutes, though it seemed much longer, the poor wretch had been dragged off.

Meanwhile, neither Melba nor de Reszke budged from their pose, although, quite near them, four husky stage-hands were struggling to overpower and drag away the lunatic. When the orchestra began again, Madame Melba's tones, at first a trifle tremulous, gave no further sign of nervous strain; Jean de Reszke's voice had not a fraction of unsteadiness. How many singers are there whose training would bring such perfect breath control?

Loyal to those she really loved, just as she was loyal to her country, Madame Melba's allegiance to her great teacher, Madame Marchesi, never swerved. And Marchesi prized it. "Of the many I have taught," she once said to me, "those who have been grateful I could count on the fingers of one hand." She alluded, I know, to the greater ones.

Presently, she told me of Eames who had studied with her, and later, over her own signature, written against her; she told of Calvé who had made her début and later her successes as a Marchesi pupil, and then gone to another teacher.

Calvé's unsought excuse for this came in a note to Marchesi, saying that her countrymen would feel more kindly toward her if she sang to them as a pupil of one born in France. This honor not falling to Madame Marchesi, who hailed from Frankfort, precluded her in Calvé's narrow vision from a credit in which musical history will be more generous.

Madame Melba, when she came to Paris in her golden days, often made her home at Madame Marchesi's in the Rue Jouffroy. If she did not stop there, her first pilgrimage on arriving in the city was to her teacher. The diva's radiant career made a vital link with the life Marchesi loved and which she, as one of the great women of the nineteenth century, had lived actively so long. And to the end, Melba made her feel how important a part she had played in her success.

In Marchesi's zenith, managers flocked to the musical evenings at her studio and in search of rising "stars." Emma Nevada and Sybil Sanderson had been pupils there; the trio, Melba, Calvé, Eames, made their successful débuts later. Long prior to that, and before leaving Vienna for the French capital, Marchesi had taught Ilma di Murska and Etelka Gerster. Only a tithe of the singing celebrities that Marchesi trained, however, were known to us in America, for they came to her from Russia, South America, England and Australia, as well as from the United States.

Gounod, Rubinstein, Massenet, the great statesmen of France, and people of the Paris world of society and letters helped make Marchesi's *soirées* there memorable. In them young girls, presently renowned, sang as pupils. When the dusk fell in her long and brilliant life, people melted away from the house in the Rue Jouffroy. "Even my colleagues never darken my doorway," she once said to me passionately. "I am not French, so I am not of them."

Through it all, Melba remained touchingly, splendidly loyal. Always she was sending pupils to Marchesi, always she was trying to find engagements for any who proved promising. Her great influence, especially at the Covent Garden Opera, made itself practically felt. It is at once a great joy and simple justice to chronicle this sympathetic, enduring association between Melba and Marchesi. That association, in itself, is sufficient reason for including memories of the one with memories of the other. In musical biography, written so often without an intimate, personal knowledge, the finer things in a great musician's life are not recorded, leaving as a result merely a formal story of brilliant successes.

Madame Melba, it was, who sent me with a letter of introduction to Madame Marchesi, for which I am strongly grateful. In turn, Marchesi gave me a letter to Leschetizky, who received me charmingly at his home in Vienna. "What kind of a man is Leschetizky?" Marchesi asked me when I called to thank her on returning. My look of surprise at this, coming from the person who had introduced me, must have been transparent, for she added with that slow, droll smile of hers. "I have never met him. But that is unnecessary. We artists understand one another." . . .

That was the period, too, when her friends as well had faded from her, one by one, but never the faithful Melba. . . .

A woman who had lived in Paris at the same *pension* with Melba in her student days at Marchesi's studio, told me of the future diva's earliest triumph. She had been asked to sing at a great house and in a musicale to which the grand world of Paris had been invited. "I was reading very late," the story ran, "and a light still shone above my door. A timid knock came. And there stood Nellie Melba in a simple white frock and tears. 'I had to tell someone,' she explained. And then related how people had that night gone mad over her singing, and an old French general had rushed up to embrace and kiss her, crying, 'You are already one of the great ones of the world!' "

While she was studying Mimi in Puccini's *La Bohème*, I happened in her New York sitting-room one day. Melba was all enthusiasm. Going to the piano she went through Mimi's music from the score, playing her own accompaniment, for in her girlhood she had studied the piano. Special portions of the rôle which appealed most strongly, she would repeat, and afterward exclaim upon their beauty. In later years, she very often sang the part, one without a single flourish of vocal display, and in preference to any other.

But how she shone in florid Italian music! The absolute assurance; the audacity; the perfection of her trill; the pearl-like evenness of her scales, not only in tone quality, but in tone duration; her exquisite *pianissimo* on open tones in alt; her dazzling delivery of bravura passages flung out with a spontaneous certainty that was fabulous. Preeminent in her field, Madame Melba reigned, as did Madame Patti, in a kingdom all her own.

MELBA, THE AUSTRALIAN NIGHTINGALE

MABEL WAGNALLS

Mrs. Mabel Wagnalls was born in Kansas City, Missouri. She studied music in Paris and piano with Franz Kullak in Berlin. Her debut as a pianist was at the Singakademie, Berlin, in 1889. She appeared in America as soloist under Theodore Thomas in 1891 and Anton Seidl in 1892, and specialized in lecture-recitals for a number of years. She was the musical editor for the Funk & Wagnalls Standard Dictionary, and the author of a number of novels and other books dealing with musical subjects, as well as a contributor to *The Etude* and various musical journals.

A memorable performance of *Aïda* was given in London, at Covent Garden, a number of years ago. The Ethiopian slave-girl, dark-tinted and slight of figure, attracted no particular attention with her first unimportant recitative notes. The audience was diverted by the fine tenor singing, the excellent contralto, and the well-drilled work of the chorus. There followed more of this ensemble, more good orchestral playing, and then an effect of melody, or rhythm, or something—that gradually caused every pulse to quicken, and stirred every soul in a strange, unaccountable way, until suddenly we realized that it was not the rhythm, or the harmony, or the tenor, or the orchestra, but *one soprano voice*, whose tones seemed to penetrate

From: Mabel Wagnalls, *Opera and Its Stars* (1924).

all space and soar to all heights and thrill all hearts in a manner that was overpowering!

The slave-girl was singing! A new star from the Southern Hemisphere was just beginning to appear in the North! A "*new name*" had been added, and was soon to be heard by "all who had an ear to hear"—Melba, the Australian Nightingale.

All critics agree that the quality of her voice has never, in the annals of music, been surpassed.

In furnishing Melba her name, which is a diminutive of Melbourne, the far continent has sprung into a musical prominence it never before attained. From a land at the outer edge of the world, a sovereign of song has arisen.

It would, of course, be artistic and effective to picture Melba's early life as one of struggle and privation. But, search as one will, not a crust or a tatter turns up in her history; She never shivered on a doorstep, or sang for pennies in the street! Let the dismal truth be told—her father was wealthy, and his gifted daughter never lacked for anything.

Nellie Mitchell, as she was known in those days, was gifted not only with a voice, but with a splendid determination to work. She practised diligently all the time in the line of her ambition, and learned to play admirably on the piano, violin, and pipe-organ. All this in spite of the diversions and entice-ments of young companions and monied pastimes. Wealth, as well as poverty, may serve to hinder progress, and it is much to Melba's credit that she had the perseverance to work unceasingly.

Even at school, during recess hours, she was always humming and trill-ing. This latter trick was a source of puzzling delight to her comrades, who never tired of hearing "that funny noise she made in her throat." The marvelous Melba trill, you see, was a gift of the gracious Fates at her birth—just back of the silver spoon in her mouth was tucked a golden trill.

The story of her childhood is best told in her own words:

"My mother was an accomplished amateur musician, and it was her play-ing that first gave me an idea of the charms of music. I was forever hum-ming everything I heard, and she was always telling me to stop, for my noise was unceasing! My favorite song was 'Coming Thro' the Rye.' I also liked 'Nellie Bly,' because my own name was Nellie!'

Incidentally, it was learned that dolls were tabued by this prima donna in pinafores.

"I hated dolls. My favorite toys were horses—wooden horses. One given to me by my father's secretary was almost an idol to me for years."

Recurring to the subject of music, Mme. Melba continued:

"I didn't *sing* much when a child; I only *hummed*. And by the way, a child's voice should be carefully guarded. I consider the ensemble singing in schools as ruinous to good voices. Each one tries to outdo the other, and the tender vocal cords are strained and tired. I, personally, did not seriously study singing until after my marriage at seventeen [*sic*] years of age."

The preparation required for Mme. Melba's career was neither very long nor arduous. She studied nine months with Marchesi, then was ready to make her début in Brussels as a star [*sic*].

All things came easy to her, because her voice never had to be *placed*; her tones were jewels already set.

"The first opera I ever heard was 'Rigoletto.' That was in Paris, when I was studying. What did I think of it? Well, I dare say my inexperience made me very bumptious, but I remember thinking I could do it better myself! In Australia I had no chance to hear operas. 'Lucia' I have never yet heard, tho that is perhaps the rôle most associated with my name."

"Lucia" has, indeed, become a Melba possession. The mad-scene alone, on a program with her name, would invariably crowd the house. It is a veritable frolic to hear her in this aria. She is pace-maker, as it were, to the flute, which repeats every phrase that she sings. It is the prettiest race ever run, and when at the finish the time-keeper brings down his baton, the audience cheers itself hoarse for the winner.

When asked her opinion of the new gramophones and the wonderful records of her voice, Madame Melba spoke with enthusiasm.

"They are, indeed, a remarkable achievement. I am looking, however, for still greater improvements, and am keenly interested in every new development." . . .

Some further random questions about the experiences of a prima donna elicited the following item. Mme. Melba smiled as she told it:

"Yes, I have some queer things said to me. Just recently a young girl of eighteen, who wished me to hear her sing, assured me that there were only two fine voices in the world to-day—hers and mine!

"But I must tell you," she added brightly, "the most graceful compliment ever paid me. It was by an Irish woman, who, in commenting on the lack of song in the native birds of Australia, pointed out that they had treasured up all their melody through the ages and then had given it to me."

Some one has said, "The ease of Melba's singing is positively audacious!" She certainly makes light of the most time-honored difficulties. She will start a high note without any preparation, with apparently no breath and no change of the lips. Faint at first as the "fabric of a dream," it is followed by the gradual grandeur of a glorious tone, straight and true as a beam of light, until finally it attains the full zenith of a crescendo.

In a bewildering variety of ways writers have attempted to describe the wonder of her voice.

"It seems to develop in the listener a new sense; he feels that each tone *always has been* and *always will be*. She literally lays them out on the air."

"Her *tone-production* is as much a gift as the voice itself."

After all, "she is Melba, the incomparable, whose beauty of voice is only equaled by the perfection of her art."

"In future years the present time will be referred to, musically, as 'in the days of Melba.' "

Like all great prima donnas, Madame Melba has a beautiful home of her own, and a country place to which she hies in the summer. Her town house is near Hyde Park, London.

Once we imagined these song-birds, during the hot months, resting luxuriantly in their various retreats—Melba in her river residence, Calvé in her French château, Jean de Reszke on his Polish estate, Eames in her Italian castle, and Patti at "Craig y Nos." But it is hardly an accurate picture, for *rest* to the artist still means *work*. They study all summer, every one of them, and entertain other artists, who work with them, or, at any rate, contribute to the perpetual whirl of music in which they live.

A very good idea of the home life of these songqueens was given to me by a young lady who sojourned with one of them for several months.

"Do you know," she said, "it was positively depressing to be near so much talent and genius. Why, in the drawing-room they would be talking seven or eight languages; and some one would improvise at the piano, while another would take a violin and join in with the most wonderful cadenzas, and then, perhaps, the piano-player would step aside and some one else would slide into his place and continue the improvisation the first one had begun; and so on all the time, until really I began to feel just about as small and worthless as a little pinch of dust."

THE MERRY PIPES OF PAN

JOHN LEMMONÉ

We have met John Lemmoné before. In addition to his long association with Melba as accompanying artist and manager, he had a distinguished musical career in his own right. He made solo recordings for Victor, and his work may be heard as flautist on several of Melba's recordings.

When Pan went fluting through the forests when the world was young, everyone followed him. Pan's popularity was never in doubt. The Pied Piper of Hamelin was another example of extraordinary success in my line, but I envy neither of them. If people have never followed the strains of my pipe, at least it has enabled me to wander the world and meet people who made or are still making history.

I am no writer. The invitation to write for *The Herald* some of my impressions frightened me. I could have played it on the flute, but with the pen—that is different. I can try no tricks, but only am able to tell in simple language some of the things which may interest my own countrymen.

For my own countrymen you are. I have lived so long abroad that many people take me for a foreigner. Ballarat was my birthplace, and my dear old mother is still living in Melbourne.

When I look back over my life there are three high-lights which leap into prominence and dwarf all my other experiences to an ordinary level. To

From: John Lemmoné, "The Merry Pipes of Pan," *The Herald* (Melbourne), June 7, 1924. Reprinted by permission of The Herald and Weekly Times Ltd.

keep a strict chronology, the first of these is the way in which my first flute came to me. It was a wonderful thing in my life, and infinitely more valuable to me than if it had come easily.

I loved music, but my parents feared the moral effect of a profession that in their estimation was beset with snares. When I was six years old, however, my father brought home a tin whistle, and promised that whichever of his three boys could first play on it, to him would be given a fife. I quickly mastered the thing, and to me in due course came the fife. It only whetted my desire for something better. I coveted with all the intense desire that is in a boy's nature a certain flute that lay in a shop window on the way to my school. It was marked 12/6. Who would ever give me 12/6? It was as unattainable as £100. Certainly not in my home could such a sum be forthcoming for such a thing as a flute.

Just across the creek bridge lay another shop, of no significance to me then. It was kept by one Wittkowsky, a gold buyer. One day, after I had gazed with longing into the shop window where my flute lay, I walked across the bridge. One of the sudden floods for which Ballarat was noted had swollen the river, and the water washed above the bridge, so that it was necessary to take off shoes and stockings to cross. I noticed some men with tin dishes, puddling dirt out of the alluvial wash brought down by the flood waters.

I asked what they were doing, and was allowed to look. To my astonishment I saw at the bottom of the dishes a thin stream of gold. It looked easy. Like a flash I was off home, and "borrowed" my mother's pudding dish and a match-box. I took a dishful of the yellow mud, and went off to some clearer water lower down. Then I got another dishful. Both showed little yellow grains of gold which I put in my match-box.

"How much will I have to get to make 12/6?" I asked the old miner next to me. He looked at my haul, and told me I had already got the amount. Off I ran to Wittkowsky, who gave me 16/6. Hardly able to believe my good luck, I rushed off to the other shop. Yes, the wonderful flute was still in the window. A second or two afterwards it was mine.

The sequel is interesting, for, years afterwards, I was playing in Ballarat with Melba. The hall in which we were was built on the exact spot where the old-time bridge had stood, and below us we could hear the creek merrily running. As we stood on the stage, she, the most famous singer of the world, and I—well, I who was deemed worthy to play with her, I said: "Here is the place where I found my first flute."

The second high-light in my life was when I stood on the stage at the Town Hall at a big concert—my first. There was a young girl on the same programme, and I played for her. Well I remember the song, well do I remember the girl. We have been together many a year since then. It was her debut, as it was mine. Her name was Nellie Mitchell. Now it is Melba.

The years rolled on, as years have a way of doing. Melba had gone away, and fame had come to her. For myself, I had succeeded, and had toured the

East with Madame Patey, the great contralto. Many will remember her. She was one of the greatest quartette I ever heard—Sims Reeves, Santley, Patti and Patey. What a wonderful combination! I played with Madame Amy Sherwin, with Mrs. Palmer, then at her best and the idol of Melbourne— with many more. But my eyes were on London.

At last I went to England. Melba was staying at the Savoy. What a dramatic change was here. When she left there was not much encouragement given to her, but her voice and her mind had won for her a unique place, and she was installed, a great lady, in a private suite at London's finest hotel. With what trembling I sent in my name to her. Would she have forgotten? Who was I that she should remember? I came into the room. She sprang up.

"How is Mrs. Palmer?" How is this one? How is that one? Till my head buzzed she kept firing questions at me. Her tongue never stopped. Then, as now, Australia was more to Melba than the rest of the world put together. When at last her desire was satisfied, and she had learnt all of Australian history I could tell her, she came to my affairs. "Let me hear you play," she demanded. I played.

"Oh, I must make them hear you," she cried warmly. Daniel Mayer was then the great man whose voice was all powerful in music. To him she sent me with a letter of introduction. The great Mayer had a headache. He had promised Melba, but I must just play a little, short piece. He was too ill for more. I played a long piece, the most showy I had. When I finished he was on his feet, and sending messages to half a dozen people—to Mancinelli of Covent Garden among others. They came on the run, for Daniel Mayer only had to whisper to be obeyed. I was launched, but it was Melba who put me on the slips.

Five tours with Patti were to follow, varied by playing with Melba at the big fashionable soirées, where the fee for her music was £500 a night. It was a wonderful life I began to lead, and books could be written about the people I met in that brilliant London society—musicians, writers, artists. But I must pass on to my association with Paderewski, whom I brought to Australia. Previously I had brought Mark Hambourg as a young man of 18, but the visit of Paderewski was epochal. Everyone remembers the splendid success of this remarkable man, who was as great an orator as he was a musician. No wonder he became Poland's choice. His was a magnetic personality. He could make people do as he chose.

Let me tell you the story of a village whose cheek gained it prominence. When Paderewski was coming to Melbourne, a gentleman in Wangaratta wrote to me, suggesting that if the pianist came to Wangaratta, the town would be thrilled. Could it not be managed? In a spirit of fun and amusement at its cool cheek, I showed the letter to Paderewski. To my surprise he was touched at the request.

"To think that a small community like that should be so interested," he said. "I should like to go if it can be arranged. I leave it to you." I replied to the letter, asking for substantial guarantee, and explaining that it was only because Paderewski was sentimental that the visit could be arranged. Alas! The guarantee could not be arranged. Nevertheless, Paderewski, rather than disappoint those who wished to hear him, bade me to arrange the special trip. It was made the occasion for a huge picnic. From all outlying places people came. They took the horses out of the pianist's carriage, and dragged him to the hall. It was a wonderful concert. Later, when he left from Auckland, Paderewski was asked what town had made the greatest impression on him. The reporter waited for the name of "Auckland." Instead "Wangaratta" was the reply, and on being pressed for a reason, the pianist replied, "It was the only town where I was not told to go and get my hair cut."

The third high-light to which I have referred is the day when I became associated with Melba by a professional and personal link, which has never been broken. Year after year I can look back on a friendship which has never been spoiled by a word that either can regret. I have been her business adviser for many years; her private business is my care, just as her musical arrangements. Under her personal command, I arranged every detail of her last opera season here in 1911, searching the world for the artists. One story I must tell in conclusion, which will give a convincing picture of the friendship which first made my life, and then kept it happy.

In 1919, Melba was about to sail for America, after a most successful season in Australia. I was ill, seriously ill, in a Sydney hospital. At her last concert in Sydney, when a bumper house was at its most enthusiastic moment, Melba stepped to the front of the platform, and, in her confidential way, she said:

"My dear old John is sick. I'd love to give him a proof of how we love him. How if we give him a special concert? I'd love to, but I can't without you. We can just do it, for my boat does not sail for five days." The day after the concert, about which I knew nothing, Melba came to visit me in the hospital. She presented me with a big silver loving cup, filled with plums. On it was a slip of paper, which read, "Put in your thumb and pull out a plum and see what your friends have sent you." I put in my thumb as directed, and found an envelope. In it was a cheque for £2113/18/. Something like a plum! She laughed at my consternation.

My pen, once started, runs on. But I have exceeded my limit. The Piper must make his bow.

PRIME DONNE

HENRY RUSSELL

Henry Russell, brother of Landon Ronald (Russell), was born in
London in 1871. Originally destined for a career in medicine, he
switched to music, which he studied at the Royal College of Music
in London. He combined his knowledge of physiology and anatomy
with music, and devised a new method of teaching singing. His
advice was sought by Lillian Nordica, Mary Garden, Ben Davies,
Alice Nielsen, and others. Melba is said to have sent him students,
including Marie Tempest, and he gained international renown by
restoring the voice of Eleanora Duse. He managed a season of
opera at Covent Garden in 1904, for which he secured the services
of Caruso, Amato, Bonci, Sammarco, and others. In 1905 he had
his own company at the Waldorf theater in London and toured
with it in the United States. From 1909 to 1913 he was manager of
the Boston Opera Company. He was associated with the Metropolitan Opera for a short time, and in 1913 directed a season of opera
at the Théâtre des Champs Elysées in Paris. He was "artistic
advisor" for the Melba-Williamson Opera Company in Australia in
1924. Claude Kingston gives us some impressions of Russell during
this period, and he might even have been the author of an unidenti-
fied and partially mutilated clipping which turned up in an old
scrap book. Even though its authorship is unknown, and although
the ends of some sentences were clipped off, an attempt at its
reconstruction seems worthwhile at this point. It reads:

From: Henry Russell, *The Passing Show*. London: Thornton Butterworth, 1926. Reprinted
by permission of Methuen London Ltd.

HENRY RUSSELL AND MELBA

I shall never cease to regret that I was not present when Melba read Henry Russell's book of recollections, in which the diva was accorded first place. I happened to be a passive witness to some of their differences of opinion during the opera season and used to note that Henry had the power of leaving her speechless, a result no one else can ever boast of.

My first realisation that all was not going smoothly between the singer and the director was at Coombe. Dame Nellie was resting after a trip to town, when the telephone rang. I happened to answer it, and called Melba to take a special message from Melbourne. She took the receiver down, and had just got out the interrogative:"Yes?" when she slammed it down hard on its hook with an uncontrollable expression of disgust, as though she were dashing something loathsome from her. "That man Russell," was her explanation, terse and sharp.

Only one thing could interest me more than reading Russell on Melba, and that would be Melba on Russell. Dame Nellie is picturesque and fervid in her choice of invective when she is really stirred, and Henry had an uncommon power of stirring her. When he first arrived, it was my luck to travel in the same train from Albury, and the diva introduced me to the Herr Director in terms of the greatest admiration. "The greatest teacher of singing in the world," was her term of distinction. The scene soon changed, and I often wonder if it was a woman who brought about the rift . . . for an extremely womanish episode happened at that time.

Everyone will remember a great party Melba gave at Coombe during the season. The world and his wife were there, and the singer wore a very special "creation" she had brought from Paris. She had spoken to many about this triumph of M. Poiret. It chanced that Mrs. Henry Russell had been to Paris at the same time as Dame Nellie. Thereby hangs the tale. The great night came, and an endless procession of cars crowded the road to Coldstream. I happened to go up with the Russells, after meeting them for dinner, and duly admiring the lady's French toilette. Arrived at Coombe, they trickled gradually to where Melba was receiving. When the two ladies confronted one another, Dame Nellie's eyes flashed, and the "mere man" was moved to ask, naively—"What, after all, is the meaning of an exclusive French model?"

Dame Nellie is too big a woman to hold lasting hatreds, but I believe the seeds of one were sown on that historic occasion.

Unfortunately, we are not able to read "Melba on Russell," but the referenced "Russell on Melba" follows from his 1926 book, *The Passing Show.* To attest to the fact that Diana Shinn (Mrs. Henry) Russell bore no grudge as the result of the affair described at Coombe Cottage, an article from her pen which appeared in a 1964 issue of *Opera News* follows the 1926 selection.

My acquaintance with Melba, the Australian prima donna, began in a rather curious way. In her memoirs she tells how she met my brother, Sir

Landon Ronald, and pays a charming tribute to his gifts as a musician. I can remember how delighted he was when the great singer first invited him to be her accompanist. I felt almost jealous of Landon, as I had never been introduced to her and at that time was an enthusiastic student of the voice. It was at the end of the London opera season, in 1895, and Melba was leaving for Paris when Landon told me he was going to see her off at Charing Cross and begged me to accompany him. We were finally introduced, and, in spite of the confusion on the station platform that made conversation difficult, Melba talked to me long enough to become interested in my work as a teacher.

"I am sorry I did not meet you before. I should like to know more about your method," she said as the train was about to leave. "Come to Paris and dine with me at my apartment in the Rue de Prony."

I accepted her invitation, although it involved an important change of my plans, as I had already taken a ticket to Germany. Two days later I kept my appointment and enjoyed an agreeable evening with her. She grew quite excited when I explained my method of teaching, and insisted on my returning the next day, when we tried several vocal experiments together. The seeds were sown of what might have proved a friendship of mutual utility. I was pleased that she was interested in my work, and glad that she could make use of my knowledge of the human throat. A correspondence ensued between us, and she expressed in the most enthusiastic terms her belief in my work. The following autumn she sent me numerous pupils. Among them was a charming American, a Mrs. Karst, who afterwards succeeded admirably in the United States.

Haddon Chambers, the playwright, was another Australian then coming into prominence. I had known him in his boyhood when he lived in rooms in a small house near St. John's Wood. He had great personal charm, was generous to a fault and had a most diverting sense of humour that endeared him to all his friends.

One afternoon he came to read me one of his plays and asked me whether I thought it would make a good subject for an opera. I forget now what my opinion was, but I remember that we discussed the singers of the day. He was a great admirer of Melba, who had just conquered London, but had never met her. He had noticed with regret her lack of dramatic power.

"What a pity," he remarked, "that she is so cold. Her voice is the most divine thing in the world, and if someone would only teach her to act, she would be perfect."

I had asked her to supper and begged him to stay and meet her. He accepted with joy, and it proved a most amusing evening. The other guests were Lady Charles Beresford, Robin Grey, Tosti and George Moore.

Few people knew more about the stage at that time than Haddon, and Melba realised at once how much she could learn from her talented compatriot. The friendship grew and the diva undoubtedly benfited by the care that Haddon bestowed on every new rôle she learnt, teaching her gradually to be an intelligent actress. I forget how long their friendship actually lasted, but I remember Melba telling me how grateful she was for his assistance and how she considered her art had improved by her association with him. For reasons, however, that I never understood and which he never explained, he suddenly ceased to be *persona grata* to her. I can only suppose that he shared my own experience and found her a trifle too exigent from time to time.

During the following years I saw a great deal of Melba. One summer I took a villa near Stresa, on the Lago Maggiore. The prospect of a few weeks' rest by the beautiful lake appealed to the weary prima donna so much that she asked me whether she might bring some friends and join my house party. I still have several of her letters in which she mentions the names of the people she wished me to invite. In those days, being the acclaimed queen of song, we treated her as royalty and made every reasonable concession to her foibles.

One hot July day I received a telegram to say that she and her friends were arriving at Locarno and asking me to meet them. I hired a launch and steamed up to that picturesque, and now historic little town, but found no trace of Melba or her party. She had got off at the wrong station and arrived at my villa before my return. We were quite a large party—Bernie Rolt, Robin Grey, his sister Dolly, Lady Stracey (the attractive sister of Lady Wavertree) and Theodore Byard. Theo, who was an intimate friend of mine, was devoted to Melba, and to please her brought his gondola all the way from Venice. I still have an amusing snapshot of him and Melba in the gondola on the lake.

The days were filled with excursions, parties, and above all, music. There were critics as well as artists among the guests, as Robin Grey edited at that time a paper called *The Musician*. Melba rose early every morning and practised conscientiously in the garden. One day a nurse from a neighbouring villa, fuming with rage, precipitated herself on to the terrace and shaking her fist at the startled singer, shouted: "You have awakened my baby with that dreadful noise, and if you don't stop I'll have you prosecuted."

Another evening when the sky was lit by an August moon, and the mountains stood like black ramparts between us and reality, Melba sang. The golden voice was borne across the silence of land and water until it reached the little town of Pallanza, five kilometres away. The following day we heard that crowds had gathered there on the piazza enchanted by the notes so distant and yet so clear.

At the end of my house party, Melba, accompanied by Lady Stracey and Bernie Rolt, left for Venice, where they were joined by Haddon Chambers. . . .

I saw nothing of Melba for some time after her visit to Stresa, though we parted the best of friends. She went to America, and when I met her again in

London, much to my surprise, she received me with obvious coldness. I had had no experience of prime donne in those days, and was puzzled at the sudden change of her attitude, still having the illusion that they behaved like normal people. Robin Grey, Byard and Haddon Chambers each gave a different reason for the change, but none was satisfactory, and I dismissed the subject from my mind, and for over ten years we passed each other as strangers. In another chapter I will tell the history of the reconciliation that took place in Boston, with the result that Melba sang several times under my direction. I saw a great deal of her after her return from America and, in fact, once again she became my guest.

This time the scene was not the Lago Maggiore, but a little farm I own, tucked away in the hills over Monte Carlo. One August day she arrived with her maid and installed herself quite happily in my modest dwelling. We had many amusing experiences together, for when Melba is in good form she is a most entertaining companion.

She often returned to the Riviera, and we might still be friends, had I not made the fatal mistake of accepting the artistic direction of her opera season in Australia. Before agreeing to her proposals I should have remembered Schopenhauer's warning: "To become reconciled with a person with whom you have once quarrelled is a form of weakness, and you pay the penalty of it when she takes the first opportunity of doing precisely the very thing which brought about the breach." . . .

Boston

During one of my later seasons concert engagements brought Melba to Boston, where she was the guest of Mrs. Jack Gardner, the famous leader of Boston's élite. We had not been on speaking terms for several years, and I was much surprised when I received a message from the prima donna through her hostess, intimating that she would like to sing at a few performances at the Opera House—but for the fact that I was director. Mrs. Gardner, who was a friend of mine, quite understood the situation, begged us to be friends for art's sake, or at least to renew diplomatic relations. I assured her that it mattered nothing to me whether Melba considered herself my friend or my enemy, and that I would be delighted if she would sing with my Company.

I assured her that the Boston Opera House was a public institution, built for the purpose of presenting the best in operatic art, and that personal feelings had no influence on my choice of artists.

The prima donna has always been known for her shrewd business acumen. I think, on that occasion, she realised that it was extremely profitable to be on friendly terms with a manager who could offer such tantalizing sums as 2,500 dollars for a single performance. Her capitulation may have also been due to the fact that Madame Alda, her compatriot, had married Gatti-Casazza. It was a curious coincidence that Alda never sang in a theatre where Melba had the controlling influence, and vice versa. Melba has never sung at the Metropolitan since her rival became the wife of the director. Alda, though her voice was never as great as Melba's, is a better actress and has a finer musical intelligence. Her flashing dark eyes and beautiful teeth add to the charm of her handsome person.

Terms and other conditions were arranged through Mrs. Gardner, and one night Melba arrived at the Opera House and found herself in the anomalous position of singing under the direction of a man to whom she did not speak. This warlike state of things did not last long. For the sake of the theatre, and not for any personal reason, I buried the hatchet.

Melba disappointed me only on one occasion and through no fault of her own. It was, as I remember, a matinée of *La Bohème*. On the morning of the day of the performance I received a message asking me to go to her hotel. "Henry, I am afraid I shall not be able to sing *La Bohème* this afternoon," she announced huskily as we met. I tried to cheer her up and told her that in order not to give the impression to the public that she and I had had a row it would be better for her to go to the theatre and try to get through the first act. I promised to have an understudy ready for the rest of the opera. She at once agreed to my proposal, and very courageously went to the theatre and dressed.

I returned to my rooms feeling rather nervous, and while trying to fortify myself with dinner received a telephone message from my secretary, asking me to go to the opera house at once, as Melba wanted to speak to me. I lived close by, and in two minutes was in Melba's dressing-room. I found her in tears. She tried to speak, and succeeded in saying in a hoarse whisper, "I can't utter a sound, my dear. You will have to put on my understudy." This took place fifteen minutes before the advertised time of the performance, and the house was packed. I told her that the only thing that would convince the public that she really meant to sing was to go before the curtain dressed in her Mimi costume and let me make an apology. This she did, and the public, although disappointed, gave her a sympathetic reception. She held my arm while I explained, as best I could, her sudden loss of voice. As we came off the stage she assured me that this was the first time in her career she had ever disappointed an audience. . . .

Australia

It was late afternoon in November, 1923. The day had been spent grappling with the stubborn roots of mountain trees, and, numbed with exhaustion, I rested on a crumbling wall and surveyed my domain. The Mediterranean, two thousand feet below, lay still and colourless, wearing an out-of-season tint of steel-grey shot with mauve. The mountains slept beneath their first blanket of snow, and only the air was alive and tingled with the icy breath of glacial streams. Autumn flowers lay in crumbled heaps in the garden, killed by the first frost of winter, though beneath me in Monte Carlo the grass was green and dotted with flowering shrubs.

Across the sodden ground plodded a servant, an ominous green envelope fluttering in her hand. It was not hard to guess its contents—a summons back to work in another field. In less than a week I called at a Dover Street Club and asked for Madame Melba, who had just arrived in London from Australia.

"I want you to go out there at once," she announced, and proceeded to outline her latest scheme. This was to engage a first-rate company, in which she would sing the principal rôles, for the Antipodes. She asked me to secure the company and go with them as director. I agreed to the former suggestion, but could not come to a decision about taking the journey myself.

A few weeks later Melba, accompanied by her Australian manager, Mr. Tait, and I met in Naples. We spent several days listening to earnest singers who desperately wanted engagements, but found no desirable voices. Melba, unfortunately, fell ill and returned at once to London, where she underwent a serious operation.

Meanwhile, Mr. Tait and I continued our journey to Milan, where practically the entire company were engaged. It is strange that this manufacturing northern city should be the centre for practically all the singers and chorus men and women of Europe. There is a vast difference between the professional and the more or less amateur chorus which I was later to use in Australia. The former are so trained that after two or three rehearsals they are able to sing in a repertoire of sixty to seventy operas. The great Galleria of Milan is like a whispering gallery, and at the rumour of the presence of a well-known operatic director in the city the clatter about the tables in the cafés grows dense and excited. Singers appear from everywhere to discuss the possibilities of engagement.

Not far away is the office of the principal agent, a man of power and great wealth. His domain is approached by a narrow, dark and dirty staircase, such as one might find in Whitechapel. In the entrance hall sits an unshaven and shabbily dressed man who demands one's business. Grouped against the wall on rickety chairs are the pathetic figures of out of work singers who spend days in this gloomy den in the hope of being granted an interview with the famous agent. In an inner room is an old-fashioned, out of tune piano. This is seldom used, for it often happens that an artist who makes an excellent impression when singing in a room proves a complete failure on the stage. Directors, therefore, usually make their choice from those whom they can hear in public performances. This makes the engagement of the débutant singer extremely difficult and precarious, as it is only a man of exceptional discernment who can tell the effect which will be produced in a theatre by a voice previously heard only in a room. Famous singers, of course, are privately interviewed and waited upon at their convenience, and, as it may be imagined, all conceivable tact is necessary on such occasions.

After we had engaged our male chorus we had yet to find a singer suitable to share with Melba the principal rôles. Madame Toti Dal Monte, that vivacious dark Neapolitan, was already being hailed by the critics as a promising artist. Her success at La Scala had been brilliant, and the Scala director was not at all anxious to release her. Finally, after much difficulty, and with the friendly help of Toscanini, a satisfactory contract was arranged and signed—just on the eve of a departure for South America. We felt rather uncertain about the engagement of this young Italian, as Melba, owing to illness, had neither seen nor heard her, and we could only hope that her personality would prove acceptable and sympathetic to the elder diva. Happily nothing could have been more agreeable than the ultimate relations between these two singers, and our fears were quite unjustified.

While we were busy engaging the opera company in Milan, reports of Melba's health from London were most disquieting, and we were filled with anxiety lest she should be unable to go to Australia. However, she was pronounced strong enough in time to make the final arrangements for the tour. It being then necessary to make my own decision, I agreed to act as director of the company. We sailed from Toulon the following October—a strangely assorted group.

When we arrived Melbourne was roasting in a tropical heat, with a north wind blowing that felt like a blast from a furnace. The city seemed a strange mixture of England and the Middle West of America, but gives a sensation of repose which I have seldom felt in any other place of its size. We established headquarters near St. Kilda, a suburb which is to Melbourne what Hampstead is to London.

I had been warned that the Municipal Theatre, which had been engaged for the opera season, was inadequate and antiquated. However, I found it a good sized building, but with no claims to the title of an opera house, and certainly not the equipment which one expects in a first-class home for lyric drama. But the inefficiencies were overcome, and we were given every assistance by Sir George Tallis, the affable managing director.

Our first undertaking was the completion of the chorus. With the hearty co-operation of Mr. Fritz Hart, the best female voices in Melbourne had been carefully schooled in the operas we were to give. The voices of the girls he chose were beautiful, and they proved to be good workers, loyal and persevering. In three months after our arrival they formed one of the best female choruses I have ever heard.

Three classes of voices form a female chorus—soprano, mezzo-soprano and contralto—and care has to be taken that no section is more dominant than another, as the harmonious whole depends on the perfect balance between all three. In the first place each division is taught its part separately under a chorus master, then the entire combination is rehearsed. When the chorus master has completed his part of the training the conductor is asked to give audition. This usually means a preliminary rehearsal with the piano, and finally with the full orchestra. The stage manager then teaches what is called the mis-en-scène of each opera, and in a well-organised house the chorus have their final rehearsals in full costume and make-up.

For many reasons it was thought advisable to bring the male chorus from Italy. This gave rise to a violent outburst of indignation from the Australian Trade Unions, and the labour party made it an excuse to re-open a controversy which had recently been raging on the subject of imported foreign labour. The papers were filled with letters of protest. "Empire goods were the best," and one patriotic citizen went so far as to point out that since Australia could produce good cricketers, they could obviously produce good choristers.

A number of Australian singers were brought together and crudely rehearsed, and we were asked to hear them. Melba, without a moment's hesitation, decided that they were not suitable for her requirements. There was not time enough to train them for the thirty-two operas about to be produced, and there was, also, the unsurmountable difficulty of teaching Colonials to sing in two different languages. This opposition and criticism greatly upset Melba, and she felt discouraged at the attitude taken by the public and the press.

Shortly after her arrival in Melbourne she asked me to spend the week-end at Coombe Cottage, her country house at Lillydale. It was a family party with the exception of Mr. Beverley Nichols and myself. Melba's delightful daughter-in-law acted as hostess, and a more charming one could not be wished for, as her delicious sense of humour and her endless good spirits enlivened what might otherwise have been difficult moments. Her husband, George, is a simple but attractive person, and scarcely the sort of man one would expect to find as the son of a prima donna, being devoid of any theatrical instincts and devoting his life to farming, hunting and polo.

Coombe Cottage, a bungalow designed by Dame Nellie herself, is beautifully situated at the foot of Lillydale HIlls, overlooking a great expanse of bush. The interior has a decidedly English atmosphere, is well furnished and extremely comfortable. One room is set aside for the souvenirs and presents the diva has received from various princes, emperors and other notables, and these are shown with natural pride to admiring visitors. The place was a delightful haven for weary people, and we spent much of our time sitting on the lawn listening to Melba's voice on the gramophone.

If Melbourne and the surrounding country has a curse, it is surely that of flies. In all my travels I have never met anything so devilish and punishing. To an ordinary European Australia's pestilence is almost incredible. These flies come not singly, nor in hundreds, but literally in hundreds of thousands. They take one's breath away, and it is impossible and even dangerous to open one's mouth in their midst. Although to all appearances they resemble the European pest, they seem to possess a quality of stickiness which I have never known in any other country. However fast one flicks them away from nose and eyes, they gather again. Such is the affliction, that nearly everybody wears fly nets, looking exactly like great green insects themselves.

One Sunday afternoon Melba caused considerable consternation by imprudently lifting her net and swallowing a fly. To everyone present the occurrence was ominous, and we all buzzed frantically about her, shouting advice through our helmets, while she coughed in the most alarming way. The offending insect was finally removed, and we subsided back into our chairs, hot, exhausted, but tremendously relieved.

On the following Monday morning we motored back to Melbourne. Melba had an appointment with Oscar Ashe at the Theatre Royal to see the costumes he had designed for Desdemona in his production of *Othello*. As she was getting out of the car she caught her fingers in the door, hurting herself so badly that she nearly fainted. Luckily the portly figure of Ashe arrived in time to catch her in his arms. It looked exactly like an outdoor rehearsal of *Othello* and Melba, who is not devoid of a sense of humour, whispered in my ear, "This will be a good advertisement for the opera, Henry. Go and telephone it to the newspapers at once."

The season opened in March with a performance of *La Bohème*, and the event caused a great deal of excitement in Melbourne. The audience was composed of the most representative people in Australia. Melba sang Mimi, and she gave an excellent performance. Although the upper register of her voice has naturally suffered from the enemy no mortal can resist, the beauty of her medium notes compensates in great measure for the loss of the high ones. It will always seem to me a pity that hundreds of young people who heard Melba during that season should have been born too late to hear a great voice in its full perfection.

THE MEANEST WOMAN IN THE WORLD

DONNA SHINN RUSSELL

Mrs. Russell's late husband, Henry Russell, owed to Melba his first pupils as a singing teacher in London, where in 1903 he became impresario at Covent Garden. From 1909 to 1914 he served as manager of the Boston Opera Company.

One afternoon in 1924, Dame Nellie Melba and I were searching for mushrooms in the vicinity of Coombe Cottage, her lovely home near Melbourne, Australia. As we walked through the long grass she turned to me and remarked with a chuckle, "It is said that the reason I gather the mushrooms on my estate is because I'm so stingy. Did you know, my dear, that I'm supposed to be the meanest woman in the world?"

I didn't reply. I had always felt she deserved the reputation; why did she joke as though it were something to be proud of?

My former husband, the late Henry Russell, was artistic director of the Melba Grand Opera Company that season, and we were house guests at Coombe Cottage, much against my will: I could not forget how badly Dame Nellie had treated a friend of mine, a promising young American girl she had brought to Italy to study with Maestro M. and then abandoned after a few months. The girl was forced to work as a servant in order to pay for her tuition, and I used to wonder how small Dame Nellie must have felt

From: Donna Shinn Russell, "The Meanest Woman in the World," *Opera News* 28, no. 9 (January 11, 1964). Reprinted courtesy of *Opera News*.

when my friend finally reached stardom. Oh, yes, her reputation for stinginess was well known.

I was silent as we walked back to the house, our baskets filled with mushrooms, my blood boiling anew at the memory of my friend's humiliation. Later that afternoon, when we were sitting in the garden, the butler brought tea and the mail. Dame Nellie excused herself as she glanced through the three letters on the tea tray. As she read the third letter her eyes filled with tears, and after a few seconds she handed it to me. "Read it," she commanded. I hesitated. "*Please* read it and tell me what you think."

The letter was from a young girl (unknown to Dame Nellie) who had hoped to become a concert pianist. Due to her mother's long illness she had been forced to abandon her piano lessons, and in two weeks all her furniture would be sold to pay for her mother's funeral. She implored Dame Nellie to help her keep her beloved Steinway. As I read the letter I told myself that the prima donna's tears were of the crocodile variety; I was convinced she would do nothing for this girl.

"It is a very touching letter," I said. "What are you going to do about it?"

Dame Nellie waited a few seconds before replying. "Helping young artists—or *anyone*, for that matter—is a very great responsibility. It would be so easy just to send a check."

"Why don't you?"

"It wouldn't be fair to her."

"What do you mean?"

"At one time I was afflicted with the vanity of goodness. It made me feel important and righteous to lavish expensive gifts upon persons less fortunate than myself. Maestro M., a wise old Italian to whom I had sent many promising pupils, took me to task for what he called my criminal generosity.

" 'You are a great singer, Nellie,' he said. 'Does your ego also crave deification? It is my conviction that all important contributions should be offered anonymously if they are to do anything for one's soul. When I was a young man I fancied myself as a benevolent member of the human race. I smothered my pupils with kindness. If they were poor, I taught them gratis and often fed and housed them over long periods of time. Did they appreciate it? Of course not! And rightly so. They had little respect for me and even began to doubt that I knew anything about voice production. I had crippled them by making things too easy for them; but I learned my lesson before it was too late.

" 'Throwing my halo into the wastepaper basket, I became a hard taskmaster overnight: I demanded my usual fee and put my students to work so they could earn it; I bullied and insulted them; I was niggardly with my praise—and believe it or not, they began to like me! When they had to pay for their lessons, they worked harder and were grateful for the extra time I gave them. I saw to it that they would not lack the stamina to meet with courage the rebuffs and setbacks that even the best singers must experience on their way to the top. Character is far more important than talent, great intellect or even genius; happily, it can be acquired. The ingredients are hardship, sacrifice, repeated failure and the courage to go forward against all odds. Only through self-reliance can anyone in any walk of life win a place in the sun. Your generosity, Nellie, is destructive. The essence of charity is to help others help themselves.' "

"After that talk with the Maestro, *did* you throw your halo into the wastepaper basket?" I asked, trying to keep the sarcasm from my voice. I was thinking that although the Maestro's credo was very interesting, it could also serve as a convenient philosophy for a miser.

"At that time I did quite a bit of soul-searching," replied Dame Nellie. "I wondered, *could* goodness be a vanity after all? What had my motives been all those years when I had granted favors so recklessly? The truth was not flattering. I owe a great deal to Maestro M. and, incidentally, to an American protégée of mine. You see, it was because of this girl that the Maestro lectured me on that day so long ago."

Was she referring to my friend? Was I to learn after all these years why Dame Nellie had treated her so outrageously? I was all ears.

"My protégée had a glorious voice, but she lacked character," continued my hostess. "She was unstable, spoiled, conceited and lazy. The Maestro had been teaching her at my expense for some time but realized that with her temperament there was little hope for her ultimate success; he suggested that I pretend to withdraw my support for a while. I was very upset. What would her admirers in America think of me for my action? She had left home in a blaze of glory and extravagant publicity. Now, no doubt, she would write to her family and call me every name in the devil's book, but in spite of how badly I felt, I agreed with the Maestro that something had to be done. Though I was to continue paying for her lessons, she must believe I had given her up as a poor risk. Maestro M. would then offer to teach her gratis, provided she would help his wife with the housework and the care of their six grandchildren. (Their mother, his daughter, had died in childbirth the year before.) My protégée was outraged at the conditions but consented because there was nothing else she could do; it was either go to work or return to the United States."

"Six grandchildren!" I exclaimed. "If I had been in her place I'd have gone home!"

"The fact that she didn't was a very encouraging sign. Six months later the Maestro told me she was dong the work of two servants—and what was more, she seemed to enjoy it. Her hands were rough from toil, but her voice had become increasingly beautiful. She was humble, stable and grateful. He refused to accept any more money from me for her tuition: she was earning her way. Many months later I arranged for her to gain experience in several small opera houses in Italy; I was gratified with the fine showing she made each time and knew that thanks to Maestro M.'s stern discipline she would one day realize her dreams."

I was near tears. I felt like falling upon my knees before this woman whom I and many others had maligned for so long. It was quite possible that my friend had been spoiled by her local triumphs. When Dame Nellie brought her to Italy, calling her a "bright promise," my friend believed that she was ready for stardom—the publicity had turned her head. The Maestro and Dame Nellie had acted wisely; I could see that now.

"After this singer became successful, why didn't you tell her about your arrangement with the Maestro?" I asked.

"Tell her? The memory of one's hardships is the sweetest part of victory; I couldn't deprive her of that! Besides, it wouldn't have been fair to the Maestro. Oh, my dear, after I was cured of the vanity of goodness, I helped many artists—as well as individuals in other walks of life—by making it possible for them to help themselves. Some failed, but others reached the goal. It was well worth the effort and money it took."

"You never gave them the opportunity to thank you?"

"Thank me? Why, bless your heart, had they known the truth not one of them would ever have forgiven me! Can't you see why?"

"I suppose they would have preferred a check. But what will you do about this girl?" I held up the letter, which was still in hand.

"I shall ask an agency in Melbourne to give me a report on her, and we shall see what should be done in her case. She may be very talented, but on the other hand she may have only an all-consuming ambition with little ability to back it up. Many aspire, but few achieve. This poor girl may be one to whom I can send a check with a clear conscience."

At that instant Pamela, Dame Nellie's little granddaughter, joined us. "Here," said Dame Nellie with great pride, "is the real mistress of Coombe Cottage. Have you a kiss for me, darling?"

Pamela stamped her three-year-old foot and cried "No!"

Dame Nellie chuckled.

"She's just like me! Stingy, you know."

* * *

The following year, Dame Nellie was on the French Riviera and lunched with us at our villa at La Turbie.

"By the way," I asked, "what happened to that young pianist?"

"Which pianist?"

"The one who asked you to help her keep her Steinway. I was with you at Coombe Cottage when you received her letter. Remember?"

"Oh, *that* one!" Dame Nellie's face was alight with joy. "Well, the agency in Melbourne gave me a wonderful report about the girl: she was talented, attractive, stable, but she lacked self-confidence. I arranged for her to work as accompanist to a brilliant young violinist whom I had been helping indirectly for some time and who was almost ready to be launched upon his concert career. I paid the girl for her work through the agency, which enabled her to continue her piano lessons, keep her furniture and pay for her mother's funeral. Now, hold your breath! A few months ago the two young people were married. It was love at first sight!"

"Did they ever find out about the part you played in their romance?"

"Need you ask? They both still think I'm the meanest woman in the world; and, that, my dear, is quite all right with me!"

ON VARIOUS CELEBRITIES

PERCY COLSON

Sing 'em Muck!

Clara Butt (1873-1936) was a giant of a woman with a contralto voice the size of a cathedral pipe organ. She had the unfortunate addiction to concert programs replete with cute little Victorian parlor songs like "A Fairy Went a-Marketing" and "Just a Ray of Sunlight"[1] which she even immortalized on recordings. The story of Melba's advice to Dame Clara has been told in many places. Since it is referred to in the following excerpt but only related in these pages in some detail (by Ivor Newton) long after the fact and in a version somewhat garbled by time, it might be well to quote a more contemporary source for a brief account of the affair. Here is the way *Musical Times* of London reported it in the issue for September 1928 (quoted in Scholes, 1947):

> The "Sing 'em muck" controversy has livened a few weeks of the "off" season. Dame Nellie Melba cabled wrathfully protesting against a statement in Dame Clara Butt's biography that the former had said to the latter, who was about to tour Australia, "Sing 'em muck; it's all they can understand." Whereupon Dame Clara cabled to Dame Nellie assuring her that she was innocent, having neither ascribed the remark to Dame Nellie, nor seen the proofs of the book in which it appeared. Exhibit No. 3 (as they say in the

---

From: [Percy Colson] *I Hope They Won't Mind* (1930).

Courts) was a cable from Miss Ponder, the writer of the book. Wiring from India, Miss Ponder affirms that the proofs were duly passed by Dame Clara.

The result of this long-distance argument is that we have three irreconcilable statements, and, one man's word being as good as another's (especially when they are women), the case must be dismissed, the parties paying their own costs. The only thing that is certain is that both these eminent singers, however emphatically they may decry the "Sing 'em muck!" principle, have consistently acted on it in arranging their programmes. The fact of their having sung a good deal of fine music as well can never alter that.[2]

Percy Colson, the author of a 1932 biography of Melba, published in 1930 an anonymous book of gossipy stories largely relating to the London musical set, titled *I Hope They Won't Mind*, from which the following excerpt is taken. In 1936 he published a sequel titled *What If They Do Mind?* with his name on the title page. Colson deserves full credit for his classic reason for believing Melba's side of the *muck* controversy; Newton gave the line to Dame Nellie, and however characteristic of her it might have been, credit should be given where credit is due.

NOTES

1. Michael Aspinall, in a "Note on Melba's Composers" issued with the Lp set of Melba's London recordings (EMI record album RLS 719), remarks that "Dame Clara Butt, clad in red velvet with diamond tiara and pearl necklace, would offer 'Dear Little Jammy Face' and 'How Pansies Grow.' . . ." If these choice items were indeed in her repertoire, at least she did not perpetuate their existence on recordings!

2. The real result was that the first edition of the book *Clara Butt: Her Life Story* by Winifred Ponder (London: George G. Harrap & Co., 1928) was withdrawn, and the offending pages (138-139) were reprinted. The first edition has become a collector's item.

In 1898, while visiting friends, I had made the acquaintance of the French [*sic*] composer, Hermann Bemberg, who was an important personage in the ultra-smart musical set led by Lady de Grey, afterwards Marchioness of Ripon. We became great friends when I went to London, and he was extremely kind to me. Few people have been born with so many natural advantages as Bemberg. The son of a rich Argentine banker who lived in Paris, he was very good-looking, brilliantly witty, and extraordinarily gifted musically. Had he been obliged to work hard, he would certainly have gone very far; indeed, Massenet once said to me: "It is a good thing for all of us that Bemberg was born rich." As it was, his songs had an immense vogue. I cannot help thinking that some of them, as also those of Massenet and Chaminade, will one day be rediscovered. Although not *great* music, many of them have both melodic charm and distinction, and they are infinitely superior to the modern "arty" song and the shoddy imitations of Debussy and Stravinsky. Both Melba and Plançon made some of their greatest successes in them. I often went with him to Lady de Grey's wonderful Sunday evening musical parties, at Coombe Court, where one heard all the most famous singers, as she practically ran Covent Garden; and, of course, all the notabilities of the day were to be seen there, too.

Bemberg gave the coup de grâce to the snobbish custom of separating the performers from the company by a red rope. He was accompanying Melba in his valse song, "Nymphes et Sylvains," at the house of a nouveau riche Jew, and as he led her on he saw the cord, picked it up, and flung it away. He was an admirable "coach," and the singers who could induce him to give them lessons counted themselves very fortunate. He coached Clara Butt for a time, in Paris, and she still sings the four or five arias he taught her. At his house I met several French celebrities, including Anatole France, a cynically urbane old gentleman, and Marcel Proust, elegant and maladif. I formed the impression that they hated each other.

It is curious how free and easy life is now, compared with what it was before the war. Nowadays no one leaves cards, the top hat has practically disappeared from the West End, except for weddings, and most of one's invitations are by telephone. Apropos of this I remember a party at the Baroness de Meyer's house in Cadogan Gardens, at which only famous music hall stars were engaged to perform. Among them were Marie Lloyd, Little Tich, and Albert Chevalier. It was a terrible fiasco. They were paralysed by the rather stiff "gilt chair tiara" atmosphere and the presence of royalty, and tried to bowdlerise their songs. The audience smiled politely, but did not know what to make of it all. Such a party would be a huge success now when all the most amusing parties are so mixed, and society women run after actors and variety celebrities, instead of its being the other way about.

Bemberg told me an amusing story of a certain great lady of Edwardian days, a great patron of music, who was well known for her very southern temperament. While staying at Como one September, she had a violent "affair" with an extremely good-looking but rather flamboyant young Italian, who was decidedly not of her own world. The following June he visited London, and, like all Italians, went at once to the opera, where he met her ladyship, and greeted her with outstretched hands and eager exclamations of pleasure. Alas, however, since September she had "loved and loved anew," and he was met with a haughty and inquiring stare! Greatly disconcerted, he said, "Don't you remember me, Madame, and the delightful time we had at Como?' She answered icily, "And since when, sir, has such an incident been considered as constituting a claim to further acquaintance?"

Of all the great artistes I ever met, I think Melba is the one who best succeeded in imposing her personality on Social London. She had many enemies, on account of her rather difficult nature and jealous disposition; but what a voice! For sheer beauty of timbre I have never heard its equal, and she always sang dead in tune; no feeling her way up to the high notes; she landed on them exactly as a boy does, and her trills and chromatic scales sounded as if they were being played by a very good flautist. I remember driving one spring morning to lunch with Bemberg at his apartement in the Avenue Jules Sandeau. Melba was there, and as we reached the quiet street she suddenly burst into song. My cocher stopped short and exclaimed: "Mais, Monsieur, c'est un ange qui chante." Personally, however, I doubt if the angels could touch her when she was at her best. I do not for a moment believe that she ever told Clara Butt to sing "muck" to the Australians, as was stated in that singer's memoirs last year. Such advice to Clara Butt would be so entirely unnecessary.

I once had the pleasure of playing the violin part of Bemberg's "Ballade du Désespéré," in which Melba and Sarah Bernhardt were taking part. We went to the Hyde Park Hotel, where Sarah Bernhardt was staying, to rehearse it. Melba arrived, smart and punctual as usual, but we had to wait some time for Sarah Bernhardt, who finally came in wearing a dirty old dressing-gown, and with wisps of grey hair struggling over her face, on which were patches of the previous night's make-up and grease paint. One quite forgot her appearance, however, when she began to recite. The concert was at Mrs. (now Lady) George Cooper's house, in Grosvenor Square. She gave two on consecutive nights, to introduce herself to London society. Among the celebrities engaged, in addition to Melba and Sarah Bernhardt, were Caruso, Kubelik, and Yvette Guilbert. Nobody gives such parties now; I doubt if there are many people who can afford to do so. Now one can hire a band for people to dance to for less than the fee of one famous artiste, and, of course, it is infinitely less expensive to ask a lot of friends to dinner and sit them down to play bridge afterwards. Mrs. Cooper, however, had just come into about two million pounds, so she had no need to study economy.

Melba always managed her financial affairs admirably. She was business-like and reliable, and never disappointed the public. She was not very easy to work with, and rather "lorded" it over everyone at Covent Garden; so much so that one season they decided to try to do without her. The experiment was a failure, and so affected the box office returns that, by the middle of June, the directors had to eat humble pie, and beg her to sing for the remainder of the season. She said, "Very well, but, as I have not a contract, I shall have to charge the fee I receive for private engagements, five hundred guineas for each performance." They had to pay it! She was not popular with her fellow artistes. An incident that occurred during a performance of *La Bohème* gives some idea of the reason. Bemberg and I were in a box that evening, and, in the second act, just as Mlle. Fritzi Scheff, who was playing "Musetta," was carefully preparing to take the high B natural at the end of the "Valse," a clear angelic voice in the wings landed on it with effortless ease and sang the rest of the phrase with her. Everyone whispered, "Melba!" There was a long wait after the curtain fell, and, finally, the manager, Mr. Neil Forsyth, came in front and announced that as Mlle. Fritzi Scheff was indisposed and could not continue to sing, Madame Melba had consented to conclude the performance with the "Mad Scene" from *Lucia*. Bemberg went behind to see what was the matter, and when he returned he told me there had been a frightful row, almost a battle, as Fritzi Scheff tried to scratch Melba's face and then had hysterics. It was awkward for the audience, as we were all turned out into Covent Garden at ten o'clock, long before the hour for which carriages were ordered, and cabs congregated to pick up those who did not possess their own conveyances.

What a cast they could muster for *La Bohème* in those days! Melba, Fritzi Scheff, Caruso, Scotti, Journet, and Gilibert. I doubt if we shall ever again see its equal. I believe that the Lady de Grey-Neil Forsyth régime was the only one under which opera at Covent Garden has ever, in addition to paying its way, paid a small dividend. Under present-day conditions it is impossible to run Covent Garden except at a loss.

Melba and Caruso in their prime certainly dwarfed all other singers in popularity, for if they were not the greatest singers of their day, in an artistic sense, they undoubtedly possessed the two most lovely voices. It is strange how often nature bestows exquisite voices on people with but little artistic talent. Caruso was not in the least musical; nor is Melba; they reduced the art of acting to its simplest proportions. Caruso, generally speaking, did not attempt to act; he just poured forth his golden notes, while Melba had two gestures: to express a mild emotion she raised one arm; for passion or despair, she raised both! I have never met a singer who fussed so much about his health as Caruso. He was always doctoring himself, and his dressing-room at the Opera was like a chemist's shop, it was so full of sprays, nasal douches, gargles, pastilles, and medicines. He was frightfully worried and bad tempered if he had the least thing the matter with him, especially if he had a slight temperature. On one occasion when I was with him he was writing to a friend, describing his symptoms, and asked me *"Come si scriva febbre, con uno o due B?"* (How do you spell fever—with one B or two?) I answered, "With one if you have only a slight temperature, but if you have a high temperature, with two." The reply amused him, and he became at once quite amiable.

ENTER
BEVERLEY NICHOLS

As Nellie Melba grew older, she liked to have young people around. She liked unconventional people with drive and ambition; she liked tenacity of purpose, and often lasting friendships were developed with those who were not afraid of her sometimes gruff ways and who would stand up to her. If they happened to be young, apparently cultured, and attractive, so much the better. It is entirely possible that part of the satisfaction of helping young musicians along was the egotistical hope that they would become successful and thereby cast reflected light on their mentor. But not all her protégés were musicians, as is exemplified by the case of a young English newspaperman who managed to slip by her defenses at an exclusive London club in order to get a story for his paper. She apparently saw what she considered "plucky" characteristics in Beverley Nichols, as well as literary abilities that might lead to a successful career. She not only granted the interview, but she invited him to dinner. Nichols was smart enough to recognize a good thing when he saw it, and nurtured the opportunity to develop a friendship that would open doors not usually opened to a brash young reporter from a gossipy tabloid.

Nichols was twenty-three, Melba sixty-two; and when the singer returned to Australia early in 1924 to work on the organization of her Melba-Williamson opera company, she cabled him, offering him a job as her secretary. Nichols claimed that he accepted the job as he was determined to persuade the singer to allow him to write her "autobiography." Whatever the case, Nichols did live at Coombe Cottage, Melba's country home near Melbourne, for about six months in 1924-1925 and did ghost-write her *Melodies and Memories*, for which effort he was to receive 50 percent of the profits. While the book is well written as a piece of literature, it is completely unsatisfactory as a biography of a world-famous opera singer, a fact Nichols apparently realized, as he blamed Melba for its more or less innocuous content and its obvious omissions, which latter could have been of considerable interest and importance.

Nichols left Melba's employ in mid-1925 and brought back the manuscript of *Melodies and Memories* for serialization and later publication in book form in the United States, and in book form in England. He also arranged for the publication of his own first book, also written in Australia, and launched himself on a writing career, during much of which he continued to lean heavily on Melba for copy. As can be seen from samples of his writing which follow, there is considerable difference in his work published during Melba's lifetime and that which came after. Melba died in February 1931; January 1932 saw the publication in both England and the United States of a novel by Beverley Nichols called *Evensong*. As we shall see, writing in 1949 about these events, he claimed that not to have written such a book "would have been a dereliction of my duty as an artist"; there might be some who would disagree that he allowed a "decent interval," as he stated, to elapse between Melba's death and the publication of *Evensong*. There is no doubt that the book was a considerable financial success, as it was later used as a play and a film, the latter with Evelyn Laye taking the part of an aging opera singer named Irela, and Conchita Supervia in the role of a young singer Irela sees as a threat to her career. The "fictitious" Irela was a vain, thoroughly nasty, malicious, scheming woman, and it wasn't until 1949 that Nichols admitted that part of the book's success "was a *succès de scandale*." The fact that *Evensong* carries the line "The characters in this novel are fictitious" may have served to avert a libel suit by Melba's estate, but the real tragedy of the whole affair is that the passing years have blurred the memory so that the character of the fictitious Irela and many of the incidents in the story have become fixed in identification in people's minds with her prototype, and so remain attached to Melba long after copies of *Evensong* have been consigned to the dustbin.

There is no doubt that novelist Nichols did a great deal of harm to the memory of the woman who launched his career, and for this reason his name is so abominated by Melba's admirers that they lose sight of the fact that the man did produce some words about the singer that should be preserved. If anyone cares to get more insight into the character of a person who had been so befriended yet could release such a stream of invective and bile as Nichols did in *Evensong*, let him or her merely leaf through the pages of the same author's *Father Figure* (1972), which claims to be "An Uncensored Autobiography," although never mentioning Melba's name. Here is described how the author made three attempts on his own father's life, and the cruel, sadistic, and inhuman revenge he took on his father after his mother's death. At least no one could accuse Mr. Nichols of inconsistency.

A MEMORY—AND SOME SONGS

BEVERLEY NICHOLS

One of the most wonderful evenings of my life was when, in the heart of the Australian Bush, Melba sang for me alone.

I ought, if I had a tidy mind, to describe how I got to the Australian Bush, and how so divine a person as Melba should be singing to me at all. But that can come in due course. For the moment I want to recapture that scene as I lived it.

There is a long room, panelled in green, lit only by the misty glow from outside the windows, fragrant with the scent of yellow roses. There are wonderful old mirrors that catch the dying sparkle of a Marie Antoinette chandelier. In the half-light so many lovely things shine dimly . . . a picture of dark, closely-clustered flowers, a case of fans, delicate as the world of fairies. . . .

I am standing at the window. There is a long veranda, and in the distance I can see, faintly outlined, the pillars of the loggia that leads to an Italian garden. Mountains, fabulously blue, rise on the horizon and everything is very quiet. Only a few hours ago the air had been rent with the shrill cries of parrots, flying to their resting-place in the forests. Even while we had dined we could hear the liquid warbling of magpies, that strange noise, like water gurgling from a flask, which brings all Australia before me as I write. And after dinner, while we had taken our coffee, the whole of the fields around had echoed with the chirping of crickets. But now . . . silence.

And then, like a moonbeam stealing into an empty room, that voice, which is as no other has ever been. . . .

From: Beverley Nichols, *25: Being a Young Man's Candid Recollections of His Elders and Betters*. London: Jonathan Cape, 1926.

Dans ton cœur dort un clair de lune . . .

The notes die away and there is silence again. I go on looking at the blue mountains. Then, from the other end of the room, a sudden laugh, the sort of laugh that people may make in Heaven, and—

"Well, did you like me?"

I laugh too. It seems so utterly fantastic to attempt to appreciate in words an art like this. Nobody ought ever to clap Melba. They ought to remain silent. The greatest things in art are above applause.

It was in, I believe, 1923, that I first had the delight of meeting her, but it was not till the season had really begun, and I found myself in Covent Garden, listening to the first opening bars of *"Mi Chiamano Mimi,"* that I really came under her spell. It was not the first time I had heard her sing. As a small boy of nine I had been taken to one of her concerts by my mother, and had greatly irritated my family by informing them, when I returned home, that I thought she sang exactly like myself.

In a sense, there was truth as well as youthful complacency in that criticism. Her voice *is* like a choirboy's, as crystalline, as utterly removed from things of the earth.

One day she said to me, with characteristic directness, "You're not well. You're poisoned. You've been working too hard. You ought to come out to Australia and help me with my Opera Season."

I denied indignantly that I was poisoned. (My doctor afterwards confirmed her diagnosis.) I said that I knew nothing about Opera. But all the same, though it was some six months later, I went out to join her in Australia—that was in the beginning of 1924.

Melba is so great a woman—I use the word "great" in the fullest sense—that one cannot possibly attempt a full-length portrait of her in a few pages. But, from the notebook of my imagination, I may perhaps draw out a few pages, roughly scribbled over with thumbnail sketches, that may make you feel you know her a little.

I shall take the sketches simply as they occur, without attempting to put them in order. The first one is labelled "energy." The face of Melba appears, rising calmly over a heavy *chaise-longue* which, unassisted, she is pushing across the room. It is one of her furniture-moving days. The whole of her boudoir is upside down. Pictures stand in rows against the walls, china is ranged along the floor, and over the chairs and sofas are scattered quantities of bibelots—pieces of jade, little mother-of-pearl boxes bearing the words *Souvenir* and *Je pense à toi*, crystal clocks, a tiny gold case containing a singing bird with emerald eyes.

The furniture-moving goes on. I endeavour to help, and am told with great frankness that I am far more bother than I am worth, and that I had better content myself with watching. And so I watch, amazed. Little by little the room takes shape. At one moment she is standing on a chair, and the next she is kneeling on the floor, doing the work of six British labourers. *Voilà*. It is done. And she is at the piano again, trilling like a newly fed thrush.

If Melba had had no voice she might have made a fortune as an art connoisseur. I have been driving with her sometimes, and have seen, on the other side of the street, a window full of antiques. "Look," I have said. "Don't you think there might be some fascinating things in there?" She looks. In the space of ten seconds her eye has taken in the entire contents of the window, and she either says "All fake," or she stops the car. I have never known her wrong. It is as inexplicable to me as the feat of the eagle which can see a mouse hidden in a field of corn a mile beneath.

So many people who like to pretend that they are artistic will tell you that they cannot bear to live with ugly things. They will say this with pained expressions, even when they are sitting, apparently unmoved, beneath a Landseer stag, on a Victorian settee. With Melba it really is pain. Whenever I see her in an ugly room I know the exact feeling of the Oyster who is irritated by a piece of sand. She is restless. Her eyes dart hither and thither. She bites her lips. For two pins she would get up and hurl things out of the window.

I shall never forget once when she was singing three times a week in the Opera at one of the great Australian cities, and was staying in an hotel in order to be near the theatre. She came down at about ten o'clock to go for a drive. I met her in the hall. As we were going out she paused in the entrance way and said:

"Those pots. Look at them. They're hideous enough in all conscience, but they're made ten times worse by being pushed out in that ridiculous position. Let's push them back against the wall."

Now wherever Melba goes in Australia there is always a little crowd in her wake, as though she were the Queen of the Continent, which indeed she is. And the prospect of moving pots in the entrance of an hotel struck me as alarming in the extreme.

I mumbled something about "waiting." She looked at me scornfully. "Wait?" she said. "What for? Come on."

Without the faintest interest in the sensation she was making, she bent over and began to move the first pot into position. I shall never forget the sparkling look of satisfaction on her face, the slight flush that the effort caused, the waving ospreys in her hat, and the cry of "There—isn't that better?" when the first pot was placed in position.

I saw a tall red-faced individual glowering down on us.

"Excuse me," he said.

"I'm Melba," she said. "I'm doing some furniture-moving for you."

He was quite speechless for a moment. Then, after a gulp he managed to say, "But Madame . . ."

"Oh, I shan't charge you anything," she remarked.

Those pots are as she placed them to this day.

The next sketch is labelled "The Singing Lesson." There are the outlines of a long bare room, a platform, some seats in front, occupied by professor and pupils. Melba sits by herself in a corner, biting a pencil. A pupil steps on to the platform and begins to sing. Suddenly the voice rings out, "Stop!"

As though she had been shot, the pupil stops dead. Melba gets up from her seat, goes to the platform, says to the accompanist, "Let me sit down a minute" and then turns to the girl.

"I'm not going to eat you," she says. Her own smile brings an answering smile to the face of the girl.

"Sing me 'Ah.' "

"Ah."

"No—'Ah'—up here, in the front of the mouth."

"Ah!"

"No. You're still swallowing it. Listen. Sing mah. Close your lips, hum, and then open them suddenly. Mah, mah, mah."

"Mah, mah, mah."

"That's better. Now higher. Right. Higher."

She takes her up the scale. At F sharp she stops. "Piano. Please, please, *pianissimo!* You'll ruin your voice if you sing top notes so loud. Better, but still too loud. *Pianissimo!*" She leans forward, one finger to her lips.

Somewhere about the top B flat the girl cracks. She blushes and turns appealingly to Melba. Melba takes no notice and strikes a note higher.

"I don't think I can . . ."

"I don't care what you think," says Melba. "Sing it."

"But I shall crack."

"That doesn't matter, I don't mind what sort of noise you make. I just want to hear it."

The girl attempts it again, the note is pure and round.

Melba rises from the piano and steps briskly from the platform. "She's got a lovely voice," she says. "A lyric soprano. She's taking her chest notes too high, that's all. Send her up to me and I'll make that all right."

I wonder how many other prima donnas there are in this world who would do that, who would put themselves to endless pains and expense, simply for the love of song.

I have yet to be informed of their names and addresses.

The third sketch is labelled—the artist. The scene is a rehearsal of *Othello.* For three hours she has been singing, directing, talking at one moment to the orchestra, at the next, to the stage hands, to anybody and everybody. The scene is set for the last act, and with her meticulous sense of detail she has been busying herself with the crimson draperies that overhang the bed. Now she is standing in mid-stage, sending her voice up to the men who work the lights. "More yellow," she is crying, "more yellow. This isn't a surgery. You're blinding me. That's better. Wait a minute. Not so much of that spot light on the bed. I am not a music-hall artist." Then, *sotto voce*, "How on earth does the poor man think that Desdemona could go to sleep with a light like that in her eyes?"

She is almost the only woman I have ever known who has an absolute horror of the slip-shod. Study her day when she is singing in opera. She is up with the lark. After breakfast she is in her boudoir, "warming" her voice, studying her rôle from start to finish. She lunches frugally, drinking only water. After lunch she drives or walks. At five there is the pretence of a meal—an omelette or a little fish. From now onwards she eats nothing till after the performance.

She is in her dressing-room from an hour and a half to two hours before the performance. Her make-up is scrupulous. She describes in her auto-biography the importance which she attaches to the minutest details of make-up, but I don't think that even her own description quite makes one realize the perfection of it. From her wig to her shoes, everything is as it should be. I have seen her reject fifty shawls for the part of Mimi, simply because they were not in keeping with her idea of the character.

Sketch four might be named Courage. I remember a day when we were driving together, and, as she stepped from the car, the chauffeur slammed the door full on to her fingers, crushing them cruelly. She cried—"Oh, my hand!" and the door was feverishly dragged open again. She bit her lip, walked into the theatre, sat down and closed her eyes. That was all. There was no hysterics, no "Vapours," not even a tear.

It is not only in physical courage that she excels. She has the sort of gay fearlessness which allows her to motor late at night through the Australian Bush with only a single chauffeur, and jewels of more value than I should care to estimate. One night she was motoring home with Lady Stradbroke, who is the wife of the Governor of Victoria. The car broke down in the middle of a forest. The chauffeur had to run off into the darkness, leaving the women alone. There they sat for a full hour. Any tramp, any of the roving, husky "sun-downers" with whom the Bush abounds, might have come along and taken all they wanted. Lady Stradbroke told me that though she herself was shaking in her shoes, Melba kept up a perpetual babble of chatter. I asked her when at two o'clock in the morning they arrived, if she had not been fearfully agitated. She laughed her unfor-gettable laugh. "Agitated? Me? They wouldn't hurt *me*. I'm Melba."

"I'm Melba." It is something to be able to say that. Something to be able to go up to an old woman selling roses in the streets of Paris and say "*C'est Melba*" and to have the roses pressed into your hands in a sort of homage. Something to know that wherever music is played or songs are sung all over the world, the artist who is playing before you is giving his utmost. Some-thing to be able to lean back in the theatre stalls at a first night, and to say to Bernard Shaw, as I once observed, "I know who *you* are" and to receive the answer: "You don't know me nearly as well as I know you."

And to remain, at the end of it all, so simple that you are never happier than when eating macaroni in a restaurant where you may have your fill for two shillings, so humble that you will kiss the cheek of the youngest débutante who, you feel, has in her something of the divine fire.

Melba, I salute you. It is not my fault that this sketch of you is so inadequate. It is yours. I cannot paint landscapes on threepenny bits.

MELBA; OR, NEVER AGAIN

BEVERLEY NICHOLS

Somebody who does not usually rhapsodize wrote to me yesterday saying: "It's a boy's voice. It has a timbre which seems to have risen, like a star, above sex, above passion, above the strife of years, into a realm of pure beauty."

He, like I, had been at Covent Garden when Melba bade farewell to the stage over which she has reigned for so many years. I did not see her on that wonderful night. I am ill at ease among masses of bouquets and grease-paint, and attendant worshippers. Besides, one was so *émotionné* that the cool air of the streets seemed infinitely welcome. But the next morning I saw her. She had been at a party till three o'clock, had risen at eight, and was dancing about the house as though she had slept for twelve hours. I told her what her unknown lover—please let me use that beautiful word, for who may not be allowed to fall in love with a voice?—had said.

"Ah, that's the Melba method! I've never swerved once from my principles. And I think I can be proud of the result. Can't I?"

I wonder if you can quite understand all that is implied in the Melba method, and, which is more, the tenacity with which Melba has adhered to it.

The Melba method began as soon as she was old enough to go out into the harsh Australian sunshine and play in the shadow of the gum-trees. For she was always humming—one of the finest vocal exercises yet discovered. She once said to me, "My mother used to beg me to stop my humming. It

From: Beverley Nichols, *Are They the Same at Home?; Being a series of Boquets Diffidently Distributed by Beverley Nichols*. London: Jonathan Cape, 1927.

used to get on her nerves. Every tune that I ever heard I would hum; and, since my opportunities for hearing music were exceedingly limited, I can imagine that my efforts must have been pretty monotonous."

The next stage in the Melba method arrived when she spent that vital nine months in Paris under the tutelage of Mathilde Marchesi. Melba has herself paid public tribute to this great teacher. But one is inclined to under-estimate the pupil's fidelity to the Marchesi ideal. Marchesi's system was one of classical simplicity, a system which went straight to nature and regarded any "forcing" as anathema. When Melba first made her dazzling success at Brussels in *Rigoletto* she had every temptation to swerve from her ideals. As she herself said, "They all came, singers, teachers, friends, enemies, and tried to make me sing as they sang. They tried to make me force my top notes, to do 'stunts,' to sing rôles which were unsuitable for me. I always refused. I always remembered Marchesi. Well—it has paid, hasn't it?"

The echoes of that "boy's" voice at Covent Garden the other day are her best answer.

The other vital principle of the Melba method, which I should like to see permanently printed on the doormat of every singing teacher in this country, has been a consistent respect for the composer. I have seen copies of songs used by other singers scored all over with alterations. I have seen phrasing hacked to pieces, diminuendos turned into crescendos, middle "C's" thrust breathlessly into the upper register. Melba has never done that. Her score of *Bohème* has a few notes in pencil by Puccini himself. Apart from that it remains a score of *Bohème*. She told me once, "I was so proud when Puccini said to me. 'You sing *my* music. You don't sing Melba-Puccini.' "

That has been always the standard rule of her life, and I like to think that it has also become the rule of some of those with whom she has come in contact. Many times have I sat by her at an opera or a concert, and seen her face contorted with agony as a young singer forces her top notes. She almost growls with indignation—not at the singer, but at the teacher who is responsible for a ruined voice. And often she has gone round afterwards to the singer's dressing-room with a few words of advice.

Those words of advice have sometimes developed into a singing lesson. Nobody who has seen Melba giving a singing lesson will ever forget it. In Australia there was a little Italian soprano with a charming lyric quality in her voice who was making the night hideous by bellowing her top notes. Melba took her in hand, and spent many afternoons at the piano making that girl sing softly. "Piano! Piano! *Pianissimo!* Softer still. Ten times more softly. Fifty times more softly. If you go on singing like this you'll have no voice at all in five years." That same little Italian singer—who seemed, when I first heard her, to be galloping down the road to ruin—has now had some of the best criticisms of any of the singers at Covent Garden this season.

There—that is the trouble about so hurried a portrait—one can only sketch a single fleeting mood. Melba is wonderful "copy," wherever she is. To see her groping about in old furniture shops with an uncanny instinct for a bargain; to see her in ecstasies over the art of Yvonne Printemps; to see her making confusion worse confounded by a sudden spasm of weeding in her garden—these things and many more I might have told. Out of pure selfishness I shall ignore them, to record an entirely personal impression.

Melba's voice, so often described as golden, has never been golden to me. It has been silver—a metal of far greater loveliness. It has the coolness of silver, and its sparkle. It is at once brilliant and chaste.

Always shall I carry with me the memory of a Venetian morning when, of the many, many times that I have heard her sing, she seemed to sing most beautifully. That fine American pianist, George Copeland, had come over from the Lido to our hotel in order to play over some songs which she was going to give at a concert the next day. The rehearsal was in a great room that looked out on to the Grand Canal. Sunlight was flooding the room, and through the open window came the lap, lap of water on the steps and the unforgettable sound—which bears with it all the deathless magic of Venice—of gondolas straining against the wooden piles.

He began to play. She sang. As she sang, she walked round the room, now in sunshine, now in shadow, her voice rising and falling in cadences of unearthly beauty. Something of the languor of Venice seemed to be echoing in those tones—something that was neither old nor young, but beyond time. Song followed song, and always there was the lapping of the water and the dappled sunlight as a hidden chorus to her plaint. The last song, I remember, was that exquisite thing by Chausson:

> Le temps des lilas
> Et le temps des roses
> Ne reviendra plus . . .

That is what I feel about Melba's voice. Never again shall we know a fragrance such as she has given us.

A VOICE THERE BREATHED AND EVENSONG

BEVERLEY NICHOLS

A Voice There Breathed

I keep trying to go forward, to push beyond the year 1925. But always some charming ghost catches me by the arm, forcing me to pause and gossip, and time stands still.

And now, instead of advancing, I must retreat even further, to the year 1923. For I want to tell the strange story of how I met the late Dame Nellie Melba. I can console myself by the thought that as the tale of our long friendship unfolds itself we shall, at last, step a little nearer to the present day.

Melba, now, is only a name to most young people, and in America she would not be even a name if it were not for *pêche Melba*. (I have often seen her in a tornado of temper, and the fiercest was when she opened an anonymous letter from Chicago containing the acid comment: "It's only the peaches that have kept *you* going. Yours sincerely, Ada Brown.")

Yet Melba's fame, at its height, was certainly as widespread as that of Caruso, Patti or Jenny Lind; and *their* legend still persists even above the roar of the jitterbugs. We may learn, any day, that some peroxide horror has been offered a million dollars to make a film of the life of Patti, squawking the mad scene from Lucia against a technicolored reproduction of Vesuvius. But nobody is likely to make a film about Melba. For which, in all humility, I thank God.

From: Beverley Nichols, *All I Could Never Be*. London: Jonathan Cape, 1949.

There is a divinity about a great soprano; it is quite unmistakable, for those who have ears to hear, and it does not exist in the modern world.

This is one of the few artistic matters about which it is impossible to argue. It is not a matter of opinion; it is a matter of fact.

Melba had this divinity; so had Patti; so in a minor degree had Tetrazzini; so had Galli-Curci, even when she was singing out of tune, which was on every day of the year except the second Tuesday in Lent. Elizabeth Schumann has *not* this divinity; she is a far finer artist—granted—but she is not of Olympic blood. Nor is Flagstad, nor Lily Pons, nor any of the rest of them.

Melba was "divine"—in the original meaning of the word, even when she was singing a scale in her bath.

One of the most dramatic proofs I ever had of this rare quality was given by a dim old record of Patti singing "Home Sweet Home". It is in the gramophone library of th B.B.C. Patti made it when the gramophone was very much in its infancy and she was very much in the reverse; she was, to be precise, sixty-eight. Yet as soon as the first notes of the voice emerged through the scratches one knew that one was in the presence of the supernatural. The voice was sheer gold—sunshine slanting through clouds. It was beyond all argument, above all analysis. Most of all, it was of a quality—like Melba's—that could not be compared. You do not *compare* goddesses with ordinary mortals; there are no standards by which to do so. Therefore, he would be a fool who attempted to *compare* Melba with any singer alive today. She was not "better" or "worse"; she was totally and eternally different. And even if Schumann—(whose exquisite artistry would make me gladly follow her ten miles in a fog, any night)—even if Schumann were to sing for a thousand years, she could never make the same incomparable *sounds* as Melba for ten seconds. For those sounds were not of this world. It would be pleasant to think that they might be of the next.

At the age of seven I artlessly produced a shrewd critique of Melba's voice. She had come to give a concert at our hometown, Torquay, and I had climbed the railings and scaled a high wall to hear her. When I returned home from my escapade I said "She sings exactly like *me*". I trust that this remark will not seem too offensive. I had a rather sensational treble, and could rattle off quantities of the elaborate traditional cadenzas from such ancient and forgotten operas *La Perle du Brésil*. (It is a pity that no living soprano ever attempts the charming "Couplets du Mysoli" from this faded masterpiece.)

The criticism was shrewd becaue Melba's was the voice of a boy rather than of a woman. It was to this child-like, sexless quality that I afterwards referred in the novel *Evensong* which created such a furore in her homeland, Australia, that effigies of me were burned in the streets of Sydney. This is the passage in question:

And then the voice came. It stole through the room like a spirit . . . there was a sense that some radiant and exquisite child had come to them from another world, and was unfolding silver scrolls of song on whose pages the pale notes glittered. Oh, the futility of words, of printed words, that flutter like dead leaves in the breath of that voice! And yet the voice, even in memory, compels those words to flutter from the lips of all those who heard her—compels the one to compare it to a flower unfolding, the other to a moonbeam dancing—and will compel all men in whose ears it echoed to search their souls for metaphors, until the last echo in the last song is stilled and even the memories of that beauty which she created are lost in the ultimate silence.

It seems odd that one should be burned in effigy for writing words like that about a woman, even if one also showed that she was human. But then, I have never understood the critics.

It was a murder that brought us together.

The year was 1923, and the whole of England was following with breathless excitement the course of the Thompson-Bywaters trial.[1] It had almost everything, from the journalistic point of view, that the public seek in a first-class murder—violence, mystery and a plentiful dose of sex. To me it was a long-drawn agony; to the end of my life I shall be haunted by the memory of the terror in Edith Thompson's eyes. However, as a working reporter, I had to be in the thick of it, and one of my jobs, apart from reporting the trial, was to persuade various celebrities to give their views on the case, and, if possible, to put their names to articles about it—(written, of course, by myself).

One day, my editor proclaimed:

"What we want is the *woman's* angle."

(Oh—that old "woman's angle", so dear to the editorial mind! Why must the "woman's angle" always be so much more saleable than the "man's angle"? Why this idiotic intellectual segregation of the sexes?)

"Who can we get to give us the woman's angle?" he demanded, fixing me with a beady eye.

I happened, at that moment, to glance at one of the news pages of the *Daily Mail*, which contained an announcement of a Melba night at Covent Garden. For lack of anything better to say I murmured "Melba?" It seemed about as foolish a suggestion as one could make, even in an editorial sanctum. For it is difficult to see any obvious connection between the art of *bel canto*[2] and the soul of a murderess.

However, the suggestion met with instant approval. "That's got it!" cried the editor. "We women—and Edith Thompson! By Dame Nellie Melba!" He banged his first on the table. "Get busy!"

In the usual daze, the usual state of embarrassment and apprehension, I got busy. I scrambled about with telephone books, *Who's Whos*, bundles of press-cuttings, trying to locate her. At the end of a morning's hard work I found that she was staying at the Empress Club in Dover Street. I put through a call, contacted her secretary and was told politely to go to hell. I went round to the club with a personal note and received the same message. In the meantime I sent a telegram, which was not answered.

By six o'clock I was desperate. We had nothing for the leader-page that week, and the editor was counting on me. So I decided on a *risque-tout* policy, and went out determined, by fair means or foul, to meet Melba face to face.

The Empress Club in Dover Street is very "exclusive", both socially and sexually. It is a purely feminine institution, and since its members are mostly elderly and nearly all distinguished the few males who enter it are equally elderly and distinguished. I was neither. So when I arrived at the entrance I paused, and glanced through the glass doorway as though waiting for a friend. The commissionaire gave me a suspicious glare. He did not look as though one could tip him, nor was he the sort who would be prone to gossip. He would surely have barred my way and asked my business, but at that moment a sabled female emerged and sent him scurrying for a taxi. It was now or never. I pushed open the door, and walked boldly past the reception desk. By a merciful providence the clerk's back was turned; the staircase lay ahead; and in a few seconds I had mounted it and stood panting on the first floor.

Now what?

The complete folly of my plan became apparent. In all probability Melba was out, or in one of the reception rooms, or even in the crowded lounge below, at which I had only taken a hurried glance. Even if she were in her room, I had no idea of the number nor the floor, and even if I were to ascertain it, I could hardly barge in without an appointment. In the meantime, at any moment a servant might appear and ask my business, or a door might open to reveal a member who would start some sort of alarm, and I should be placed in a ridiculous and humiliating position. Compared with the stark and deadly dilemmas which have been the daily lot of the modern younger generation, my embarrassment must seem trivial. But it was genuine enough at the moment.

I walked along the corridor. Nothing happened. A staircase lay ahead. I walked up it and made the circuit of the second floor. Still nothing. Another staircase . . . another corridor . . . and then, miracle of miracles . . . the Voice.

It echoed, very faintly, through a door that lay at the extreme end of the passage. Hardly believing my good luck, I tiptoed nearer. This was the sort of coincidence for which journalists pray all their lives. But by the time I reached the door, I had forgotten all about journalism, all about everything except the Voice. It seemed then, as it has always seemed since—long after she is dead, even through the frayed veil of the gramophone—less like a sound than a light, a silver beam of light that hovered in the air, tracing patterns of unearthly beauty.

She was singing the addio from *Bohème*—the aria which of all others I associate with her most intimately, and which, in the years to come, I was to hear her sing more times than I can remember. Long afterwards, at the end of a strange and wonderful night, when she had sung one of her many farewells, she was to stand in her dressing-room, a tired old woman, with diamonds blazing round her neck, against a background of orchids and lilies and red roses; and she was to send everyone out of her dressing-room so that she might speak to me alone.

"Beverley", she said, "I want you to make me a promise".

"What is it?"

"I want you to promise never to hear any other woman sing *Bohème*".

There were a number of replies I could have made . . . polished, flattering, as a courtier might reply to a queen. But I could only mutter: "I promise".

For a moment she said nothing; I had a fear that she would break down; her lips were tight set and her eyes stared straight ahead, as though she were searching the future and found it bleak. But the old Melba quality triumphed.

"That's that", she snapped. And then—on an ascending scale, like an angry thrush—"For God's sake, where's my maid?"

However all those things lay far ahead. We must return to that moment when I stood, young and inky and irresponsible, worshipping outside the door of her room.

Addio . . . Senza Rancor

The silver light faded in an incomparable diminuendo.

Suddenly, the door opened. I found myself blinking into the startled face of a middle-aged woman. And I heard the Voice demand, in tones that were far from silver:

"Who the devil are *you*?"

* * *

Melba introduced me to a new world, or rather, to a very old world. Just as Ned Lathom had given me my first glimpse of the sparkling, sequined crew who danced over the borders of Mayfair into the blue lights of Bohemia, just as Mrs. Greville was later to introduce me into a soberer and far more solid society, where a dinner-table could be, and often was, a centre of power-politics, so Melba, with a gesture, swept me back into the world of the Edwardians.

It was a peculiar experience for a very young man. I imagine that there can be nobody of my age or upbringing who has spent so many hours in small, shiny cabriolets, almost stifled under a mountain of sable rugs, listening to gossip about famous beauties who, if they were not actually in the grave, were sitting very close to the edge. They became so familiar to me, these ghosts, that I could only think of them by their Christian names. There was "darling Gladys"—pronounced Glaydis, who was the famous Lady de Grey, the adored of Jean de Reszke, and one of the last great leaders of London society. Lady de Grey sounded quite fabulous; she combined beauty and power with a sort of lofty naughtiness which must have been irresistible. My favourite story about her is laid in Paris. One night she had a whim to visit a quarter which was not at all the sort of quarter to be visited by ladies, in those prim days. There was no question of going in disguise; her height, her beauty, her breeding were not to be hidden under any conventional cloak. So what must be done? Obviously, the streets must be railed off, the French police must be called into service, and—for as long as the mood of naughtiness endured—the quarter in question must be the private preserve of her ladyship. Which was exactly what happened. To me, this is enchanting; it has the authentic ring of 1789.

Then there was Alfred de Rothschild—all gilt and plush and glamour, a sort of aesthetic Jew Süss, who used to pay Melba £1000 for a few songs after dinner, and having paid it, would take back the cheque, reinvest the proceeds, and return it to her a few weeks later, doubled. She often used to quote to me his favourite remark: "I made my money by selling too soon." I have often recalled it—too late.

Nor can I forget "darling Flo" who, as Mrs. Hwfa Williams, was best known to the world as one of King Edward's favourite hostesses. Darling Flo was something of a poppet, and I used to like going down to her house at Coombe, where, across the smooth-shaven lawns, the royal figure had so frequently stalked. She was—or seemed to me—immensely old, she was almost stone deaf, and she was invariably in a state of chronic impecuniosity. In spite of these drawbacks she was as gay as a cricket. She always talked a weird sort of Italian baby-language which she had made popular in Edwardian society (you can hear echoes of it in Vita Sackville-West's brilliant period-piece *The Edwardians*). Instead of saying: "I am tired", she would say "Flo is fatigato". Her husband was always called "Grey mousey". And "grey mousey" was often extremely "fatigato", particularly when the baliffs were drawing near.

"Millie" (Duchess of Sutherland), "Feo" (Lady Alington), "darling Daisy" (the Princess of Pless), and of course "Alice" (the Hon. Mrs. George Keppel), I came to know them all, by proxy. And, on the whole, I rather liked them. But I would not have listened so attentively to the stories about them if I had not realized there was money in them.

Melba, I decided, must write her autobiography, or rather, must permit me to write it for her. Her brain was a treasure-house of the sort of material for which editors, as Fleet Street had taught me, were prepared to pay through the nose. Hers was still a great name in England and America; the gossipy autobiography was at its highest peak of popularity; all I had to do was to take down these stories as she told them at the dinner-table, string them together, sprinkle them with an appropriate coating of sugar—for it was essential, if we were to obtain really large figures for the serial rights, that the central figure should be presented, not only with a golden voice but also with a golden heart—and then, take them into the market to seek the highest bidder.

There was only one drawback to my plan. Melba was sixty; she was touchy about her age; and when I first outlined the plan to her, she reacted unfavourably.

"It's a little early for *that!*" she snapped. "Anybody would think I was a hundred".

"But people write their autobiographies at any age".

"Not *me*. I know what people would say".

So did I. They were already saying it. But I also knew that if I could present her with a *fait accompli*, the glamour of appearing in the role of authoress would be irresistible. And so, a few months later, when she suddenly cabled from Australia asking me to go out to help her run her farewell opera season, I accepted.

It was to prove one of the major follies in a life that has been full of folly. But at the time it seemed a sensible thing to do, in spite of the arrival of a number of anonymous letters kindly suggesting that I must be her lover.

As a rule, any major move in the life of a writer provides him with "copy". From the stimulus of new sights and sounds the brain creates new patterns, or rather, it rearranges the old ones; for art is only the extension of the artist's personality in various forms of fancy dress. And one would have thought that a young writer, when handed a large continent for his inspection, would have been able to extract from it at least the material for an occasional short story.

But Australia gave me nothing—literally nothing, probably because I saw it through the bars of such a very gilded cage. Not that the continent has ever been a major source of inspiraton to the artist. Apart from that solitary and neglected masterpiece, *The Fortunes of Richard Mahoney*, by Henry Handel Richardson, Australia has always proved as arid in inspiration as its own deserts. True, there is D. H. Lawrence's *Kangaroo*, but even Lawrence's most hysterical disciples have never claimed for it much merit. As for painting, there is Hans Heysen, who plays pleasantly with the lights and shades of the ubiquitous gum tree. I have a pretty Hans Heysen that hangs in my study; I know of no other Australian artist worthy to hang beside him.

I hasten to add that I have no right to lay down the law, as I never saw the real Australia. Travelling through the continent with Melba was like travelling through France with Marie Antoinette; on the few occasions when it was possible to peer through the windows of the barouche a jewelled hand was laid on one's arm, demanding attention. There were momentary glimpses that I had—in periods of escape—which were stimulating and suggestive. I remember, for instance, a long, rough bar in Perth, with shavings on the wooden floor, filled with crude angular figures that had drifted in from the bush. It was a holiday; they were all in black, with sweeping black sombreros, swilling tumblers of whisky, cursing each other in their broad Australian accent—of all human intonations the most repulsive. This picture never fades; it has the sharpness and precision of a drawing by Cruikshank, to whose period it seems to belong. And though it is only a pin-point on the canvas of memory it has that luminous quality which might one day glow into a story.

There were glimpses, too, of startling natural beauty. From time to time I managed to escape to the woods when the mimosas were in bloom. (It is characteristic of Australia that the lovely word "mimosa", as light and feathery as the flower it celebrates, has been nationally rejected in favour of the ugly "wattle", which sounds like a kitchen utensil.) The time of the mimosas is Australia's *heure exquise*; it brings to the traveller the same sort of rapture as when, in the Holy Land, he finds whole hill-sides draped with the scarlet cloak of anemones, or when in Northern Bengal he walks under trees whose branches are laden, as by snow, with shining hosts of wild white orchids. The time of the mimosas is a time of light; the countless shades of yellow seem to blend into one great festival of sunshine; and as the wind blows through these winding, golden galleries, as a million silver leaves turn and flutter against a sky of pellucid blue, one is very near to heaven.

But such moments were few and far between. For ninety-nine hours out of the hundred I was chained to Melba's side, endeavouring to keep within reasonable bounds a temperament which grew more and more explosive as the opening of the opera season approached.

Perhaps I had better say a word about the background. We lived at Coombe Cottage, with a family background of George (her son), and his wife and daughter. Coombe was a pleasant, rambling building in the Colonial style, about twenty miles from Melbourne. I have a memory of tall, airy rooms, with highly polished floors in which one could see reflected the sparkle of the chandeliers. There was some good Louis Seize furniture, and a couple of Mason and Hamlin grand pianos, which were a constant source of joy. There were also a couple of English footmen, who were not a constant source of joy, because they hated each other and were always complaining of "the 'eat". Melba doted on one of them, oddly enough, because he looked so dissipated. "William looks so *pale*", she used to say to me. "So distinguished!" And then she would exercise her ingenuity in inventing all sorts of reasons why William presented this appearance.

I could find nothing in the Australian bush—by which we were entirely surrounded—which was likely to make *me* look very pale, still less very distinguished, and perhaps this was the source of my general *malaise*. I was bored to distraction, particularly at nights. We would come back from a day's rehearsal in which everything had gone wrong . . . ("that trombone, my dear, ought to be *deported*. . . . I refuse to believe that he doesn't do it on purpose") . . . and after a very heating dinner, often in solitude, we would sit down to a game of dominoes. Outside there was the lush Australian night, with all its purple shadows, and occasionally, from the distance, would come the call of a laughing jackass—which, in moments of especial bitterness I felt should be turned into Australia's national anthem. Mingled with this sound, from time to time, would come other sounds, human sounds, female sounds, to put it bluntly, shrieks—suggesting that William was up to something that would make him look even more pale and distinguished in the morning. And there we sat, playing dominoes.

"Was it for this", I asked myself—placing a six-five against her double six, and thereby relieving myself of a potential debt of elevenpence—"was it for this that I became President of the Oxford Union?" (More shrieks from the bush.) "Was it for this that as a schoolboy I sat up late at night under a placard traced with my own hand announcing the fact that 'Bismarck used to work till dawn'?" (A positive fusillade of shrieks from the bush, drawing from Melba the observation that: "William obviously has good blood".)

However, it was too late to draw back now. Besides, my main object in coming to Australia, to write Melba's autobiography, was slowly but surely accomplishing itself. I had managed to overcome her opposition, partly by enlarging on the wonderful publicity she would get, but mainly by persuading her that the book would not be classed as "Autobiography" but as "Memoirs". And though an "autobiography" might be very ageing— indeed, an open confession of senility, a book of "memoirs" was a sign of vitality, of positive sprightliness. Besides, I pointed out, it might be very profitable for her, as I was to do all the work and she was to take half the proceeds.[3]

She had curious ideas of what might interest the public. When I asked her to give me a few frank words about Tetrazzini, whom she detested and despised, she waved her hands and said:

"Say she was a charming artist! A *delicious* artist!"

I pointed out that only yesterday Melba had said that she looked like a cook and faked all her top notes.

"I can't *possibly* say things like that. I must be *generous*".

"Then what shall we say about Caruso?"

"Say he was a charming artist! A great voice! A *superb* voice!"

"But what about his habit of squeaking rubber balls in your ear when you were dying in the last act of *Bohème*?"

"Really! I couldn't say such things! So vulgar!"

And so it went on. Everybody had to go down as charming and delicious, whatever her true opinion of them might be. I felt that this was carrying the golden-hearted pose to extremes; nevertheless, I stuck to it manfully.

But one night I felt that I had had enough. It had been a particularly wearing day; she had indulged in a new wig for the role of Desdemona, and at the matinée it had kept on slipping over her forehead, stifling her, and making the final attentions of Othello almost superfluous. In addition, she had eaten a large and not quite ripe "Grannie Smith" apple—"so delicious, my dear Beverley, you do not eat nearly enough fruit"—and it was still—if the reader will forgive the word—"repeating". As a result, our dinner *à deux* had been a scowling and silent occasion, and afterwards she had flounced off to her room in a huff. No, she did *not* feel "up to" dominoes.

So I too retired, to jot down the memoirs of the previous day, which had been a fairly fruitful one. But suddenly I could bear it no longer. I looked round the lonely bedroom with its incongruous French furniture, its tiny bookcase of volumes of operatic reminiscence, and its mantelpiece loaded with photographs of Edwardian musical celebrities . . . ("A ma chère Nellie—souvenirs d'Adieu—Tosti", "A la voix de ma vie—Jean de Reszke", "A tout jamais—Caruso") . . . and I said to myself: "To hell with it all. I've had a life myself. It's as good as hers. It's better. It's gayer, livelier, more highly coloured. I'll write it!"

There and then, in my pyjamas, I went over to the desk—shook my fountain pen, which was empty, dipped it in the ink-pot which, naturally, like all ink-pots in the houses of prima donnas, was full of dust, iron filings and a quantity of lead pellets, seized a pencil, and wrote the first words of the first book which was to entitle me to join the rococo crowd that gains the eminence of *Who's Who*.

Twenty-five seems to me to be the latest age at which anybody should write an autobiography.

Yes—it was certainly a gesture of defiance. And maybe you who are reading these words will say that the young author was right, and that the first book of memoirs should also have been the last. But having started I cannot stop. The memories crowd too thickly about me.

Evensong

One day—it was Melba's birthday, and though she never told anybody her age, the anniversary always put her in a despairing mood—she said to me with a catch in her throat: "You have never heard me sing." It must have cost her a great deal to make that confession. She meant, of course, that I had never heard her in the days of her glory.

But I *was* to hear her in the days of her glory. I am not attempting a paradox; I am narrating a miracle.

It happened a year later, which means that we must now leave Australia—not, I should imagine, with much regret.

The miracle must wait for a moment, while I attempt to fill in the background.

I came back alone, via America, stayed long enough in New York to sell the memoirs to *Liberty*, and—which was more important in the long run—to sell *Twenty-Five* to George Doran. After which I returned to London, to my old job.

But not quite to my old job. Whatever Australia may not have done for me, it did at least give some power of self-assertion. One cannot live for half a year with a prima donna without a violent reaction. To everybody's surprise, including my own, I bounded into Northcliffe House like a lion, and asked Falk for a great deal more money than I had ever had before, got it, demanded to be made dramatic critic, and got that too.

"Soon you'll be showing us how to sing Faust," observed Falk, grimly.

Bouncing out again, I gave notice to the landlady of my flat, and—fortified by the advance from *Liberty*—took a seven-year lease of an elegant little house in Westminister. As if that were not enough, I went out very early on the following morning and bought a small motor-car. . . .

As a final gesture I acquired a manservant, and this was one of the few gilt-edged investments I ever made. Reginald Arthur Gaskin is still with me, which probably says more for his sense of loyalty and friendship than for his business acumen. . . .

A house—a car—a manservant; one was progressing. Sometimes, like all young men who earn their living by the pen, I had tremors of anxiety. I would pause at the front door, and stare up at the house, with its windows that had to be cleaned, its roof that had to be repaired, its rates that had to be paid, and I would think: "All this, and the car, and Gaskin and heaven knows what else, has to come out of my head. I have no other means of support than selling words on paper. What will happen if one day the world will no longer pay for those words?" Then, as though to dispel these forebodings, a girl would dance down the street in a red hat, or a snatch of song would echo from a neighbouring window, and I would tell myself that the very thought of failure, now, was grotesque. The world was too full of "a number of things," and I had no doubts of my capacity as a reporter.

And now we can tell the story of the "miracle" which I mentioned at the beginning of the chapter.

Soon after returning to London I decided to take a short holiday in Venice. Australia had parched my mind; I wanted a deep draught of European civilization.

Hardly had I arrived, and established myself in a tiny apartment overlooking the Grand Canal, when a telegram came from Melba:

TOUCHED THOUGHT ARRIVING EXCELSIOR EARLY NEXT WEEK YOU MUST JOIN ME.

The cryptic beginning of this message deserves a moment's explanation. Melba had a Scotch aversion to wasting money on telegrams; she would spend half an hour, as though she were doing a crossword puzzle, trying to delete unnecessary words. Sometimes she cut out so much that the telegram, when it arrived, was completely incomprehensible to its recipient, with the result that he or she had to send another telegram seeking an elucidation.

One day, in a moment of inspiration, she thought of the phrase "Touched thought." This, being interpreted, meant "I am touched by your thought."

"That says everything!" she cried, clapping her hands. "Don't you agree?"

I did not. To me it had a slightly psychic echo, as though she had been fiddling about with ectoplasm, but naturally I did not say so.

So, in future "touched thought" it was. Sometimes, in moments of expansion, it would become "deeply touched thought," and occasionally, to persons of special importance, "deeply touched your thought."

One dreadful mishap resulted from this practice. Melba received a letter from a woman who had just arrived from Australia, asking her to dine on the same night. With the letter (as an excuse for the shortness of the invitation), was an immense basket of yellow orchids, which even in those days must have cost at least thirty guineas.

"I certainly shan't dine with that woman," cried Melba, snatching the basket and hurrying it into the drawing-room. "She's one of the people who say I drink. Send her a telegram—'Regret indisposed.' "

I glanced at the glittering blaze of blossom. "Oughtn't you to thank her for the flowers?"

Melba snorted. "You can add 'touched thought.' It'll all come into twelve words."

Although "touched thought" at a penny a word seemed a hardly adequate acknowledgment of thirty guineas' worth of superb Cymbidiums, these were the words which I sent over the telephone. Unfortunately, they were not the words which arrived at the other end.

Here is the telegram as it was actually delivered—to a woman, remember, who had made the suggestion that Melba drank (which was, of course, absurd).

REGRET INDISPOSED TOUCHED PORT

Maybe that telegram was worth the Cymbidiums; she dined out on it for weeks.

I must apologize to the reader for the tardiness of the miracle. Here it is at last.

Melba arrived in great form, and in spite of my feeble protests I was swept out of my quiet apartment and transported to the Excelsior on the Lido. ("So much more healthy, my dear, all those mosquitoes. Who lent you the apartment? Catherine d'Erlanger? Well—what can you expect?")

The connection between the Baroness d'Erlanger and mosquitoes would not have suggested itself to anybody but a prima donna.

Soon the familiar bustle was in full swing. Gondolas arrived, filled to the brim with roses, behind which could be seen elderly Italian admirers, usually impoverished noblemen, twirling their moustaches. Composers arrived, also of the greatest antiquity, bowing and creaking in her salon, and producing from their pockets, like conjurers, songs which they had dedicated to her. These, with the most touching thanks, she promised to sing. As soon as they had gone she threw them into the waste-paper basket with the single word "Muck!"

And then, of course, there must be a concert. Moreover, the concert must be held on the Grand Canal. How romantic—to sing in a gondola by moonlight! What a wonderful story it would make! "I shall wear my new Worth, with the silver cape. You will be inspired, my dear Beverley!" I doubted it; in fact, I thought the whole idea was crazy. Melba, normally, had a very proper horror of singing in the open air; her voice, particularly at that period, was not of the fabric with which she could afford to play tricks. As for singing on the Grand Canal—it was fantastic. She would have to compete with the hooting of the steamships, the cries of the gondoliers, and all the bustle of a great city. She thought that all these things would automatically stop as soon as she began to sing, as though she were a sort of vocal Canute. I knew better. I had not the courage to tell her so, which was a pity, for when the concert was given, after endless fusses and bothers, it was a most regrettable farce.

But a few days *before* the concert the miracle occurred.

I had been charged with the business of finding an accompanist. That proved easier than one might have expected, for George Copeland, a superb American pianist, was staying in Venice at the time, and said that he would be only too honoured to play for her. The task of finding a piano was more difficult; pianos in Venice are few and far between; and perhaps that is just as well, for the mists of the lagoons enter into their souls, and cause them, when played, to emit sounds like the wailing of the damned. It was only after several days of search, tiptoeing through strange palazzos, under ceilings by Tiepolo, and braving a quantity of these highly decorated infernal machines, that I eventually found a fairly adequate Steinway. It was in an apartment on the Grand Canal.

And now at long last for the miracle, which happened on the following day when Melba, Copeland and I arrived at the apartment to rehearse. It could not have had a more unpropitious beginning. It was very early in the morning, just after nine o'clock, and the concierge had gone out marketing, so that we had to wait for nearly half an hour in the hall, while Melba fumed and fretted against the impossibility of Italy and everything Italian. When he at last returned, he evidently regarded us with the gravest suspicion, as though we had come to steal the *bibelots*, and only consented to leave the room after a substantial bribe. To make matters worse, Melba had a rash on the back of her hand, which was due to an over-indulgence in *scampi à la Milanaise*, and she kept on scratching it and muttering under her breath.

Copeland went to the piano. "What shall we begin with?"

"It doesn't matter."

"The Duparc 'Clair de lune'?"

She shrugged her shoulders, nodded, and walked to the window.

"This is going to be hell," I thought, settling myself in an obscure corner.

He began the lovely lilting accompaniment. She took a deep breath, lifted her chin, opened her lips.

And then—I must fall back on the phrase—the world stood still.

For the voice that floated into the room was the voice that dimly, as through a veil, I had heard in the old gramophone records; here it was, in all its untarnished glory, the voice of the young Melba. So sudden was the shock, so totally unexpected the impact of this rapturous sound, that for a moment Copeland's fingers stumbled, for he could hardly believe his ears. Then he too was swept into the magic—and for a while the three of us were away on wings, out of the world.

I dared not look at her. I stared out of the window on to the waters of the Canal, thanking God for this moment. The whole world seemed to be bathed in silver—silver on the water, silver on the sails, most of all in the air we breathed, for it was as though the room were shining with music. In a sort of dream I realized that people were beginning to stop outside, with fingers to their lips; gondolas were edging silently towards the window, and in them the gondoliers stood with wide eyes and open mouths, as though they were in some angelic presence.

The music ended; the little group outside remained silent, spellbound; there was only the lapping of the water on the steps of the canal. Then, with exquisite tact, Copeland played, very softly, the introduction to the lovely aubade from the *Roi d' Ys*. And again, the voice came, flawless, with the dew on it. And now I slowly turned to watch her. She had on her face an expression of the most extraordinary surprise; she seemed to be not so much singing as *listening*; her eyes strayed round the room, she even turned behind her, as though seeking the source of this enchantment. But always the music flowed on. At the end, quite carelessly, with that incredible assurance which once caused Jean de Reszke to coin the phrase *l'attaque impertinente*, she sang the trill on G, drifted to the top C, held it diminuendo . . . fading, fading . . . till it vanished like a star that is quenched.

And now Copeland grew bolder. Something, quite evidently, was happening, something that might never happen again. It was something that could not—*must* not—be put into words; to speak would have been to break the spell. We were held together only by a thin thread of music, and only while the music lasted were we safe.

He played the opening phrase of "Depuis le Jour"—an aria which some critics, today, pretend to find shallow and pretentious, perhaps because they have never heard it sung as Melba sang it then. Between her and Copeland, at that moment, there must have been some sort of psychic understanding, for the opening phrase of the aria, as the reader will recollect, consists only of a single spread chord and its fifth; it is little more than a key note, and unless the singer were waiting for it there is no reason why she should know what she was expected to sing. Yet without a moment's hesitation the voice echoed the phrase and soared into the lovely song, that is like a winding staircase of melody, losing itself in heights that are unattainable to ordinary mortals. . . .

> Depuis le jour ou je me suis donnée
> Toute fleurie me semble ma destinée

I was near to tears.

"It can't go on—it's impossible," I muttered to myelf. "Something will snap. It's uncanny. It may be the end . . . it may be the swan song." Almost I wanted her to stop.

But it went on.

By now, the listening crowd stretched far out into the canal, held there, spellbound, in the bright sunlight—utterly silent. At least, that is how my memory recalls it. Obviously there must have been *some* sound apart from the lapping of the water—the occasional hoot of a *vaporetto*, or the cry of a gondolier sweeping out a *piccolo canale*. But the effect was of silence, of fingers to the lips. Even the bolder spirits, who tied up to the steps, steered their way in silence, and then stayed still, staring up to the sky.

The song died away in an incomparable diminuendo.

> Et je tremble délicieusement
> Au souvenir d'amour.

Then for the first time Copeland spoke.

"You are singing . . . exceptionally," he whispered.

She nodded. She still wore that strange expression of bewilderment, as though she were asking herself "Who is it who has been singing? Whence is the music coming?"

He spoke again. "Do you feel . . . like this?"

To my astonishment, and to my dismay, he sketched the opening phrase of the recitatif from the Mad Scene in *Lucia*. "But no," I wanted to cry, "that is madness. She has not sung it for ten, for twenty years. It is the supreme test—it is exhausting even for the youngest, most brilliant coloratura. You are setting her an impossible task, you will shatter this wonderful moment for ever."

He paused. The echo of the chords trembled in the air.

Then, she nodded. And she sang.

It was the culmination of the miracle. Many times have I heard the Mad Scene—by Tetrazzini, by Galli-Curci, by Toti del Monte. Engraved on my memory are all the spiral staircases of its roulades, the fountains of its cadenzas. I know all its pitfalls—the devilish little breath-traps in which it abounds. Never, never have I heard it sung as Melba sang it then, at the age of sixty-one, in the middle of the morning, unrehearsed, with a rash on her hands.

And then, without any warning, in the middle of a scale, she stopped. The silence was so sudden that it hurt. I turned to see what had happened. She was standing there, with her hand to her throat, staring before her, as though she were looking into some great distance.

Slowly she shook her head. I saw her lips move; she whispered, "No more." She seemed to be speaking not for that moment only, but for all time. "No more," she said again. "This," I felt, "is the last farewell."

Copeland was crying, quite unashamedly. The moment was so overwhelming in its emotion that I felt that something must be done, and done quickly, to save it from bathos. And then I remembered the crowd outside. I went up to her, took her by the hand, and led her to the window. As soon as they saw her there was a burst of cheering from a thousand warm Italian throats, and all the tightly packed gondolas blossomed with fluttering handkerchiefs and waving hands. "Viva! Viva!" they cried. "Bis! Bis!"

But there could be no "bis." It had been for the last time.

* * *

Perhaps these memories should end on this note of high romance; but it would be a false one. She was not a romantic woman, there was hardly a grain of poetry in her temperament, which was shrewd and down-to-earth, and even the word "Farewell," for her, was little more than a business asset.

She played astonishing tricks with this word. To the man in the street the word "farewell" means what it says; to a prima donna it means anything she cares to make it. If Melba gave one Farewell she must have given fifty. Once I reproved her for this practice, with grievous results. She used to get me to write appropriate little messages to the press on these occasions, and one day, shortly before the latest of the many Farewells, she rang me up in a state of great excitement and demanded to see me at once. I was very busy, and was irritated to discover, on my arrival, that all she wanted was yet another of the familiar *adieux*.

I suggested, rather tersely, that perhaps we might use one of the messages we had used before.

Her eyes opened wide in what appeared to be genuine astonishment.

"But I have *never* said Farewell before!"

This was really a little too much. I mentioned the last occasion.

"You must be mad! *That* was 'prior to the Australian tour.' It said so distinctly on the placards. And the one before that was 'prior to the American tour.'"

"And this one?"

"This one is Farewell to the Albert Hall. That means it's Farewell for ever." Her voice choked with emotion. "I shall never sing in London again."

She did, of course, constantly.

One of the most poignant gramophone records ever made was on the occasion of Melba's Farewell to Covent Garden. That really *was* a Farewell, for she never sang in opera again. It was an unforgettable occasion; the packed audience, led by the King and Queen, glittered as it had seldom glittered before and had certainly never glittered since. But the most glittering thing of all was the voice. It happened, thank God, to be one of her "good" nights, and they were getting few and far between. For days before I had sweated blood in case there should be any of the tell-tale signs that I knew so well—the forcing of the notes E and F where the middle register merges into the top, the woodiness of the high notes when they were sung forte, most of all, the agonizing crack in the addio. But as soon as she opened her mouth I sighed with relief, sat back and relaxed. It was going to be all right. How much more than "all right" it was is proved by the gramophone disc, which is a recording of parts of the actual performance. Even in this the voice has an unearthly sheen, it is like a spirit drifting slowly away into a moonlit distance.

On the other side of the disc is Melba's Farewell Speech. I feel a special interest in this as I wrote it for her. We had a fierce row about it. She had written a speech herself which she read to me, with great pride. It was quite dreadful. It was so filled with royal highnesses, excellencies and what not that it sounded like a court circular.

I said to her: "You want to cut out all those people. There's only one man you need mention—Austin."

"What about Austin?" she snapped.

"You pointed him out to me the other day. You told me that he'd shown you into your carriage at the stage door for forty years. He's your man."

"I've never heard of anything so ridiculous in my life."

Nevertheless, she did as she was told. And Austin brought down the house.

It was inevitable, when Melba died, that I should write a novel about a prima donna. Not to have done so would have been a dereliction of my duty as an artist. A great hullabaloo is always raised when a novelist or a playwright introduces into his work some character who is obviously drawn from life. That is a lot of hypocritical nonsense. There are no manners in art—there is only style. The men or women whom he has chosen should feel honoured, even if he has transfixed them like butterflies to a board.

It is possible to be a gentleman on Mondays and a cad on Tuesdays; the finest artists are cads all the time. Boswell had his days off—there are passages in those salty pages when I feel his pen wavers, pauses and halts, brought to a full-stop by the sudden tug of gentility at his elbow. Thank God they are few and far between.

So, after a decent interval had elapsed, I went down to Roquebrune and wrote *Evensong*. I stayed alone at a little hotel called the Maison Imbert, in a tiny room perched on the edge of the cliff, writing three thousand words a day, in conditions of complete perfection—sunshine, solitude, the scent of roses, a glass of red wine by my side. *Evensong* was easier to write than any other book I ever attempted, for though the story I invented was completely imaginary, I knew the central figure so intimately that she took sole charge of the action. Nor, must I add, did I create a caricature. If some of Melba's friends who, afterwards, were bitterest in their comments on my picture of her, could glance, even for a few moments, at the letters which she wrote to me about *them*—letters hastily scribbled in pencil and filled with the most hysterical abuse—they might not be so loud in their own accusations.

When *Evensong* was published it had a considerable success, as a book, as a film and as a play. And I should be the last to deny that part of its success—though I hope only a minor part—was a *succès de scandale*.

I was on the stage of the Arts Theatre, rehearsing Maurice Evans in the first act of my play *Avalanche*, when I first learned of the furore which *Evensong* had created in Australia.

A young reporter from some press agency suddenly bounded out of the wings waving a sheaf of telegrams in my face. "Say, Mr. Nichols," he said, "Australia's gone up in smoke about your book."

That seemed very gratifying. But as I read the telegrams, I was not so sure. They passed the bounds of reason; they were like the reports of a witch-hunt. Even the respectable *Argus*, which is a rather stodgy Australian equivalent of *The Times*, had delivered itself of a leading article which portrayed me as a blend of Nero and Crippen.

If only the Australians could have heard how Melba herself used to rail against her own country! If only I had possessed a gramophone record of the mocking, bitter invective which she poured out upon Australia and everything Australian! By comparison, Mrs. Trollope's assaults on Victorian America were the sweetest milk of human charity.

I found myself in the curious position of having to defend her own countrymen against her onslaughts.

"They may be crude," I would say, "but they're incredibly warm-hearted and hospitable, and they're obviously anxious to learn."

She brushed such protest aside.

"They're hopeless . . . hopeless!" According to her, there was not a single house in Australia which showed the least evidence of taste. There was only one restaurant in the whole continent where one could eat a civilized meal—and that was an obscure little Italian joint in a Melbourne side-street. No—there was *one* other—a tea-shop in Sydney, where one had excellent lobsters. Melba used to eat far too much lobster, and after each feast she would sit back, smacking her lips and saying: "Delicious—like *nuts.*" But an hour or two later, when she was paying the price of her indiscretion, her face would cloud, and she would say: "I'm quite certain there was something wrong with those lobsters." There was, of course, nothing wrong with them, except that she had eaten the better part of mine as well as her own.

"Why did I ever come back? It is a desert—there is nothing, *nobody!*" How often have I heard such cries of despair—rising in an incomparable treble that was made all the more appealing by the faint hint of an Australian accent.

And yet, she must have loved something about it, for it was there that she returned to die, in the shadow of the Blue Mountains, near the hall in which, as a schoolgirl, she had given her first concert. There was a fair amount of applause at that concert, but she told me that the only criticism she received came from one of her school mates. It was hardly a compliment. "Nellie!" said the child severely, "I could see your drawers!"

She was a strange creature—stormy, arrogant but somehow endearing. What sort of woman she would have been, without her voice, no man can guess. It does not matter very much.

NOTES

1. I have written a full account of this remarkable case in *Twenty-Five* (Jonathan Cape).

2. *Bel Canto*, as a matter of passing interest, was the title given to the German edition of *Evensong*, which, with most of my other German translations, was afterwards banned by Hitler.

3. It was. When it was at last finished, under the title *Melodies and Memories*, the American magazine *Liberty* bought the serial rights for a sum which was not much for Melba, but was a lot for me.

INTERVIEWS

Melba was always good copy. Numerous interviews with the singer can be found in the files of the Australian press. A few samples will serve to set the tone.

MELBA LOOKS BACK ON MAGIC MOMENTS IN HER GREAT CAREER

FRANK A. RUSSELL

There was nothing of the "falling star" about Melba as she talked to me in the music room at Coombe. Around us, and in every other room, there were beautiful objects, the acquisition of which recalled milestones in the remarkable career of the woman who was preparing to close one chapter—not the last—of it.

"The greatest trouble of the artist who is nearing the close of her career is to secure a graceful exit," said Dame Nellie, after explaining her reasons for the momentous step she was about to take. "It is tragic to wait till the audience have clattered out, and the electrician begins to snap off the lights.

"I prefer to say my farewell while people can still feel pleasure in what I can do; to leave them with a recollection that does justice to me and to them."

Remembering certain world-famous artists whom I had had the misfortune to hear at their last and worst, I could not doubt the wisdom of her decision. Something of the sadness of her renunciation involved touched me, but not for long. For suddenly Melba's voice rang out in an aria from *Traviata*. The voice was Melba's, but with a difference. No one had ever heard her notes crack before. The song ceased, providentially, and Dame Nellie burst out laughing.

"That was how _____ sounded when I heard her in London," she explained, "and yet she had a world tour afterwards. And this is how poor old

From: Frank A. Russell, "Melba Looks Back on Magic Moments in Her Great Career," *The Herald* (Melbourne), October 13, 1924. Reprinted by permission of The Herald and Weekly Times Ltd.

_____ sang, while she still was reckoned a great artist." Once more, in the same aria, Melba with delightful comedy, distorted the music.

"But Patti! Ah! Patti!" And the true, sweet Melba notes fell softly on the air, phrasing true, tone delightful. She trilled to a close, with a whisper— "Dear Patti!"

I asked a question, and the years rolled back for me as Melba recalled the rich past, embroidered with triumphs. Since 1884, when she had sung in Melbourne as Mrs. Walter [sic] Armstrong, and only one critic had dared to prophesy great things for her, if she should leave her own country, she had made the world laugh and cry. Obscure daughter of an unknown Australian might have appeared to most English people an apt description of the young girl who arrived with her father, David Mitchell, to see if London would not give her the opportunity Melbourne denied her.

"I was very unhappy in those days," said Dame Nellie, as she completed a sad little picture of her arrival in London, which turned coldly away from her.

"My father was against my taking up professional singing. I had pestered him and pestered him to give me the chance, and he gave in to me, as he nearly always used to do. But it seemed a hopeless fight. Doors would not open, and no one cared to listen to me and try me out. It was the crossroads for me. Do you know that it was only the veriest chance that saved me from returning to a humdrum suburban life after all my fine ambitions? It really was. My father was quite determined to go back, and I had not a penny apart from him.

"I will go if Marchesi says I am not likely to make a success," I bargained, and at last he agreed. Madame Wiedermann had given me a letter to Marchesi, her own teacher, and it is to Madame Wiedermann that I owe what followed.

"I sent my letter, and an interview was arranged. Marchesi looked at me when I came in. She was not cordial." Once more Melba became the comedienne, and with pursed-up lips and puffed-out cheeks she acted the part of the great little teacher of singing.

"I sang that very aria from *Traviata* I sang just now, and, to my horror, in the very middle of it, Marchesi turned and marched out. I thought my goose was cooked. My last hope had departed, when in popped Marchesi again, dragging by the hand a little man, whom I found to be her husband.

" 'Have the kindness, madame, to sing that song once more,' she said, and I sang it again. Marchesi turned to the little man and said sotto voce, 'Did not I tell you, she is a star?'

"That was my first great moment," pronounced Melba, whose life thereafter was to contain "moments" enough. "Think of what it meant to the little provincial singer, who was about to be dragged back to Melbourne a fizzle. It was wonderful!"

"And the next great 'moment?' " I asked. Then Melba began to describe the past. In vivid phrase she made live for me the successive steps by which she became the idol of the musical world. It was as though we sat in a darkened room and looked out and down a lit corridor to the brilliant chamber of her youth.

"There was another stumbling-block," she explained, and it seems extraordinary to reflect that this was the rooted objection of her Scotch father to any participation in theatrical performances. Marchesi wished to train her for opera, whereas Mr. Mitchell would only yield a consent, unwilling at that, to concerts and oratorios. However, woman's wit triumphed, and the studies for opera went on in secret.

"The next great moment was my real debut in Brussels," Dame Nellie went on. "I sang the role of Gilda in *Rigoletto*. It may seem foolish to you, but I honestly had not the faintest idea of what was in store for me. The first shock was in seeing my name so large and important! 'But why? why?' I asked. 'Because you are the star, Madame,' was the reply.

"The next day was a tremendous one for me. I had sung in a dream; the people were pleased; there was a furore, but what I could not believe was that I had become famous. Me! Impossible!

"It seems another person, as I look back. I remember another big 'moment' in the Paris Opera House. Two of my sisters had just arrived from Australia. They had not any conception that little Nellie Mitchell was a personage, and when the curtain went up and down about sixty times, and they saw hundreds of people yelling and applauding as only a French audience can, you may imagine their surprise. The *Figaro* next morning had a special paragraph about their consternation. What a night that was! Gounod himself was in the house. Let me tell you this. A triumph is not a triumph until one is able to demonstrate it to one's family—always the last to believe that their duckling is a swan.

"One's country is the same as the family in this respect," smiled Melba. "Success has to be underlined by the world at large before your own country will believe in it."

Dame Nellie, who knows her world, admires the United States, because it looks out for its own. To be an American is in itself a title to regard; but to be an American with talent is to have a sure claim to admiration and advertisement. Australia might well take a leaf out of their book in this respect.

"Would you like to see my very first public criticism?" she asked.

The criticism, from the Richmond *Australasian*, was written when Melba was ten. It deserves a place in our historical archives.

"Little Miss Mitchell, a young lady of ten years, who did not content herself with singing in first-rate style 'Can't You Dance the Polka?' but also accompanied herself on the piano, was, we think, the gem of the evening, and rightly deserved the spontaneous encore she received and responded to by singing 'Comin' Thro' the Rye.' It took the audience by surprise to hear such sweet notes coming from a mere child. The incomparable Miss Mitchell, in singing 'Barney O'Hea,' quite outdid her former effort. She is indeed a musical prodigy, and she will make crowded houses whenever she is announced again."

The critic was right. She has had a few crowded houses since.

Later, walking through the Coombe gardens, I asked Melba what would have happened if Marchesi had been inaccessible.

"What would have been your choice of a career if singing had been denied you?"

"I should have gone in for decorating," was the instant reply, and she told me with glee of a magnificent offer she had received from a big London firm to decorate for them.

On the whole, however, the world will agree that Melba's best decoration is that she weaves magically on an operatic score!

MELBA ON LIFE AFTER DEATH: "THE TRUE, ETERNAL ME"

NELLIE MELBA

Music Which Showed Spirit World

In an article in the *Weekly Dispatch* on "When I Am Dead" Dame Nellie Melba writes:

" 'Grinning at the roots of daisies,' What did that mean? Well I remember when I heard the brutal phrase first. I was a child, walking the Australian bush, listening to grown-ups discussing a dying acquaintance. The phrase burnt itself into my childish mentality, causing a grotesquely vivid, frightening picture. In my independent mind it caused an early silent rebellion against my Presbyterian parents' unbending creed, with its Scottish gloom and conventional heavens and hells, in accordance with which my father, fearing contamination, hurried me and mother to a side street when Roman Catholics passed.

"I couldn't believe the dead would really burn in hell; I couldn't believe that God was so cruel. When a child I imagined God to be a tall, grey-bearded man, with eyes of infinite tenderness, seated on a throne of gold against the flaming crimsons and purples of an Australian sunset which merged into divine glory behind his head. That vision has not faded. It seems more human now than H. G. Wells's veiled being or the Spiritualists' abstract deductions.

From: Nellie Melba, "Melba on Life after Death: 'The True, Eternal Me,' " *The Herald* (Melbourne), October 26, 1925. Reprinted by permission of The Herald and Weekly Times Ltd.

"I AM IMMORTAL"

"I always instinctively believed in life after death. I cannot believe that God, who painted the rose, hung the stars in the summer night and breathed eternal music into the sea, is capable of mocking creatures by denying immortality.

"I do not understand why he sends a child to die lingeringly of disease, but in my instincts there flames up a torch, like moments of great emotion, shedding light through the open door leading to eternity. It is then that I know I am immortal.

"Music can light such a torch. Once, listening to Parsifal, I was thrown into a trance, when I entered the spiritual world. Only the music stopping recalled me. I know the best in me will live and the worst die. There may be fires to pass tempests to face, but there is something that fire cannot burn nor storm quench. Call it soul, ego, astral body—what you will. I call it the true eternal me."

MELBA'S INDICTMENT: "OUR MUSICAL REPUTATION A MYTH"

NELLIE MELBA

Ashamed of Us

Australians pride themselves on their musical reputation. We have produced a Melba, a Florence Austral, an Ada Crossley, and their resounding fame has reflected glory on the country whence they came. But have we any real title to be considered among the really musical nations?

Dame Nellie Melba, who returned to Melbourne yesterday after a week's visit to Adelaide, was in a mood to have answered these questions in the negative. Her son, Mr. George Armstrong, met her at Spencer Street.

"Friedmann was giving concerts over there," she explained, "and I felt ashamed of my countrymen and women. What neglect! Here was one of the finest artists in the world—wonderful man, and yet he might have been a nobody, so far as public interest was concerned. I did what I could, but it was saddening to see such apathy.

"What do we Australians want, if a Zimbalist, a Friedman is not good enough for us?"

> "Are we only going to patronise musicians if they are made fashionable? It looks like it."

From: Nellie Melba, "Melba's Indictment: 'Our Musical Reputation a Myth,' " *The Herald* (Melbourne), September 5, 1927. Reprinted by permission of The Herald and Weekly Times Ltd.

"It is time someone—one of themselves—told Australians some of their shortcomings. A visitor will not hurt their feelings by telling the truth; a foreigner they will not listen to. Well, they shall listen to me."

"ONLY A MYTH"

"It hurts me, it shames me, for my fellow-Australians to see a man like Zimbalist or Friedmann come here both men who never play but to packed, enthusiastic audiences, and to have them realise that our musical appreciation is only a myth. We have been so fortunate in hearing the world's best, but how long can we expect such men and women to travel all this way to coldness and neglect?

"It is scandalous. It is part of the slackness that is getting hold of this country. I will have more to say about it—no, not just now, but soon. I owe so much to this country that I owe it also to her to have the courage to speak out, even if the truth hurts.

"If more of us big people—yes, I can say that—dared to speak out, it would do a great deal of good. I love my country too much to be silent."

WHERE IS HAPPINESS? IS IT IN FAME?

NELLIE MELBA

Happiness is to be found in a thousand ways, and fame is only one of them. If fame in itself were the only path to content of mind, I suppose my content would wane gradually as the years pass, and other singers take the audiences of the world by storm; but that is not the case.

I need not say that I, whose life has been spent singing to the world, am filled with sadness now that I realise that I must sing my last before the public I have learnt to love. But it is a happy kind of sadness if such a thing is possible—it is not regret; I do not say to myself—"I would like to have all my fame over again." That would merely be selfish and morbid, and the very antithesis of happiness. Rather I will look forward with happy anticipation to the young singers who will sway the world tomorrow as in the past. I looked forward to my own ambitious future. I would even like to tell them some of the things which they can avoid, which brought me sorrow because I did not avoid them.

Asking too much of fame is one of these. Years ago, when I ran about in the sunshine, humming, always humming, a tomboy of the Australian bush, my dreams showed me myself as the centre of an applauding throng, hemmed in with masses of bouquets, surrounded by acclaiming friends, ideally happy. I pictured myself then, taking wonderful singing parts in the world's most famous operas. I was wild for joy when, quite early in my career, I was given the role of Brünnhilde in Wagner's *Siegfried*. I realised

From: Nellie Melba, "Where Is Happiness? Is It in Fame?" *The Herald* (Melbourne), September 10, 1927. Reprinted by permission of The Herald and Weekly Times Ltd.

that it was divine music, and for me the chance to become famous in a night, but when I took the part, I found that I ought never to have attempted it. The physical strain was too great, and, had I continued to sing it, I should have lost my voice in a very short time. One critic said that it was "like seeing a piece of Dresden china attacked by a bull." You can imagine my feelings of utter misery next morning when I saw the unfavorable reports of my performance in the papers—those papers which I had prayed would welcome me as a coming prima donna. I cried, of course, but it taught me one of the most valuable lessons in life. I learnt not to be heartbroken over failures, for, however many times one may fail, there are still unbounded chances of success in the future, and the successes are all the sweeter when they come. I learnt to value my failures just as much as my triumphs, and that quality is essential if you would find happiness.

Where is happiness? Why, it is to be found in the world all about us, in the stillness of a summer night, in the pride of a good thing done, in the flush of a summer dawn, the following of an ideal, the strong grip of a friend, the perfect heart of a rose, or the wild sweetness of a song. It is always very near, you may come upon it at the very next turn of the road, it is often within the reach of you if you but stretch out your hand. The secret of finding it? I cannot tell you. I know that fame alone does not bring it, and I know that it is within the reach of all, rich or poor, celebrated or unknown. Only have courage and conviction, tenacity and kindliness, a ready smile and a willingness to lend a hand to one less fortunate in the race. It lies partly in doing your job, with all your ability, refusing to despair however black things may seem, and going half-way to the next turn of the road yourself. Often it is surprising to find how quickly happiness comes tripping more than half-way to meet you.

There was a time when I thought that if I were ever acclaimed by the world as one of its great singers, if in fact, I ever won real fame, I should attain the greatest happiness possible. Do you know what achievement of that fame has meant to me? I have had to deny myself pleasures of every kind, I have had to wander from capital to capital in the wearying spotlights of the world, when other women have been able to choose the joys and the wonder of home. I have had to face hostility, to hear lies and not answer them, to be the victim of scandals, which tortured the more because they were so utterly undeserved, and force a smile when it was my woman's privilege to weep. This is Fame. But I do not regret it—the sunshine was the more joyous in contrast to the shadow.

No one could find happiness in eternal sunshine. We all of us resent the sorrows of life, but without them we should have no keen appreciation of its joys. Had I not had times of shadow, I should never have been a great artist. I should never have gained the happiness which followed increased confidence when I began to find that my interpretation of roles, like Desdemona in Verdi's *Othello*, was becoming something more than a mere matter of singing, something which I felt was instinct with the passion of life itself. I have lived for art, I have turned everything good or bad to the service of my art, and in so doing I have found happiness. It would seem that this elusive thing comes not merely when one is working for fame, but when one is working sincerely for anything. It is useless to rail at the pain of life, because happiness will follow and contrast it.

Always in these dark moments one learns something. One's character is deepened. One approaches a step nearer to that perfect understanding and tranquillity of mind, triumphant over circumstances, which is the only true happiness.

THE DEATH OF NELLIE MELBA

Melba made her final trip to Australia in the fall of 1930. She became ill a few days before her ship, the *Cathay*, arrived at Perth's port of Freemantle, and she was so ill that her doctor forbade her landing. This was duly reported in the *New York Times* on November 5, and almost daily bulletins on her condition continued to appear, carried by the wire services throughout the world. On November 11 it was reported that she had been placed in a Melbourne hospital; subsequent reports stated that she had returned to Coombe Cottage at Lilydale. In January 1931 she decided to pay her sister Annie a visit in Moss Vale, N.S.W., but when she got to Sydney she was too ill to go on and was placed in St. Vincent's Hospital. Here it was found that she was suffering from paratyphoid, apparently contracted the previous year on a visit to Egypt. Again, the world's newspapers carried daily bulletins, culminating with the front-page headlines of February 23, 1931: "DAME NELLIE MELBA DIES IN AUSTRALIA." There followed a stream of editorials, obituaries, and career reviews by noted critics in the musical magazines of the day, a sampling of which is presented in the section that follows.

THE ART OF MELBA

W. J. HENDERSON

When the news of Nellie Melba's death was published Monday morning some authorities could find no way to speak of her except to compare her with Adelina Patti. But as they had already done the same thing with Marion Talley and Lily Pons, the comparison had little value. Nor did anyone first establish the premise that Mme. Patti was the standard by which all other singers were to be judged. Doubtless when some of the obituary writers went back to the 1893 files of their own papers they were amazed to find that Mme. Melba's début was treated in from a third to two-thirds of a column. Marion Talley received six times as much space and Miss Pons from three to four times as much. The art of ballyhoo had not been fully developed in the gay nineties. Nevertheless Mme. Melba enjoyed a long and famous career.

Old operagoers can remember her in the zenith of her glory. Her latest appearances in New York were not to the advantage of her reputation. Mme. Melba made her stage début at the Théâtre de la Monnaie, Brussels, October 12, 1887, as Gilda in *Rigoletto*. Dubious statements have been made about her age. It was said at the time of her first appearance to be 26. Agnes Murphy wrote a biography which bears out this assertion by giving the year of her birth as 1861. Thus she must have been 32 when she came to the Metropolitan. Whatever the number of years, the voice was in the plenitude of its glory and it was quickly accepted as one of the great voices of operatic history.

From: The New York *Sun*, February 28, 1931.

The quality of musical tone cannot be adequately described. No words can convey to a music lover who did not hear Melba any idea of the sounds with which she ravished all ears. Maurel used to say of the voice of Tamango, "C'est la voix unique du monde." One could equally as well have said of Melba's: "It is the unique voice of the world." This writer never heard any other just like it. Its beauty, its power, its clarion quality differed from the fluty notes of Patti. It was not a better voice, but a different one. It has been called silvery, but what does that signify? There is one quality which it had and which may be comprehended even by those who did not hear her; it had splendor. The tones glowed with a starlike brilliance. They flamed with a white flame. And they possessed a remarkable force which the famous singer always used with continence. She gave the impression of singing well within her limits.

In Handel's time the composer adapted his rôles to the voices in his company. Doubtless some of the success of the amazing Faustina and Cuzzoni was due to this. Melba, however, had to take her operas as she found them, and achieve her fame by singing them in her own way. Her voice was of the full range needed for the colorature and light lyric rôles of the modern repertoire. It extended from B flat below the clef to the high F. The scale was beautifully equalized throughout and there was not the slightest change in the quality from bottom to top. All the tones were forward; there was never even a suspicion of throatiness. The full, flowing and facile emission of the tones has never been surpassed, if matched, by any other singer of our time. The intonation was preëminent in its correctness; the singer was rarely in the smallest measure off pitch.

The Melba attack was little short of marvelous. The term attack is not a good one. Melba indeed had no attack; she opened her mouth and a tone was in existence. It began without ictus, when she wished it to, and without betrayal of breathing. It simply was there. When she wished to make a bold attack, as in the trio of the last scene of *Faust*, she made it with the clear silvery stroke of a bell. Her trill was ravishing. On the evening of her début at the Metropolitan she sang in the cadenza of the mad scene a prodigiously long crescendo trill which was not merely astonishing, but also beautiful. Her staccati were as firm, as well placed, and as musical as if they had been played on a piano. Her cantilena was flawless in smoothness and purity. She phrased with elegance and sound musicianship as well as with consideration for the import of the text. In short, her technic was such as to bring out completely the whole beauty of her voice and to enhance her delivery with all the graces of vocal art.

She was not a singer of what is called "dramatic" manner, though not devoid of sentiment or the ability to express a gentle pathos. But her interpretative power was superficial. She conquered rather by the sensuous spell of the voice, by the brilliancy and fluency of her ornamentation and the symmetrical lines of her delivery than by the awakening of feeling in her hearers. Her limitations did not prevent her from undertaking a wide variety of rôles. Immediately after her first Lucia she sang Nedda, Semiramide, Juliette, Gilda. Comment at the time was that she was deficient in sentiment in the last named part. But it must be borne in mind that much more was expected of singers then than now, and that Mme. Melba surprised her hearers in later rôles.

In her second season she sang Micaela, Marguerite, Elaine in Bemberg's opera of that name, and the Queen in *Les Huguenots*. It may mean nothing to contemporaneous operagoers, but the cast of that production of Meyerbeer's masterpiece is historical—Nordica as Valentine, Scalchi as the Page, Melba as the Queen, Jean de Reszke as Raoul, Edouard de Reszke as Marcel, Plançon as St. Bris and Maurel as de Nevers. There was without doubt never before or since such a star cast. Present-day operagoers may get a hint of its caliber from the statement that every member of the roster could be ranked with Caruso.

Mme. Melba did not sing Violetta in *Traviata* till December 22, 1896, when she astonished her public by the degree of pathos she developed in the second act. It was, however, all in the singing; the action throughout the opera was unequal to the musical exposition. It was on December 30 of the same year that she made her lamentable attempt at a dramatic Wagnerian rôle. She sang Brünnhilde in *Siegfried* on the evening when Jean de Reszke impersonated the young Volsung for the first time on any stage. What prompted Mme. Melba to undertake the Brünnhilde has never been known. She herself was at one time credited with having charged Mr. de Reszke with persuading her to make the experiment, but the story was generally disbelieved. Those who knew Jean de Reszke intimately pronounced it incredible. The prima donna did not sing the part a second time.

Her first *Aida* was accomplished on January 24, 1898, and, although she was not then or at any other time able to create any illusion in the rôle, her beautiful singing of the music enabled her to retain the part in her repertory for some years. What is more strange is that she first sang Rosina in *Il Barbiere di Siviglia* on January 28, of the same year. The opera, now a familiar one, had not been given at the Metropolitan since 1890 when the Rosina was Adelina Patti. Mme. Melba's impersonation found favor. To be sure she was not the scintillating, coquettish, enchanting Rosina fashioned with bewitching spontaneity by Patti, but she was sufficiently vivacious to sustain interest and despite hoarseness in the opening measure of "Una voce poco fa" she had a vocal triumph. In the lesson scene she was warmly applauded for her delivery of Massenet's "Sevillana." For an encore she seated herself at the piano and to her own accompaniment sang Tosti's "Mattinata," which became inseparably associated with her lesson scene from that time.

Since this is not a biographical sketch, it is unnecessary to follow Mme. Melba through her various opera and concert seasons. But it should not be forgotten that the Metropolitan was not the sole New York stage of her triumphs. In 1907 she sang Lucia, Gilda, Mimi and Violetta with Oscar Hammerstein's company at the Manhattan Opera House. This writer then noted a little deterioration in the voice. It had acquired a slightly acidulous quality. The soprano was 46 years of age and the alteration of the voice was not a matter for wonder.

Those who heard this celebrated singer in her latest appearances here can have formed no true conception of her greatness. That she was not an artist of constructive imagination is undeniable. That she was a mere "diva" of the older type, who walked on and off the stage and enchained audiences by sheer outpour of tones, is equally undeniable. Melba had much more than that to give her public, though beyond question the incomparable voice stood before all else. But this singer was a good musician as well as a complete mistress of the technique of singing.

Good musicians are not as numerous on the opera stage as some music lovers believe, for the reason that young persons with voices refuse to go through the labor essential to the mastery of musical theory and practice. All they desire is to learn how to make pleasing sounds with their voices and then let patient coaches take care of the rest. Neither voice teachers nor coaches can turn out Melbas. They are self-made. They appear only at intervals. One of the remarkable features of the record of the Metropolitan is that the roster of its company once contained at the same time the names of Sembrich and Melba.

The present writer had not the honor of Mme. Melba's acquaintance, but from those who knew her well he heard many stories of her amiability, of her generosity, of her genuine kindness to beginners struggling to get their feet on the first rungs of the ladder she had climbed.

MELBA'S VOICE

Melba was one of the great singers, "by the grace of God." Elderly opera-goers of today like to look back upon them and to hold up as exemplars of the great art of song the "bel canto" that they insist is no more. That custom, it has been pointed out, is as old as the art of song itself. The art has always been going to the dogs; and it would be easy to search through the memoirs and recollections and criticisms of aged croakers and find an unending series of jeremiads—jeremiads always invalidated by the rise of some new star just as the old ones were disappearing below the musical horizon. One can only hope that history will repeat itself; that Nature has not broken the mold and—quite as important—that mankind has not forgotten or disregarded the way to bring natural endowments in voice to the summit of artistic achievement, and will refrain from new demands in new music that the human voice cannot meet.

The strict and strenuous training required to arrive at perfection was undergone by Nellie Melba, though she had one of those almost unique natural equipments that fitted her voice to attain perfection with the least of scholastic guidance. Some great singers have attained greatness through the long and laborious conquest of a recalcitrant organ. Melba's was not such a one. A year sufficed to bring her to a pont that has taken others, quite as great, many years to reach. She was at once recognized to have attained, in her way, something akin to perfection that only a riper experience was needed to complete. She came to New York first in 1893, six years after her European début, having already reached the height of her fame. She first

From: "Melba's Voice" (Editorial), *New York Times*, March 1, 1931.

appeared at the Metropolitan in *Lucia di Lammermoor*. Those were great days at the Metropolitan, made great by great singers—the days of Jean and Edouard de Reszke, Plançon, Lassalle, Sembrich, Lehmann, Nordica, Eames and others of that kind. Mme. Melba was at once recognized as belonging to the royal lineage; there was no doubt about it, there was no discussion.

Melba was one who would have completely met Rossini's standard of great singers, whose three demands were for voice, voice and voice. She was never an operatic actress of communicating warmth, of convincing power. In some of her parts she even displayed a sort of *gaucherie*. But the qualities she did possess were hers in the highest measure, and they gave the completest satisfaction to those who heard her for what she was. She held entire sway in New York, not only at the Metropolitan but also at the Manhattan Opera House; and she made history here that cannot be forgotten by those who were part of it, and that will long be a tradition with those who were not so fortunate in their life-span.

MELBA'S ART OF SONG

OLIN DOWNES

Her Career in Perspective—The Age of Voices Gives Place to the Age of Machines

It is undeniable that the age of great singing has departed and that one of the last figures of this age was Nellie Melba.

No one knows to a certainty the year of her birth, but her career came as a culmination of an extraordinary period of song. Within that period the world knew one other voice as phenomenal for a man as Melba's was for a woman. The man was Enrico Caruso. He made his debut in Opera in 1894 and sang to within a few months of his death in 1921. Melba made her first appearance in opera in 1887 at the Monnaie in Brussels, and made her last appearance at Covent Garden June 8, 1926, before an audience deeply moved, consisting of all ranks of citizens, from commoner to King.

Melba was born with a phenomenal gift, which needed the artistic coaching of Marchesi more than it needed any actual vocal training to bring it to perfection. It has been said that in the whole history of opera there is no more exceptional figure, and that is presumably true. We can have no precise information of the great singers of the seventeenth and eighteenth centuries, in the golden age of bel canto. We will never know exactly how a Farinelli or Senesino or Faustina or Cuzzoni actually sang, although plentiful records of the period, and, what is most convincing, the music written for them, bear witness to their incredible skill.

From: Olin Downes, "Melba's Art of Song," *New York Times*, March 1, 1931.

But the memory of Nellie Melba in the early 1900's, and the recollections of the veteran operagoers who heard her sing before that, establish beyond a doubt or peradventure the existence of a voice which could hardly have been more beautiful, coming from a human throat, and a marvelous, instinctive art that matched the voice in the ease and spontaneity with which it was employed. This was a woman created by nature to sing. No woman's voice exists today, or at least is known on any stage, which remotely approaches it for sheer golden beauty and a resonance, from the lowest to the highest note of a two and a half octave range, that was as clear as a flute or a mountain stream.

If the audience wanted dramatic passion, depth of feeling, inner revelation, it turned elsewhere; but the voice and art of Melba were of such unique enchantment that the listener was lost in the sheer joy of his experience, and from within himself supplied such meanings as the heart desired when she sang. By all the chronicles and experience of the living who heard not only the later group of the Nordicas and Calvés and de Reszkés and Sembrichs and their great and distinguished feminine contemporaries of the vocal art, but also their forerunners, the Pattis and Albanis and Nilssons and the great Lehmann, Melba's had a pure siren beauty denied to any other voice her century produced. Fortunate the generations that heard her, for we shall not hear her like again.

* * *

All sorts of reasons have been advanced for the dearth of voices today, the principal one being the haste and lack of thoroughness in the modern singer's education. This, in turn, hinges upon modern economic conditions, which, instead of freeing man from labor, force him to harder labor than ever before, with earnings of security and contentment in inverse ratio to the effort required. Is not the fundamental reason for the decline of singing the state of the human mind in the age of machinery and mass production? We not only live by machines, but we rely more and more upon instruments to produce our music. It would probably be found by careful examination of the records that instrumental resource and virtuosity in the last fifty years have increased as much as the standards of vocal performance have declined in the same period. In a similar way the personal rapport of artist and audience, and the intimate effect upon that audience of the singer's art, have greatly weakened. The master of the situation is the conductor, despot of a hundred instruments. They all serve him in expressing his ideas; they overwhelm the audience. And now, replacing the human control of instruments, we have the mechanical control of the machine and the employment of nature's superhuman powers to convey the sounds made by the machines to the multitude.

* * *

The kinetic power, the synthetic tendencies of the period, find expression through media with which the voice cannot possibly compete, until it looks as if the singer, or even virtuoso, who used to stir our emotions and kindle our dreams by means of his individual art will be one day as rare as the horse and carriage. A new age carries the conquest of time and space and the command of inconceivable dynamic power to a pitch with which the appeal of the human voice has little to do. And when the voice is employed with instruments it is usually expected to adapt its needs and demands to theirs. That is the general trend, which is not the trend of a period when human beings instinctively sing. The age commonly called Victorian and unromantic, which begins to appear in perspective a highly romantic period, was the one which produced Melbas, or at least kindred stars of the vocal heaven. It is hard to conceive of our times doing so.

Certainly, the period is not propitious for singers' development. The Italian master who kept his pupil on vocalises for seven years and then told him he could sing any vocal music in existence could not make a living today. In that many years the young singer studies a half dozen operatic roles, bursts upon the stage of a lyric theatre and is paid handsomely by the house and by record and radio companies for his product. Shortcomings of technic and defects of the voice are to be remedied as he goes along—or they will not be remedied. Usually the public appearance is made not only before the singer is thoroughly prepared for it, but at a cost of bad and ineradicable habits which eventually ruin the voice. This is hardly a generality. It is a fact ninety-five voices out of a hundred. Does the youthful aspirant retire to a quiet spot, live in a simple, healthful way, cultivate a strong body and quiet nerves and a balanced mind, and develop, without tension or haste, a manner of singing which is as natural as breathing itself, and as beneficial to the physical organization? Does he wait till the music of a rôle has been so completely absorbed that it is a part of him, and the task of meeting its vocal problems one that can be accomplished with technical security and a voluptuous pleasure in pouring the music from his throat?

He does not. Neither the actual conditions, nor spirit, nor tempo of our times permits of this. And then there is the cursed nervousness, introspection and incredible physical demands of modern operatic music. Melba herself fought free of it. On just one occasion she tried a Wagnerian part and quickly desisted, feeling that with all her technical ease and mastery she was completely unable to cope with the demands of the music. Emma Calvé told us once of a similar experience with Anton Seidl. Seidl dreamed of Calvé as Isolde. Calvé memorized the rôle and there was one rehearsal with orchestra. Following that rehearsal Calvé retired to the privacy of her chamber and did not sing again for fifteen days.

This is not to say that Wagner cannot be sung. A thousand times it has been proved that he can be. He even is, on rare occasions. But the new and prodigious demands of dramatic music on the voice began with Wagner, and the dramatic music of today is in many cases much more inimical to the development of beautiful tone and technical ease than his hardest passages dreamed of being.

This can be said: It is harder to sing well today than in any previous musical period the world has known. The technique and capacities of the voice are confused with or are pitted against those of the instruments. Preparatory training is not and cannot be what it was, although a thorough technical training was never so necessary. But worst of all, the temper of the period does not encourage the impulse to sing.

Of course, this is a passing state. There are eternal verities of human nature which temporary expedients of civilizations will never change. One of these is the incomparable and searching appeal of the human voice and that form of expression which is the alpha and omega of music-song.

Song was when music began, and song will be as long as the art endures. When the beautiful voice appears, the world pauses, whatever its occupation, to listen. The eloquence of that voice, its mysterious and irresistible appeal, is one of the most fundamental expressions of the race. Writers of fugues and symphonies, learned historians and technicians, the laborer in the field, the philosopher in his den, will be stirred out of themselves and into another world of beauty and feeling at its sound. There was that in the voice of Nellie Melba; and when great voices appear again they will accompany another era in music.

MELBA'S WILL

WILLIAM R. MORAN

The last will and testament of Dame Nellie Melba, a thirteen-page type-written document signed November 5, 1928, makes interesting reading. Wireservice reports at the time the will was made public estimated the singer's worth at approximately $1,000,000, which was less than expected. It was stated that Dame Nellie had suffered great financial losses during the World War, owing to the wiping out of her German and Austrian investments, and that she had sustained major losses in England, the United States, and Australia at the time of the 1929 stock market crash.

The will makes thirteen specific bequests of jewelry and art objects to her son and daughter-in-law, three sisters, two brothers, four nieces, a sister-in-law, a grandniece, and her beloved granddaughter, Pamela. Pamela also received "all my jewellery trinkets and personal ornaments not hereinbefore otherwise effectually disposed of," which trinkets were said to be worth something like $70,000. Some insight into Melba's usually well-hidden sentimentalism is afforded by the statement "It is my particular wish that my said granddaughter shall have and always retain the blue bag given me by the late Alfred Rothschild and also the kettle I have always carried with me on my tours."

There were some thirty-five cash legacies to family, friends, servants, protégés, and others listed as "of the Hotel Ritz in Paris" or "of Covent Garden, London," who must have been specially remembered for some service rendered.

The will also provided for six life-time annuities, one of them to her old friend John Lemmoné. A gift of $40,000 was to be invested to provide a scholarship at the Albert Street Conservatorium in Melbourne, "in the hope that another Melba may arise." There were also gifts of funds to support a park, a children's hospital, and a kindergarten.

After provision for her son, his wife, and his heirs, the will states: "In event of failure of the Trustees with regard to the ultimate residue of my estate, my Trustees shall hold the same upon trust to pay . . . for the promotion and encouragement of all branches of music in Victoria including the cultivation of the voice, and I express the wish that my Trustees shall, if practicable for this purpose, apply the same for the Promotion of Grand Opera in Melbourne including the purchase or building of an Opera House."

MELBA'S CAREER A LONG SUCCESSION OF TRIUMPHS

JOHN ALAN HAUGHTON

Australian Diva, Whose Voice Is Recalled
as Unique among Great Voices, Won Highest
Fame in Spite of Early Opposition from
Family and Late Beginning—Was Queen of
Song in an Era of Great Singers

Nellie Melba, the most widely celebrated coloratura soprano of the closing
decade of the Nineteenth Century and the opening one of the Twentieth
Century, died in St. Vincent's Hospital, Sydney, Australia, after a few
weeks' illness of an obscure malady which she contracted a year ago in
Egypt and which baffled the skill of her physicians. She was in her seventieth year.

The position occupied by Melba during her prime was that of an acknowledged queen of song. It was an age of great singers, great sopranos
especially. Contemporaneous with her were the Americans, Emma Eames
and Lillian Nordica, also Emma Calvé and Marcella Sembrich, all sopranos,
yet she was unique among them.

The voice itself was one of crystalline purity and extraordinary evenness
from bottom to top. She quickly rose to the pinnacle of her profession, once

she found in Mathilde Marchesi a teacher whose method suited her voice, which was to a degree "naturally placed." That it was capable of expressing the greatest gamut of emotion cannot be said and her singing of songs which required varied tone color and temperamental expression left something to be desired. One remembers it as having been larger in volume and lighter in color than the beautifully used voice of Mme. Sembrich. It had a less characteristic quality than that of Mme. Eames. Unlike Mme. Nordica and Mme. Calvé, who started their careers as coloratura sopranos, but developed into dramatic sopranos, Melba remained a coloratura to the end of her days, although she was very successful as Mimi and Desdemona, neither of which has any coloratura passages, though neither is a really dramatic role.

DID LITTLE REGULAR PRACTICE

Again, unlike most great singers, Melba did not permit her voice to rule her completely. She once told the writer that she never did any lengthy, systematic practice—just a few scales and trills to keep it "oiled." She also said that she followed no set regimen with respect to eating on the days she sang. "I eat sensibly at all times," she said, "therefore, I see no reason for making any change!"

In spite of limitations with respect to dramatic instinct, the voice of Melba had an empyrean quality that lifted its hearers out of themselves. There is no voice of the present day that remotely approaches it.

Helen Porter Mitchell, to give the singer her correct maiden name, was born at "Doonside," Richmond, near Melbourne, May 19, 1861. Both her father and mother, the latter of whom died when she was a child, were musically cultivated, though her father's Scotch Presbyterian principles made him frown upon music as anything more than part of religious worship or home diversion.

MADE APPEARANCE AS CHILD

Nellie's musical leanings began at an early age, and she picked out tunes on the harmonium in her father's home almost as soon as she learned to talk. Her first public appearance was in a charity concert arranged by her aunts in the Melbourne Town Hall. The infant prima-donna sang "Shells of the Ocean" with such effect that an encore was demanded and she responded with "Comin' through the Rye."

Later she was sent to the Presbyterian Ladies' College in Melbourne, and there her first systematic musical instruction began under Mme. Christian, who later entered a convent. Her singing was not encouraged, but she was taught piano and organ and theory.

From the time she was a small child, she seems to have had a natural trill, and her young friends used to say, "Nellie, make that funny noise in your throat." This incident was used by George Moore in his novel *Evelyn Innes*, as was another which will be mentioned later on. She also cultivated whistling to a point of virtuosity, and to this she ascribed her unusual breath control when she became a singer. It is said she utilized this ability when learning new roles, thus saving her voice.

Passing from the hands of Mme. Christian, Nellie began studying with a Signor Cecchi. She had such faith in her own ability as a singer that she arranged a charity concert in the drawing room at Doonside. Although she was singing in church, a public appearance in concert, even in a drawing room, was against her father's principles, so, as fast as his daughter invited people to come, he requested them to stay away. When the hour of the concert arrived, only two persons applied for admission, but the singer went through her entire program as though singing before the largest audience in the world. On another occasion when she was to appear at a concert in Sorrento, a seaside resort, to pay for a new cemetery wall in the town, the money for preliminary expenses was used up and none was left for bill posting. Nellie waited until nightfall, and then, armed with a bucket of paste, brush and posters, went about the town doing her own bill-sticking.

MARRIES IRISH PLANTER

When barely twenty-one, on December 22, 1882, Nellie married Charles Nesbit Armstrong, the son of an Irish baronet, in Brisbane. Mr. Armstrong was a sugar planter. It is said that her father was in favor of the match, hoping that her singing aspirations would thus easily be disposed of. Such was not the case, however, as Nellie continued her lessons with Signor Cecchi for a while and later with Mme. Charbonnet Kellermann, mother of Annette Kellermann, the swimmer. About this time she sang and played piano numbers at the Government House, and the Marchioness of Normanby, wife of the governor of Victoria, said to her: "My child, you play the piano beautifully, but the time will come when you will forsake the piano for your voice." Melba is said to have regarded this statement as the turning point of her career.

On May 17, 1885, Mrs. Armstrong sang at a benefit concert of pupils of Signor Cecchi in aid of some indigent musician. This led to an engagement by a local impresario for a series of concerts, four a week at ten pounds, or about fifty dollars a week. She was quite satisfied with this arrangement. It is interesting to note, however, that on her return to Australia some seventeen years later, this same impresario had to pay her 2350 pounds, or about $11,750, for a single concert. The same year she sang in the *Messiah* in the Town Hall in Sydney and convinced her father of her capabilities.

LEAVES AUSTRALIA FOR EUROPE

The following year Mr. Mitchell was appointed Commissioner to the Indian and Colonial Exhibition in London, and he invited his daughter and her husband and their infant son to go to London with him.

In spite of her high hopes, Mrs. Armstrong failed to make any impresson on London. Sir Hubert Parry would not even give her an audition. Sir Arthur Sullivan, after hearing her sing, said that if she would study he might be able to give her a position in the chorus of *The Mikado* the following year. Carl Rosa made an appointment to hear her, but forgot it. Melba, characteristically, declined to make another appointment. Wilhelm Ganz, however, heard her sing and gave her an engagement in Prince's Hall, where she sang June 1, 1886, still without creating any impression whatever.

Both her father and husband then attempted to convince her that her aspirations would come to nothing. Nevertheless she staked everything on one last throw . . . and won!

Before leaving Australia, Mrs. Armstrong had been given a letter of introduction to Mathilde Marchesi by the wife of the Austrian ambassador in Melbourne. Armed with this letter, she went over to Paris and sang for Marchesi. Made over into fiction, the entire scene has been preserved in George Moore's *Evelyn Innes*. After hearing Mrs. Armstrong sing, without making any comment, the veteran teacher ran to the steps and called to her husband. "Salvatore! Come down! I've found a real star!" Returning to the astonished young singer, she said: "If you'll stop with me a year, I'll make something wonderful of you!"

STARTS LESSONS WITH MARCHESI

Mrs. Armstrong accordingly set to work and began the study of operatic roles at once. Marchesi, always quick of temper, bullied her to tears very often, but none the less, she taught her how to use her voice. It was at one of her salon musicales in the Rue Jouffroy the following December that Helen Porter Mitchell Armstrong became "Melba," by which name she was known forever after. The name, made from her native city of Melbourne, was used as being more euphonious than her own. Ambroise Thomas, who was present, heard her sing the Mad Scene from his *Hamlet* and prophesied great things for her. Shortly after, Maurice Strakosch, who had so much to do with the making of Patti's career, heard Melba singing "Caro Nome" one day during a lesson. He was visiting Marchesi's husband and said to him: "Salvatore, I want that singer. I don't know whether she is tall or short or pretty or ugly." A contract was signed with him which, if memory serves, caused Melba some inconvenience, but he died a year later.

After only nine months' preparation, Melba made her operatic début as Gilda at the Théâtre de la Monnaie in Brussels, on October 13, 1887. She had only three stage rehearsals, but in spite of this, her biographer states that her success was instantaneous and overwhelming. There is, however, some doubt about this. She sang in Italian on account of her indifferent French accent. The same season she also appeared in *Traviata*, *Lucia*, *Lakmé* and *Hamlet*. Her stipend was about $600 a month.

SINGS AT COVENT GARDEN

Sir Augustus Harris, hearing her, offered her an engagement at Covent Garden, where she appeared as Lucia on May 24, 1888. Her success was very mild indeed and, curiously enough, the British critics spoke more of her acting ability, which in later years was considered most mediocre, and ignored her singing. She appeared in several other operas without much more success, and at the end of the season gave up her contract for the following year.

Back in Brussels she took up her career there. Paris tried to get her for the first performance of *Roméo et Juliette* at the Opéra, but Brussels would not release her and Patti sang instead. Her Paris debut was as Ophélie in *Hamlet* on May 9, 1889. She was paid $1,200 a month, which she considered "princely." Berlin and Madrid offered her better terms, as did the Gaite-Lyriqué for light opera, but she decided to remain at the Opéra. That Spring she sang again at Covent Garden with more success, appearing as Juliette with the de Reszkes, then at the height of their fame, and was commanded to sing at Buckingham Palace. She appeared as Elsa in *Lohengrin* during this season. Her only appearance at the Opéra-Comique in Paris was on December 11, 1890, when she sang Micaela to the Carmen of Calvé at a benefit for the Bizet monument.

In February, 1891, she was invited to St. Petersburg to sing *Lohengrin*, *Faust* and *Roméo and Juliet* with the de Reszkes. The Tsar Alexander ordered all these operas to be remounted and restudied for them.

CONQUERS CABAL AT LA SCALA

Her first Italian appearance was at La Scala in *Lucia* on March 16, 1893. There was a cabal against her, and she was threatened with poison and every sort of personal indignity. She ignored all this, however, and although facing at first a chilly, inimical house, she triumphed completely. During this engagement she met Verdi and coached Gilda, Aïda and Desdemona with him. She also promised Leoncavallo to create Nedda in the London premiere of *Pagliacci*, which she did with great success, and Mascagni to create Luisa in his *I Rantzau* in London. This latter, however, was a failure.

Melba's American debut was made as Lucia at the Metropolitan on the evening of December 4, 1893. It was only a partial success. The following month she sang in a performance of *Tannhaüser* in French and in February in *Lohengrin* in Italian. The season ended that year with *Faust* on February 23, the de Reszkes and Melba being in the cast. The enthusiasm was such that at the end of the Prison Scene, a grand piano was hauled onto the stage and Melba sang "Home, Sweet Home" to the accompaniment of Jean de Reszke! The following year she was a member of one of the phenomenal casts in which every role was filled by a star of the first magnitude. *Huguenots* was given with Nordica, Melba, Scalchi, the de Reszkes, Plançon and Maurel. She also sang Desdemona for the first time, to the Otello of Tamagno and the Iago of Maurel. At the opening of the Music Hall in Baltimore that season she sang Bohm's "Still wie die Nacht," telling the audiences as she sat at the piano to accompany herself that this was the first time she had ever sung in German in public. Her first appearance in Massenet's *Manon* in this country was made at the Metropolitan on January 27, 1896.

FATAL *SIEGFRIED* PERFORMANCE

The following December 30 Melba made one of the great and historic mistakes of her career. On the advice of Jean de Reszke, she had been study-ing the role of Brünnhilde in *Siegfried*. Her one appearance in the part, with Anton Seidl conducting, very nearly wrecked her voice. She sang a few more times during the month of January and then retired for a long rest on the French Riviera.

In 1897-1898 Melba made an extensive tour of the United States with the Damrosch-Ellis Opera Company, singing *Traviata* and *Barber of Seville*. Ignoring accuracy of detail, in the Music Lesson Scene, Melba used to have a concert grand piano wheeled onto the stage and would accompany herself in various songs, some of which were scarcely commensurate with her dignity as an artist.

She had studied Mimi with the composer in London, and said it was she who advised him to see the play *Madame Butterfly*, which was then running in London and from which one of Puccini's most famous operas was made. She sang in the first Covent Garden performance of *Bohème* in 1899. The writer remembers very vividly hearing her in the work that same summer. At the conclusion of the Puccini opera Melba would don the nightgown of Lucy Ashton and coming before the curtain would sing the Mad Scene from *Lucia*.

WITH CARUSO AT MONTE CARLO

Melba's first opera with Caruso was *Bohème*, which she sang at Monte Carlo in February, 1902. During this engagement she sang in Berlioz's *Dam-

nation of Faust which was given with Renaud as Mephistopheles and Jean de Reszke as Faust. In September of that year she made her first visit to Australia since she left it to study for the stage. Her return was like the triumph of royalty, and her father was so overcome with excitement that he suffered a paralytic stroke.

When Oscar Hammerstein had his Manhattan Opera House in process of building, he approached Melba with a proposition to sing with his organization. Melba gave no definite reply one way or another. The first season of the Manhattan Opera, as is well known, began as a complete failure financially. Hammerstein cabled to her in London after the opening of the season, and against all advice she decided to come to the Manhattan. "I like his pluck!" she is reported to have said. She was paid $3,000 a performance and all traveling expenses. Her début at the Manhattan in *Traviata* on January 2, 1907, turned the tide for the house. She later appeared in *Lucia*.

During her first performance there she was amused and interested at hearing during the applause the Australian bushman's call "Coo-ee!" It transpired that an Australian government official whom she had known as a little girl was passing through New York on his way to England and took this way of welcoming her.

Melba's popularity in *Bohème* was such that tickets are said to have sold for $30 when she appeared in it. At the close of the season of 1907 Melba returned to Australia for another visit. She toured America in concert with Kubelik in 1913.

With her engagement at the Manhattan Opera House, Melba's operatic career virtually came to an end in this country, although she returned to sing special performances with the Chicago Opera in 1919-1920. During this engagement she appeared only in *Bohème* and *Faust*, and although the public was interested in her still, it must be admitted that the once superb voice was no longer what it had been. She appeared occasionally in both concert and opera in England and also in Australia. Her formal farewell was made in a gala performance at Covent Garden in 1926, amid scenes of wildest enthusiasm. She appeared once again in public in Australia the following year when she sang "God Save the King" at the opening of the Australian Parliament by the Duke of York.

CREATED "DAME" NELLIE MELBA

Melba was always an intense nationalist and expressed herself very strongly in Paris over the anti-British feeling during the Boer War. She also had much to say with regard to the treatment of Dreyfus. During the World War she earned over $500,000, which she donated to the Red Cross. For this she was given the title of "Dame," which corresponds to Knighthood, in April, 1918.

Her marriage was not a happy one, and soon after her operatic début she was separated from her husband and son. In 1900, Captain Armstrong, then a rancher in Texas, obtained a divorce. Shortly after this, the singer and her son were reconciled, and at the time of his marriage in 1906, she is said to have given him a castle in Ireland for a wedding present.

Melba's funeral was held on February 26 in the Presbyterian Church at Lilydale, near Melbourne, where her father lived after giving up Doonside, the home of her childhood. An immense crowd lined the streets during the funeral, and hundreds of wreaths from well-known persons all over the world were carried in open carriages. She was buried in the Lilydale Cemetery, next to her father.

POST-MORTEM

In over fifty years that have passed since Nellie Melba's death, hardly one of those years has gone by without someone, somewhere, breaking into print with something new about the Australian singer. For a time, she frequently appeared as the subject of a chapter or two in the memoirs of someone who had worked with her or knew her professionally. It is indeed remarkable how many lives her life touched to leave impressions that lasted through the years. Some of these recollections seem worth collation from their scattered sources, and I present a sampling here. The years are now taking their toll of those who had firsthand experiences with the singer, so some of the stories will begin to reappear with the inevitable distortions of the twice- or thrice-told tale. Even so, it appears that Melba will continue to be "good copy" in the years to come.

NELLIE MELBA

HERMAN KLEIN

One of the most respected and best known of the music critics and vocal teachers of the latter part of the nineteenth and first part of the twentieth centuries was Herman Klein, born in Norwich in 1856. His *Thirty Years of Musical Life in London, 1870-1900* (1903) is a classic reference work for the period. He wrote an important biography of Adelina Patti (*The Reign of Patti*, 1920), and his *Great Woman Singers of My Time* (1931), from which the following excerpt is taken, and *The Golden Age of Opera* (1933) are sought-after works today. Klein was long a proponent of the gramophone as an aid in vocal teaching, and he attempted to have Lillian Nordica record vocal lessons for the American Columbia Phonograph Company when he became their "musical advisor" in 1906. From June 1924 until his death in March 1934, he contributed a monthly column to *The Gramophone*, in which he reviewed current vocal recordings and discussed vocal technique of the past and present. In a lifetime devoted to music, he had an expert's opportunity to hear the great singers of several generations, and his opinions are worth noting today.

From: Herman Klein, *Great Woman Singers of My Time*. London: George Routledge & Sons, Ltd., 1931. Reprinted by permission of Routledge & Kegan Paul Ltd.

I am one of the few living persons—certainly the only English writer on musical subjects—who happened to hear Dame Melba sing at Princes' Hall, Piccadilly, in 1886, when she was still Mrs. Nellie Armstrong, of Melbourne, New South Wales [sic]. Remembering well what an untrained vocalist she then was and the lovely natural quality of her voice, I can give full credit to Mme. Mathilde Marchesi for the improvement which was manifest in the singer's style on her return to London two years later.

The clever old teacher had been wise enough, where the production of tone was involved, to "let well alone". She had seen at once that in this case it would be impossible to better the work of nature. She did not even attempt to darken the rather white timbre of the medium register, but left it bright, silvery, glistening, just as she had found it. Instead of paying attention to that, she cultivated without forcing the head notes in her own characteristic, Garcia-like way. She extended their tessitura without converting the musical *soprano leggiero* into a *soprano sfogato*. She taught her pupil a perfect scale and a delicious shake, and made of her a facile, flexible, brilliant vocalist.

It was a quick transformation. In little more than a year after Melba had begun study with Marchesi in Paris she was ready to make her début in opera. One or two of the French critics had heard her at semi-private concerts, and wrote only simple truth when they declared her to be one of those rare beings who sang like the birds—"comme le rossignol". Yet Paris was not to be the scene of her earliest successes. It was from the Théâtre de la Monnaie, at Brussels, that the news of her extraordinary triumph as Gilda in *Rigoletto* (October 12, 1887) was trumpeted forth to the world. As her teacher, who was present, said in her book (*Marchesi and Music*), "The very next day and afterwards it was nothing but a chorus of praise everywhere; the entire press of Brussels declaring the young *artiste* to be a star of the first magnitude".

She was now known as "Melba"; and the reports of her success had speedily reached Augustus Harris. That rising impresario had taken no interest whatever in her when she first visited London and sought to secure an engagement with him. British opera-goers still remained unmoved by the advent of an Australian soprano who had been creating excitement across the Channel. They refused to flock in crowds to Covent Garden to witness her first appearance there on Queen Victoria's birthday, May 24, 1888. The audience was a large and fashionable one, certainly; and a great deal was expected of the débutante by the habitués who had heard and read reports about her. But the critics, accustomed to take such things *cum grano salis*, assumed their usual calm, judicial attitude and, what is more, preserved it until they had written their notices. The latter were careful without being enthusiastic.

The opera was *Lucia di Lammermoor*. It progressed for the best part of two acts "without incident". Nor was it until after the Mad Scene that the house began to wake up and indulge in warm applause or displays amounting finally to what is termed an ovation. The sextet went well, however, and was cordially received. My own impressions were of a mingled description. I found the amateur had given place to the artist; I thought the quality of her voice was exceptionally beautiful; but, on the whole, the singer left me cold.[1]

With this opinion the general verdict was in full agreement, even though not expressed on all hands with the same frankness. On the other hand, Mme. Melba succeeded instantly in winning the suffrages of Society. She made more friends among the wealthy patrons of the "Royal Italian Opera" than any new prima donna of that period, whatever her nationality. These friendships, which she never failed to foster and utilize, were to stand her in good stead all through the only difficult or uphill portion of her career.

But more valuable by far, in an artistic sense, to one who was still comparatively a stage novice, was the practical advice that she received from the famous Polish tenor who was her constant associate during her second season at Covent Garden. Then it was that she really began to master certain fundamental principles of her art of which she had previously commanded little more than a smattering. From him she acquired the old Italian system of breathing, which Mme. Marchesi too frequently allowed her pupils to pick up as best they could. Until that time Melba had been a vocalist *et praeterea nihil*. Jean de Reszke practically taught her how to act, how to impart ease and significance to her gestures, how to move about the stage with grace and dignity.

Jean de Reszke had sung in Gounod's opera for the first time in Paris during the previous winter (1888-89), with Adelina Patti, when *Roméo et Juliette* was transferred from the Opéra-Comique to the Opéra. I had had the good fortune to be present at that historic *première*, and was able to make comparisons. I knew full well that the glamour, the excitement, the amazing "atmosphere" of that night could never be recaptured, either at Covent Garden or at any other opera-house. But a Roméo such as Jean de Reszke must perforce inspire any Juliette, however inexperienced, however unequal to him in dramatic calibre. And so it proved. He and Melba had rehearsed together with such sedulous care that not a tiny point in their stage business was overlooked. So perfectly did their voices blend, so faultless was their intonation, so identical their phrasing, that the long series of duets proved a joy from first to last.

Looking back now upon this interesting event, I cannot help thinking that the advance which it showed touched in many respects the high water-mark of Dame Melba's achievement as a lyric artist. She may have essayed more exacting parts—some that did not suit her at all; only one or two that fitted her quite so well. But no one save Patti ever sang Juliette's waltz-air with the same extraordinary ease, with the same *insouciance* (there is no English word for it), or the same pearl-like clarity of execution in *appoggiature,* runs, and cadenzas.

Because he inspired her, Melba always appeared to greater advantage with Jean de Reszke than with any other tenor. When he was the Faust her acting in the Garden and Prison scenes would wax warmer and even a trace of passion might glow in her silvery tones. In less familiar music the incandescence would be missing. It was so in Goring Thomas's *Esmeralda* (given at Covent Garden in French in 1890), when she sang the title-rôle to Jean's Captain Phœbus; and in Bemberg's new opera *Elaine* (1892). Yet even when the vital spark was lacking, its absence could be over-looked in the enjoyment of Melba's "glorious medium" (so Jean de Reszke used to describe it), the exquisite *coloratura,* the facile flow of girlish and delicate yet vibrant head tone. Hence could one delight in her "Caro nome", her "Jewel Song", her Mad Scene in *Hamlet,* her "Willow Song" in Verdi's *Otello.*

The ambition to sing heavier rôles led her now and again to essay tasks that lay physically beyond her. She should never, for instance, have attempted Wagner. Her first venture in that direction was at the Paris Opéra, where, so early as '90 or '91, she sang Elsa to the Lohengrin of Ernest van Dyck. A few months later she undertook the part at Covent Garden, struggling through the opening act under an attack of nervousness that nearly upset her. In the duet with Ortrud she plucked up courage somewhat, and in the wedding scene she wore a cloth-of-gold gown that dazzled all beholders. But, on the whole, her voice was naturally too light for the music of Elsa; she was unable to cope with its declamatory needs. Her experiment as Brünnhilde in *Siegfried* came near to injuring her voice permanently. That, however, did not happen in London but in New York.

Dame Melba's legitimate triumphs were won in those less exacting rôles which really lay within her means. One of the best of these was Nedda, a part that she took when *Pagliacci* was first produced at Covent Garden in May, 1893. Leoncavallo—not, as a rule, a particularly demonstrative Italian—went into such raptures over her delicious rendering of the *ballatella* that, after leading the demand for a repetition, he could not forbear rushing behind forthwith to embrace her before the end of the act. In the second tableau Melba acted with a spirit and *entrain* very rare with her, and sang magnificently. The excitement of the scene allowed full scope for her dramatic idea, which was to present Columbine as a kind of second-rate provincial actress. Altogether it provided a vivid realization of Leoncavallo's conception.

Melba's Nedda in a sense foreshadowed her yet more popular embodiment of Mimi in *La Bohème,* which was not seen, however, until six years later. She had in the meantime added to her repertory such important characters as Violetta, Micaela, Rosina in *Il Barbiere,* and the Queen in *Les*

Huguenots; while in 1904 she created at Covent Garden the heroine of a short opera entitled *Hélène*, which was written expressly for her by Saint-Saëns.

But in none of these parts did she make the same strong impression as in Puccini's early opera. The earnest, sentimental nature of the devoted *grisette* appealed to her strongly, and the music, at once straightforward, melodious, and touching, brought out all that was sweetest and purest in the voice of the Australian singer. No wonder she repeated here the hit that she had made in the part with the same Musetta (Zélie de Lussan) in America the previous year. It was in scenes from *La Bohème* that Dame Melba last appeared upon the stage of Covent Garden when she bad her operatic farewell to the British public in the summer of 1926.

Thirty-eight years is a lengthy span for the career of an opera singer. Few have equalled and still fewer have exceeded it. Stamina, not age, is the test in these cases; and if Melba's voice retained its silvery timbre and resonance for a period beyond the common, it was the result of her exceptionally unartificial, effortless method of producing it. For the same reason, coupled with the amazing ease that marked her execution of the most difficult *tours de force*, her singing never failed to give the listener unalloyed pleasure. Hence the fact that she became one of the most popular artists of her day.

Among the things that contributed substantially to her fortune was the gramophone, of whose potentialities she was perhaps the first singer to be a successful and profitable exponent.

NOTE

1. This is how I summed up the Australian singer after the season had terminated: "Mme Melba possesses a flexible high soprano voice of resonant timbre and extensive compass; her means are under perfect control and her vocalization is of a brilliant order. There can be no doubt that her powers as a singer are above the average; at the same time her style, judged from the loftiest standpoint, is disfigured by certain mannerisms and to an extent deficient in that indescribable something which we call charm. Her *tours de force* are dazzling enough, but her accents lack the ring of true pathos; she sings and acts with admirable intelligence, but in both the gift of spontaneous feeling is denied her. This definition is essential in order to explain how it was that Mme Melba, despite the warm reception accorded her at the outset, failed to maintain the advantage she had gained and establish herself among reigning operatic favourites." (*Musical Notes*, 1888.)

PEN SKETCHES

SIR LANDON RONALD

We have met Sir Landon Ronald before. Following is a selection
from his second book, *Myself and Others* (1931), published in the
year of Melba's death. Ronald's frank appraisal of Melba as a
singer and artist warrants attention.

When I read in the newspapers the beautiful tributes that were written
about my old friend, Nellie Melba, after she died, the first thing that
occurred to me was that I would have given anything if she could have read
them herself.

To those outside her intimate circle she was always prone to boast that
she never cared "tuppence" what any critic wrote about her, but this was
not really true. She cared very much, and as long as I can remember, she
was very sensitive about those who attempted to belittle her art. I think the
reason was not so much that she resented criticism, but that she knew that
she was a great singer and that she had worked extremely hard to attain the
immense position she held in the public estimation.

I have heard people talk about what a marvellous thing it must be to be
born with a gift such as Melba had, but little they knew of the work that
was necessary before that gift reached the state of perfection which made it
unique!

From: Landon Ronald, *Myself and Others: Written Lest I Forget*. London: Samson Low,
Marston & Co., Ltd., 1931. Reprinted by permission of Purnell Books.

With the death of Nellie Melba, as far as I can see, the days of the great Coloratura Soprano are finished. Certainly nobody has taken her place so far, and although I am the first to acknowledge that there are many and great operatic singers to be heard at Covent Garden and elsewhere in these days, yet I emphatically say that there is not another Melba.

Of course there is no denying that she had the gift of one of the most glorious voices that God ever placed in the throat of a woman. It was not the size of it, because it was in no sense a big voice, but it was the amazing purity, the golden quality, and the perfection of breathing and production and other essentials that go to the making up of a great singer.

I was associated with her for close on forty years, and the point that stands out in my memory more than almost anything else is the amazing change that came over her, temperamentally, during the last ten or twelve years of her artistic career.

Thirty years ago, Melba was often described as singing like a bird, but with a cold personality that had a freezing effect upon her audience. There was a certain amount of truth in this. She appeared almost to resent the tumultuous applause that was showered on her, and often used to tell me how intensely she disliked the tricks and antics of her fellow *prime-donne* of that period, and that she would never in her life degrade herself as an artist by imitating them.

And yet it is only a few years back that her whole attitude on this point changed, and I can remember her being most effusive to her audience at the Albert Hall, and even blowing them kisses at the end of a concert.

In her earlier days, again, she abhorred making speeches. . . .

Years later, as I say, she went to the opposite extreme, and would make very happy little speeches either at a public dinner or to an audience, and thoroughly enjoy doing so.

Melba as a companion was simply splendid. Whatever she may have appeared to those who knew her but little, her friends will ever remember her as being full of fun, enjoying life, and being a very homely and very Bohemian woman. She had a rare gift of mimicry, and would often convulse us with laughter by her imitations of some of her colleagues.

She was in no sense a great musician, and although in the early days I often begged her to sing some of the great classic songs of Schubert, Schumann, Brahms and others, it was only towards the end of her life that she turned to singing some modern French songs and in an interview blamed the British public for liking "Good-bye" and other songs which she had sung to them for years, and made enormously popular.

Considering the colossal success she had as a concert singer, it may seem odd for me to say that I am absolutely convinced that she was nothing but an operatic singer. In rôles such as "Traviata", "Lucia", "Marguerite" in *Faust*, "Ophelia" in *Hamlet*, "Mimi" in *Bohème* and many others, she was simply unequalled. It is not for me to pronounce any opinion of her as an actress. She always seemed to me neither better or worse than the average operatic singer is as an exponent of dramatic art.

I deplore still the passing of one of the greatest operatic singers of all time, and even now I find it difficult to realise that I shall never hear that lovely voice again, or revel in the fun and jokes that she loved so well in her own home.

She led the life of a Queen of Song and enjoyed every day of it. Besides the gift of a wonderful voice, she had splendid health, riches, and was fêted wherever she went. Could anyone who liked that sort of thing ask for more?

MELBA'S FAREWELL
AT COVENT GARDEN

WILLIAM R. MORAN

"Nostalgia" is a popular word today, its meaning having shifted in modern parlance from its older connotation of homesickness toward that of a general worship of things past. Everyone from the baker to the candlestick maker is busily promoting synthetic recollections of a not too distant past, with these efforts directed largely toward a generation too young to have personal experience of the product. Surely it is easier to sell books on, or models of, the horseless carriage to those who never had to start or drive the things! But nostalgia is not always a synthetic commodity. The phonograph has reached the sophisticated age where today we can take part in historical events that were preserved on recordings. This can certainly bring recent history closer to us, and with a real sense of involvement, by allowing us to eavesdrop, as it were, in a far more dramatic way than we can participate through the printed page.

There are probably few events that were such veritable orgies of sentimentality (today's "nostalgia"?) as the night of Tuesday, June 8, 1926, when His Master's Voice captured on eleven wax plates some of the goings-on within the walls of the Royal Opera, Covent Garden, London. The occasion was the farewell performance of Dame Nellie Melba, the Australian soprano who had made her debut in this house just a few days more than thirty-eight years before.

Historians have a way of pointing to a certain event or date and designating it as the "close of an era." Actually, massive changes in life-style usually come about by a more gradual transition. The seeds of the so-called Edwardian era had been sown and were well on their way to flourishing by the time of Victoria's death in 1901, and there was little indication of the close of that era on the assumption of the English throne by George V on Edward's death in 1910. By the time Melba made her European operatic debut in Brussels in 1887 and had sung her first performance at Covent Garden in *Lucia di Lammermoor* in 1888, there had been a reversal of the old mid-Victorian view that singers, musicians, and others "of the stage" were a risqué lot that the better class did not want to associate with socially.

Victoria herself had been largely responsible for this change in viewpoint, as she took great delight in enlivening her social functions by "command performances," which took place at Windsor and the other royal abodes and which drew on the finest in London's artistic world. Melba was a special favorite of the old monarch. Her presence was in demand at private parties held in London and at weekends at country estates, and by the mid-Nineties she was the acknowledged Queen of Covent Garden. "Melba nights" were something special, were sold out long in advance, and frequently were attended by local and visiting royalty.

Writing in 1932, the year after Melba's death, Percy Colson had this to say:

A Melba night at the opera some thirty years ago! It recalls not only that thrillingly lovely voice, and the personality and magnetism which caused Melba to rule over Covent Garden with all the power and prestige of such queens of song as Catalani, Jenny Lind and Patti, but also a social epoch which, though we knew it not at the time, was fast drawing to its close, and which was stricken to death in that fatal blow of 1914.

When the Gramophone Company persuaded Melba to make commercial recordings in 1904, it was an event that was much advertised. Her records were distinguished by a mauve-colored label and bore a replica of her signature. The Victor issue of these discs in the U.S. also bore the special label with the banner "VICTOR MELBA RECORD." They were supplied in an imitation leather envelope provided with an isinglass window through which the label could be read; a picture of the singer appeared when the record was withdrawn. A twelve-inch single-faced Melba record sold for $5.00, the ten-inch size for $3.00. (Caruso records sold at that time, for example, bore the regular Red Seal labels of the period and sold for $3.00 and $2.00, respectively, with no special envelope.)

Melba's first domestic recordings for Victor, which were made in 1907, appeared with the standard Red Seal label, but her name was given merely as Melba in a type size larger than any other used in the title block. Only in his single duet with Melba, from the first act of *La Bohème*, does Caruso's name appear in the large type along with hers. Melba's name was one to be reckoned with. Not only was she considered one of the world's greatest sopranos—perhaps the greatest—but she was a personality and the symbol of a way of life. In many ways, certainly, she typified the Edwardian age to perfection.

Much happened in the thirty-eight years between Melba's Covent Garden debut and her farewell performance, and World War I was of course the most cataclysmic of the period's events. Colson describes the changes in this way:

I have always regretted going to hear [Melba] after the war. It was in June, 1923, and the opera was *Faust*. It was the saddest evening I ever spent at Covent Garden. Where was the brilliant audience which was wont to frequent the beautiful theater—the exquisitely dressed, bejewelled women, the smart men? All vanished. . . . In the stalls there were young women holding their hats, and men either not in evening dress, or wearing dinner jackets, and I could not bear to look at the boxes. Faust was played by a third-rate American [*sic*] tenor, or rather tenorino, named Johnson, and when Melba appeared, matronly enough to be Marguerite's mother, I could have wept. The art was still there, but the voice was only the ghost of that silvery wonder of former years.

The farewell performance on June 8, 1926, had been announced well in advance with the initial prospectus of the season, which was published December 5, 1925. The program was to consist of Act II of Gounod's *Roméo et Juliette* (with its famous balcony scene), Acts III and IV of Puccini's *La Bohème*, and the opening of Act IV of Verdi's *Otello*, with its long scene for the soprano. Percy Pitt was to conduct the Gounod, Vincenzo Bellezza the Puccini and Verdi.

The matter of casting, however, was not soon settled. For her Roméo, Melba chose the American tenor Charles Hackett. For her companions in *Bohème*, she wanted some fellow countrymen. Browning Mummery and Frederic Collier, both Australians, were already at hand on the Covent Garden roster for the roles of Rodolfo and Colline and presented no problem. But Melba had taken a liking to a young Australian baritone, John Brownlee, who was then singing his first roles in a small French opera house, and she made up her mind that he was to be her Marcello. Melba called him at seven o'clock one morning in Paris and issued the invitation. She asked if he knew the role, to which Brownlee replied affirmatively, even though he had never even heard the opera! He recalled:

I went home, my head swimming. Here was I, an unknown, inexperienced Australian singer, and I was going to sing before the King and Queen in my debut at Covent Garden. I'd always learned music fast, and I knew the part of Marcello at the end of the week. We rehearsed in Melba's place with Maurice Renaud, the great baritone, who helped me a lot and gave me some of his costumes. It was an experience. Even rehearsing was exciting when Melba was around.

It was quite a night to make one's debut. The King and Queen were there, the

Prince of Wales, and other members of the Royal Family. Practically the whole of England had come to Covent Garden that night to pay homage to Melba. The auditorium was a sea of gowns and tiaras and uniforms and decorations and white shirtfronts. The atmosphere was charged almost beyond endurance. A lot of people had come with dire forebodings. They were afraid it would be a pathetic spectacle and wished it were over. Some were sorry for the old girl of over 67 [she actually was just a little over 65] and for what they thought would be Melba's ordeal.

It didn't turn out that way. Melba's ordeal became Melba's triumph. She confounded her staunchest admirers. She sang so beautifully that years seemed to recede as in a fairy tale, and there stood again the great prima donna of a quarter of a century ago. The voice had almost a youthful charm and freshness. The heavenly legato was still there, and the wonderful technique. It was a miracle. The people who had come out of a sense of duty were as in a trance. Then they went wild with excitement.

After the last act of *La Bohème*, the curtain came down and the stagehands quickly arranged onstage all the flowers that Melba had received. When the curtain went up, she stood in front of a six-foot high sea of flowers. In all my life at the opera, I've never heard another ovation that had such overtones of love, affection and adoration. Only the supposed cold English can bestow such a tribute upon an artist whom they worship.

And thanks to the art of electrical recording, imperfect as it was, we can be a part of that scene today.

It is not known just when Victor's English affiliate, His Master's Voice, made the decision to attempt a recording of this historic event. The first experimental recordings by the new Western Electric system had been made in the U.S. in February 1925. The first "live performance" recordings had been made at the Metropolitan Opera House in New York at a concert March 31 of the same year, and—as the companies licensed to use the new system had to build up a catalog of newly recorded discs—public announcement of the advent of electrical recording was actually delayed until November 1926. HMV had recorded the first full-length symphony by the new process and had released the disc in December 1925 to a roasting criticism by *The Gramophone*'s Compton Mackenzie and others who thought the new recordings "sounded more like a complicated cat fight in a mustard mill than anything else." By the spring of 1926, however, a smattering of better recordings, accompanied by better-tempered reviews, had been produced.

Apparently feeling nothing ventured, nothing gained, HMV decided to record Melba. Chaliapin made his Covent Garden debut May 25, 1926, in *Mefistofele*, and HMV planned an experimental run at a repeat performance May 31, presumably to try out the equipment for the great Melba affair a week or so later. Immediately one new problem arose: Chaliapin was under exclusive contract to HMV for recordings, but other members of the cast (Bianca Scacciati and Francesco Merli) were exclusively Columbia artists. No compromise was reached in this situation, so all that was recorded were some bits and pieces of the performance in which the rival company's artists did not appear. The results of this "session" were nine twelve-inch sides (matrix nos. CR 382-390), of which four eventually were released. In spite of problems with balance between the orchestra and the singers as they moved about the stage, the sides were impressive.

For the Melba night of June 8, the issue of exclusive contracts again was raised. Her Roméo was Hackett, under contract to Columbia, so unfortunately no attempt was made to record that portion of the performance. (Today, with both the HMV and British Columbia labels under the same aegis, that of EMI, this problem has disappeared.) Eleven twelve-inch sides were cut. (Details are shown on page 463.)

July 1926 saw the publication of DB 943, containing the *Bohème* "Addio" and the farewell speech. Compton Mackenzie wrote in *The Gramophone* for August:

Of the vocal records [for the month] the most sensational are the two made at Covent Garden by His Master's Voice. The disc of Dame Nellie Melba singing Mimi's "Addio" and her speech of farewell on the other side, definitely mark a new epoch in the power of the gramophone. . . . I wish to express nothing except our profound homage to a great singer and a great lady and our intense appreciation of what the Gramophone Company has done in preserving that solemn occasion forever. This record may wring tears from those as yet unborn, for I cannot believe that the world will ever grow too old to be touched by the sincere emotion of a great artist. A record like this may not draw the sting of death, but it does rob the grave of a complete victory.

The next of the farewell recordings to receive publication was DB 1500, which was first listed in the October 1931 *Connoisseur Catalogue*: the first part of the *Otello* "Willow Song." Because it was coupled with a previously released side (CR 412), it was assumed that it was the only remaining unissued side that had been approved by the artist. Presumably it was issued in commemoration of her death, which had occurred in Sydney earlier the same year. Thus it was a surprise to find the *Bohème* quartet (CR 413) making its tardy debut in dubbed 45-rpm seven-inch form on 7ER 5201, along with the three previously released recordings, in September 1961.

For many years, the Gramophone Company would press special editions (at a special price) of discontinued recordings. If one ordered by matrix (and not catalog) numbers, those in charge of such things apparently ran the orders through the factory without bothering to check up to see if the requested pressings had been passed by the artist or not. Thus it was that a few knowledgeable collectors came into possession of pressings of the entire set of the Melba farewell recordings, and inevitably the complete set has found its way onto various "pirate" LPs. And in 1976, at long last, the full farewell performance was "officially" issued by EMI as part of the HMV Treasury series album 'Nellie Melba: The London Recordings 1904-26" (RLS 719, five discs, available as a Capitol import).

Listening to the complete set of recordings today, most auditors agree that they contain some exquisite singing, and the number of places that show strain or faulty intonation are remarkably few. Actually, some of the unpublished sides seem flawless, except perhaps for an occasional imbalance in volume or a faulty cut in or out of the microphone at the beginning or end of a side. Certainly there is nothing on these records to mar the memory or reputation of Nellie Melba, and there is much of value and interest.

Points of comparison with earlier recordings are afforded by only three of the sides. Melba had previously recorded "Addio" with piano in London in March and again in November of 1904, and with orchestra in the U.S. in March 1907, January 1909, and November 1910. While there are minor differences in phrasing, there is remarkably little change in Melba's voice over the period of time represented by these acoustical recordings and that of June 1926. Aside from the "Addio," the rest of the 1926 *Bohème* material is new to the Melba discography and, of course, lends a new perspective to her ensemble work. The *Otello* selections had been previously recorded (the "Willow Song" in truncated form) in 1909 and 1910 by Victor; once again, comparison does not detract from the farewell performance. These recordings, unique in the history of the phonograph, captured a moment of artistic consequence and a technological development poised on the brink of its triumph.

HOW I SANG WITH MELBA

AILWYN BEST

It was my cousin Susan (Lady Susan Birch) who suggested that Dame Nellie Melba might hear me sing. I was 19 at the time, and was enjoying my last year of school at Winchester. I was told by my housemaster that special leave had been granted for me to travel up to London. I was to go straight (he laid great stress on the word "straight") to Mrs. Benjamin Guinness's house in Carlton House Terrace, where there was a large salon and a grand piano.

I set off, feeling (as may be imagined) very proud, but also extremely nervous. I took with me some English songs by Quilter, and some Handel: *Acis and Galatea*. There was a setting of Shelley, "Love's Philosophy", with a high A which could show off my upper range—a good, rousing song which would help me to overcome nervousness; and the two tenor arias in *Acis* I had sung at the School concert. In a moment of wild optimism I slipped in one or two Italian operatic arias. Anyway, the diva would only want me to do a scale or two and sing one song; she would be taken off to lunch by my cousin, and I would then catch the train back to Winchester. I would be told that I had a nice voice and must study hard, and that would be all.

What actually happened was so fantastic that I could never have imagined it, even in my wildest dreams.

It was 1926, the year of Melba's farewell at Covent Garden. London had just paid her an overwhelming tribute as the *prima donna assoluta* of her day. At 67, she had sung extracts from Desdemona's and Mimi's roles at her

From: Ailwyn Best, "How I Sang with Melba," *Opera* 21, no. 12 (December 1970).

farewell performance. The critics had written of "the noble art of singing—even now, no younger singer can compare with her in the steadiness and perfect intonation of her incomparable voice". I had read these notices; and knew a number of the marvellous recordings she made when she was 48. Her singing in the duet in Act I of *La Bohème* with Caruso was to me sheer perfection. Even now I have never heard anything approaching it. And I was going to meet her—and sing for her! With these thoughts in mind, I arrived at Carlton House Terrace.

There was no drawing back now. Summoning up my courage, I rang the bell. The butler led me up to the first floor and into a spacious, elaborately decorated room with the shutters folded over the windows to keep it cool. All the furniture had been pushed back against the walls—leaving the middle of the room empty. The floor was polished hardwood—good for sound, I thought.

In the far corner was a grand piano: a small man dressed in a black suit was sitting at the keyboard. He got up and came towards me. "How do you do?" he said. "My name is Harold Craxton". Luckily, I knew who he was. He had made some records of the Delius Cello Sonata with Beatrice Harrison, and was one of the best accompanists of the day. In the most charming way he went on: "And you are the young man who is gong to sing, and I shall have the pleasure of playing for you. Let us see what you have brought. Ah, yes, a good selection. Do not try to make too much noise—the quality is what counts. What will you begin with?"

Before I could reply, the front door below us opened loudly and a sound of animated women's voices burst up the staircase. There was a laugh—a high, silvery laugh, and then: "Let's try!" Immediately a long steady trill began—on about E or F. Softly, then swelling to a forte, then dying away—coming nearer as the singer came up the staircase. It was hauntingly magical. It ended abruptly as she reached the landing—the classic *messa di voce* that is seldom heard in public nowadays. "Nellie, that was wonderful!" Another laugh—and the two women came forward into the room. "Come and be presented", said my cousin.

I made myself go forward and bent over the hand that Melba held out to me. She was of medium height, dressed in something dark, with a rope of pearls round her neck. Her face, under its broad-brimmed picture hat, was not at first sight beautiful, but it was charged with vitality and missed nothing. I was being weighed in the balance. Apparently the impression was not altogether unfavourable, for she smiled.

She also wasted no time. "Now", she said briskly, "Sing me something".

With that, she went and sat down with my cousin on the sofa on the far side of the great room. I suddenly felt hideously alone and ready to crawl under the piano, anywhere, out of sight of those eyes and that imposing, erect figure on the settee. But I had forgotten Mr. Craxton. Like all true artists, he was ready to help. He took me by the arm and led me over to the piano. "Shall we start with the Quilter?" I nodded, unable to speak.

I took several deep breaths, and tried to think of the song. Harold Craxton played the opening bars with *bravura*. I caught his mood and plunged into the music.

> The fountains mingle with the river,
> And the rivers with the ocean,
> The winds of Heaven mix for ever
> With a sweet emotion;
> Nothing in the world is single,
> All things, by a law divine,
> In one another's being mingle,
> Why not mine with thine?

Awful. Oh, dear. Rather short of breath. Still, the last high A wasn't too bad.

"Now something else".

Mr. Craxton started the introduction to "Love in Her Eyes Sits Playing" from *Acis and Galatea*. This is written for strings, but Mr. Craxton played it like the artist he is. I was less nervous now, and, with a recent recording by that fine tenor Tudor Davies in mind, I tried my best, although with my inexperience and as yet undeveloped technique, I could not take all the long phrases in one breath. However, the aria at last came to an end, and I waited for my dismissal. But I was not to be let off so easily.

"That is better", I heard Melba's incisive voice across the room. "You are breathing better. I like your voice. A true *tenore lirico*. Now sing something that really shows it off. Have you any Italian opera? Sing that".

How I blessed the afterthought that prompted me to bring those arias!

As soon as I began "Recondita armonia" from *Tosca*, she became more interested. This she knew; this was her world.

Recollection becomes confused. But I must have sung for a good hour. Suddenly, she got up and came over to me.

"Splendid", she said. "You must come and sing with us this afternoon". I stammered out that I was quite unprepared, but she cut me short. "Nonsense", she said. "You will do very well. Now come on and we will have some lunch".

My cousin explained that Melba had consented to give an afternoon concert that day with an Australian protégé of hers who had sung Marcello with her at the farewell performance of *La Bohème*. I could hardly believe that I was to be one of the artists and would actually be singing with her. It all seemed unreal.

"Where is the concert to be?" I asked, thinking that it might be at a private house party somewhere nearby. "Wormwood Scrubs Prison", came the astonishing answer!

We had lunch; I think it was at the Ritz, but I cannot remember. There was much laughter. Melba sat opposite me, and kept everyone amused with her wit and her stories of famous people, some of which were hardly in the "drawing-room" category. I fear I was much too preoccupied to listen. It was all so exciting and unexpected; I was tasting success, and was content to bask for a while in reflected glory.

A vast car whirled the party to Wormwood Scrubs. At the prison we were taken to an anteroom, where a young, dark, powerfully built man was introduced. He was the Australian baritone, John Brownlee, later to be world-famous, who had just made his debut at Covent Garden. Lady Susan's husband, Wyndham Birch, had also joined the party. Melba had changed into a long, elegant white dress. I do not think she wore much jewellery (perhaps some of the audience would know too much about it!). We all trooped onto the platform and sat on a row of chairs. The prison theatre was, to my excited eyes, enormous, but it cannot have held more than 500 people. It was packed, and the applause was deafening.

John Brownlee led off with Maude Valerie White's "King Charles"—a good rousing song. I can still hear his manly, resonant tones and steady legato. I followed with Siegmund's "Spring Song" from *Die Walküre*. I was possessed by Wagner at this time and imagined I could sing all the heroic roles in the repertory! Luckily, the "Spring Song" is lyrical in style, and no serious mishap occurred.

Of Melba's singing one must write with diffidence; I had few critical standards, and impressions fade after so long. She sang firstly, as far as can be remembered, the "Jewel Song" from *Faust*, in French, in which she was perhaps not in her best form. The wonderful voice seemed veiled, and even a little unsteady. But the final trill, and high B natural, for which she roused herself, had much of the old verve and brilliance which can be heard on the HMV recording made in 1907. She then sang "Si mes vers avaient des ailes" by Reynaldo Hahn, which has also been recorded. This song is a gem, and should be much better known. It would make a perfect "encore" song for a soprano. She sang it beautifully. Intonation, legato, and expression were alike faultless, and the voice floated out with that effortless, disembodied quality that was one of the attributes of this extraordinary singer. A moment of absolute silence—and then the crash of applause. Melba, I think, repeated this song—it is very short—to everyone's delight. It was remarkable to feel the tenseness and appreciation of the audience, made up almost entirely of prisoners. She sang one or two other things which I cannot unfortunately remember; and she finished with "Swing Low, Sweet Chariot". I can still hear in my mind how she sang "coming—coming—coming for to carry me home" with a gasp in between the words. Not everyone would dare to do this! But the audience refused to let her go. She repeated the last verse. They were eating out of her hand by this time. She kissed her hands to them. The applause seemed never-ending.

There she stood—this amazing woman whose career had been one long blaze of glory; whose singing had been unsurpassed during two generations of great voices; who by great natural gifts, backed by hard work, determination, and sheer force of character, had created for herself a legend. Her star was setting fast, her singing triumphs were over; but the legend, her monument, remains.

MELBA'S LAST VISIT
TO COVENT GARDEN

WILLIAM R. MORAN

Josephine O'Donnell joined the staff at the Royal Opera House, Covent Garden, London, in 1926, the year of Melba's famous farewell at that theater. Ten years later she wrote a book of memoirs which she called *Among the Covent Garden Stars*. One of her stories concerns an off-season audition which was being held in the house. Hopeful singers had come from all over the British Isles on the chance of getting on the Royal Opera House "small parts" list for the upcoming international season. At this period, the opera house was used during the winter months as a dance hall, and the seats in the auditorium were covered by an expansive dance floor, presenting one great unbroken surface across which the already nervous applicants had to make their way to present their music to the audition pianist. At the back of the auditorium were the managing director and members of his critical staff. On the day in question, in the midst of the auditions, O'Donnell spotted a stranger, wrapped in a fur coat, striding the length of the hall and making towards the director's table.

I started in pursuit, but was surprised to see that Colonel Blois, after one quick glance, had started up and was coming to meet the intruder with outstretched hand.

"How awfully nice of you, Dame Nellie!"

"Ssh! I'm here incognita! A little bird told me you were hearing some voices, and I'm so interested."

She took the chair which Eustace Blois, a great favourite of hers, pulled forward beside his own, and then listened intently.

Presently a slight, fair girl began to sing. The voice, though not powerful, was clear and true, but persuaded, like most beginners, that she could never be heard at the end of that vast, empty space, she began to force and the top notes became shriller and shriller.

Her aria ended, the girl walked back . . . , and I was about to give Colonel Blois the next name when Melba came up to me.

"Do you think we could have that child back for a moment?" She walked towards the piano. "May I?" The accompanist, somewhat surprised, rose, and Melba, seating herself at the piano, beckoned the girl to her side.

"Now, my dear, would you run up a few arpeggios for me? Just quite softly." She ran her hands over the keys. Higher and higher, but the voice was still perfectly sweet. "Ah—pianissimo, pianissimo!—There, you have sung several tones higher this time, and quite easily!"

She stood up, and placing a hand on the girl's shoulder said: "You have a charming voice, my dear—but you won't force it, will you?"

Then, smiling back at Colonel Blois, she turned the fur collar up round her ears once more and went out to face the fog. This was really Melba's last, but not least gracious, appearance at Covent Garden.

PERCY PITT ON MELBA AT COVENT GARDEN

J. D. CHAMIER

Percy Pitt was an English composer, organist, and pianist, born in
London in 1870. His early studies were in Leipzig and Munich, and
on his return to England he became chorus master for the Mottl
Concerts and organist at Queen's Hall. Later he became répétiteur,
assistant conductor, and finally conductor at the Royal Opera,
Covent Garden. He directed the Grand Opera Syndicate, conducted
the Beecham Opera Company, and was artistic director of its successor, the British National Opera Company. For many years he
was associated with the Gramophone Company, acting as orchestra
director and piano accompanist for many recordings by Tetrazzini
and other famous singers. In 1922 he was made musical director of
the B.B.C., an association maintained until his death in 1932.

The selection presented here is from a biography of Pitt published
in 1938. It is interesting for two comments: first, that Melba was
considering the role of Tosca as early as 1903 (she never did sing
it), and second, the reference to Higgins' talk with Melba with
respect to Tetrazzini. For years, the story has been circulated that
Melba tried to prevent Tetrazzini's singing at Covent Garden.

From: J. Daniel Chamier, *Percy Pitt of Covent Garden and the B.B.C.* London: Edward
Arnold (Publishers) Ltd., 1938.

It was still what Herman Klein called "the golden age of opera." Albani had made her last appearance at Covent Garden in 1896, and the de Reszkes in 1899 and 1900; but within a few years before and after Percy Pitt's appointment there had been many interesting débuts, of which perhaps the most important were Ternina (her London début) 1898, Saléza the same year, Scotti 1899, Bonci 1900, Caruso 1902, Mary Garden's first London appearance the same year, Titta Ruffo 1903, Destinn, Selma Kurz and Sammarco 1904. Calvé, Eames, Brema, Kirkby-Lunn, van Dyck, van Rooy, Renaud, Plançon, and Journet were still or already singing. As for Melba, she was a charming Institution. She had first sung at Covent Garden in 1888, and for twenty-five years thereafter sang there every summer season, as regular in her coming as the swallows. Percy Pitt first met her in 1903, when she brought him a young American soprano, Elizabeth Parkina, for an audition. As a result Melba asked him to coach her in La Tosca, a part which she wished to add to her repertoire. He found her delightful to work with, hard-working and intelligent as well as a thorough artist. She always arrived practically note-perfect at the earliest rehearsal calls for a new opera. In 1904 he directed the first production of Saint-Saëns' *Hélène*, written expressly for her, though not one either of the singer's or composer's best performances. He also accompanied her at musical parties, and they became good friends; for the present it was "Dear Percy Pitt," though "come to see me," she wrote, "because I *like you.*"

She quarrelled with him once; but after a few days' coolness asked him gaily what he was "sticking out his stomach for."—"If you don't know, who does?" was his reply; to which Melba's peace-making rejoinder was, "Don't be a fool, let's be friends!" She could be "disconcertingly frank"; and if, being Anglo-Saxon and good-humoured, she was not so terribly disconcerting as some foreign stars in moments of frankness, an occasional tinge of apprehension in managers and directors was betrayed in one of Higgins' letters to Percy Pitt. "I have just had a long talk with Melba," he wrote reassuringly, "who is in a very good temper and quite reasonable. We shall have no trouble about Tetrazzini as far as she is concerned."

Trouble among ladies! Did not Percy Pitt say there was no such thing to be feared nowadays? The voices of these two ladies, in any case, were so different that they had no reason not to love each other.

21. Tetrazzini versus Melba: Stars in Opposition; or, The "Record" Operatic Duel. From *Punch*, 1908.

AT THE N.S.W.
CONSERVATORIUM
OF MUSIC

W. ARUNDEL ORCHARD

Mr. Orchard was Director of the N.S.W. Conservatorium of Music
for many years.

On several occasions we co-operated with visiting singers, notably, Dame
Nellie Melba in solos from Mozart, Verdi and Puccini. Her peerless singing
of the Mozart and her unusually dramatic moments in the *Othello* numbers
were events that remain.

On one occasion she was rehearsing Elsa's "Dream" with us. Suddenly
there were some jarring notes and she whispered to me, without moving her
head, "Was I wrong?" "You came in too soon," I said. So she turned to the
orchestra, curtseyed and said to them, "Gentlemen, may we have that
again? Poor old Nellie's memory is going!" How charming of her and what
tact! Knowing only too well the burden of repetition to the players, she
immediately gained their goodwill and they spontaneously applauded, and
very willingly did anything she wanted. Indeed, a great woman. As an
instance of her great care and desire to give only of her best, the following is
worth recording. She was to sing "Depuis le jour," from *Louise*, and feeling

From: W. Arundel Orchard, *The Distant View* (1943).

a little below par she arranged to have the orchestral parts down a tone. This was done, and she rehearsed with the new parts and was satisfied. But on the night of the concert she said, "I feel fine, so we'll use the original parts!" And there it was. She took no unnecessary risk, and her preparation for possible trouble made her comfortable and sure of herself and in the end all went as she desired.

On another occasion we were rehearsing selections from Puccini's *La Bohème*, and I had begun the prelude to Mimi's song when Dame Melba stopped me and said quietly, "Those parts are arrangements—where did you get them?" When I told her they were sent to me by her agents she called out to John Lemmoné, who was in the hall, "John, where did you get these? Wire to Melbourne at once for the original scoring." To me she said, "Too bad to have bothered us with these things, can we rehearse to-morrow?" The point of this is that, for purposes of expediency, someone had sent the wrong orchestration and she realised it—no wonder she was supreme.

When in Sydney, Dame Nellie generally called to see me at the Conservatorium. As this was usually in winter time, she seldom left her car, preferring to send for me to go and sit with her in her roomy and comfortable conveyance warmed with a radiator and fur rugs. And there we sat, chatting about the things she wanted to know. Very wisely she took no risk of a chill by walking through the long and bleak corridors of the Conservatorium.

By way of contrast, incidents at rehearsal with Dame Clara Butt and Kennerly Rumford are interesting. With Dame Clara we were rehearsing "Softly Awakes My Heart." Towards the end she came in too soon after a few bars rest, so she looked at me and called out in her Amazonian voice, "That's wrong!" "Yes," I said, "you were too soon." "Rubbish," she replied. "I have sung this with the Composer. We'll have it again." So we repeated and she was still wrong. "Too soon," I said. "Nonsense, I can't be," said the Dame. So I turned my stand so that she could see the score. The orchestra was getting annoyed, as they knew it was her fault. So they played too loudly and I had to hush them up. Again the passage was tried and this time, as she followed the score, things went right; but she was most ungracious about it. Really, it was only one of those momentary slips liable to occur with anyone. The point was her manner in comparison with Dame Nellie's. . . .

On April 13, 1927, we played at Dame Nellie Melba's farewell concert, contributing orchestral items and accompanying her in opera excerpts from *Bohème, Othello,* and *Figaro,* also playing with Lindley Evans in Cesar Franck's Symphonic Variation for pianoforte and orchestra. Stuart Robertson, her associate artist, was the only other singer besides Dame Nellie. The Sydney Town Hall was packed to the door, and Melba sang her items as she alone could sing them. . . .

The year 1931 began badly with the illness and unexpected death of Dame Nellie Melba. It was a sad time, and we all felt it very deeply. Melba was more than a great singer, she was an institution and did more to bring Australia before the world in the early days of this century than anybody or anything else. In many ways she was a diplomat besides being a great Australian, and her name will live for many a long day.

FINDING ANOTHER MELBA

ROLAND FOSTER

One-time secretary to Clara Butt, Foster was a well-known voice teacher for many years in Sydney.

Ever since that vocal phenomenon known to the world as Melba rose to the highest place in the vocal firmament, ambitious teachers and fond parents all over Australia have cherished hopes of producing a successor to that unique and incomparable star. Singer after singer has been "discovered," carefully groomed, publicly lauded and sent overseas to famous teachers in the hope of gaining similar honours. Nevertheless, despite some few outstanding successes and a number of distinctly creditable achievements, Melba's reputation as Australia's most celebrated singer still remains unchallenged, although nearly sixty years have gone by since her European debut.

One wealthy Melbourne mamma took her eighteen-year-old daughter all the way to Paris and sought an interview with Melba's teacher, Madame Marchesi. "What would you charge for making my daughter sing as well as Nellie Melba?" she blandly enquired, supremely confident, as many people are, that money and influence can open up the way to success.

"Madame, you have come to me under a misapprehension. I am a teacher of singing, not a magician," declared Marchesi after having heard the young lady sing.

From: Roland Foster, *Come Listen to My Song* (1949).

Another common delusion is that the ability to sing some well-known aria from Melba's repertoire indicates the possibility of following in those exalted footsteps. An amusing example of this belief was provided by a conversation between two painters at work outside the Conservatorium which I happened to overhear one day. A girl in an upstairs studio was executing the high flights and flourishes of "Caro Nome," so dear to the heart of every aspiring soprano. "Just listen to that, Bill," said painter number one, pausing with brush in mid-air, "another blinkin' Melba!" "Too right!" agreed his mate; "there's one in every suburb if they only had the same chance as Melba had."

The same chance! Many girls have had chances as good as and even better than Melba's, without achieving more than a fraction of her success. Neither Melba's wonderful voice nor the extra-ordinary technical facility that she acquired would have made her pre-eminent amongst operatic sopranos without the possession of other rare qualifications, backed by will-power, courage and determination in the face of parental opposition and in spite of lack of public encouragement at home and an unfavourable reception on her first visit to London. Consider the circumstances of Melba's early career, which gave little indication of her future greatness.

It was as a pianist, not a singer, that she first became known in Melbourne's social circles, for Melba herself, contrary to the wishes of her father, cherished hopes of a professional career at the keyboard. Lady Normanby, wife of the then Governor of Victoria, was the first to suggest that the as-yet-undeveloped voice might repay serious cultivation, whereupon Melba, who at the age of 21 had become Mrs. Armstrong, with characteristic energy turned her attention to vocal study.

After a period of training, small engagements began to come her way, as they do with most young singers, but not until nearly three years later did her professional career really begin with a concert tour under the management of George Musgrove, who paid her £20 a week, at the rate of £5 per concert. Seventeen years afterwards, on her triumphant return to Australia, Mr. Musgrove had the pleasure of handing her the somewhat more substantial remuneration of £2,350 as her share of the proceeds of a single Sydney concert, a record figure for Australia.

Before leaving Australia Melba gave some concerts on her own account, at several of which the receipts did not cover expenses; her farewell appearance in Melbourne arousing no great amount of interest or enthusiasm, as shown by the net receipts of sixty-five pounds, a paltry sum in comparison with the six thousand pounds which Amy Castles was estimated to have made from three concerts before her departure Londonwards thirteen years later.

When appearing in country towns the accompanist usually played a group of solos. After one concert the local reporter came round to enquire the title of the pianist's encore. "Pabst's Variations on a Theme from Eugene

Onegin by Tchaikovsky," John Lemmoné, who was Melba's manager, informed him. "Would you mind repeating that?" asked the scribe, more familiar with varieties of poultry than piano pieces. John obligingly gave him the title again. It appeared in print next day as "A fast team of variations of unknown origin by Checkoffsky."

Melba's father, having been appointed to an official position in London, offered to pay for a year's tuition abroad on condition that, if unsuccessful, she would return to Australia. So at twenty-five years of age Melba reached the great metropolis accompanied by a husband and a baby son, to find herself apparently unwelcome and unwanted. Letters of introduction brought small result. Neither Sir Hubert Parry nor Carl Rosa, the operatic impresario, could find time to hear her. Alberto Randegger, the celebrated teacher, declined to accept her as a pupil; and Sir Arthur Sullivan was so little impressed that he suggested the possibility of a chorus engagement at the Savoy Theatre after a year's further study! Her sole public appearance at one of the minor concert halls was pronounced "decidedly amateurish and mediocre" by a leading critic—who in after years became one of Melba's greatest admirers. Not a very promising introduction to the great world of music, was it?

Depressed, though not dismayed by the frigidity of London's musical atmosphere, Melba, realising the necessity of further study, betook herself to Paris, there to be hailed by the eminent teacher, Madame Marchesi, as a future star. The acute ear of this wise old lady evidently discerned some latent quality, hitherto unrecognised, in the young singer's voice, which she set out to develop with results of which the musical world soon became aware. In less than twelve months Melba had mastered two operatic rôles and made an astonishingly successful debut in Brussels. Thirty pounds a month was the modest figure on that first contract, soon to be replaced by one of much more generous proportions. Within ten years Melba had established herself at the top of the vocal tree and was receiving £300 a night at Covent Garden and 500 guineas for private concerts given by social celebrities who vied with one another in securing the most distinquished—and most expensive—artists of the day.

Melba, whose favourite recreation was dancing, was a familiar figure in the ballrooms of the great. But she also took plenty of outdoor exercise and was careful of her diet, which (according to an interview in a London magazine) consisted mainly of café au lait, toast, mutton-chops, beefsteak, greens, fruit and light wine. "I never touch cereals, bread, potatoes, pastry or candy. They upset me," she said. "I have coffee and toast every morning for my breakfast. I eat fruit three times a day. I only eat broiled meat, and I take it with salad. I never, never drink anything cold; and, as I don't fancy cooked water, I live on coffee, tea and wine."

To Australians of the present generation Melba is just a name, a legendary figure of the past, but those who heard her in London will never forget the furore that she created at the zenith of her career. A "Melba night" at Covent Garden was a great social function as well as an important musical event. From the hundred and ten private boxes, a glittering assemblage of women decked in priceless jewels looked down upon an equally brilliant array in the thousand stalls, British and foreign military and naval uniforms mingling with the sober black of their masculine escorts, most of them people whose names would correspond closely with the list of those present at a Court Ball. Hundreds of these notabilities, too, could be counted amongst Melba's personal friends.

Accustomed from girlhood to the usages of good society, the prima donna bore herself with ease and assurance in the exalted circles headed by H.R.H. the Prince of Wales, soon to become Edward VII, who had specially interested himself in her career and whose example was speedily followed by countless people of high degree. Lack of the necessary social graces has proved a handicap to many aspiring singers. I could name several with really great voices who failed to reach the highest rank because of crudities in speech and manner, or inability to adapt themselves to a cultured environment.

The thorough musical training which Melba received in childhood was one of her greatest assets. No parent should therefore neglect this highly important angle of their children's education, which may influence their whole future lives. Lack of musical knowledge is a tremendous handicap to young singers, ninety-five per cent of whom know little or nothing about music and consequently start from a long way behind scratch. It is no exaggeration to say that a large majority of those who wish to begin vocal training at eighteen, twenty or even later cannot tell the difference between a semibreve and a semiquaver, or read the notes of "God Save the King" if the words are not attached. Sharps and flats mean nothing in their young lives, the only scales with which they are acquainted being of the fishy variety. For this reason alone, thousands of really beautiful voices have gone to waste. Of what advantage would it be to possess a Steinway concert grand piano or a thousand-pound violin if you could learn to play only simple elementary tunes? And that, unfortunately, is the position in which many possessing really fine voices find themselves through lack of early musical training.

The increasing abundance of brilliantly gifted instrumentalists makes it hard to understand the comparative dearth of musically qualified singers, though in respect of general intelligence, it is frequently evident that Providence sometimes bestows a beautiful voice as compensation for a limited supply of brains. "God put everything in her throat and nothing in her head," said a world-famous teacher about a singer of this type.

From the successes already won and the exceptional promise shown by such gifted young pianists and violinists as Eileen Joyce, Enith Clarke, Joyce Greer, Beatrice Tange, Mewton-Wood, Claire Simpson, Perry Hart, Alison

Nelson, Leonard Hungerford, Richard Farrell and others, it would seem that unless Australian singers look to their laurels they will find themselves in the near future overshadowed by the rising generation of instrumentalists, for whom, owing to the increasing number of orchestral concerts, better opportunities of becoming known are available.

That there will ever be another Melba, so vocally supreme, so socially distinguished and the fortunate possessor of both rank and wealth, is very doubtful, because the conditions and circumstances under which Melba's international reputation was made have gone for ever. The crowned heads of Germany, Russia, Bulgaria and other European countries who gave her Royal recognition have vanished, and with them the Russian grand dukes and duchesses, the German princes, princesses, counts and barons, and those of other countries, with all their pomp and state.

In Melba's day grand opera was the exclusive province of the noble and wealthy. The aristocracy and plutocracy of a dozen different countries besides Britain itself contributed to the upkeep of Covent Garden by subscribing for boxes and stalls; American, South African and South American millionaires willingly paid hundreds of guineas to be in the social swim; visitors from all parts of the Empire booked their seats months in advance, and all the great hotels were filled to overflowing.

In the theatre itself the real devotees of opera were to be found, not among the "society" crowd, but higher up in the half-guinea and upper circle, the seven-and-sixpenny amphitheatre and the half-crown gallery with its wooden benches and protective iron rails—actually the best place for hearing, although you got only a distant view. The salary list was colossal, with Melba at £300 a night, Caruso £250, Calvé and Destinn £200 each, and fifty or sixty other principals on a descending scale from the hundreds to the twenties per performance. Several highly paid conductors; an orchestra of a hundred; as many more in the chorus and corps-de-ballet; stage hands and electricians numbering over a hundred; front-of-the-house staff; advertising, printing and heavy rental brought the expenses up to a positively alarming total. How many thousands of pounds deficit had to be made up annually only the guarantors could tell.

In later years Sir Thomas Beecham and some of his wealthy friends footed the bill. But times have changed. For its continued existence opera must depend upon the support of the many instead of the wealthy few. No longer can the half-dozen remaining great opera houses afford to outbid each other for the services of reigning stars. Opera is on the way to becoming democratised, just as it has been in Russia, Austria and other countries.

Still, even though hundreds of pounds a night may no longer be obtainable on the operatic stage, the vocal favourites of to-day have other means of restoring the balance—radio work, the films, gramophone records and international tours, as the careers of Grace Moore, Lily Pons, Militza

Korjus, Lawrence Tibbett, Jan Kiepura, Gladys Swarthout and various others have shown. In the operatic sphere Australia has good reason to be proud of the brilliant achievements in two hemispheres of Marjorie Lawrence, Florence Austral, John Brownlee, Elsa Stralia, Joan Hammond, Strella Wilson, Astra Desmond, Arnold Matters, Frederick Collier, Horace Stevens, Kenneth Neate, Harold Williams and others who have helped to maintain its vocal prestige overseas.

As time goes on there will be others of equal renown, but those who aspire to fame must realise that in this world of ours to-day musicianship, artistry and intellect are more important than the voice itself. It is not a question of how good your voice is, but: How well can you sing?

MELBA'S GEESE WERE NOT SWANS

THOROLD WATERS

"You've spent a good many years in London. How is it we never met before?" was Dame Nellie Melba's query within a minute of my introduction to her. The question was a natural one, for the preliminary thought of most of the youngsters going to Europe for musical careers, as I did, was to seek the favor of Melba if they could. The reply startled her a little.

"Dame Nellie, you were right on top, getting four hundred guineas a night. . . ."

"Five hundred!" she corrected in a flash.

"Five hundred. Yes, of course, Dame Nellie. And you couldn't possibly do anything for a beginner aiming at a guinea or two. Then, why bother you?"

"That's the sanest way I've ever heard it put," the diva declared, with twinkling humor. "If a lot of the others had been as sensible, what a lot of misgivings and misunderstandings it would have saved us all!"

This was the beginning of a clearer analysis of the psychology of Melba, that fascinating complex of the woman with the iron will and mastery, vehement charitable impulsiveness, imperturbable determination to retain the throne she had won, and the heart of a whimsical child. For Dame Nellie was a pleased child, if ever there was one, when things were right. In that sense, she never grew up.

At our very last encounter, just before Melba went to her beloved Paris and London for the last time, I noticed that she had secured an immense

From: Thorold Waters, *Much Besides Music* (1951).

lampshade that she required for platform use in a concert which, as fate determined, was to be her final one in Melbourne. She had it in a music dealer's, looking for someone to wrap it up.

"Big hats coming in again, Dame Nellie?" I suggested.

"Yes," she said with a giggle. "Shall I try it on?"

And she paraded the shop with it held above her.

After one of the intervals of the memorable initial Australian performance of *Turandot* I met her in the foyer of Her Majesty's rhapsodical and yet tremendously anxious to know what others thought about Puccini's posthumous opera. "Don't look at those dreadful things!" she exclaimed, with a flourish of despairing hands towards several monstrous post-impressions which desecrated the walls, "but tell me whether you like *Turandot*."

"Wonderful!" said I. "That first chorus is a stroke of genius. Except the ones in *Boris Godounov* it's the only chorus I know of that really comes alive. And how I'd enjoy playing one of those three magical figures, Ping, Pang, and Pong."

"So would I," said Dame Nellie. "Oh, if they'd only let me play Pong!"

The child speaking through the woman of sixty-seven. Would that all of us could remain children in heart as long as Melba did! And here is another, more serious, touch of the child, a little diffident and doubtful of its own judgment, coming uppermost through the strong personality of a Queen of the World. It was the morning after her last protégée of any consequence, the American singer Elena Danielli, had made her Australian debut. Danielli had gained much praise for the realistic acting she added to her attractive if somewhat nervous singing as Nedda—and realism in the operatic school of verismo of Leancavallo and Mascagni is the best of the battle over.

"Do tell me. You are quite sincere in what you said about her?" asked Melba, hanging with more than a shade of anxiety upon the reply.

"Quite, Dame Nellie. It wouldn't have been said otherwise."

"I'm so glad to hear you say that," was her response. "One can never completely trust oneself." This from the mightiest arbiter in the world of song! Yet every day I hear the most drastic affirmations by positivists who have never sung. It delighted me, during that magnificent opera season, to be told by Melba's daughter-in-law, Mrs. Armstrong, that each morning "Mardi" (grand-daughter Pamela's name for her) spread the newspaper over the billiard table at Coombe Cottage and rested finally with hand pointing to my reviews. "There! That man knows!" she would comment.

Thus is one led back to a phase of Melba's many-sided character about which there has been ceaseless misunderstanding, and in its turn this will lead on to a little homily to singers and other musical artists on the value and dignity of self-reliance. Never in the history of great singers has there been one who permitted herself to be so needlessly interested—if only fleetingly—in so many lesser singers from her own and other lands. As I have shown, it became a matter for her amazement when she found that one of the long tribe of Australian singers who went to England in her wake had failed to "look up Melba."

The expectation of so many that the successor to Adelina Patti would be able to push them forward became pathetic. The wonder was that she lent a temporary hand in one after another of these cases. A woman in her exalted place had nothing to gain by it; in some ways it was inevitable that she should lose, for of a truth it led to a deal of misunderstanding, some of it very wilful, among her fellow-Australians as to the efforts Melba should, or should not, have made for them.

Bear this in mind; it was she who blazed the big track, although other contemporaneous Australians were attempting to push through it ahead of her, or about the same time. She did not get on it or forge so far past the others through the aid of any generous sister in song in London or Paris, but by dint entirely of her own resoluteness and initiative in the face of several absolute discouragements—of which Alberto Randegger's refusal to accept her as a pupil, and Sir Arthur Sullivan's "thumbs down" on her effort to enrol as a minor unit in Savoy opera are classic instances. Yet almost from the very first night of triumph in the Théâtre de la Monnaie in Brussels was Melba interminably besieged by an ever-increasing battery of young women with voices which most of them imagined were equal to hers.

Among all these voices was one that I have always considered inherently more gorgeous in its dramatic tapestries and wonderful aptitude for florid display apart from the broader curves of singing. It arrived in Paris while Melba was still consolidating her own position on the throne. A little war of rumour has ever since been rife as to what happened in this case of Amy Castles and in others such as that of the contralto Regina Nagel, who went to Paris on the strength of her singing, off-stage, of "Ben Bolt" in *Trilby*, but ran into vocal disaster in the studio of Melba's martinet teacher, Marchesi. Yet the fact indisputable, apart from these individual cases, is that Melba, the imperious, the blunt, the temperamentally changeable, as I have so often heard her described, actually tried to help certain young Australian singers when other Australians of considerable reputation made a fine ostentation of affording help they never gave.

"Words, idle words!" Cordial introductions to expensive singing tutors who could reciprocate these courtesies on the "You scratch my back and I'll scratch your back" business principle, sheaves of purring missives from England to Australia describing the lovely home and kindness and busy life of charming Madame This and dear Miss That; how many times have I seen it working out to just nothing at all for the enravished young aspirant! Yet these were the very artists who, perched comfortably on lower branches of the tree than Melba's exclusive one, were in a far better position to help newcomers along the way to the little fees and the smaller fame.

The child in Melba made her singularly impulsive in taking up singers when they came to her. Her geese, as we know, were none of them swans, and her fidelity to the outworn and snappy Mathilde Marchesi long after that veteran had ceased turning out her Melbas, Calvés, Gersters and di Murskas was in actual fact rather tragic for some of the voices, but Melba at least went beyond the formula of idle words. I have known this impulsive woman to bestow handsome assistance in instances she has deeply regretted afterwards, but temperamentally she could not resist those impulses, strong wine as they proved for the heads of the youngsters. And when the young-sters became foolish, as so often they have done—well, the great Melba, all the world in thrall to her, was scarcely one to suffer fools gladly. Of course, she was too great a personality to bear malice towards them, but the mere fact of dropping from her immediate orbit hurt their vanity grievously in various cases, thus leading to spiteful talk which probably never reached Melba's ears at all. To be quite honest, she was afflicted by far more than her fair percentage of fools.

There was a man whom she praised in Australia and told, seemingly without any suspicion of his domestic circumstances, that he might do well in the concert field in England. When he turned up in London and called to inform her that he had arrived, and with him his wife and "we are seven" family, all Dame Nellie could ejaculate was: "Well, of all the damned idiots! Take them back at once." Well, wouldn't anyone?

But put this alongside her determination to do the best for Elena Danielli, whom I met in Munich in 1930, bubbling over with adoring gratitude to Melba for creating the chance for her in Covent Garden. Put it alongside the launching of Stella Power with all the eclat of a Royal Albert Hall appearance and big provincial tour to follow as "the little Melba"—not that I commend anybody being styled the little anything. Put it alongside her decision ten years before that to send a struggling New Zealand soprano to Paris, to Marchesi and the costumiers and beauty specialists, face lifting and all, which was followed up by inducing the then Prince and Princess of Wales, by no means insatiable music patrons, to bring all fashionable London at their heels to the girl's recital. That the young singer launched with such a regal gesture was thereafter unable to stand up to it was, as I see the affair, just one more instance of a shortage in younger women's own temperament and self-reliant qualities.

And then, consider the magnificent amity of Melba on a certain opera night of which I fancy a *Bohème* programme, ferreted out from among my accumulation of many, furnishes the illustrious cast; it included Melba, Caruso, Scotti, Journet, and that almost incomparable operatic comedian, Gilibert, and yet I recall the experience as the most painful in a long round which has not been at all times joy.

The Musetta was Melba's protégée Elizabeth Parkina. She had developed a throat malady which eventually ended her career. Probably she was the most dependable Musetta that Melba's Mimi ever had beside her. But on this night she completely marred a scene of *La Bohème*, scandalised the fashionable Covent Garden audience by her palpable incapacity, had to be replaced for the remainder of the opera, and was then informed by the authorities of the great theatre that she would never appear on its stage again. "In that case," stormed Melba, "I will never appear here again myself."

It turned out that, after taking a drug at the bidding of the throat specialist to enable her to sing, the girl was persuaded by a fellow artist to drink a glass of champagne. In the next *La Bohème* cast the Musetta was the same, singing with her accustomed gay abandon to the Mimi of protecting Melba.

I have tried to conjure up something of the real Melba, and in the course of it have shown how essentially kind and generous she was within prima donna limitations. In more than enough instances the people she was kind to did not realise the moment for combining gratitude with self-reliance. Possessing no reliance—the very first need of anyone storming the citadels of fame—they found themselves swinging eventually in mid-air at the end of Melba's apron-strings; having no gratitude they forgot the lift they had been given by those apron-strings, and their own insufficiency made the grip relax. Gratitude, we all know, is the pleasant sense of favors to come.

But the moral of all this is, as Melba obviously agreed in the little colloquy of which I have made a text at the beginning of this chapter, it really is no use at all going out to seek reputation in the arcades of music unless you are able to stand on your own two feet. If a Melba will lend you an arm for a while, well and good, but that is not to be expected of her indefinitely. And few arms were more friendly to young singers than Melba's.

THE LAST
OF THE BOHEMIANS

CLAUDE McKAY

McKay was an Australian editor and newspaperman.

The first time I met John Lemmoné, Melba's personal manager, was in Brisbane. I was set down to interview Melba for the *Observer*, the *Courier's* evening paper; she was to arrive by liner from America in the early morning. But at eleven o'clock the ship had not yet arrived at Pinkenba, and my story had to be with the sub-editor at one o'clock. The liner was still a couple of hours away. So I asked John Lemmoné to be Melba for the purposes of the interview, and we vamped up a column together.

George Musgrove was the impresario of this concert tour. Many years later I got to know this remarkable man as intimately as it was possible to know him. There was nothing small in his make-up, and though he seemed a saturnine individual in his more genial moments he was a delightfully entertaining talker. His sense of the dramatic would manifest itself when recalling incidents in which he had figured. One such was when he was in his office at the Princess Theatre, Melbourne, and a card was brought to him by the stage-door keeper. The name on it, David Mitchell, conveyed nothing to him. However, he said, "Show him in."

An elderly man entered and Musgrove asked what he could do for him.

"You have just come back from Europe, I understand," the visitor said,

From: Claude McKay, *This Is the Life: An Autobiography of a Newspaperman*. Sydney: Angus & Robertson Publishers, 1961.

"and from your knowledge of these things could tell me what I would like to learn."

Musgrove asked him what he wanted to know, and Mitchell continued, "It's about my daughter. Is she as famous as the papers make out?"

"First," replied Musgrove, "you might tell me who your daughter is."

"She calls herself Nellie Melba," the old man answered.

Mitchell, who was one of the wealthiest men in Victoria, was said to have cast off his daughter because she wanted to be a singer and left her to dree her own weird. He looked uneasily at Musgrove.

"All I can tell you," said Musgrove, "is that your daughter is one of the great ones of this world. She is the Queen of Song, and at her feet are kings and lords of the earth." And he went on to tell Mitchell what a Melba night was like at Covent Garden, at the Metropolitan in New York, and at the brilliant opera houses of Europe. The old man, shaken, quietly thanked Musgrove and went his way.

In the triumphal tour that Musgrove directed David Mitchell was a devoted follower of his daughter. He went everywhere with her, basking in the reflected glory. He was seen amongst the crowds, observing the homage paid her; he drove with her to concert halls, helping to clear the way through the throng. And Melba delighted in his exultation, giving him her affection and laughter and jollying him along. Nothing gave her more enjoyment than to let him know that she could take care of the bawbees! At a week-end party at Coombe Cottage, Lilydale, where long after this I was Melba's guest, she mentioned that her father had foreclosed on a mortgage on a local butcher's shop and was running the business with a manager. A cold saddle of mutton was on the sideboard at a Sunday luncheon at which David Mitchell was present. Before us all Melba said, "I had to change my butcher. I got that saddle of mutton ninepence cheaper than I could get it at father's shop." . . .

The Golden Years of the Theatre

Melba's grand opera season hit Sydney with an impact such as had never previously been experienced in Australia. Box-office queues ran right round a city block. We booked the gallery at ten shillings a seat, and it was packed for every evening performance by two o'clock in the afternoon. We found room for a piano in the gallery, and there, while waiting, students entertained themselves with music and song. On one afternoon I induced Melba to climb the gallery stairs. She sat down at the piano and accompanied herself, singing to the rapturous crowd. They stood and cheered her as she left.

Melba was immensely popular in the theatre. On the first day when she put in an appearance at a rehearsal the stagehands were gaping at her.

"Like to hear me sing, boys?" she asked.

Would they! The orchestra was rehearsing *La Traviata*. Melba sang her big first-act aria. Then she went off into the wings, returned and bowed to the stage crew. After that nothing for her was ever too much to ask of them.

With John Lemmoné, who held her in great awe, I looked after the publicity for the season. Melba had taken a house at Rose Bay—the castellated residence built by the Bennetts when the *Evening News* was proving to be a gold-mine. But it was dark and damp, and during the season Melba went down with laryngitis, and was unable to appear for several nights. One day Lemmoné came to me in great distress. He had received a note in Melba's scrawl, saying:

Isn't it disgusting? The people say I am drunk. What can be done about it?
Yours, heartbroken,
Nellie Melba

I asked John to leave the letter with me and I'd think it over. He did so. That night I called on Heney, then editor of the *Sydney Morning Herald*. I showed him Melba's letter. He asked what could be done.

"Print it facsimile," I said, "with a note that Melba has laryngitis, rebuking anyone who holds the uncharitable thoughts that many do."

Heney hesitated. I told him I represented Melba, and assured him he had full authority to do as I requested. With all the indignation I felt, I remarked that it was a shameful way to malign our most famous Australian woman, and urged him to administer the reproof. After a while he agreed.

Next morning John Lemmoné came hot-foot to see me.

"What have you done?" he moaned. "I've never been so upset in my life! Good God! What will Melba say? You'll have to come along with me and see her, and may God have mercy on your soul!"

We drove out to Rose Bay and were shown to Melba's bedroom, where she was sitting up in bed, the *Herald* in front of her.

"Who did this?" she demanded.

"I did," I confessed.

"Come here!" she commanded. "Lean over."

This I did, expecting the worst. She threw her arms round me, kissing me on both cheeks.

"I knew John wouldn't have the audacity to say anything," she said, laughing, "and I would never have thought of this myself."

When Melba reappeared a few nights later the house stood up and cheered her for minutes. She always said that this was the reception that moved her most deeply of all.

From then on I was in high favour, and when the company went to Melbourne she asked that I go also. She was told that Sydney couldn't spare me. The day before the opening night she wired that if I wasn't on the express that same evening she wouldn't appear. I was on the train, all right!

In Melbourne I signed a contract to go with Melba to Europe as her secretary. About this time J. C. Williamson came back from abroad. I didn't see him immediately on my return to the Sydney office—which was then in Castlereagh Street, adjoining the Theatre Royal—but one evening, after finishing work for the day, I encountered him walking up and down outside the office door. He strolled along with me to the Australia and asked me would I join him in a drink. That was the only time I had ever heard of him entering a bar.

"What's this I hear of you going to Paris with Melba?" he said when our drinks were poured.

I told him it was so. I had reached a dead end, anyhow. He said I would be unwise to be at the caprice of a woman, especially a woman as celebrated as Melba. Would another few hundred a year keep me?

"But," I said, "I don't see how I could honourably ignore my signature."

"Leave that to me," he said. "I'll arrange it with Melba." And he did.

Beverley Nichols became Melba's secretary on her return to London, and was with her long enough to write her into his novel, *Evensong*.

I had never met a woman of more abounding health than Melba. She took great care of herself, but didn't coddle. At Lilydale she was first to be up and about every morning. She would be out in the garden with the dawn, in high spirits, and had the gift of being able to remain energetic the whole day long. When I was in London in later years and heard that she had been carried ashore at Perth, I felt it must be the end. I wrote her obituary for John Gordon, editor of the *Sunday Express*, and left it with him in case the worst happened. I was on my way to Australia when he printed my "Memories of Melba".

MELBA

IVOR NEWTON

A list of the great accompanists of the past fifty years would certainly include Coenraad V. Bos (born in 1875), Frank La Forge (1879), Michael Raucheisen (1889), Gerald Moore (1899), and Ivor Newton, who tells us, rather coyly, that he was born "early in the 1890s." His experiences working with some of the great singers of the period are told in a fascinating manner in his book *At the Piano*, from which this selection is taken. For the most part, his wealth of stories comes from long personal contact with the artists with whom he worked closely: His chapter on Tetrazzini is a real gem, and the one about Conchita Supervia is a classic living portrait. One suspects, however, that his association with Melba was a brief and passing one, as his picture of the Australian singer is fleshed out with material that came to him from others and is marred by some slight inaccuracies.

Often in my early days, I heard opera goers dismiss one new soprano after another with the remark, "I'm fastidious—I was brought up on Melba." In other words, they were accustomed to a voice of unique purity and freshness, with some of the qualities of a highly cultivated treble, used with a perfect artistry that prevented any musical mistakes. How can Melba's voice be described? I have heard it called both "golden" and "as bright and

From: Ivor Newton, *At the Piano—Ivor Newton: The World of an Accompanist*. London: Hamish Hamilton, 1966.

chaste as glittering silver." There is no doubt that its unique quality, once heard, was never forgotten. Melba was, moreover, a woman of precise if somewhat limited tastes whose fastidiousness went hand in hand with strict musical discipline. I am still proud and happy to remember that she encouraged me when I was still fairly new to my career.

The telephone call which one day summoned me to go and play for Dame Nellie was, for me, a royal command, and having been summoned to the presence, I soon learned to choose my words carefully when I was talking to her. One day I ventured, while we were rehearsing, to remark on the perfection of her phrasing. She looked at me and said, "That is why I am Melba."

Clara Butt was the voice of the British Empire, but Nellie Melba was something more rare and dazzling, the idol and the ideal of audiences wherever European music was to be heard, from her native Australia across the globe. She came to the musical world with the power of her own commanding personality and the authority of a prima donna who had been coached in their operas by Verdi, Puccini and Leoncavallo, and who had won the hearts of Gounod, Delibes and Massenet for her singing of their music. She was the first singer of international standing to take the gramophone seriously and the first to broadcast "to the world," though the world of those early days of radio had a circumference of only a thousand miles. She began her broadcast with a "Melba trill" to allow her listeners to tune in.

Totally intolerant of inefficiency, so that Beecham declared that he liked to have Melba in the cast of an opera because she made everybody on the stage behave well, she saw to it that everything around her was well organised. Every detail of her day was arranged in such a precise and orderly fashion one would have thought she would have been a successful business woman. But her personality gave her the quality of being so much larger than life that she would never have been satisfied with a career outside the public gaze. Oddly enough, her speaking voice was hard, loud, and in no way lovable, but it seemed to embody part of her personality.

Melba made her presence felt at my first appearance in the Queen's Hall. I was accompanying Dmitri Smirnoff, the leading tenor of the Imperial Russian Opera, whose singing with the Russian company at Drury Lane had attracted a good deal of attention in spite of the presence of Chaliapin. Smirnoff, distinguished both in appearance and in his singing, had recently been appearing with Melba at Monte Carlo and evidently she admired him greatly. On this occasion she was sitting in the stalls and, when the programme ended and it was time for encores, she walked up the steps to the side of the platform and began to stage-manage the proceedings. This was my first meeting with her, and in spite of what I had heard of her I was not prepared for her brusque directness. She watched Smirnoff hesitate for a moment over his encores, and then took charge.

"Give 'em *'La donna è mobile,'*" she commanded. Then she turned to me. "You won't need music for that," she said.

When I knew her rather better, she said, "When Smirnoff sings in *Rigoletto*, you have the rare experience of seeing a tenor who has the grace and bearing you'd expect from a Duke of Mantua."

Working with Melba was not easy; her strictness, perfectionism and technical mastery made demands on her colleagues and accompanist as exigent as those made on her own skill and temperament. But it was not necessary, when she was at work, to guard against difficult moods, tantrums and temperamental storms; she was too disciplined an artist to allow externals to interfere with work. What roused her anger was anything slovenly or inappropriate. She told me how, sitting with Puccini in a box at La Scala during a performance of *Tosca*, she turned to him when *"E lucevan le stelle"* was applauded until it was given an encore and asked, "Why do you allow this sort of thing? It breaks the continuity." The composer replied, "If I didn't, it would break their hearts." One sometimes felt that all hearts could break as long as things were done in the Melba way. My usual classification of singers as being either emotional or intellectual does not, I must admit, apply to Melba. No one could have called her an intellectual singer, in spite of her strictly disciplined approach to her art. "I shall sing the opera exactly as Gounod wrote it; I hope that you'll conduct it in the same way," were her words to the young Eugene Goossens when, before a performance of *Faust* which he was unexpectedly called upon to conduct, he went to ask her how she would sing Marguerite and if there was anything about her interpretation he ought to know. On the other hand, she was certainly not an emotional singer; the extreme purity of her voice prevented that, and as for acting, someone unkindly said her "quaint little gestures" were her substitute for it.

To her discipline was joined a sense of realism unusual in a great prima donna. She faced facts and liked other people to do the same. She sent the young singer, Elena Danielli, a protégée of hers, to an audition at Covent Garden, hoping for the rôle of Violetta in *La Traviata*. Danielli returned full of disappointment. "They have asked me to sing Xenia" (a small if telling part) "in *Boris*, with Chaliapin," she said. "Well," said Melba briskly, "that's better than a slap in the face from a wet pudding cloth."

Melba accepted homage from her public as something no more than her due. As her voice gradually lost its phenomenally sweet, clear high notes, and the elaborate coloratura of many of her great rôles became taxing—a fact which Melba noticed before the mass of her admirers—*La Bohème* was a gift from the gods to her. Her voice might no longer be capable of the acrobatic exertions it had tirelessly performed in the past, but it remained fresh, pure and ageless, and Mimi suited it to perfection. It was Melba who forced *La Bohème* upon a reluctant Covent Garden management in 1899, and was responsible for its British success; the work had been heard before, in a Carl Rosa Company production, in Liverpool and subsequently in London, in an English translation *The Bohemians* but had made little impression.

Melba's reign at Covent Garden lasted for many years, and her power over the management was so real that she was consulted about such details as the colour and design of new curtains. Sir Thomas Beecham (another autocrat) described the situation which arose when he ordered that "her" dressing-room in Covent Garden was to be repainted without her knowledge. For a long time her contract contained a clause declaring that no artist appearing at Covent Garden was to receive more than she did, so that she was paid in guineas to Caruso's pounds. This was the age when every well-dressed man wore a tie-pin, and it was with tie-pins that Melba rewarded her male colleagues and subordinates. A tenor or a baritone high in her favour would receive a tie-pin with her initial "M" in diamonds; the less exalted found that the initial was in gold, while for attentive stage-door keepers it was in blue enamel.

Melba had all the experienced artist's sensitivity to an audience's reactions. Once at an afternoon concert in Caernarvon, the audience was stolid rather than responsive. With half the programme behind her, she determined to break down the barriers. She addressed her apparently staid Welsh listeners. "All my life," she said, "I've been hearing about the wonderful voices of the Welsh, and their magnificent choral singing. I wonder, may I ask you to sing for me? Perhaps you would sing *Aberystwyth*."

The audience rose like one man and the splendid tune rolled overpoweringly forth with a fervour that almost raised the roof. The rest of the concert was an overwhelming triumph for Melba.

In Australia as well as in England she imposed authority over the country and its social life as well as over the musical theatre.. "The Melba Opera Company" toured the Australian cities with artists of the first rank, drawn to the antipodes by Melba's prestige.

After she had sung with Dino Borgioli at Monte Carlo, she ensured his engagement in Australia by means of a telegram which read: "We must have Borgioli. Fine voice, good legs." Borgioli told me of Dame Nellie's speech on the last night of the season in Melbourne that year. She stood, surrounded by bouquets, thanked the audience for its support and gave her special thanks to her "dear public" for attending performances on the nights when she was not singing. But it was not only Melba's voice which made her Australian operatic ventures successful, although the Australian tradition of music began with her; her sheer efficiency as an organiser made a real success of whatever she handled with concentration.

When I had been lunching in Sydney with Lord Wakehurst, then Governor of New South Wales, Lady Wakehurst said, "You must show Mr.

Newton the Melba Room." I was taken upstairs to a most luxurious bed-room, with a splendid view over the garden and the harbour. Lord Wake-hurst explained that, as Dame Nellie lived in Melbourne, whenever she came to Sydney, it had become her custom over the years to herald every visit with a telegram to the Governor, "Please can I have my room?"

Only once did Melba shake the Australian people's devotion to their star. When Clara Butt and Kennerley Rumford were about to tour Australia for the first time, draining the country of money with fourteen concerts in Sydney, another fourteen in Melbourne and as many in every other city as its population warranted, the Rumfords asked Melba's advice. What sort of programmes, they wondered, would Australians like? "Sing 'em muck," said Melba, bluntly. "It's all they understand."

Forty years later, when Clara Butt wrote her *Memoirs*, she recalled the advice she had been given by the greatest musical personality Australia had produced, and caused an uproar. Cables of denial sped across the oceans from Australia, for loyalty had somehow to be recovered. "How could I have said that?" asked Melba plaintively of the Australian press. "I have always had the greatest admiration for the taste and discrimination of my Australian audiences." A mutual friend asked Melba if it were true that she had really given Clara Butt this dangerous advice. "Of course not," retorted Melba; "in Clara's case, it wasn't necessary."

Although her directness and forthright vigour were very Australian, she was completely *au fait* with Europe and the ways of the European *beau monde*. She lived in an atmosphere of Edwardian elegance and, socially, was as precise and correct as she was in matters of music. She never accepted an engagement to sing at a musical party at any great house in London unless she received an invitation, so that her social position, even though she was one of the artists, was never in doubt. When Tetrazzini sud-denly soared like a rocket to fame, Melba's animosity towards her per-mitted no exchange of compliments; *Punch* published a cartoon of the hostile prima donne fighting a duel with gramophones.

Before her final tour she fell out with Lionel Powell, who was also Tetraz-zini's manager, and went to Ibbs and Tillett, who arranged her farewell progress throughout the country. She invited me to play for her, and when I naturally mentioned this to Lionel Powell, he looked at me somewhat belligerently. "You can't do that," he said, "I'm relying on you for Tetrazzini's tour at the same time." As both Powell's and Tetrazzini's names sounded unpleasant in Melba's ears, my reply refusing her offer could not tactfully mention either; I have never found a letter so difficult to draft.

She could be thoughtless too, to those who were not her rivals. On one of her tours, a manager, afraid that advancing years might cost him his job, tried to disguise the wear and tear of age with a little make-up. One evening she caught sight of him as she left her dressing room to go to the platform.

"Good God," she cried, without a moment's reflection, "you've more on your face than I have!"

In later life, her self-knowledge could be disconcerting. After one of her very last concerts, a gushing woman in the artists' room rushed up, crying. "That was wonderful! You've never sung better in your life!"

"My dear lady," said Melba grimly, "I assure you that I have—often." I met her once in Munich when I was on my way to Salzburg. "When you get there," she said, "look out for a soprano named Adele Kern. Her high notes are as beautiful as mine—or, rather, as mine used to be."

When entertaining friends, Melba was always ready to sing. But when she herself was a guest, a different principle applied. I was once playing at a party in a country house when Melba, who was staying near by, had come over to dinner. After dinner, our hostess said to me, "Do you think we could get Melba to sing?" "That depends," I said, with considerable hesitation, "upon who asks her." I looked around at the distinguished men present and suggested that Edward Carson, the famous lawyer and politician, might be able to persuade her, for I thought that she might succumb to his musical brogue. Our hostess, however, favoured Lord Hewart, the Lord Chief Justice, as her emissary. Hearing what his duties would be, Lord Hewart asked me to brief him for this delicate mission. I suggested what I thought would be a tactful line of approach, and, at the first opportunity, Hewart walked over to Melba and engaged her in conversation while we watched anxiously from a distance. Melba seemed to be in excellent spirits, and our hopes of success rose considerably. But gradually we noticed her face becoming firmer and firmer and her smiles less expansive. A few moments later Lord Hewart returned to where I was standing. "No good," he whispered in my ear. "Put that down as my greatest failure as an advocate."

At her farewell performance in Covent Garden, King George V and Queen Mary were in the Royal Box and the audience was madly rapturous. Melba was sixty-five, but the programme was unsparing and nothing could have borne more undeniable witness to the brilliance of her technical control than her ability, at that age, to deal with the second act of Gounod's *Romeo and Juliet*, the third and fourth acts of *La Bohème* and the Willow Song and "Ave Maria" from *Otello*. The applause was very moving and the mass of flowers that reached the stage magnificent. Amongst them was a huge kangaroo in flowers, and when an admirer in the stalls threw a posy up to her, Melba's Australian breeding came out and she caught it with the skill of a Don Bradman.

Her speech, the last time her voice was heard in the opera house in which she had been most at home, was excellent; "My darling public," she begged, "at all costs keep Covent Garden as your opera house—for my sake." As befitted a queen about to abdicate, her speech forgot nobody, not even the stagehands or the doorkeeper who, she said, "for forty years has never failed to escort me to my car."

At that farewell performance, John Brownlee, one of her protégés, made his debut singing Marcello to her Mimi. Years later, in Australia, he took me to see her grave. Carved on her tombstone beneath her name, are the words "*Addio, senza rancor.*" No one could have thought more appropriate for her epitaph than those of Mimi's touching farewell.

OPERATIC HIGHS AND LOWS

CLAUDE KINGSTON

The J. C. Williamson organization, one of the world's oldest theatrical companies, had its headquarters in Melbourne. It is "The
Firm" mentioned in this chapter, taken from Claude Kingston's
book, *It Don't Seem a Day Too Much*. Kingston began life as a
pianist and church organist; he eventually became "Celebrities
Manager" for the Tait brothers, who ran the Williamson company.
The title of his book may need some explanation. He tells us in an
author's note that he took it from a song, "My Old Dutch," made
famous by the British music hall entertainer, Albert Chevalier
(1861-1923). In the ballad, the humble cockney tells in his own
simple words of his love for his wife:

> We've been together now for forty years,
> An' it don't seem a day too much;
> There ain't a lady livin' in the land
> As I'd swop for my dear old dutch!

Kingston's fifty years in the business of entertainment in Australia brought him in close contact with a seemingly endless list of
musical personalities, including Paderewski, Chaliapin, Flagstad,
Galli-Curci, Heifetz, Tibbett, Crooks, Schipa, Kubelik, and many

From: Claude Kingston, *It Don't Seem a Day Too Much* (Adelaide: Rigby Ltd., 1971).

others. "The power behind the scrum, invisible but ever present," Yehudi Menuhin wrote on an autographed photograph in 1935 to the man who had managed his tour, arranged his hotel bookings, smoothed his path, and generally acted as wet-nurse. Kingston's breezy style is well exemplified in the following excerpt from his memoirs. He died at the age of ninety in 1978.

Some people, including music-lovers, insist that grand opera is infantile rubbish. If everything about life and art has to be strictly logical, like a geometrical design, these stern realists are possibly right but life and art would be dreary if they travelled all the time on straight unwavering lines. Anyway, an astonishingly large number of ordinary mortals seem to go on delighting in grand opera with all its extravagances. I confess I am one.

I know the stories of many of the popular operas are irrational. I also know there are occasional incongruities on the operatic stage—for example, a fat tenor singing a passionate love song to a fat soprano. Do these things matter? The grand opera world is one of make-believe, as enchanted in its own way as the fairy-tale world of Hans Andersen, and those who love it accept it for what it is and close their eyes to the absurdities. At all events, grand opera has lasted for a long while and I believe it will last for a long while yet.

I have had a hand in presenting every grand opera season in which The Firm has been involved since 1924. My memories are chiefly of people—of artists like Toti Dal Monte, Lina Pagliughi, Joan Sutherland, Rina Malatrasi, Dino Borgioli, Apollo Granforte, Joseph Hislop, John Brownlee, and a score of others but, above all, of that unsurpassed prima donna and unexcelled businesswoman, Dame Nellie Melba.

Melba and The Firm joined forces to stage the two grand opera seasons which took Australia by storm in 1924 and 1928. I had been acquainted with her since 1918 when the flautist, John Lemmoné, her associate artist and business manager for many years, introduced us. I had met her several times in the years between and she had always been friendly in her blunt and uneffusive way but it was when we were preparing for the 1924 season that I first came to know her well and saw behind the artist the astute businesswoman who made of Melba the supreme prima donna of her time.

Most prima donnas—and also quite a few male stars of grand opera—are like petulant children. They want their own way at any price, they cry for the moon and expect somebody to run and fetch it for them. Not Melba. There never was a stronger-minded woman, so of course she wanted her own way, but not at any price; being practical and intelligent, she left other prima donnas to build cloud castles and concentrated on going out after attainable things.

What she accomplished is a matter of history, and some day, I hope, Australians will recognise her for what she was—a great woman who had an immense impact on this country's musical development.

The Firm put me in charge of publicity for the Sydney part of the Melba-Williamson 1924 season and I burnt some gallons of midnight oil laying plans. I thought I knew something about theatrical publicity but alongside Melba I was a tyro.

We went from Melbourne to Sydney by the express a few days ahead of the company. She asked me to get a statement ready for reporters from the Sydney newspapers who were to join the train at Moss Vale, some two hours from Sydney. I drafted one for her.

Having read it through she said, "You've got a lot to learn," and tore it up and tossed the bits of paper in the air. "I'll speak to them."

I was abashed and also a little hurt. I had thought the statement a good one—a clear summary of the highlights of the coming season with due mention of the stars who would be singing. All right, Dame Nellie, I thought, let's see you do better!

The express stopped at Moss Vale and the reporters crowded into Melba's compartment. She received them with royal graciousness. One of them asked a leading question about the opera season but Melba brushed it aside. "Bother the opera!" she said. "What I want to talk about are the fleas on this beastly express. It's alive with them."

She then told the hard-scribbling reporters that she had not slept a wink because of these voracious fleas. "I'm bitten all over," she exclaimed. "Would you like me to lift my skirts to prove it?"

Nobody was ungallant enough to make her do that. It was just as well, I suspect. No fleas had bitten me and if they had attacked Melba she had not mentioned it until then.

The reporters scuttled away and wired off vivid accounts of Melba's battle with the fleas of the Melbourne-Sydney express. Every newspaper featured the story and plastered Sydney with posters about it. The railway authorities protested that nobody else had complained and said they were mystified why their fleas had singled out Melba, but they undertook to purify the train at once.

Was it legitimate publicity? I prefer to let moralists answer that. All I know is that the talk about Melba's fleas reached a thousand people for every one who would have bothered to read of Toti Dal Monte's dazzling coloratura and that practically not a soul in Sydney or New South Wales was unaware that we had arrived to launch a grand opera season.

And long practice had shown Melba that when you want to make people take notice of an opera season anything goes.

The 1924 and 1928 seasons owed much of their success to Melba's drive, imagination, and hard-won knowledge. They, and The Firm's 1948 season also, owed hardly less to that remarkable man Nevin Tait. He had a pro-

found knowledge of grand opera and a magic touch which somehow—
don't ask me how—transformed a good company into a great one.

He made his home in London for over fifty years as The Firm's resident
director abroad and was always there except when he came out to Australia
as Artistic Director of our opera seasons or made sorties to the Continent in
search of talented people. He was thus largely responsible for engaging the
long line of celebrities we imported.

I remember that Henry Russell was misguided enough to try to usurp
Nevin's place in 1924. Russell, an able but pushful English impresario and
singing teacher, arrived in Australia some weeks ahead of Nevin and lost no
time in announcing himself to the Press as Dame Nellie Melba's personal
representative (which he was) and Artistic Director of the company (which
he was not). The issue was quickly settled once Nevin arrived but only after
a most shocking row. I don't know if it was to mark his victory that Nevin
gave the most wonderful supper party I have ever attended. He invited
between thirty and forty of us to a private dining-room at Menzies Hotel
and treated us to such a meal as only a man who was an artist in living
would know how to order; each course was accompanied by a superlative
wine. Need I say that Henry Russell was not there? Russell stayed in Australia as Melba's personal representative until, having succeeded in quarrel-
ling with her also, he found himself on his way back to Europe at short
notice.

Nevin Tait had a winning way and consummate poise. Nothing could
disturb his outward calm, not even the kind of misadventure which befell
him on a night when one of the companies was playing Aïda in Sydney.
Dame Nellie Melba and I were standing at the back of the dress circle.
Holding a packed house enthralled, the singers and orchestra were just
reaching a tremendous climax in one of the big scenes when Nevin Tait,
immaculate in evening dress and looking like anything but an Egyptian in
ancient Memphis, appeared on stage.

Most men trapped in that blaze of lights with music crashing all about
them would have yielded to panic and gone stumbling back to the shelter of
the wings in ludicrous haste to escape. Nevin Tait walked right on across
the stage as if nothing untoward were happening. Some of the audience tit-
tered but if could have been far worse; they would have collapsed in
guffaws and thrown the whole performance into chaos if he had done what
impulse must have bade him do and run for it.

He told me later he had been discussing a detail of casting with somebody
in the wings. Wanting to cross to the other side, he made a false entry and
found himself not behind the backdrop but in front of it. It happened as
simply as that.

Standing beside me at the back of the dress circle, Melba made some
sulphurous comments when she saw our elegant and imperturbable Artistic
Director strolling across the stage. I shall not repeat her words. They were

not set to music but they were more telling than anything in the whole wide range of grand opera.

Working beside Melba in the 1924 and 1928 opera seasons I learnt an immense respect for her artistic integrity, her perfectionism, her personal probity, her moral stamina.

Her business acumen was astounding; it would have done credit to an international banker or the chairman of a great department store. And she had one uncanny gift which I have never met in any other woman or any man. She could work through a sheaf of begging letters quickly and separate the genuine from the bogus without faltering. Being in the public eye, she was a natural target for both professional cadgers and decent people down on their luck who did not know where to turn for help.

Every morning she would come to my office with the day's collection of letters pleading for aid. She would read them with care, tearing up one with some such remark as, "I don't like this handwriting or the person behind it. No!" Then perhaps tossing the next one across my desk and saying, "This woman's in real trouble, Claude. We must help her." The money she distributed, anything from five to fifty pounds, came out of her own pocket. One day, I remember, the total was more than £400.

I knew better than to gossip about her generosities. "If you ever mention this to anyone," she warned me once, "I'll never speak to you again." Phil Finkelstein, who was for many years in charge of The Firm's publicity in Melbourne, was the only other man in the know, so if either of us had talked, retribution would have been swift and certain.

Whenever I was able to test Melba's judgment on anybody who wrote to her for help I found it unerring, but her assessments of close associates were not always infallible. For all her perception she let her heart rule her head at times if she formed a strong personal liking for some man or woman. Beverley Nichols was an example. He was in the early twenties when Melba met him, a young Fleet Street newspaper reporter and an aspiring writer, and she brought him out to Australia at the time of the 1924 season to "ghost" her autobiography, *Melodies and Memories*. She paid him a good salary, introduced him to scores of influential people, took him to stay at her Victorian home, Coombe Cottage, near Lilydale, and in general treated him like a prodigal son. Soon after her death he published a novel called *Evensong*. It had a wide success. The central character was an ageing prima donna locked in a battle for supremacy with a young one. The real-life models were obviously Melba and Toti Dal Monte, and everybody who had been associated with the 1924 Melba-Williamson season knew it. I thought it quite disgusting but perhaps I am biased; I had seen something of Nichols while the 1924 season was playing and found nothing about him to like.

I am glad to say that many of the young artists and other young people

Melba helped—and she helped a large number—were loyal to her and loyal to her memory. The Australian baritone, John Brownlee, was one. She advised him to go to Europe and study when he was an unknown twenty-three-year-old; a few years later Melba, having taken great pains to put him on the world singing map, brought him back to Australia as one of the principals of the 1928 opera company.

I was glad to see Brownlee do well in his native land. My association with him had begun even before Melba's. When he was eighteen or nineteen I heard him at a concert in his home town, Geelong, and that night I engaged him to come to Collins Street Baptist church as baritone soloist in an Easter presentation of *The Crucifixion*. It was his first engagement in Melbourne.

I am bound to admit however that I was never an unrestrained admirer of Brownlee's singing. I found his voice rather monotonous, and although he was a conscientious singer he had not the fire in his soul ever to be a great one.

Few things exasperate me more than the stories which still go the rounds to the effect that Melba was sometimes the worse for drink.

I know the origin of those tales. They were put into circulation by another Australian singer who was fond of the bottle herself. This woman, who was some years younger than Melba, had an excellent voice; if she had been born with more character—a little of Melba's fibre, let us say—she might have reached the top. Disappointed at falling short, she let envy eat into her and set out to blacken Melba's name by whispering the baseless yarn that Melba drank. Scandalmongers clutched at it and noised it around, and soon many Australians accepted it as true.

I have been more or less closely acquainted with hundreds of men and women who knew Melba well. Some liked her and others detested her but they have all been at one on her supposed tippling; they agree that it began as a mischievous fabrication and grew because certain people like to see their betters deflated and abased, whether justly or not.

I worked on the 1924 opera season for twenty-eight weeks in Sydney and Melbourne. I saw Melba every day and usually three or four or five times a day, and I always escorted her back to her hotel after the performance. Yet at no time did I see her take more than one glass of champagne at a meal or any other sitting and never anything else.

The stories that she drank should not need to be refuted. Her artistic and business record is the best proof of their falsity; she could not have survived in either field if she had got under the weather even occasionally, let alone often. She was still singing tolerably well in her sixties, at an age when most singers have long been finished. In 1924 she sang the leading roles in such operas as *Faust*, *La Bohème*, and *Otello* a number of times, and neither her ageing voice nor her ageing body could have stood the strain had it been weakened by toping. But of course the little yelping poodles who always yap at the lion—from a safe distance—were there to yap at Melba. They still do. Why not? Their only hope of being noticed is to try to pull a giant down.

Although Melba was an iron disciplinarian and stricter with herself than anyone else, she was never a prude. She did not care a damn about the conventional morality of any action, only about its influence on the doer's efficiency. Anybody in her companies who drank too much was automatically out but she closed her eyes to the amorous adventures in which some of our stars continually indulged—sexual diversions did not dim the glory of their voices or make them late for rehearsals. If one of the prima donnas and a leading tenor, say, opted for one night or many nights of love together Melba shrugged and said in effect, "Good luck to them!" Had they gone on a drinking spree she would have been furious and packed them off back to Europe by the next boat.

One night in Sydney I escorted Melba to her suite at the Hotel Australia after the night's performance. We took the lift to her floor and were walking along the corridor when a naked man came out of a room fifteen or twenty paces ahead of us. We both knew him well; he was a most distinguished Australian and every second person in Sydney could have put the right name to his face at a glance.

I suppose he did not see us. He certainly did not look our way or give any other sign that he knew we were approaching. I never could bring myself to decide whether he was in a golden haze after too much champagne and unaware of his surroundings, or simply magnificently self-possessed. He strolled unhurriedly across the corridor, opened a door and took his nakedness inside, then closed the door quietly but firmly behind him.

"Did you see that?" Melba asked.

"Yes," I said.

That was all either of us ever said about it. We both knew that the bedroom into which the naked night-walker had disappeared was occupied by one of our prima donnas. I could not but admire his taste. She was a beautiful woman.

Troubles come in different shapes and sizes when an opera season is under way but one thing is as certain as tomorrow's sunrise: troubles always come. Sometimes they erupt long before the company even assembles, and that is what happened in 1928.

With all the preparations for the season well in hand (or so I innocently supposed), I decided to take a short holiday. I needed a break; I had worked for some years with only an occasional day or two away from the job, and I was stale. My wife and I decided to go to Cowes on Phillip Island, in Westernport Bay. We had hardly begun to unpack in the Isle of Wight Hotel, eighty-odd miles from Melbourne, when I realised we should have gone much farther. Sir George Tallis (who had been deservedly knighted in 1922), one of The Firm's Managing Directors, came through on the telephone from Melbourne. Tallis was as calm, as courteous, and as unflappable a man as any I ever knew but that day he was almost stuttering with emotion as he told me the awful news: The curtain might never rise on the opera season unless a strike by the Australian chorus could be settled.

"It could cost The Firm a hundred thousand pounds," he said. "You'll come?"

I went and told Ella the holiday was over.

Sir George Tallis and John, Frank, and Charles Tait were awaiting me at The Firm's offices in Melbourne. They were four horribly worried men.

"You know the people in Sydney," said Talis. "Smile at them! You mustn't fail. Money is no obstacle if you can settle this thing quickly."

I caught the express that evening knowing I had never had a weightier mission for The Firm. Time was so short. Dame Nellie Melba had left London for Australia, the Italian principals would be sailing from Europe any day. Without the chorus we would have to call the season off, pay heavy compensation to all the stars and other people we had on contract, and lose tens of thousands of pounds which we had already spent. Tallis's estimate that it would cost us £100,000 was conservative. And as a last bitter pill The Firm's prestige would be battered. Already the newspaper headlines were like the tolling of a death-bell.

The cause of the crisis was simple. The Firm had made a contract with E. A. Mowle, a Sydney choral coach, to train and supply the opera choruses and to act as chorus-master. Then, without consulting him, our European representatives had engaged a number of seasoned Italian opera choristers to act as chorus leaders and stiffen the less experienced Australians. Mowle's pride was wounded and, having said "No chorus!" he had withdrawn into his shell.

I had never met Mowle but I found him at the New South Wales Conservatorium. He was a gentle and scholarly little man. I liked him at once. We could have settled the whole thing after a few minutes' talk except for one complication: it had become a political issue.

"I can't do anything now," Mowle told me. "It's in Mr. Mahoney's hands."

Mr. Mahoney was William Mahoney, a New South Wales Labor Member of the House of Representatives.

"Surely we can arrange something?" I pressed Mowle.

He said he'd talk to Mahoney. The upshot was that after three days' skirmishing Mowle told me he had fixed a meeting between Mahoney and me in the lounge-bar of the Hotel Australia.

Mahoney and I got along well from the start. I bought him a drink and told him my side of the story. He bought me a drink and told me his side. He was a good rugged type of Australian, pleasant enough but determined to fight what he considered to be a capitalist attempt to downgrade the Australian choristers for the benefit of a bunch of spaghetti-eating Italians. He had his facts well marshalled and expressed himself in terse lucid English.

"It's a pity to let this trouble go on," I said. "It's doing nobody any good—not Mr. Mowle or his choristers or The Firm."

"Well," said Mahoney, "the Australians seem to be getting a rough trot."

I told him The Firm had nothing but admiration for the Australians. "We're not trying to push them out," I said. "All we want are the Italian chorus leaders. That will make things easier for the Australians and save everybody's time."

"Yes," said Mahoney, who was a dyed-in-the-wool Labor man but no extremist. "I can see that."

"Then let's agree on a settlement and put out a statement," I urged.

In a few minutes we hammered out a settlement which protected Mowle and his choristers on the one hand and The Firm on the other. Then we went along to a writing-desk near the lounge-bar and drafted a short Press statement.

I telephoned Tallis in Melbourne. He could hardly contain himself. He almost whooped with relief. When I got back to Melbourne next day he stopped just short of flinging his arms about me. "You've saved the season," he kept repeating. "You've saved the season."

Little Mowle and I became lifelong friends.

Oh, yes, troubles always come! Behind the scenes every opera house is a battleground. Not the least reason is that prima donnas are more often than not vain, capricious, and wayward when they are not playing their parts on stage. The more talented the prima donna the more pampered she is apt to be and therefore the more demanding and unreasonable. As a synonym for a spoilt or selfishly irrational person the term "prima donna" is, I assure you, singularly appropriate. The exceptions such as Melba, who knew her own value but never let success turn her head, and was a businesswoman first, last and all the time, are conspicuously few.

There was a particularly fierce contest of wills between two of our prima donnas in the 1924 season. The ladies were Toti Dal Monte and Augusta Concato, and the bone of contention, if I may so express it, was an inoffensive little Pekinese dog. A Melbourne opera-lover left the Peke at Her Majesty's Theatre ticketed with a card inscribed "To my favourite prima donna" or something like that—a flattering but imprecise direction. The donor evidently intended the Peke to be a token of gratitude for the joy that the singing of one of our prima donnas had given him and for one reason or another all the others vacated the field in favour of Dal Monte and Concato. There was the riddle. Did he mean Dal Monte or did he mean Concato?

Each laid claim to the gift dog and neither would yield. They fought over the poor little animal like two furies and nearly dragged it in two. Nobody in authority had the courage to make a decision in favour of one or the other but someone ordered the dog to be impounded until they settled the issue between themselves. The battle went on morning, noon and night with the rivals screeching at one another on the flimsiest pretext. Not, let me say, that either Toti or Augusta cared two grace-notes about the Peke as a dog. The motive of the dispute was quite different. The Peke was a badge of merit and each was determined to have it, not for itself but for what it represented.

I shall not detail all the shifts and manoeuvres in that deadly battle but Dal Monte got the Peke in the end. Nobody was really surprised. Under her plump and smiling exterior she was quite a steely little lady.

Love tangles are inseparable from a grand opera season. I suppose the atmosphere of an opera house encourages romantic thoughts in anybody naturally inclined that way, especially in prima donnas. Dinh Gilly, the French baritone who became one of the great singing teachers of his time after his retirement from the operatic stage, once said of the prima donnas he had known that "if they hadn't lovers around them they used to drag the scene shifters into their dressingrooms before their mad scenes." An over-simplification perhaps, but basically true.

While one of the Melba-Williamson seasons was at its height I went to bed in Melbourne one night and fell into a sound sleep. My bedside telephone woke me about three in the morning. A woman's voice pouring out a flood of frantic Italian greeted me when I put the receiver to my ear. The caller was one of our prima donnas and she demanded that I go to her on the instant—there was not a moment to lose. With visions of murder, suicide, and sudden death, I called a taxicab, threw on some clothing and hurried to the city hotel where she was staying.

The poor girl was having hysterics when I arrived and it took me some time to discover the reason. Then it all came out. Her lover, a baritone of no particular note as a singer but a muscular fellow with a powerful attraction for women, had placed his wife's photograph on the mantelshelf of the suite he and the prima donna were sharing and would not let her remove it. I needed all my tact to settle that argument but when I left the hotel the crisis had passed and the lady and her baritone were once again on smiling and amorous terms. Little of the night remained, and I was heavy-eyed next day.

I recall another lively scene in Sydney. A court had ordered one of our prima donnas to pay heavy damages to the wife of a man singer for alien-ating his affections. She was burning with righteous indignation. It seemed the affair, having started as a grand passion, had diminished in ardour and the prima donna was ready, even eager, to return the erring husband to his wife. She complained bitterly because the unreasonable wife refused to take him back and insisted on a money settlement.

It must not be thought that the course of true love never runs smooth in the grand opera world. Toti Dal Monte and her husband, Enzo De Muro

Lamanto, the lyric tenor, provide good evidence of that. I have followed their marital career with special interest because I helped to push them toward the altar.

It was during the 1928 season that I noticed the close friendship between them. One night after a performance of *Lucia di Lammermoor* in Melbourne, in which Toti was Lucia and Enzo was Edgardo, I said to her, quite casually, "I think you should marry Enzo."

"If you think so I will," she said with her beaming smile. "You must arrange everything for a wedding in Sydney at St. Mary's Cathedral."

Delighted that these two likeable people intended marrying, I gladly accepted her instructions. I did not know what I was letting myself in for.

The company moved to Sydney and soon after our arrival there Toti came to my office to talk about the wedding. She told me she wanted it to be quiet with a reception for not more than thirty guests at Romano's. I must have been naïve. I took her words at face value and innocently put the arrangements in hand. Within a week she told me there would be not thirty guests but two hundred. I drew a deep breath and revised the preparations. A few days later Toti came to me again with a new list of guests: it had grown to five hundred.

Sydney has never seen another wedding quite like it. Australians loved Toti; she was not only a magnificent singer in most of the popular soprano roles of Italian opera but also a woman of effervescent personality who won hearts wherever she went. St. Mary's Cathedral was filled to the doors, and 15,000 or more people jostled in the surrounding streets and parks listening to a running description of the ceremony piped over loud-speakers. That immaculate restaurateur, Azzalin Orlando Romano, sometimes known as "Azzalin the Dazzlin'," was a personal friend of Toti and Enzo, and the reception he organised was a dazzling event.

It was a wonderful wedding, the equal of anything even a grand opera composer or librettist ever imagined, and the costs were in proportion. A few days later the bills started coming in and they kept on coming. I mentioned them to the happy husband but Enzo shrugged. He did not intend to pay anything, The Firm could pay, he said—hadn't the wedding been a grand advertisement for us and well worth every penny it would cost us? And he turned his back and strolled away. It had undoubtedly been good publicity but neither I nor my associates in The Firm saw it as a legitimate charge on our advertising budget, particularly since Toti was being paid an astronomical fee every time she sang and Enzo was doing nicely also.

We decided to postpone a settlement until the season ended and the company was breaking up. The day of reckoning came after a series of farewell performances in Perth. I was not relishing the showdown but as it turned out I had been starting at shadows. I have never been sure if Toti and Enzo were doing an elaborate leg-pull when they refused to pay the bills in Sydney or whether they were serious but had second thoughts. I must give them the benefit of any doubt because after the last performance in Perth they came to my office, all radiant smiles, and treating the whole thing as a piece of comedy handed me a cheque in full settlement.

Along with the cheque they presented Nevin Tait with a gold cigarette case and me with a very lovely and expensive clock as a mark of goodwill and to remind us of their wedding. We were touched but neither of us nor anybody else who was there needed any keepsake to help us remember that wedding.

In fairness, I am bound to say that prima donnas are not the only opera-singers who throw violent fits of temperament. That fine baritone Apollo Granforte (what a Tonio he was in *Pagliacci!*) who came out in 1924 and again in 1928 and in 1932 could explode like the most mettlesome coloratura soprano when his *amour-propre* was hurt.

He came hurtling into my office in Sydney one morning waving a copy of the *Sydney Morning Herald* and nearly foaming at the mouth. We had put on *Lucia di Lammermoor* the night before and the *Herald* critic had given the performance a good notice; he had made some flattering comments on Granforte's singing and acting as Enrico so at first I could not guess why our star baritone was so irate. Then the penny dropped. As usual, the *Herald* had illustrated the review with photographs of two or three of the principals but that morning Granforte's picture had been omitted. He bellowed at me in Italian, clawing at the newspaper and ripping it to pieces. The uproar was terrific. Nevin Tait, whose room was next door, put his head in and de-manded, "What's all this?" but did not linger when he saw Granforte danc-ing in front of me gesticulating and strewing my carpet with torn news-paper. He backed away, closed the door, and left me to placate Granforte if I could.

Knowing few words of Italian I did not understand what Granforte was saying except that he wanted to murder the *Herald* critic and probably me too. But I did know that *Si* meant *Yes* in Italian and I felt I could reach for no better word in this crisis. So whenever he ran out of breath and paused to refill his lungs I said "Si! Si!" as soothingly as possible.

He ranted on for about eight or nine minutes and then collapsed, breath-less and voiceless. He had expended much more vocal energy than in sing-ing the chief baritone role in a whole opera and he slumped down in a chair like a blown-up rubber figure that has sprung a leak. I walked over and patted him on the shoulder and said "Si! Si!" Then I went in next door to see Nevin but before closing my door behind me I turned back to Apollo, nodded understandingly and repeated "Si! Si!"

When next I saw him he was his usual sunny self. He seemed to have for-gotten all about the *Herald's* affront. I smiled at him and he smiled back. For one moment I was tempted to murmur "Si! Si!" but I decided not to push my luck too far.

AS THEY REMEMBERED HER

JOHN THOMPSON

On the occasion of the one hundredth anniversary of Melba's birth, John Thompson, Senior Feature Producer of the Australian Broadcasting Commission in Sydney, put together a remarkable program by clever editing of tapes made from interviews. Here is the way he tells about it in his book.

Introduction

Some years ago I began doing radio biographies of outstanding Australians who were no longer alive but were still vividly remembered by friends, enemies, and acquaintances. All these programmes have been recorded on long-playing discs for the national archives, and some of them form the basis of this book.

Biography by word of mouth has been made possible with the development of tape recorders. My method has been to choose some celebrated person and then, usually over a long period, to record the reminiscences of people best able to tell me about him. What was he like? How did he walk and speak? How did he act in private? What made him tick?

The end result in each case was an intimate word-picture. One personality was revealed in the mirrors of many other personalities, all differently

From: John Thompson, *On the Lips of Living Men*. Melbourne: Lansdowne Press, 1962.

angled and all differently coloured. And each programme was held together by a minimum of linking narration spoken by myself.

Much more was recorded than I ever expected to use, and in due course my tapes had to be studied with great care in order to select the most lively and illuminating passages. Then came the delightful task of arranging these passages so as to create a logical and compelling symposium or conversation-piece, using the actual words and voices of the people with whom I had spoken. Hours of spontaneous talk had to be cut down to a total of sixty minutes or less, good material often had to be sacrificed for the sake of time or for the sake of unity, but there was no other restriction save the prevailing standards of good taste as applied to broadcasting.

The initial work of interviewing was of absorbing interest, because it brought me in touch with scores of unusual people. The associates of extraordinary persons are seldom ungifted or humdrum and a glance at the pages of this book will discover many names which have been important in their own time and not a few which will count for something in Australian history. Their reminiscences were often extremely searching, and for me—and afterwards, I hope, for the public—they enabled some splendid Australians to be understood and appreciated. A proportion of what I was told was probably wide of the mark, since memory is uncertain and interpretation fallible, but with each contribution the central personality emerged more clearly, even when speakers contradicted one another and even, sometimes, when issues were misunderstood.

My programmes could not have been made without the expert skill of my good friends the radio technicians of the P.M.G.'s Department. Again and again they bore with me through long sessions of dubbing and editing. Our first step in each instance was to assemble in the desired order on one tape, or a succession of tapes, all the best passages from my original recordings. My own linking narration was dubbed in where it was needed. Then, with scissors, we began tidying up. Modern magnetic tape can be edited like film, and a skilful man will eliminate blemishes or redundancies of speech so that excisions are never suspected. It is easy, by the same token, completely to distort what a speaker says, but we were scrupulous in not changing the import of what was originally said by my contributors. The whole aim of our editing was, as it were, to cut off the fat and leave the final programme incisive and packed and lean.

Normal spontaneous talk is surprisingly longwinded and repetitious, studded with "ums" and "ers" and full of uncompleted sentences and parentheses that get out of control. This is especially so when a speaker is thinking things out and defining his ideas as he goes. It does not necessarily detract from the interest of what is said, but it does slow up the act of communication. By skilful editing, however, most speech can be contracted without loss, the more so as it is quite normal for a groping speaker to light suddenly on a phrase or a striking image which crystallizes what he is driving at. Instantly his voice becomes charged with feeling, and all self-consciousness disappears. Such are the most precious moments of human talk, when words and voice are touched with inspiration, and it was around such moments that the liveliest and most moving parts of my programmes were organized.

In preparing the scripts of these programmes for publication in book form, some rearrangement has been necessary. Some of the sequences have been varied, and my linking narrations have been incorporated in individual prefaces. The contributions of the speakers have been printed verbatim and entire, save for an occasional correction of grammar or the addition of a few words necessary for lucidity—rather less, indeed, than is often done in preparing speeches for *Hansard*.

Dame Nellie Melba

It would be a poor compliment to a great personality to pretend that Melba had no failings. She was ambitious, proud, domineering, and she was sometimes ruthless. She was capable, too, of great kindness and generosity. She was an indefatigable worker, and she was a woman of penetrating intelligence. She had all the unconventionality, and all the authority, of a genius who knew she was a genius. She succeeded, unlike most re-creative artists, in leaving her mark on the musical life of her native land, where she is still a living force, thanks to the teachers she taught and the performers she helped and trained.

She was born Nellie Mitchell on the 19th of May, 1861, in Melbourne. Her family was wealthy, and she received a first-class education. Her marriage to a Queensland grazier was unsuccessful, and she did not remain with her husband after the birth of a son. At the first opportunity she sailed for Europe, where she studied with Madame Marchesi and assumed the stage name of Madame Melba, after her native city. Within a few years Melba became recognized as the outstanding lyric and coloratura soprano of her day. She flowered and flourished as a singer in the last years of Queen Victoria, and she reached the height of her career in the reign of Edward the Seventh. Never in history have the fortunate ones of the earth seemed more secure than in that brief epoch of plush and of lavish gilding, of osprey feathers and bell toppers, of hansom cabs and of gaslight, of princes—and prima donnas. Among the prima donnas, Melba was the greatest of all. She was by far the most famous of living Australians, and she did not lose touch with Australia. She frequently revisited her homeland and she established a residence at Coombe Cottage, near Lilydale, where the garden to this day is exactly as it was when she lived. During her latter years she was sometimes known to complain that she was already best remembered only for a dessert, Pêche Melba, invented and named for her by the master of master chefs, Escoffier. But she need not have sighed, I think, for she will long be remembered for her voice, her fame and her strength of character. She was envied and often maligned in Australia, but her death (which occurred in Sydney in 1931) was deeply and sincerely mourned.

The reminiscences in the following pages were supplied by students, colleagues and friends. J. Sutton Crow has long been a respected name in Melbourne's musical circles. Edric Henty and Basil Hart knew and admired Melba when they were young men. The late Peter Dawson often sang with her and was a friend for many years. John Brownlee, the famous baritone, began as one of her protégés. John Amadio, the flautist, admired and was admired by Melba. Sir Bernard Heinze, Director of the Sydney Conservatorium of Music, is of course known far and wide as a conductor—and as a wit. Wilfrid Thomas, who still sings a little, is a highly successful broadcaster. Lindley Evans the pianist was Melba's concert pianist for a period of some years. Ruth Ladd, singing teacher at the Sydney Conservatorium, carries on Melba's principles of instruction. Among those who were taught by the diva are Queenie Ashton, the well-known Sydney radio actress, Gertrude Johnstone of the National Theatre in Melbourne, Marie Bremner of musical comedy fame, Florence Yates of Sydney, and even Gladys Moncrieff whose splendid voice captured a whole generation. Helen Wood, who has gained an overseas reputation with her unusual paintings, is the daughter of Melba's sister the late Mrs. Lempriere. Phil Finkelstein is a man of the theatre, and worked for many years with Williamson's. William James, composer and pianist, was, until his retirement, Federal Director of Music for the Australian Broadcasting Commission. Lauri Kennedy the celebrated cellist, and his wife Dorothy Kennedy, were greatly assisted by Melba. Browning Mummery had one of the outstanding Australian voices of his day. Una Bourne, like Lindley Evans, was Melba's concert pianist for a period. The late Percy Grainger, needless to say, was a virtuoso pianist and one of the most notable of Australian composers. Dr. A. E. Floyd was for many years organist of St. Paul's Cathedral, Melbourne, and subsequently endeared himself to tens of thousands of listeners by his weekly broadcasts of magnificent recorded music.

J. SUTTON CROW

She could be most dignified, and at other times she could throw dignity away.

She could even be quite rough. She used to talk to Marshall Hall in such a way, telling him what to do, that I though, "By Jove, I don't know that I'd like that if I was a conductor."

EDRIC HENTY

She was a rather severe character. She never smiled much or anything like that, you know. She gave the impression of being rather a ruthless character, didn't show very much affection at any time. But on the other hand she had a particularly kind nature which I don't think was ever properly appreciated.

PETER DAWSON

She had terrific personal authority, and it was absolutely natural, inborn. It was the same with her charm, a thing that couldn't be acquired. And she was on the snobbish side too, sometimes.

JOHN BROWNLEE

I think the word *electrical* is really what explains Melba more than anything else. Things were always happening, it was always exciting, wherever Melba was.

QUEENIE ASHTON

She had a delightful sense of humour, but I wouldn't say it was at all refined. She loved things that were a little risqué. A lovely sense of fun, and she'd come out with a few swear words occasionally, you know. She didn't mind.

Her laugh, of course, was raucous. It really was. Extremely raucous. You couldn't think of that laugh coming from the woman who had that beautiful singing voice. She was terribly John Blunt, you know. She'd just speak her mind, and when she said to me, "My God, girl, your voice has been ruined. I don't know what Dinh Gilly has done to it," she used a deep rough voice. You couldn't think that it was the same voice she sang with, because of course when she sang a beautiful voice came out.

GERTRUDE JOHNSTONE

I think the great thing in her was her tenacity, and she would have been a success in anything that she had undertaken. If she'd had a milliner's shop, well, hers would have been the best milliner's shop in the street.

RUTH LADD

She said to us one day "I must have perfection." And she turned to Fritz Hart and she said "Fritz, if I'd been a housemaid I'd have been the best in Australia—I couldn't help it. It's got to be perfection for me."

BASIL HART

She had a tremendous amount of physical energy and also a very quick brain. As a business woman I think that she would probably have been able to run the I.C.I. or any of the big business concerns. Her energy was such that she could wear out any three younger people in the course of the day. Always on the go.

HELEN WOOD

She was a perfectionist, and I've seen her at the theatre spending hours of time not only attending to what she had to do herself—her own job, which goodness knows was hard enough—but looking at the lighting, looking at the dressing, seeing how the stage was going to be set, attending to the scenery, seeing that it was fresh—and because she was so good at those things she was impatient with people who were slovenly. I've seen people do a slovenly job or walk on to a stage badly or drop out of character—sort of relax and get tired when they should have been getting into character to go on with the part again—and these things would irritate her. And I think quite rightly.

LINDLEY EVANS

When she was 25 she sailed for Europe, in 1886. She was bent on an operatic career, and she began studying with Madame Marchesi in Paris. It was at a concert in Marchesi's house that she first used the name of Melba, and it was there that she got her start. Marchesi had so many students that entrepreneurs from all over Europe used to visit her studio in order to look them over. So one day somebody turned up and Marchesi said that she'd got a young Australian. So the young Australian was produced, and she sang. This chap was very interested in her and he immediately offered her a contract, and that was that. Not very much later someone else came in and he not only offered her a contract but offered her an engagement to sing in Brussels on a certain Saturday night, which Marchesi told Melba to sign. But Melba said she couldn't sign it because she'd already signed one for the other man. But Marchesi said "Oh don't worry about him; he's a great friend of mine and everything will be all right. I'll fix it." So Melba signed the second contract and duly went off to Brussels. No sooner had she got to Brussels than she was confronted with a writ which the first man had taken out to prevent her from singing, and there she was, living by herself, with this opportunity which she had come across the world for, and the whole foundation seemed to have been taken away from beneath her. Nothing to do—nothing! What *could* she do? So she was in her room, hardly caring what happened, and days went by until the Friday night, when suddenly there was a commotion below and she walked out of the room to see what was going on, and someone was calling her name. It was some maid, or some friend who knew the circumstances, who had come to tell her that the first man had dropped dead. So she went on with her engagement, and the next day she was famous throughout Europe. She created such a terrific sensation that opening night in Brussels that that was the beginning of it.

RUTH LADD

Much later in life she used to invite us girls, her students, to luncheon at Coombe Cottage at Coldstream. And I always remember her saying at lunch one day, "Did I ever tell you the story of how I received my first contract for Monte Carlo?" Somebody said, "No." "Well," she said, "I had made my début in Brussels and it was a great success and then there really was nothing much doing and I was wondering more or less where the next money was coming from." So she went down to Monte Carlo where she heard that the Prima Donna had made a flop of the season and the manager apparently was very anxious and wanted really to find somebody else. However, he wasn't going to let Melba know that, and Melba wasn't going to let him know that she was anxious to get the job. She arranged things so that she met this man, and he asked her to afternoon tea somewhere. They went to some restaurant, and of course at last the conversation, as it was meant to do, came round to this flop the other woman had made. The manager said, "You wouldn't consider it, I suppose. I hear you've done extraordinarily well in Brussels." So Melba said, "No, no, I've just finished the season there and I feel that I'd like a rest now. I've got my French maid and my son George with me, and we just want a rest." Nothing more happened then, but this man said, "I trust you will come and have tea with me again?" So Melba said yes, she'd be happy to, you see. So another date was fixed. Once again they hedged, and at last he said, "You wouldn't consider an engagement if I made the offer tempting enough, you wouldn't consider taking on this season?"

Melba said, "Oh well, it depends entirely upon what you consider a tempting offer." So he made her what, at the time, was quite a fabulous offer, and she said, "Well, if you like to treble it, yes." So he said, "Right!" And they turned the menu over and made out the contract there and then. She told us that at lunch.

JOHN AMADIO

I shall never forget her voice. Of course she was miraculously controlled. The one outstanding quality she had was the steadiness of her voice. If you hear any of her old recordings put on now, even with the imperfect recording of her day, you'll notice the wonderful pure steadiness—like Caruso!

SIR BERNARD HEINZE

A young fresh beautiful voice. Full of lustre, full of beauty, clear and pure. And that was one of the most extraordinary things about her voice, I think more than anything else, the absolute purity of it. There was no effort visible to the naked eye. There was of course a physical effort of her own, but it created no disturbance to her physical being. The sort of thing that one sees so frequently in other artists, you know, the flushing of the face or the filling of the throat—nothing of that sort with her. The thing flowed freely and with the greatest possible beauty. It was helped of course by the fact that she was a woman of extremely good constitution. She was a powerful woman but not fat. She was a well built and big woman but it was all good strong earnest being.

PERCY GRAINGER

I think she had a very high standard of workmanship. She herself worked very hard at anything. Knew all details and had mastered, I think, every technique of her art. Her voice, of course, was a very distinctive one. Oh my goodness, it was. I'm not particularly fond of opera singers as a rule, but I must say I have never heard anything to compare with the beauty of Melba's voice, in any branch of singing. The top notes of course were very ringing and telling, as they are with a good many fine sopranos. But the curious thing with Melba was that her lower notes and middle notes were equally telling. They had a quality all of their own; and even when she was singing with a big orchestra, she was never wiped out. She had a tremendous carrying power and a tremendous beauty of tone and very great refinement of workmanship in everything she did.

DR. FLOYD

Of course, I never heard her in the middle of her great operatic career. I first heard her here in Melbourne a little over forty years ago, I think, when she was getting on for seventy. And I remember that when she began to sing I said to myself, "Is this the great world-famous Melba?" And then I gradually realized that she had switched over from the coloratura arias with which she'd made a great name in her heyday in Europe—she realized that she had to treat her voice with consideration—she'd switched over to atmospheric French songs, which gave her unique opportunities of using the best part of her voice. And it had an indescribable quality. I think the nearest to a true description that I've ever read is in that rather disagreeable book written by a man who was at an earlier stage a protégé of hers but who later wrote a rather disagreeable novel. I think it was called *Evensong*. But he does in the course of the book give a description of a party in a big house in London, Melba present, and somebody persuaded her to sing. Perhaps her hostess. "And," says Beverley Nichols, "she stood up, and there came on the air that voice like a disembodied spirit, like a little boy's voice that seemed to come—" I don't know whether *he* says this or whether it's what *I* say in a very deliberate effort to tell the truth as I see it—"seemed to come from everywhere and nowhere. There it was in the air—poised, and perfect."

WILFRID THOMAS

I met her when I was quite young, not long before she died. And it was quite unexpected. In those days, of course, the great thing about her as far as we were concerned was that she was the first Australian artist to go abroad, to go to Europe and to tell the world and show the world that we could produce something more than sheep and convicts and boomerangs and aborigines and so on. We had this legend of champagne, and Grand Dukes throwing diamonds the size of the crown jewels from the boxes, and all this romantic stuff, and I think that the sum total of it all was that we didn't regard her with tremendous affection but more with awe, you know. I was more or less terrified of her when I first met her. And it happened in a singing studio—a music studio in Sydney—at lunchtime one day. I was practising there with a pianist friend of mine named Dick Thew and the door was flung open and there, framed by the varnished lintels, stood this diamond and fur character— the Queen of Song—and she advanced in a most imperious manner, and behind her coming out of the shadows were her manager John Lemmoné and Mabel Batchelor, who was the lessee of the studio. She advanced towards me and she said, "What's your name?" you see, and I said, "Wilfrid Thomas." I was terrified. And she said, "How old are you?" I said, "Twenty-one, Madam, please." And she said, "My God! I wish I were." Then she said, "All right, sing." So we dug into the old music bag and pulled out my most ambitious aria, a Handel aria called "Hear me, ye winds and waves," with a big dramatic introduction on the piano. And I sang "From the rage of the tempest out of the seething water, so far the gods protect me." And she said, "I don't want to hear any more!" Ugh! I was very crestfallen. She said, "Don't you know any ballads?" And I said, "Oh yes," and we pulled another song out of the bag, a little hunting song by Franco Leoni called "Tallyho," and it goes something like this:

There's a noise of galloping over the hill
And the hunter's horn rings merry and shrill,
See here they come with a view hulloo,
Hounds and horses and huntsmen too,

Galloping, galloping, galloping,
Galloping, galloping, galloping,
Galloping by.

I was very proud of this song. And while I was singing, Melba hoisted up her skirts and started to dance around the studio, prancing around with her hat tipped on the side of her head, yelling out "Tallyho! Tallyho!" which . . . well, now we'd be very amused, wouldn't we? This, of course, completely shattered me. This was the great Empress. I couldn't believe that this great dignified character should behave in such a manner. Anyway, she then pulled up and walked towards me, staring me in the eye, and she said, "Your consonants, your diction." She was trying to give me a lesson, but I didn't realize it at the time. She said, "I've never forgotten what Ellen Terry said to me, she said, 'Melba, have you ever been tipsy?' " See? Accentuating the labials, the consonants. I just didn't know what to say when she said this to me, and then she swept Dick Thew off the piano stool and pulled her gloves off and started to play scales and vocal exercises which I had to sing. And then, when she'd had enough, she plonked the cover of the piano down and pulled on her gloves, stood up and, hardly saying goodbye or anything else, stamped out of the studio, and Dick and I just looked at each other, flabbergasted.

We didn't know what had happened to us. It was like being struck by lightning. And then, a few seconds after this, Lemmoné came back into the studio and said to me, "Madam likes you."

GLADYS MONCRIEFF

When I was a girl, while I was still a student, I was invited one afternoon, I didn't know why, to sing two songs in the empty Theatre Royal. There were no lights on in the stalls. It was very dark, and I couldn't see anybody, but at the end of the two numbers Mr. Ward came on the stage and with him was Melba. Of course I was very excited. And she sat down at the piano and for about half an hour she gave me a lesson. I was doing scales and little exercises for her, and all of a sudden she said, "Now sing this for me," and I sang up and up and up and got up to top C. "Oh," I said, "I couldn't go higher." And she said, "Come on. Come on." So I went up another semitone and then I sang C sharp and then I went up to D. And she said, "Now come on, up to the next one." And I was so afraid, but anyhow I sang the next note. She said "There!" and jumped up from the piano. She said, "That was E in alt. And that is wonderful," and she said, "Mr. Ward said he's going to do something very wonderful for you when he signs you up, and if he does it I think your future career is assured."

Mrs. Hugh Ward taught me singing, and I remember too that Melba gave Mrs. Ward some little exercises for my voice which had a break in the middle register. It was wonderful for me, because I'd go so far and then this break would come, and then there wouldn't be any voice and I'd sing right up high; but she bridged it right over. Eventually people used to say it was the best part of my voice—the middle of the voice.

PETER DAWSON

I remember how she liked to organize things and take charge. Many years ago I was engaged to perform at a Charity Concert in England. Well, I went along to sing and I sang a set of Parry songs. Nellie was sitting in front of the hall and there were all the elite sitting in the front with Nellie, as big as you like. All very pleased. And I came on and was about to start. She said, "Peter!" she said, "wait a minute, don't start yet. No." So I stopped and I looked and she said, "There's no light on you. Where are the technicians—where are they? Where are the electricians? Bring the electricians. Come on." And I was still standing there. And I thought, "Good God, what's this?"

They began scampering around, and she said, "Look! that border—bring that border over there, and do this and do that and the other," you see, and "Take that away there. You want some light on this, you can't see Peter Dawson. He might be a trapdoor spider." Of course I was enjoying all this, and then she said, "Now that one over there—yes, that's right. Now, just a minute." And she got up from her seat and walked back three or four rows in the aisle, and then she said, "Yes, that's better. All right, Peter," and she came back and sat down. So I said, "Thank you very much, Madame Nellie," I said, "can I start now?" She said, "Yes, go on, it's all yours." So I sang these Parry songs.

I remember Melba singing with Caruso. *Bohème*! My goodness, the way she used to carry when she walked off the stage, carrying that top C right through when she went, and you could hear it still going away in the distance—magnificent! A hush, and up they would go! They would wave their programmes and throw their hand-kerchiefs up, and oh, it was really remarkable. The Melba nights! The gala nights! The gala nights when they had roses—all the theatre decorated with beautiful roses—and people could hardly breathe, the atmosphere was so charged with the rose aroma that it affected the singing. And the scintillating diamonds, the diamonds of the aristocracy who attended the old Covent Garden. The atmosphere was simply marvellous.

The dressing rooms were all in corridors, but the biggest one of course and the largest was Dame Nellie's. She was the principal singer and nobody could depose her and she could, well, she could stop any singer from coming there to sing. One that was mentioned, I think, was Tetrazzini. She hadn't a chance of getting in with a tin opener while Nellie was there. But as soon as Nellie went, in came Tet. Well anyway, this dressing room. It had MELBA in great letters: MELBA! SILENCE! SILENCE! on the door; SILENCE on the stage. And everybody used to watch. Whenever she came out of her dressing room to make her entry to the stage, they crept away like mice out of sight. The stagehands wore plimsoll shoes so that they wouldn't make any noise, they never dropped anything, never did a thing. She didn't see anybody, only the actors and actresses who were with her—the singers. But then of course a time came when a lot of the stagehands resented this. They didn't like her because they reckoned it was brutal treatment. And she had a little piece of plate glass on the side of the stage—a little plate glass shelf—and she used to suck a piece of Australian wattle gum. She'd take it out of her mouth and put it on this little shelf, and then go on to sing. Of course, one of the stagehands, one of those clever Alecs, he swapped the wattle gum for a chew of tobacco, see! And she came off the stage and put that in her mouth and oh! fireworks, me boy! Oooh! Everybody got the sack! Everybody was sacked! A terrible thing to do, you know! Murder!

Anyway, they were all back next day. She forgot all about it, and there you are.

You know, the story is true, when Caruso, in *Bohème*, was about to sing "Thy Tiny Hand Is Frozen," he got his dresser to put a hot sausage in a tin on a spirit lamp. It was a hot sausage, and Caruso came on stage and had it in his hand. He took hold of her hand—"Your Tiny Hand Is Frozen"—and put the hot sausage in her hand. God! She flung it up in the air and it bounced round the stage just like a mouse. The audience wondered what it was, bouncing around, and of course Caruso had his back to the audience, and Melba was ropeable. "Oh, you dago so-and-so," she said. He laughed and said, "English lady, you like the sausage?"

Ah, what a power that man had! And Nellie always said, "Tenor?" she said, "Baritone—high baritone! He's no tenor. A baritone!" She wouldn't have it he was a tenor. But he was what you may call a tenore robusto, and he could sing a top C—my goodness! And he was such a jolly man! Nellie was quite friendly with him, but . . . er . . .

WILLIAM JAMES

To her rivals Melba, outwardly, I would say, was cold in approach. She would never let anybody get above her at all. There was one young tenor who was under the same management as Melba in London, and their manager was putting on a Sunday afternoon concert in the Albert Hall. I was engaged to play for this young tenor who was getting his first real chance in London at the Albert Hall, and singing with Melba, which of course was a tremendous thing. He was singing an Italian aria—I think it was "Che Gelida Manina" from *Bohème*—and the first thing Melba said to him was, "What language are you singing in?" He said, "Italian, Madame." She said, "I am very sorry, but I am the only one singing in Italian this afternoon." Well, this poor fellow then had to come out and on the spur of the moment, sing it in English. But that—that was Melba. I don't think she did it for any ulterior motive. It was only that she must be on top of everything.

LAURI KENNEDY

I remember, though, that she was the only one who pushed me on to take encores at her own concerts. She would stand in the wings and she would say, "Go on, go on, go on, bow again, and then go and play another encore for them." Most artists are not usually given that way, you know.

DOROTHY KENNEDY

I remember one occasion (without mentioning names, but it was a very great artist) when my husband was being recalled. There was terrific applause and the accompanist took on a little number that he thought would be appropriate, but when this big artist appeared in the wings and saw it he snatched it away and said, "Oh no, you play this." He handed him a lullaby or something, which of course settled any further encores for the young cellist. That man was up to all the tricks, but Melba would never do a thing like that.

PHIL FINKELSTEIN

She had a wonderful sense of the value of publicity, and I remember an occasion when she was invited to lunch at Government House. Along St. Kilda Road her car broke down, and all the efforts of the driver couldn't start it. Did Melba hop on a tram? No. Did she hitchhike a ride from another passing motorist? No. Melba stopped a butcher's cart that was coming along and climbed up and was driven to the front door of Government House on the meat wagon, all dressed up in her finery. What a story! I rushed it to the papers, which duly gave it a wonderful spread and Melba got her publicity, not that she needed it but she loved it.

SIR BERNARD HEINZE

I remember one time Sir Edward Cunningham telling me that she came to see him at the Argus, and she said, "Edward, I haven't seen any reference to my presence in Australia in the last week or two." "Oh," he said, "there's been a good deal go in." "No, no," she said, "not enough! Not enough! I don't care what you say, for me or against me, but for heaven's sake say something about *me*." The great thing was *not* to be dismissed without notice. Of course, it was a pretty hard world, and she had had to fight her way in order to get to the top.

PETER DAWSON

She did get to the top, and she made a great deal of money. She was one of the lucky ones. She got a royalty of half a guinea on every record that was sold for a guinea, and hundreds of thousands of records were sold of her. Imagine how the wool grew while she slept, eh? And then of course she had a lot of things that she sort of gambled in. Shares in this and shares in that. Somebody told me that one time she owned all the taxi cabs in Melbourne.

LINDLEY EVANS

I remember that she was very matter-of-fact and very downright when she engaged me to travel with her overseas as her concert accompanist.

I got the feeling, "Oh well, this is strictly a business affair and that's all there is to it." But I hadn't been in London more than a week or so when she casually said to me one day, "Look," she said, "if you're ever short of money you come and ask me. I've plenty of money." So you see it wasn't quite what you might think. You had to get to know her, and I knew her so well.

She was quite difficult to work with, in some ways, and at first I thought I'd never stand it, because she was a person who knew exactly what she wanted and was determined to have it at all costs and any price. As you can imagine, she was frightfully pernickety over things. For example, she was learning some French songs, some new French songs. Well now, she spoke French and Italian as fluently as she spoke English, and yet when she had learnt those French songs for the first time and she knew them as well as it was possible to know them from the musical side, she then, before she sang them in public, called in a cultivated Frenchwoman to hear her sing and to make sure that her French was impeccable. That sort of thing was typical. We used to rehearse and rehearse and rehearse until things went sideways. She even noticed such things as your dress. I always used to have to turn around each night when I came into the artist's room so that she could see that everything was all right from the sartorial point of view.

She was a highly strung woman, and I remember an occasion, just before a concert in Sydney, when she was really worked up. She rang me up in the morning —it was a Saturday—and she said she was feeling very nervous about the night's concert, and she wanted to go out for a drive, and would I go with her? Well, I picked her up in George Street. We started off up George Street and got as far as King Street and she said to the driver, "Turn up King Street." And we turned up King Street and she said, "Turn down Castlereagh Street." And I thought, "This is a funny sort of a drive." As we were moving along Castlereagh Street she said to the driver, "Stop at the Australia." And she turned to me and said, "You know, I don't want to go for this drive. I'm feeling quite worried about this concert tonight." She said, "I think I'll go home and rest." So I said, "Very well." The chauffeur couldn't stop in front of the Australia—it was a Saturday morning and there were thousands of people everywhere—cars everywhere—and we got right to the corner of Martin Place before we could find a spot. We stopped there, and she said, "You can get out here," and as I got out she handed me a big portmanteau. She said, "Give that to the man in the Australia." Well I was walking along to the Australia to dump this thing in the luggage room, when I met someone whom I hadn't seen for a long while, and I said to this chap, "Hold on a minute till I put this thing down." So I put the portmanteau down against the building and we stood on the side of the kerb for ten or fifteen minutes, talking. Then I picked up the bag and walked into the Australia. I remember that in those days it cost tuppence to leave a bag, so I dumped the bag in and I got a ticket for tuppence. That was the end of it as far as I was concerned, until that night at the concert in the Town Hall, and as soon as I came into the room she said, "You're a bright one." By this time I'd had lots of experience and I wasn't worried. I said, "Well, what have I done this time?" She said, "Do you know what was in that bag that I gave you today?" And I said, "I haven't the vaguest idea." And then she said, "Oh, nothing very much, you know. Only this," and she pointed to a bracelet round her wrist, "and this"—a diamond tiara. "And this"—a necklace. Forty thousand quid's worth of jewellery and I'd left it lying around in Castlereagh Street.

UNA BOURNE

Her jewels were perfectly magnificent. We used to have quite an interesting time together, after a concert, when she would tell me the history of the different things. This one given, you know, in Russia. Decorations also received in all parts of Europe. And her dresses were very elegant. I don't think we can say that she specialized in any particular type of frock, but it was always something with a long elegant line that helped her to look dignified and a bit taller than she really was. But a distinctive feature was that instead of gesticulating with her hands as so many concert artists do, she would always carry a fan and hold it poised very lightly between her hands.

When she came to London for any length of time, she always rented some well-known person's house where she entertained royally, really and truly Royalty there as well as all the society people. It was a unique point about Melba that she had that wonderful social position in which they all adored her and came to her parties and loved being there. She toured as a royal person even when she was the concert artist. She was treated in that way the whole time, and I think that is why Australia should feel that she was a wonderful ambassadress for the country.

BROWNING MUMMERY

One of the great nights of her career was the Farewell at Covent Garden in 1926, when Melba was about sixty-five. I was one of the Australians who sang with her then—Frederick Collier was another, and John Brownlee sang too—and I can remember the night before: I think I was singing in *Carmen*, and as we came out of the theatre the queue was forming then for the Farewell Performance. They sat all night in the little seats outside the theatre. And of course the atmosphere in the theatre was tremendous—tremendous!

JOHN BROWNLEE

King George and Queen Mary and the Prince of Wales and all the members of the Royal Family were in the Royal Box. Every woman in Covent Garden that night was wearing her diamond tiara and every man had on a white tie and tails. Probably people had come from all over Europe to pay tribute to Melba on that occasion, and, at the end of the perfectly extraordinary programme that she went through, the curtains came down, and when they opened up again the stage was literally covered from one side to another with all the floral tributes that had been sent in for her. And it was really the love and affection of a vast audience who were demonstrating what they felt about Melba on that occasion.

UNA BOURNE

It was really a marvellous event, but what impressed me tremendously was that the critic at that moment on the *London Times* was a very good musician and he worded his review in this way: He said, "Had this been the début of a very very fine young girl—we would have given great credit to it. We can hardly believe it's the end of a thirty-year career."

BASIL HART

One of the most remarkable things about Melba was that in her fifties she launched out on a *new* career. She became a teacher. One day in 1915, during the first World War, she rang my father and said, "Fritz, it's Melba speaking, Nellie Melba. I want to start a school of singing at your Conservatorium." She did that, and I think it's important that people should realize that Melba did not receive one penny for any of the work that she did at the Conservatorium. It was all voluntary work. She founded a school. She trained the teachers, Mary Campbell, Anne Williams, and they in turn have trained other teachers to follow on in the Melba method. For instance, I can think of Ruth Ladd who is doing such excellent work at the Sydney Conservatorium.

RUTH LADD

Melba was an absolute inspiration as a teacher. We all used to meet in the hall twice a week and sometimes three times a week for lessons, the idea being that it was admirable for those people who intended to teach to listen to the lessons of other people. We all had nicknames, which was rather funny, and Madam would say, "Come along, Little Mouse. I'll give you your lesson." So Little Mouse would get up and stand on the platform and have to sing. We had another one called the Rabbit. She lives in Western Australia, a girl with a magnificent voice. I myself was known as the Duchess, not because of my magnificence but because of my resemblance to the Duchess of Leinster.

Well, those lessons were magnificent experience. Nothing but perfection pleased Dame Nellie. She wouldn't listen to anything else. At any forcing of the voice she would immediately clap her hands over her ears and say, "Don't screech like a cat. If you force your voice you cannot come to this class. I will not take the responsibility." And of course she was always stressing the importance of a sound musical knowledge. Many many times people came for auditions and she would say to the young singer, "How old are you?" "Sixteen." "Go away and learn the piano till you're eighteen and come back to me when you have some musical knowledge." Of course, Melba herself was a magnificent pianist before she was a singer at all. And she was an excellent violinist and was an organist, too.

GERTRUDE JOHNSTONE

She was a first-class teacher. She had a very very strong feeling for musical phrasing and that kind of thing, and she demanded very good diction. She used to say, "It's brains, brains, brains, then voice." And she'd say, "You must live, you must feel, you must read, you must have background to become a singer. You've got to think."

FLORENCE YATES

She was quite dogmatic, I'd say. Very much the teacher. And she insisted on good hard work and that was all there was to it, and if you didn't work she just didn't bother any more. But if you did work she would help you.

DOROTHY KENNEDY

If you helped yourself after she'd given you a lift or encouragement in any way, or if you achieved something, she was so proud, you know. There were instances where people just didn't do anything if she wasn't at their back all the time, and she said to me, "I can't stand these spoonfed people if they won't strike out for themselves." People like that, she just dropped them. There were no two ways about it.

LAURI KENNEDY

But think how many she helped. And how many Australians! I remember a programme she arranged at Earl Farquhar's house, or some other big person's, and all the artists were Australians. It was a remarkable affair because there were three queens, the Queen of England, the Queen of Norway, and the Queen of Italy, and after the concert we were presented—each one of us was presented to Queen Mary. What was remarkable about Melba was her terms of familiarity with Royalty over there, and the presentation that night was very funny, because naturally Royalty doesn't know what to say to you at times, and Queen Mary couldn't think of anything to say to me, so she looked at me, and she said, "You have a wonderful touch." Well, maybe I have and maybe I haven't, but the Queen followed this up and said, "I suppose you have a wonderful instrument." And Melba nudged her—positively nudged her in the ribs—and said, "He'll have a better one, Ma'am, when he can afford it," fishing, of course, with the idea that the Queen might give me a Stradivari or something. But that didn't eventuate, I'm sorry to relate.

MARIE BREMNER

When I was at the Conservatorium there were about sixty or seventy students, and Melba had designed for us what we called our "Long White Nightgowns." They were on the whole fairly plain, straight up and down white uniforms, and on the left breast pocket we wore a badge which she had designed herself. It was of green ribbon, a most attractive colour, and it had a fine blue and white line on the edge of the ribbon, and in the centre of it was a laurel wreath, with the letter "M" in blue. Above it was a dove, a white dove, with a spray in its mouth, and underneath was, in a scroll, "Con Amore." Our studies and our singing lessons and everything we did at the Conservatorium, were to be approached "with love."

We saw a tremendous lot of her when she was in Australia because she used to visit the Conservatorium at the most unexpected times. You never knew when she was going to drop in, and it was rather frightening to be having a lesson, when the door would open and there she would be; and she would say to the teacher, whoever it happened to be, "I'll take over," and she'd brush the teacher aside and sit down to the piano to give you a lesson. I was having a lesson one day when she came in, and she taught me a little song called "Obstination" by Fontenaille, and even now I can hear her, when I sing that song, I can hear her singing it in her lovely clear liquid voice—well, it wasn't liquid, really, it had a *silver* quality which we have never been able to repeat in the world.

There was a young girl who was brought to her one day, a girl called Wilma Berkeley, and Melba was taken with her voice and said she would like to help her and would like to give her a concert. She said to her, "Now I will help you, so go away and get yourself a trousseau and a dress, and let me know what it's like." So she came up one day—she was a very shy person—and Melba said to her, "Well, have you got your dress?" And she said, "Yes, here it is," and she showed the frock she was going to wear, and Melba said, "No, you can't wear that. That's only good for a school concert." And she said to Mary Campbell, "Mary, do your stuff," and with that she went out of the room. Well, Mary bent down and picked up from underneath the grand piano a gold box. She put it on top of the piano and said "There you are, Wilma, that's for you." And Wilma Berkeley opened it, and after she'd taken away the tissue paper there was everything that she was to wear at her concert, from the chaplet of gold leaves for her hair to the gold shoes she was going to wear on her feet. The girl, of course, was quite overcome. And they were all in perfect measurement. Melba had done that surreptitiously, on the side. She was a most generous person but she hated to be thanked for anything. In her bluff manner she'd more or less brush you aside and say, "Oh tut tut tut tut, that's all right, that's all right." And then of course, she was so generous to other people, John Brownlee, for instance, you remember.

BASIL HART

She loved to make friends of her students. They were terribly frightened of her in many ways but she used to have annual parties up at Coombe Cottage for the Conservatorium girls. These days we would call them barbecues. Perhaps a hundred girls would go up to Coombe Cottage and they would be out in the grounds there and be cooking their chops around fires, and Melba would be there with a chef's cap on, dashing about, full of good humour.

GERTRUDE JOHNSTONE

Lovely parties we used to have. Afterwards the driver of the car would report that we were singing all the way home, and then we would hear about it the next morning. "That's not the thing to do. You won't have any voices left if you do that." But her home was beautiful—it really was lovely.

She was wonderfully generous to me. You see, while I was still a student I was approached by the people who were planning to form the Italian-Australian Opera Company. They told me they needed a coloratura soprano. Of course I was very thrilled at the idea of it, but I was late for my lesson because of going to an audition with the agent. When I arrived I was full of enthusiasm to tell Dame Nellie, but she was furious with me. How dare I come late for a lesson? And so all my ardour was frozen and she never heard of my audition till I was actually away in Queensland singing with the company. Again she was furious with me. I should have told her everything, you see—but it wasn't always very easy to tell her everything. And when I came back to see her, she said, "You're not a student. You're a prima donna now. You don't need me," in a very hurt voice. But after a short time, she got over it and gave me marvellous cadenzas for things that I later sang on the other side of the world. She could get very cross with you, and you remembered it when she was cross, but she actually gave me the special cadenzas that she herself with Madame Marchesi had evolved, and she made me take copies so that I should have them when my opportunity came, which was a wonderful thing to do.

MELBA REVISITED

MAIE CASEY

A Reprise and a Coda

In the preceding pages, we have seen how John Thompson of the Australian Broadcasting Commission was able to secure interviews with a number of Australians who remembered Dame Nellie Melba for a broadcast on May 19, 1961, celebrating the one-hundredth anniversary of the singer's birth. It seems fitting to conclude these contemporary comments with the words of another well-known and greatly admired Australian, the Lady Maie Casey, whose death in her ninety-second year, on January 21, 1983, closed a remarkable career as writer, artist, aviatrix, and wife of Lord Casey. The former Ethel Marian Sumner Ryan, daughter of a Melbourne surgeon, married Richard Gardiner Casey in 1926 and in full measure supported him in a long partnership dissolved only by his death in 1976. The two were complementary to one another. Lord Casey's diplomatic and other posts included those of first Australian Minister to the United States, British Minister of State in the Middle East, member of the War Cabinet of the United Kingdom in World War II, Governor-General of Bengal, and, finally, Governor-General of Australia from 1965 to 1969.

From: Maie Casey, *Melba Revisited*. Melbourne, privately printed, 1975. Reprinted by permission of her family and estate trustees.

In 1975 Lady Casey published privately a little booklet
entitled *Melba Revisited*. It is through the kindness and with the
approval of her family and estate trustees that the following
excerpts are quoted from this work.

My first sight of Madame Melba, already known to me through my parents
as an important woman with a flute-like voice, was when I was about nine
years old.

My Swiss nurse and I went to pick up a dress for my mother from the
show-rooms, in or off Flinders Street, Melbourne, of the Misses Clapp,
famous dressmakers of the period.

As Berthe Tissot and I stood waiting in the wide hall a woman stepped
into it. I can see her now standing by the door, elegant, waisted, erect, with
a face that compelled attention. She talked with a welcoming Miss Clapp.
Then she turned to me. "How is Charlie?" she said.

At that time I spoke French as often as I did English and was slightly
taken aback by her question. Perhaps I would have expected her to say
"Comment va Monsieur votre père" or at least "How is your father . . .
your papa." I did not realise until afterwards how human it was for her to
speak to me in this way.

Throughout our lives it is the unexpected, the dramatic, that stays in our
memory; the ordinary slides quickly away. And so I have remembered
clearly my first meeting with Madame Melba, her words and her lovely
mouth as she spoke.

The next time I saw her was from a great distance. While at school in
Paris a few years later I went with other girls to sit high up with the gods at
the Opera House to listen to Verdi's *Rigoletto* [June 11, 1908]. This was a
special occasion; the singers were Enrico Caruso, Maurice Renaud and
Nellie Melba.

The beautiful lusty human voices of the tenor and the baritone rose
towards us full of enjoyment and masculine vigour. The voice of Melba,
remote, incredible, joined theirs from some other sphere. It soared above
the orchestra like another musical instrument, pure, disembodied. No
human voice was this.

No wonder our hearts stood still as we listened. No wonder someone
should have said of us, "Quite like a bouquet of flowers, those still young
girls!"

I thought then of Melba in the hall of the Misses Clapp in Melbourne and
of her lovely mouth through which these incredible sounds now came.

During the months I was at Mme. Chevalier's school at Neuilly we went
also to hear and see Sarah Bernhardt in l'Aiglon and in Adrienne
Lecouvreur.

One afternoon I persuaded a docile teacher from our school to take me to
call on Mme. Bernhardt in the Boulevard Périrè. Alas, we got no further

than the front door where a serviteur guardian stood against the background of a large hall hung with paintings and filled with furniture and objects of art.

Melba who had become in the late eighteen eighties a friend of the great actress often entered these portals and she wrote a description of one of the rooms in that marvellously over-cluttered house.

In Paris I heard Gustave Charpentier's opera *Louise* where Mary Garden sang the aria "Depuis le jour," surely for a singer one of the most difficult. But it was not until recently when I was given by Melba's grand-daughter Pamela Vestey two early records of Melba singing it, one with piano accompaniment, one with orchestra, that I was reminded how wonderful it could be with her miraculous precise head notes.

Hero worship stirs in most of us at moments of our lives when we encounter something superbly done, in whatever field. In music, in the many arts revealed by the eye including that of movement. In human behaviour.

When I was eighteen I was befriended for her lifetime by Mollie Sanderson, an Englishwoman married to Sir John Sanderson of Sanderson, Murray, ship-owners. Mollie in Melbourne taught me most of what I know about music. She played the piano, the violin, and was a considerable singer of German lieder, French songs and some arias.

Mollie became a friend of Nellie Melba's in Melbourne, in London. Sometimes I was allowed into the fringe of this friendship. Mollie Sanderson had a magnetic personality and much beauty; tall, dark, with flashing brown eyes and white teeth. Her hands which I admired and sometimes drew had fingers with waists; almost as though pale gloves had been drawn over skeletal bones. She had a strong attraction for men, whom she usually preferred to women. But her love and appreciation of music, her intelligence and wit and her fearlessness appealed to Melba of whose equally powerful personality many were afraid. They were two women of almost the same metal.

Early in this friendship I went with the Sandersons to a night party at Coombe Cottage, Melba's spread-out one-storey house near Lilydale under the protection of the Dandenong Ranges in Victoria. On a flat roof reached by an outside staircase some of us supped in the moonlight, then wandered through the exciting rooms below. We danced on a wooden floor under the moon and stars. It was another occasion rare enough to be remembered even without the presence of Madame Melba in a glittering dress draped with long ropes of pearls. . . .

Mollie spoke often of Melba, of her abilities outside the field of music: as a businesswoman, as a woman of personal discipline. She spoke of her as a singer whose voice never spilled over its notes and moved from register to register as imperceptibly as the notes of a flute. A voice without holes.

Sometimes she mentioned the astonishing contrast between the vigorous vivid woman and her remote angelic voice—almost a white voice.

In 1885 Mrs. Nellie Armstrong had been enthusiastically acclaimed in Australia as a rising young soprano but it was not until she came to the great teacher of singing Mathilde Marchesi in Paris in 1886 that the potential of her unique voice was recognised. . . . It was at a party given at her Paris home for Nellie Armstrong that the significant name of Melba was first heard.

Marchesi taught her not to force her voice, not to sustain a note beyond its climax; through her guidance Melba's voice preserved its freshness and purity until almost the end of her life. With much else she showed Melba how to stand easily on a stage, with weight on the balls of the feet rather than on the heels and how to move her arms and hands with restraint which she did with grace. Sarah Bernhardt also gave her friendly advice on the gestures of the body and on pronunciation; she considered clarity of speech to be as important to a singer as it was to an actor. So precise became Melba's diction and so exact was her ear that she sang with perfect pronunciation in French and in Italian. And very few other than the French can ever pronounce the lovely word "amour."

Many years later during Melba's visits to Australia much that she had learned from Mathilde Marchesi, and from Sarah Bernhardt, was incorporated in a pamphlet "The Melba Method" by Dame Nellie Melba, with a grateful tribute by her for the help of Professor Fritz Hart and Miss Mary Campbell.

She used this during her teaching of young singers at the Melbourne Conservatorium. Her personality comes clearly through this succinct and unexpectedly moving guide to students.

Mollie Sanderson stressed Melba's innate sense of drama, the sense of the actor, a gift essential to public figures on or off the stage. It was sometimes said of her that she was stilted and artificial on the stage. But so were most of the stylised operatic singers of that time. Their movements, their gesticulations—in the pattern of Greek mime—were as disciplined and acceptable then as was the technique of their singing.

In 1920 Melba was living in an elegant house in Old Queen's Street, London, looking out on the Mall. She was then Dame Nellie Melba.

One night she invited Mollie Sanderson and me to dine with her at the Savoy Hotel. We followed her almost royal progress into the diningroom accompanied by two singers, Peter Dawson and John McCormack: the vigorous Australian woman with her lively if not altogether compatible friends.

Dame Nellie, graceful, erect, was more solid than I remembered her. I sat opposite to her at the round table and looked at her luminous dark eyes, her lightly aquiline nose, her mouth as she smiled. I listened to her voice traversing the magnificent barrier of her teeth. It was not like that of many Australian women, high and slightly nasal although when she sang it had a touch of that necessary and exciting nasal quality.

Her voice was clear without accent of any kind. Pamela Vestey who was twelve when her grandmother died remembers her speaking voice as "higher and lighter when she was happy or excited and lower when she was sad."

Through Mollie Sanderson the intermediary I knew also Melba's son George and his wife Evie. Mollie was fond of them both and had become godmother to their daughter Pamela. She considered George to be as musical as his mother with an unerring selective instinct.

I would see the Armstrongs from time to time. Soon after I married in 1926 Evie and I met by chance in Piccadilly outside the Ritz Hotel in London. She was a beautiful woman with a deep husky voice and blue Irish eyes circled by dark lashes. She had a relevant wit.

Another unusual encounter because she said to me, "How nice that you have married Dick Casey. I don't think he will go off and leave you!" I had not thought of that.

A few years ago when Evie Armstrong and her daughter Pamela were in Melbourne I said to Evie: "How lucky it was that Melba liked you!" "Darling," she said to me, "Melba *chose* me for George!"

I understood why when I played an early record Pamela had given me of a Miss Evelyn Doyle singing "I know a lovely garden" accompanied on the piano by Madame Melba. Evie had a warm endearing young mezzo voice and she sang carefully and well although a little nervously.

Apart from my remembrance of Melba's singing voice, which always stilled me, I listened through these early records to the music she sang for her private pleasure. Amongst them "D'une prison" by Reynaldo Hahn and Mozart's "Il Re Pastore.". . .

When Melba had become the renowned singer who held the world not only by her voice but by her personality, she was a welcome guest in some of the interesting English houses of the day. This was not usual at that time. Singers, musicians, actors were invited professionally into private houses to reveal their talents for the enjoyment of special guests. They came, they received large fees, but they went without mixing with the guests, an arrangement that suited them. Gifted, disciplined, busy, they had little time or desire for social life. For occasional friendships, yes, for society as such, no. . . .

Melba transcended this pattern, largely because of her willingness to do so through her Australian friendliness. She was particularly attracted to children and young people as they were to her. Her appeal came as much perhaps from her vitality as it did from her voice and fame.

Who can resist vitality? It draws us like the sun.

Some letters she kept were written with romantic devotion by young persons to whom she had given affection and encouragement.

One reply from her in 1910 reads:

Blounts, Marlow,

Dear Eton Boy

I wonder if Mr. Broadbent teaches you to spell awful with two l's? Do ask him from me.

Yours truly
Nellie Melba

A letter dated March 25, 1910 came from Belvoir Castle, Grantham.

My dear Nel Mel

A line of welcome home, really an affectionate one. The Girls are writing to you, I know, so your plans will be disclosed to them. I am at Death's Door from an illness (not infectious!) but I salute you most warmly,

Yours aff.
Rutland

It was his youngest daughter, the Lady Diana Manners, who had brought Madame Melba into friendship with the Manners family.

She has been good enough to write for me the following wonderful piece: By Diana Cooper, 1974:

What can I remember of Melba?

It is so long ago. I suppose aged about twelve, I admired her passionately.

Bohème, sung by Melba and Caruso, was the first Opera I ever saw. I can see it now as I saw it then and 50 times over the years. Identically—(the old sets were only changed this year for the better by Julia Oman). These two bulky world-famous artists, who could hardly kiss standing up to their sudden love in the first act's attic (more easily of course when Mimi lay dying in the attic bed) took me by storm. Her notes were agile, sustained and perfectly pure (Caruso's were passionately earthbound and as vigorous as Youth itself in Excellcis).

Covent Garden was excitedly moved and applausive. I was a mop of tears and from that moment in love with the Prima donna.

How we actually came to know her I can't remember: probably by this very spoilt child prodding and nagging at her mother to bring her into our lives. So Melba became a constant visitor to the house. She realised no doubt the total worship of this precocious, pert, affectionate young girl—she would bring me smiles and trinkets from Australia and fondle me, and for a birthday O! wonders of wonders! from the great Melba came a huge horned gramophone simulating mahogany with all—yes *all* her records, as well as a few Caruso songs and *Pagliacci* and the quartette from *Rigoletto*. There must have been 20 of them. Every single night for six weeks in the small house under the wing of Haddon Hall we played every one of them; no sooner had my tone-deaf father and one of his foggies retired to play besique than my mother, two sisters, one brother, Uncle Charles and Harry, Mrs. Page our governess and a guest or two settled down to our Euphoria.

This gramophone, after the old phonograph with tubular wax records belonging to the next-door patient I palled up with in a nursing home years before, that squeaked like a pig being slaughtered with no relation to human sound, was a revelation of reproduction. We had a pianola at Belvoir worked by one's feet—the noise was real enough but the emphasis, accent and soul was left to the ignorant pedler to create: but the "last word" in gramophone seemed to us a miracle—the echoing truth, the living voice. "Can I change the needle Mummy?" I had the pride of ownership and the glory and snobbery of the great Melba having given it to me.

She came later to Belvoir, greatly welcomed. She was alas! too professional to be musical fun. "On ne badine pas avec la musique." Unlike Chaliapin a later passion of mine who could not cease from playing on, and with the piano, jokes and snatches, glees and heart rending phrases and guises. He would bring to my back garden in London four hefty choirmen "pour ballader un peu"—all the back windows of the street open to share the delight.

Melba took her gift more seriously but during a stay would conscientiously devote an hour of song to us and the staff (the staff, including gardeners, carpenters, stablemen, foresters and one upholsterer, would number 50 at least). She would sing Goodbye Summer and many an old favourite.

About the time when Melba entered into the warmth of the Manners family she stayed in a ducal Palazzo in Venice. On a moonlit night a known voice rose towards her from a floating gondola. It was the voice of Enrico Caruso singing from Puccini's *La Bohème* with uninhibited zest.

Melba rose from a party and stepped on to the balcony of the Palazzo to join the wonderful tenor voice with hers in the music they both knew so well. And so they sang on together in the night from gondola and balcony—voices in space.

Another spontaneous concert was heard when Melba visited Honolulu much later.

An island fête was held for Dame Nellie Melba who had been lent a beach house on the distant side of Diamond Head. In the evening beach boys came to sing and play ukuleles and guitars. Melba began to hum softly and then her voice rose above theirs in the night air. Again what a setting for sound. . . .

In 1927 Dick and I came to Australia from London where he was representing Prime Minister Stanley Bruce at the Foreign Office and on the Committee of Imperial Defence. His task was to move the Federal Department of External Affairs from Melbourne to Canberra.

We dined one night with Melba at Coombe Cottage, entering with a sense of excitement through the strong iron gates drawn together by her initials.

But it was not only the famous singer we had come to see. It was the lively intelligent woman, particularly for Dick who was not much interested in music. We were greeted at the entrance by the old butler and then by Dame Nellie. The long ropes of pearls still flowed over her bosom.

As a background in the beautiful rooms of the Cottage were paintings and drawings of her on the walls, and small tables holding silver-framed photographs of the important figures of her wide world. Crowned heads (some to be uncrowned), presidents, dukes, musicians and singers.

She was particularly pleased to see Dick who knew and was fond of her son George. Like Mollie Sanderson she was accustomed to and probably preferred the company of admiring men although she had a warm understanding of women through the girl singers she had taught at the Melbourne Conservatorium.

Once more we dined with her. Both these dinners were for six persons around a table lit by candles, with talk of world interest.

Before we left on our second visit Melba went to the piano. She played a little, then she sang for us, not the airs so many were accustomed to hear but music more rare. For me she sang some of the aria "Depuis le jour" from Charpentier's opera *Louise* in a voice that still held its beauty.

It was said that when she was singing sometimes to herself in the garden of Coombe Cottage the thrushes would come and listen to her.

From now on this story is of fragments from Melba's life told me by some who had known her.

In 1930 she became ill of a fever that for a while was not identified. Finally it was diagnosed as para-typhoid by Evie's brother Dr. William Doyle of Sydney. Nowadays it would probably have yielded to knowledge and treatment.

From Coombe Cottage where she had arrived from London with George and Evie Armstrong and their small daughter Pamela, she went for a short time to a private hospital in Melbourne controlled by a matron Melba named The Great White Hawk. Here a friend of mine was working as a young graduate nurse. Occasionally she looked after Melba and they enjoyed each other.

This nurse entered her room one day with a radio which was transmitting one of the singer's songs. Melba was transfixed with horror. She said: "*This is how it should be sung!*" She sat up in bed and the physical machinery of her neck and throat came into faultless action. Fascinated by this highly trained physical process, the movement of the muscles seen at close quarters, my friend was almost as impressed by the technique as she was by the range and still lovely sounds of the voice.

Melba returned to Coombe Cottage with an attendant nurse, Miss Teresa Wardell, grand-daughter of the famous architect, W. W. Wardell. She came to know Melba well and to love her, respecting her courage, intelligence and kindness.

On Christmas Day 1930 a few guests had been invited to dinner and at the last moment it was found that there would be thirteen at the table. Hurriedly a small table was set to break the number. The dinner was quiet, rather formal with little gaiety. As Melba left the room with Teresa Wardell she said softly: "It was a Death Feast!"

In 1973 I called on Miss Gertrude Johnson in Melbourne. She was a distinguished soprano who had sung with Melba at Covent Garden, and was one of the first to sing opera for the B.B.C. She was also the founder in 1935 of the National Theatre movement of Australia. An early protégé of Melba's, she was delighted to talk about her.

Gertrude Johnson was a tall woman of strong personality—handsome, erect, white-haired but otherwise nearly untouched by age. I imagined the effect her high impressive figure must have made long ago on the stage of Covent Garden.

She spoke to me of Melba's endowment as a singer and then, as Mollie Sanderson had, of the woman of discipline, the pefectionist. There was the story of a girl she was coaching who had arrived to see her five minutes ahead of time. Melba told her that it was as inept to arrive early as it was to arrive late. She was not ready for her!

Gertrude Johnson agreed with me that many unfair and untrue things had been said and written of Melba. But slaughter was the usual fate of tall and vigorous poppies. Melba was high-spirited and decisive; because of her life of adulation she became somewhat spoilt and impatient in small ways. But remembered trivia cannot destroy the great figures of the past. The glory remains.

Melba was generous and kind to persons she liked. She was enjoyed and loved by those who really knew her. Gertrude Johnson who had worked and sung with her emphasised how much she owed to Melba's advice and technical help, so freely given. She said of Melba, "She could be a duchess or a larrikin!" Said I: "We can all be larrikins—we Australians!" "Yes," said Gertrude Johnson, "But not all of us can be duchesses!"

What of Melba's private life? Inevitably it was subordinated to her disciplined life as a singer.

Apart from her involvement with musicians and singers, and the friendship she received from many, there were four men who were important to her. Her father, her husband, her son, and a young Frenchman.

Primarily, her father David Mitchell (1828-1916) who came to Australia from Forfarshire in Scotland as a qualified stone-mason, penniless as were many of our forebears.

He established himself as a builder in Richmond, Melbourne and he began the Cave Hill Quarry and lime works at Lilydale where Melba was later to make her Australian home. In 1907 she bought a small cottage with some land around it and it grew with her needs into the lovely Coombe Cottage. It was close to the great landmark of white cave that reached towards the summit of the hills.

In Melbourne amongst smaller enterprises David Mitchell built Scots Church, the Exhibition Buildings and the late, lamented Menzies Hotel.

His daughter Nellie was his favourite child, for her intelligence, her strong character, for her angelic voice when she sang. He himself had a bass voice and played the violin; his Scottish wife, *née* Isabella Dow, taught their children musical theory and the use of the piano and organ.

When he travelled to buildings sites and into the country he sometimes took Nellie with him. It was in Brisbane in 1882 with her father that she met Charles Armstrong (1858-1948) and in spite of opposition she married him. He was the sixth son of Sir Andrew Armstrong, Baronet of Gallen Priory, Kings County, Ireland.

Charles had been to sea as an apprentice before the mast but after a few voyages he left the ship and began to buy and sell horses in Queensland. He became one of the best horsemen in Australia. He was a handsome man with sparkling blue eyes, was full of vitality, humour, intolerance and charm.

The two strong personalities were too much for each other and after the birth of a son their marriage was virtually over. Maybe the dominant Charles became jealous of his wife's developing career. They both adored their son George and shared him for many years, differing totally on his upbringing.

As a child he accompanied his mother to Paris and Brussels; later his father took him to America where he lived with an Armstrong cousin in Texas, Oregon and California. He became an experienced horseman and stockman. George returned to his mother in England when he was twenty-one.

In 1890 Melba met Louis-Philippe, Duc d'Orléans, great grandson of the last French King and Pretender to the throne of France.

He was twenty and Melba, then an acclaimed singer, was twenty-nine. They became friends; they had much in common—simplicity, vigour, humour.

He was born in England in 1869 at York House, Twickenham, the eldest son of the Comte de Paris, came to France when he was two and remained there until he was seventeen when he was exiled. Returning to his country officially when Frenchmen of his age were being conscripted he was not accepted into the French Army. Instead he was arrested and sentenced to two years in prison. After a short term he was released and he went back to England.

His story was a sad one. He had much to give to his country, not necessarily as royalty but as a citizen of France.

But because of his intelligence, his qualities of leadership as an explorer in the north-east of Greenland, in Arctic and Equatorial waters, in other areas; because of his tall handsome good looks and his increasing support by French Royalists the Republic feared him.

The ardent desire of this exile that his body might be permitted to lie in the soil of France in private burial or be dropped into the sea off the coast of France was refused. He was buried in Sicily where he died of pneumonia in 1926.

The Duc d'Orléans married in 1896 the Archduchess Maria Dorothea of Austria, grand-daughter of the last Palatine of Hungary. There were no children of the marriage.

The enduring respect and affection he and Melba felt for each other shines out of a letter he wrote to her in French when he was fifty.

> Ritz Hotel
> Piccadilly
> London W.1.
> Tuesday, 25th March, 1919
> Evening

My dear Nellie, what can I tell you of the tender emotion that I have felt again after so many years? It seemed to me that it was yesterday that I said au revoir to you and that I found myself near to you the same, in spite of the age I then had nearly thirty years ago.

I was so happy to find you in spite of your sufferings moral and physical the *same Nellie* who has never changed and who remains in my life, sometimes so sad, the only constant and faithful friend towards whom—even in the delirium of death I so closely escaped—my soul and heart reached across space. For you know me and understand me! In spite of all the world has done to separate the one from the other. I am satisfied because the confidence you give me is my recompense. Thank you again for the few moments in which you have really made me happy in evoking the best years of my youth that I have relived through you and with you. I count the minutes that separate me from the moment when I will see you tomorrow evening, I hope for longer than this evening? I have so many things to say to you that I cannot write. But that tomorrow evening will come of themselves from my lips when I am near to you. I do hope you will give me time to tell you all that I have in my heart.

Meanwhile, my dear Nellie, I kiss most affectionately your pretty hands and am always your old

> Tipon.

When we revisited Coombe Cottage in 1972 to see Evie Armstrong and Pamela Vestey who were in Australia for a short time, I saw a sulphur-crested cockatoo sitting moodily in the corner of a high cage on the veranda with his back turned to the world.

I observed him with caution and respect then greeted him gently. He scuttled towards me at the sound of my voice and we exchanged a few

22. Melba's Own Photograph of Louis-Philippe, duc d'Orléans

words. Perhaps he had not heard many women's voices in the last years when Coombe Cottage was seldom habited. He had been Melba's own cockatoo and was now an old bird although his shining black eyes and smooth plumage belied it.

I felt honoured that he had come towards me and welcomed me although I did not believe for a moment that my voice held any trace of the sounds of the great singer.

MELBA'S ADVICE ON THE ART OF SINGING

It is inevitable that all great singers are asked for advice by those contemplating a singing career, and a frequent request is to explain their "method" of singing. Melba was no exception, as her advice and counsel were continually sought over the years by students as well as by journalists in need of copy. I have gathered here a representative sampling of her advice to singers, the first written some eight years after her debut. In the chapter "The Care of the Voice," the singer, in her staunch loyalty to Mme. Marchesi, claims that she went to the Parisian teacher "without a single vocal lesson." It is also interesting to note the roles of Aïda, Elsa, Semiramide, and Elizabeth in *Tannhäuser* in her list of successes. The next two chapters, "Advice on the Selection of Music as a Profession" and "On the Science of Singing," were both included in the 1909 Murphy biography. A lecture on diction, which Melba gave at the Guildhall School in London, has been reprinted as it appeared in a Melbourne newspaper in 1911.

We have seen, in previous accounts, that Melba's interest in teaching began to assert itself during the war years, when she found herself spending more time in Australia. Actually, she had attempted to make recordings of singing lessons on a visit to the Victor Talking Machine Company's laboratory in Camden, New Jersey, in October 1913, but the one disc that was cut on that occasion was never issued. (This may have been made at Victor's suggestion: In 1910 the American tenor Evan Williams had made a serious effort to produce a series of recorded singing lessons, none of which was issued; Ernestine Schumann-Heink had cut three trial "vocal lessons" in September 1913, likewise never published. With Melba's effort also a failure, Victor engaged, in 1915, the services of the well-known New York singing teacher Oscar Saenger to prepare a series of recorded vocal lessons, the recording of which occupied nearly two years. These records were announced in May 1917 and were carried in the Victor catalogs until 1928.)

The January 1914 issue of *The Etude* carried an article titled "A Talk with the Girl Who Would Be a Prima Donna: From an

Interview Secured for *The Etude* with the Renowned Diva Mme. Nellie Melba." This article was reprinted under the title "Common Sense in Training and Preserving the Voice" in the book *Great Singers on the Art of Singing* by James Francis Cooke (Philadelphia, 1921). Melba first asks the question, "How can a good voice be detected?" in answer to which she warns against listening to friends and relatives. "The only one to judge is a skilled musician, with good artistic taste and some experience in vocal matters." She notes that musical intelligence is as important as the possession of a fine voice. "Very few people are musically gifted. When one of these people happens to possess a good voice, great industry, a love for vocal art, physical strength, patience, good sense, good taste and abundant faith in her possibilities, the chances of making a good singer are excellent." Melba stresses that children's voices are delicate "despite the wear and tear which children give it by unnecessary howling and screaming" but she comments that children are very susceptible to impressions which will remain into adulthood. For this reason she recommends taking children to hear great singers, since although a great deal will be forgotten, "the better part will be unconsciously stowed away in the subconscious mind, to burst forth later in bautiful song through no different process than that by which the little birds store away the song of the older birds." Melba stresses the importance of a thorough musical education and notes that her parents fortunately insisted that she study piano, organ, and harmonic composition. She notes that she can play any score through and can learn operas by herself so that she can form her own interpretation. "The times I have depended on a *répétiteur* have been so few that I can hardly remember them." She states that the first vocal practice should be so simple that there is no forcing. "In avoiding strain the pupil must above all things learn to sing the upper notes without effort. . . . It is imperative that when a soprano sings her head tones, beginning with F sharp and upward, they shall proceed very softly and entirely without strain as they ascend."

In discussing the preservation of the voice, Melba offers one of her most important secrets: *Never give the public all you have.* "The singer who sings to the utmost every time is like the athlete who exhausts himself to the state of collapse. . . . I have never strained, I have never continued rôles that proved unsuited to me, I have never sung when I have not been in good voice. . . . It is not so much *what* one practices but *how* one practices." In answer to the question "Is the art of singing dying out?" Melba answers that "unless more attention is paid to the real art of singing, there must be a decadence in a short time. . . . The voice seems to demand a kind of exercise leading to flexibility and fluent tone production that is not found in the ultra-dramatic music of any of the modern composers." She warns that young singers start out with good voices, but if they undertake the works of Strauss and Wagner without an adequate period of preparation, they will experience serious vocal difficulties. Thus she recommends music of the older Italian composers who "demanded first of all dulcet tones and limpid fluency." She goes on to make the point that the heavier Germanic roles should be undertaken only by experienced and well-trained singers, not by beginners.

Melba concludes this interview by saying that her greatest incentive has always been opposition. Her family's objections to an operatic career only made her more determined to prove that she could succeed; competition from other singers who sang the same roles merely made her determined to surpass them. Opposition and competition should never be a fear; final triumph will be greater the more one has overcome.

In April 1922, an Adelaide, South Australia, newspaper, *The Advertiser*, began a series of six articles written by Dame Nellie Melba to explain "the Melba Method." The fact that the first article also includes the announcement of a forthcoming tour by Mme. Melba may or may not have had anything to do with the publication of this series. At any event, with the exception of the first section of the series, which was reprinted almost word for word in 1926, it is believed that this important discussion is reprinted here for the first time in permanent form.

In 1926, the Sydney and London music publisher, Chappel & Co., Ltd., issued a sixty-three-page book titled *The Melba Method* by Dame Nellie Melba, part two of which contains a music for vocalises for low and high voice. The first part contained a reprinting of the first of the 1922 articles, plus additional text, all of which is reprinted herewith. In 1983, Beverley Nichols stated in a letter to the author that he had actually written the text for the 1926 publication, which is curious since the series was certainly initiated before Nichols came to Australia. Perhaps Nichols' role was in editing Melba's earlier text.

THE CARE OF THE VOICE

NELLIE MELBA

Madame Nellie Melba (*née* Mitchell) was born in Melbourne, Australia, in 1865 [*sic*]. Her stage name is derived from that of her birthplace. Her parents, people of wealth, conservative Presbyterians of Scotch descent, were possessed of considerable musical talent, which they exercised solely in private. Instrumental rather than vocal music appealed to the family taste, and the young girl was encouraged to practise the pianoforte, violin, organ, and harp, while her vocal gifts were made light of. Nevertheless, she was sought for as a singer at church and charity concerts, and warbled as easily and gladly and unconsciously as a thrush in a hedgerow, although as long as she remained at home she could not study singing, because her family feared she would go upon the stage if her voice were cultivated, and their aversion to the theatre was so great, that she was subjected to constant discouragement in every direction likely to lead to it.

At the age of eighteen [*sic*] Nellie Mitchell entered into what proved a most unfortunate marriage with Captain Armstrong. Subsequently Mr. David Mitchell was appointed commissioner from Australia to the Colonial Exhibition held in London. His daughter accompanied him, and, while there, sang so successfully [*sic*] at a concert given in Freemasons' Hall, that her delighted critics advised her to qualify herself for a public career.

Soon after she placed herself under the instruction of Madame Marchesi, in Paris. A few months later, Maurice Strakosch, who heard her singing, offered the young student a five years' engagement. The death of the impre-

From: Anton Seidl, editor-in-chief, *The Music of the Modern World* (1895).

sario broke up the plan, and shortly after the manager of the Brussels Opera House heard her sing at one of Marchesi's receptions, and offered her an appearance under his direction. Therefore, after a period of training covering barely nine months, the young Australian made her début in the Belgian capital, in October, 1887, at the Théâtre de la Monnaie, as Gilda in *Rigoletto* and was at once hailed by both press and public as the successor of Patti and Nilsson.

In the spring of 1888 Madame Melba made her English début at Covent Garden, with overwhelming success. Since that time her history has been the simple record of artistic triumphs, one of the greatest occasions having been her appearance as Ophelia in *Hamlet* at the Grand Opera, Paris, in 1889. The following year she won her laurels in Milan, at La Scala.

After a tour of Holland and Scandinavia which has never been equalled artistically or financially in either country, Madame Melba in the Metropolitan Opera House, New York, achieved with the most critical and exacting audience in the world, a success which has been repeated in every large city in the United States.

Madame Nellie Melba is a coloratura singer, pure and simple. Her voice is a high soprano of great range; it is brilliant rather than sympathetic; true, flexible, of admirable *timbre*—a perfect instrument which Nature, helped by study, enables the possessor to use with astonishing facility and surety. The ease with which Melba sings is greatly facilitated by an admirable method, but no method ever gave its prodigious spontaneity to that fountain of silvery tone.

Talent and voice of this order find their best medium of expression in lyric opera—opera in that *cantabile* style in which highly embellished themes are most abundant. In such rôles as Lucia, and Gilda in *Rigoletto*, or in the rôle of Marguerite of Navarre in the *Huguenots*, this prima donna is at her best; while her opportunities are somewhat less in operas of a later school, in which song becomes the vehicle of dramatic expression rather than the sole end of the composer's art. In loveliness and brilliancy of tone, combined with absolutely unforced and correct vocal emission, Madame Melba has scarcely been excelled. After an operatic career of seven years Melba's voice is as fresh, of a quality as delicate and fragrant, as when she made her début. In the conversation which was to be recorded in these pages she spoke very simply and earnestly: "It is not poetic," she said, "but it is plain truth, that upon the condition of the stomach depends chiefly the condition of the voice. Now, stomachic disorders are mainly caused by unsuitable food; and about my food I am most particular. It requires a little self-denial, of course, to abstain from rich dishes and wines; but my fare is invariably of the simplest kind. Plenty of chops and steaks, fresh vegetables and fruits.

"Then, exercise, indoors with dumb-bells, when the weather is bad; but always in the open air if fine, and there walking is best. No ordinary rule of health may be disregarded by the singer, and every sensible person must know more or less what contributes best in his individual case to health and well-being.

"Another secret of the freshness of my voice is that, while I save none of my other muscles, but take much physical exercise, I use my voice for the public only. When young artists undertake a new rôle they immediately begin to sing it. They hack and hack at their voices, not for purposes of execution, but merely to memorize what they might better do with their fingers on the keyboard. Oh, you do not catch me simply memorizing on my voice what can be as well done on a mechanical instrument!

"When the music is fixed in my mind then only do I use my voice upon it. Further still, except at rehearsal I always use my voice pianissimo. If you practise forte, you can not sing pianissimo afterward. Therefore, pianissimo in private, and the forte is sure to come all right in public. Of course, while the average voice is being developed, scales, solfeggi, and vocalization over its full compass, are essential; but once the voice has obtained its growth, my experience is that if you sing in public you should save it completely in private."

Of placing the voice Melba spoke earnestly:

"I especially advise young singers above all things to look after the proper posing of the voice. When I first went to Marchesi, in Paris, without a single vocal lesson I sang as well as I do to-day, but for one break in my voice. Marchesi corrected that at once, and placed the registers properly. If this had not been done I should have totally lost my voice. Singers will know of themselves where the break lies between their registers, and if the teacher tries to force the voice over the break there is sure to be something wrong. The probable result will be permanent ruin of the vocal organs. Many a voice is thus ruined in the first stages of tuition. It is quite possible to sing as an artist and yet be an exception to the ordinary rule as to the place where the registers change. A natural peculiarity in this respect should not be disregarded. I carry my middle register to F sharp, half a tone beyond the prescribed limit. If I were a teacher and advocated this in any special case, I should have the whole fraternity abusing me. But I know my own voice.

"While I have been on the stage I have sung in eighteen different rôles, and have studied several in which I have not appeared. I like them all. If I begin the study of one and find I do not like it, I drop it at once. I can make nothing of a rôle with which I am not in sympathy. Of course, one has naturally a weakness for those in which one has achieved the greatest success. But I seem to have been equally successful in mine—Aïda, Elsa, Lucia, Gilda, Semiramide, Elizabeth in *Tannhäuser*, and Elaine, and Juliette—Gounod himself taught me that part—and Marguerite as well.

"Certain rôles may suit the voice and not the temperament of the artist, or the reverse. I mean, that one's nature may be one of passionate intensity, and one's voice of a quality unfit for the strain of expressing exalted sentiments, intense feeling, and profound emotion. A man with a light high tenor voice could not hope to sing heroic rôles with any considerable success; neither could a heavy dramatic soprano make much effect in opéra-comique music. A singer should pay regard to the type of her voice (for that is the medium of expression), and ignore inclination to impersonate characters for which the voice is unsuited, even though Nature may have bestowed every other endowment required for those parts. When possible, I always study my rôle with the composer. Gounod was my friend. I studied with him, with Mascagni, with Thomas, with Delibes. If I cannot reach the composer, I study what the music says to me of the meaning of the libretto. I do not go to the scene of the story, study the class of people to which the characters belong, or even read of it from books. I try to get the composer's meaning, rather than to make a conception of my own of what the part ought to be. I work this out in my own mind, not from observation of scene or people."

ADVICE ON THE SELECTION OF MUSIC AS A PROFESSION

NELLIE MELBA

It having been represented to me that a public expression of my views on the question of young aspirants entering on the study of music in foreign lands might serve in some measure as a corrective to the admitted unwarranted exodus, I gladly join my voice with those who have already endeavoured to remedy an evil the extent of which is little known outside the circle of the victims themselves. Where an English or American student of music has adequate financial means and a reasonable quota of common sense, I would strongly recommend a period of foreign study, for whether the natural musical endowment of such a student be small or great, nothing but benefit can result from the experience. The youth or maiden of circumscribed talents will soon be made to realize the limitations of his or her qualifications, and while this advent of truth may be claimed to have a salutary effect on the mediocrity, it also invariably awakens the greatly gifted to that broader understanding which is the basis of genuine art.

The message, however, which I am now sending to the British and American student is particularly addressed to the inexperienced girls of the Empire and of the great Western Republic who, without the necessary financial means, and having no friendly circle in the foreign cities to which they journey, too often become the victims of their own temerity, and help to add to the prosperity of the ever-increasing circle of unprincipled agents and teachers. Just here I should like to say that few people show greater patience with, and

From: Agnes G. Murphy, *Melba: A Biography* (1909). First published in *The Lone Hand* (Melbourne), February 1, 1909.

kindness to, the most obscure of their clients than do the established concert and opera agents and teachers of Europe and the United Kingdom; but, unfortunately, it is not by these men and women of repute that the over-anxious and ill-equipped student of music elects to be advised. The essential elements of the position make it otherwise.

To the young American or English girl hungering for musical study in Europe I can only repeat what I have been already called upon to say to the young people of Australia, where the abundance of admirable voices has led to something like a human stampede to the old country. There, as in America, it has become the custom to send to Italy, France, Germany, or England any girl or youth who exhibits some degree of musical precocity. The circumstances in both countries are analogous. In the majority of cases the American amateur is sent out on a mission of research and conquest, through the ignorant enthusiasm and prejudice of relatives and friends who have no means of knowing the moral and physical humiliation and suffer-ing to which their incompetent advice helps to consign those who are its dupes.

Britain and America have contributed a creditable contingent to the ranks of famous artists, and may be expected to consistently continue, even improve on, that contribution. Yet it is incidental to these successes that there exists a multitude of failures. In the contemplation of those who have reaped a lavish measure of success, the lamentably and incomparably greater number who sink to obscurity—or worse—are allowed to pass un-noticed. Only those who have succeeded are considered, and emulation of the elect supplies a never-ending and ill-conditioned procession of novices in pursuit of ready honours. If there exists a royal road to triumph, it is found almost as rarely as the blossoms of the century plant—too seldom to be of any use as a practical help to the vast majority, most of whom make their search blindfold.

The average English and American student, like those of my own coun-try, arrives in Europe without the measure of talent and the supply of money indispensable to a European career (for even those specially gifted require financial means to tide them comfortably over the necessary term of study and waiting), and in numerous cases the unfortunate aspirant sinks to a deplorable condition of poverty and despair. In the different large foreign cities, I have known, and still know, numerous instances where young Britishers and Americans have arrived full of ardent hopes, fostered by the foolish laudation of careless or ignorant friends, but who, in a condition of penury, are ready to accept relief from any kindly disposed source. A very brief interval too often separates the heyday of their joyous anticipa-tion from the gloom of their shattered dreams.

The lot of these unsuccessful students is peculiarly hard, as they have generally cut themselves adrift from home and friends and old associations, and journeyed great distances, to find the unavoidable goal of failure, through the routine of misery and privation. The students who are not fortunate very naturally try to hide all evidence of their failure, especially in the land of their birth, and in this way hundreds of other aspirants are led to stumble on, under the old illusion as to easy laurels.

Little more than a year ago, Mr. James E. Dunning, the United States Consul at Milan, through the Department of Commerce and Labour at Washington, brought before the American people the calamitous condition of numbers of young Americans who had travelled to Italy in quest of musical fame. In his moderate and well-considered report, Mr. Dunning dwelt on the hardships to which these young people are constantly reduced through the inherent difficulties of their arduous undertaking—difficulties intensified a thousandfold by the snares spread for them by the designing hangers-on of the profession. What is true of Milan is true in a somewhat similar degree of Paris, Berlin, London, Vienna, and the other great cities, where private and official sources are constantly being appealed to for the assistance of these bankrupt students.

The germ of the trouble is the over-confidence of the aspirant who refuses to be advised, and declines to profit by the wretched experience of others who have tried and failed. Each novice, in the thraldom of inexperience, believes that his or her case will be the exception to the quoted rule, and to those who point out that passable proficiency in amateur efforts may not be capable of the expansion necessary to professional success, an impatient ear is turned by the ambitious though inept student.

Carried away by the outward glamour of a successful artist's life, they set at naught the counsel of those who would guide them, attribute the sober views of their advisers to over-anxiety, and invariably suggest that it is such interference that has wrecked the career of many an embryo genius. Of the many called, they may be of the few chosen, is their argument; and so they rush on, learning too late the supreme difficulties, if not the hopelessness, of their quest.

Different other causes contribute to this regrettable state of affairs, among them the exaggerated importance which many people, besides the performer, attach to the satisfactory rendering of a little drawing-room music, the facility with which accounts of these and other petty little efforts are circulated as successes in some newspapers on both sides of the Atlantic, and the general but decreasing unwillingness of the American and English public—as represented by their resident managers—to accept musicians of purely local renown in the most important music rôles. These three causes are in the main responsible for the numbers of disheartened dependents who, year after year, make a most undesirable addition to the American and British colonies in the chief centres of Europe.

The girl or youth—but more especially the girl—whose accomplishments expand to their utmost attractiveness under the genial influence of the home circle, is too often the one who is least fitted for the struggles, the labours, the sacrifices of a professional career, especially when entered on in a foreign land. The very qualities which are her strength in the world of her sympathetic friends become her weakness in the too often blighting sphere of cold, or designing, or indifferent strangers. It is not easy to imagine a sadder lot than that of the young musical aspirants whose once ardent hopes are wrecked in an alien land. All their efforts have been directed towards an illusion, and the training on which they have spent their available time and money, instead of being a help, is an actual hindrance to their advance in any of the rougher walks of life. In this way valuable human energy is wasted, and individuals and families who might have been made happy through its proper direction are reduced to humiliating, even degrading, conditions of dependence. The parents and friends of any average amateur of music should well weigh their words before encouraging any such performer to enter into a professional life, either at home or abroad. The satisfactory rendering of a solo at a family soirée or local concert is not sufficient indication of qualifications for a career where brains, courage, tact, industry, resolution, and physical vigour are at least as essential to success as a beautiful voice or exceptional technique.

I would, therefore, advise greater wisdom in the selection of candidates. More care should be taken not to send abroad students whose talents are never likely to justify the enterprise, and in no case should the novices be allowed to depart without sufficient money to carry them in comfort through an extended term of study and probation.

Then, again, Press opinions on students' efforts at concerts got up for experimental purposes are almost always, and of necessity, misleading. The young singers or players naturally select the two or three numbers in which they are calculated to appear to most advantage; no performer likely to clash with them in any way is given a place on the programme; the hall is packed with interested friends whose enthusiasm creates a false atmosphere, which not unreasonably leads the less experienced critic—who is generally selected for minor events—into writing a notice somewhat more encouraging than his calmer judgment would endorse.

The arranged absence of any superior talent, the ardent applause of prejudiced friends, and the kindly opinion of a critic ready to make the best of what to him is an unimportant occasion, are the points incidental to these entertainments that count towards the summary of their success.

One of these concerts is often allowed to dictate the decision as to a career, yet they are almost always but well-meant efforts at forcing a selection which should never be made.

When the selection has been made, however, and the young aspirant goes abroad, and becomes the centre of one or two similar musical exploits in Paris, London, or Berlin, it is then that special evil is wrought by the misleading reports sent to the homeland by careless but kindly correspondents. The young amateurs who remained at home, and who had no very flattering opinion of those who had been sent abroad, on reading of the latter's success, form a hasty opinion as to the ease with which the great musical world is conquered, and straightway enter on the task themselves. The ubiquitous duties of foreign correspondents too often make it incumbent on them to accept second-hand information, and in this manner even the most conscientious among them are sometimes misled. I would urge on all contributors to the Press the wisdom of carefully editing every story of musical success which happens to be outside their own personal knowledge. In this way I believe much could be done to alleviate the conditions to which Mr. Consul Dunning and others have called attention.

As for the American apathy towards the native-born musician whose gifts have not been sponsored by the European public, it reveals a condition which has a parallel at least in all English-speaking communities. I suppose few would dispute that the greatest of American artists are those who have won recognition in foreign lands, and in that way the preference for such, however much to be regretted, may be said to be based on the selection epitomized in "the survival of the fittest." In the days to come, when music as an inspiration and recreation of the people will have an older pedigree in Great Britain and America, the public of these countries will probably be more ready to abide by their own verdict in the creation of their favourites, and perhaps show some of that ardent preference for the artists of their own race which is manifested by the peoples of Italy, France, and Germany.

The higher the standard of the British and American music institutions, and the greater the efficiency of the professors engaged therein, the sooner will the element of unreason be minimized in the British and American preference for music artists of foreign reputation. England and America are already fortunate in the possession of great facilities for the cultivation of music, but there are numerous opportunities for the extension and higher development of these facilities, many of them provided for in the newly formed British Musical League and in Madame Nordica's admirable American proposition. In her proposal there is the elemental basis of a great national conservatoire, which would supply local students with additional stimulus, and save many of them from the disappointments and hardships which so often fall to their lot in foreign cities.

I imagine that some of Madame Nordica's critics have taken the reference to Bayreuth too literally. Personally, I see no reason why an American national home for opera, embodying some of the best features of Bayreuth, should not be a matter of accomplishment, and as such become a splendid help to great numbers of students. But my interest lies specially in the phase of her scheme which deals directly with tuition. It is impossible to outline exactly every detail in the preliminary summary of such an undertaking, but the setting up of any centre of musical education formulated on lines that aim at the highest results—always remembering my strong plea for individual, in preference to class, tuition—and where the greatest teachers of

Europe might be induced to preside for certain terms, is a step that should appeal largely to the American people. It would give the student, the manager, and the public greater confidence in the home-developed singer or instrumentalist, and in this way alone would do something to correct the unreasonable exodus of music aspirants with which I am specially dealing.

I am also glad to have this opportunity of expressing my interest in Mr. Henry Savage's plan, which has resulted in the establishment of a Paris bureau where American musicians in Europe are able to secure desired information and advice, and I hope some English enthusiast may be induced to follow his example. At this centre Mr. Savage's staff keep a record of all young students arriving from America, and provide lists of teachers, schools, agents, managers, coaches, accompanists, translators, diction masters, and places of abode to which they may go assured of fair dealing and friendly reception. As matters have existed up to now, even the students of exceptional talents, on the completion of their musical education, have too often drifted into sad obscurity for want of competent guidance.

Still harder has been the fate of the student whose gifts are but of the average order. Should the bureau be continued on the lines which Mr. Savage's own high personal reputation warrants one in assuming, there can be no doubt but that it will confer incalculable benefit on numbers of worthy young Americans, whose ambition leads them to respond to the uncertain call of European competition.

For all young British and American amateurs having sufficient means to see them in comfort through a term of foreign study, but more especially those possessing exceptional natural gifts, I, of course, strongly urge the advantage of a term of residence and research in the great music centres of the old world. The study of the French, German, and Italian languages, so necessary to the operatic artist, is always more thoroughly carried out in the countries where they are the native tongue. The chances to study under the most famous masters, and the opportunities to hear the greatest works interpreted by the greatest artists, are also comparatively easy and numerous in Europe, while in the atmosphere of the famous seats of music there is an incentive which no other condition can so surely supply.

For the student of mediocre talent and little money these advantages, however, are entirely over-shadowed by the privations and disappointments which, in their case, are but the preliminary to failure. I repeat, then, that the greatest discretion should be exercised in the nomination of students for European study, and I insist that even an unusual voice or admirable technique is not in itself sufficient to warrant an undertaking, the success of which, apart from liberal expenditure, also demands several exceptional qualities of body and mind.

ON THE SCIENCE
OF SINGING

NELLIE MELBA

Musical knowledge continues to spread with rapidity and effect, but I think the greater chances of success thus opened to numbers of followers is very largely—too largely—discounted by the scores of inept executants and professors who, without even the most ordinary qualifications, proclaim themselves teachers and interpreters of an art which demands in its apostles the fitness of very liberal attainments. What should be a learned profession is recklessly overcrowded by ignorant exponents, who are inconceivably accepted even by those who would vehemently resent any semblance of charlatanism in any other serious calling. The unqualified performer is the natural result of the unqualified teacher, and while no test of ability is exacted from the vast body of professors, so long will music suffer through the ignorance of its adherents.

Many amateurs, and especially women, are no doubt attracted to the profession of music by the high, perhaps extravagant, rates of remuneration paid to successful performers and teachers. It is something of an anomaly that a field where the monetary appreciation is so high should be the one where proven fitness is not essential to entry. If we had more competent teachers, we should have more great singers; and I shall never cease to urge the necessity of placing the tuition of singing on a more exclusive basis than that on which it now exists. The acknowledged professors in all the great cities should resort to some means to shut out from their ranks the tyros

From: Agnes G. Murphy, *Melba: A Biography* (1909).

whose research too often does not extend beyond the superficial smattering gleaned in a year or two from questionable authorities.

In all other learned professions—and even in mechanical callings—different technical tests are imposed before a person is accepted as an authority in that profession or calling. In music the insistence on any test is, unhappily, not the rule, but the exception; especially is this the case in English-speaking colonies and communities. Casual observation, backed up by unlimited confidence, too often suffices to win a large measure of public support, the charlatan, by the very essence of his method, having a much more easy course than the cultured specialist, who has made a heavy outlay of time, talent, and money in obtaining qualifying knowledge.

It is my practice to hear as many young singers as possible in the different cities I visit, also in London, the city of my home, and everywhere I am grieved by the injury I see done through ignorant tuition, for in the vast majority of cases I find methods in vogue which are entirely at variance with the health of the delicate vocal cords. We do not accept tuition in architecture, chemistry, or law from any casual dabbler in these professions, but we welcome the gospel of vocalization from those who have not even a perfunctory acquaintance with the science of singing. Students should remember that a good general knowledge of music does not imply a knowledge of voice-production based on scientific principles, and until they come to look for that scientific basis in their teachers, nondescript singers will continue to be crowded on a patient, perhaps culpable, public. Physiological principles are the necessary groundwork of correct vocalization. Through them defects are more surely detected and remedied, and the restoration or development of a maimed or immature organ definitely achieved. Physiology is absolutely essential to preserve the health of the vocal organs and protect the voice from injurious influences; but in saying this it must be understood that I am dealing with the science, not the soul, of song.

Having said so much about incompetent teachers, I return to the question of inept pupils. Too many girls and youths are encouraged to adopt music as a profession merely because of its gentility as a means of livelihood, or because their voices have contributed to the pleasure of the family circle, where the compliments of a few relations or friends are taken as sufficient warranty of fitness for a professional career. Before young vocal aspirants decide on this difficult undertaking, I strongly recommend the seeking of high and unprejudiced counsel, preferably from a singer who is familiar with the requirements and difficulties of the calling, and who is intimate with the conditions which obtain in the great centres of music. In endeavouring to arrive at a decision, it is well to remember that there are more failures through lack of common sense than through lack of talent. The person who aims at a public career, especially in opera, must have character supported by reason and control, otherwise the progress which a good voice and certain technical knowledge temporarily insure always stops short of great results. I freely acknowledge the value of opportunity, and if opportunity knocks but once at most men's doors, it is ostensibly of primary importance to be prepared for that call. Even that *rara avis*, the born singer, might dissipate Heaven-sent gifts for want of opportunity, while the vocalist of highly cultivated talent might never emerge from obscurity without it. Conditions of musical knowledge and physical health being equal, the student of alert mind, who is prepared for her chance, and goes some way to meet it, is the one who is surest of success.

Mental lethargy is fatal to advancement, and no young musician has a right to rely for preferment on the exertions of others. Those who have attained the qualifications of technical equipment essential to success, and who do not achieve it, are generally those who fail to strike out for themselves. Industry as well as knowledge is necessary to the successful novice, and no one is justified in the belief that she or he will sing by inspiration, no matter how prodigal Nature may have been in the bestowal of her gifts. And if diligence is essential for the highest development of the born singer, it must be regarded as of a thousandfold greater importance to the vocalist whose endowments fall short of that inspired creature.

One of the first fields for the employment of the beginner's energy is physiology. No student should be content to proceed without gaining a reasonable knowledge of the anatomy of the throat and the sensitive and complicated physical mechanism that produce the singing voice. For myself, I at one time became so completely absorbed in this study that I could practically neither think nor speak of anything else. An understanding of the delicate functions of voice mechanism is a rational and logical plea for perfection in singing, and was always embodied in the methods of the old Italian masters, whose general accuracy has been reduced to a much surer science by some of their present-day followers. Those who know the structure of the larynx and the muscular mechanism of the parts called into action by the production of the voice, will find themselves in possession of knowledge essential to correct attack. The application of the air-blast to the vocal cords should be a detail of exact science, not a haphazard circumstance. In a warm general recommendation of the old Italian method, I do not hesitate to condemn the white voice and tremolo so favoured by some Italian singers.

Great success in singing is impossible to the vocalist who does not thoroughly understand breathing, attack, the use of the registers, the structure and functions of the parts above the voice-box, and the relation of chest expansion to the production of tone. As I have so often said, a beautiful voice is only the basis of vocal progress, in the perfection of which correct breathing is the greatest technical essential. Faulty breathing can even negative the expression of noble thought which a soulful, but incompetent, performer may be struggling to put into his work. It is utterly impossible to demonstrate in song the beauty of either a singer's voice or mind without proper breath control. Tone, expression, resonance, phrasing, are all dependent on respiration, and girls and boys of musical tastes, even when too young to be permitted the free use of their voices, should be fully taught the principles of taking breath.

During the years of childhood and adolescence the science of breathing is a peculiarly appropriate study, for, other conditions apart, correct breathing is highly conducive to good health, and owing to the greater elasticity of the body during the growing years, the chest is then much more readily developed and expanded. As the diaphragm is the chief muscle of inspiration, special care should be devoted to any exercises that promote its strength. Expiration is considerably more difficult of control than inspiration, and consequently calls for the most careful practice.

Exact vibration of the vocal cords can never be secured where the breathing is hurried or faulty, and any conditions likely to produce either should be rigidly avoided, particularly at the time of a singer's first entrance on the stage or concert platform, which even under the happiest circumstances is always a moment of nervousness and doubt. The timid singer will always find her forces strengthened on such occasions by taking a few very deep breaths on stepping before the public, and by choosing for the opening number—where a choice is possible—music that is free from exacting initial bars.

To my mind, a girl should never enter on the serious routine of voice culture until she is seventeen years of age. Before that time even a moderate share of work is likely to interfere with the proper development of the vocal organs, and perhaps cause certain injury. Only the other day Madame Mathilde Marchesi recalled the fact that the too frequent use of her marvellous voice in youth had prematurely impaired the middle register of Jenny Lind. If one so divinely gifted as she suffered through prodigal use of the voice during her early years, how imperative must be the necessity for care in the case of those whose endowments fall immeasurably below her unique standard!

On the other hand, we have to-day several artists of world-wide fame who, because of a reasonable economy of their vocal means in their young days, and their consistent adherence to a correct method, are singing as freshly now as they did twenty years ago, while others, who started with equal or greater natural endowments, have become painfully defective in their artistic work through ignorant use of the vocal organs.[1]

A most helpful factor in the study of music, especially for an operatic career, is a knowledge of foreign languages, and as they can always be most successfully acquired in the countries where they are the native tongue, I consider that a sufficient reason for the advocacy of foreign study. Terms of residence in the music centres of Italy, France, Germany, Austria, Russia, and the consequent familiarity with the work and traditions of the great masters of these countries, give the student a certainty, an authority, in her work which cannot be obtained in any other way. The subtleties and complexities of the art more easily possess the mind where music has long been fostered, and where it has become part of the national life, rather than the luxury, or perhaps affectation, of a class.

All these countries possess great teachers of singing, but I personally consider Madame Mathilde Marchesi, of Paris, the greatest of them all. I repeat my oft-expressed opinion that she is a marvel of scientific method, a most remarkable personality for whose place no city of the world has yet revealed a probable successor. Through the elder Garcia, who developed his method from the tenets of the earlier great Italian masters, Mathilde Marchesi conceived the spirit of her own principle of tuition, which may be roughly indicated in a few words: "Change to the middle notes on F. Begin the head notes on F sharp. Once on the head notes, always practise pianissimo."

Madame Lilli Lehmann I hold to be the greatest teacher of German vocal art. Every Italian city boasts of highly qualified masters, and if I were dealing with the possibilities of vocal tuition in London, I could name several most admirable teachers. In my own studies I have been most fortunate, for in the operatic rôles with which I am most closely identified I have had the invaluable assistance of the composers themselves—Gounod, Verdi, Delibes, Ambroise Thomas, Leoncavallo, Puccini, Massenet, Saint-Saëns. Holding, as I do, that the singer's mission is to interpret the message of the composer, and not to mutilate or embellish it with extraneous ideas, I naturally consider the opportunity of securing the composer's assistance as a fortunate chance which cannot be too highly appreciated.

From the outset I advise young singers to look after the posing of the voice. They will know better than anybody where the break occurs, and they must see that the teacher does not adopt an extreme course in the endeavour to bridge it over prematurely. Any attempt at unduly precipitating the blending of the registers must result in injury to the voice—indeed, permanent injury is in this way often done during the initial stages of vocal study. Some enthusiasts have described my own voice as of one register.[2] I mention this to draw attention to the result that may be achieved by careful thought and industry, and as an incentive to the many students who discredit the possibility of hiding the natural break.

I am a great believer in the wisdom of fully recognizing every novice's individuality, but the general rule as to the register changes is a safe one for almost every student. There are exceptions, of course, and, as for myself, I carry my chest register up to F and change on F sharp, which is half a tone beyond the usual limit. When I went to Madame Marchesi, she at once recognized this natural peculiarity, and allowed for it in the scheme of my tuition, her discernment giving me a speedy chance to demonstrate that exceptional register changes do not constitute a bar to success. One point of guidance easy of remembrance is that any method that tires a student, that entails a sense of strain, is sure to be wrong.

The most valuable voices often present the most striking superficial difficulties, and only the most accomplished teachers should be entrusted with the task of their removal. It often happens that even where the voice is properly posed, there still remains a weakness where the registers change, and bad teachers frequently endeavour to produce an enlargement of tone by constant practice of this feeble section of the voice. I am strongly opposed to this policy, and I urge equal exercise of the whole organ as the best method of securing uniformity of tone. But if there should persistently remain a natural blemish, far better to retain the voice with its trifling inherent weakness, than chance its entire destruction through the enforcement of a tax which Nature indicates as oppressive. During the development of the average voice, scales, solfeggios, and vocalization over its entire range are absolutely essential to its proper growth; but once the period of vocal maturity is reached, I am sure all students who sing in public will be wise to reserve their voices as much as possible in private.

Young aspirants often write to me, and in commenting on the freshness of my voice and the spontaneity of my singing, assume that these conditions are the result of some occult knowledge entirely outside the possibility of their achievement. The secret lies in the fact that I never taxed my voice in the way peculiar to the great majority of inexperienced vocalists. My gospel has been to give the body ample exercise, and the voice ample rest. This, as I have indicated, is particularly necessary for the students who have already begun to sing in public.

Before even attempting to hum over any music, I am always careful to phrase it on the keyboard and commit it to memory. Young singers too often take a new song or rôle to the piano, and, without any knowledge of it, begin to use and waste the voice in a preliminary that could be equally well accomplished on a mechanical instrument. They chop and hack at their voices, not in any effort at vocal accomplishment, but merely for the purpose of memorizing. It is only when the words and music are firmly engraved on my mind that I use my voice on them, and even then I spare it as much as possible by practising the top notes quite pianissimo, except on the rare occasions at rehearsal where the full voice is needed. Practising high notes forte is one of the most pernicious customs of vocal study, and as a general rule it may be safely laid down that it invariably minimizes the possibility of those refined, soft effects which are not only a charm, but a necessity, to artistic singing. During practise students should always hold their forces well in reserve, and if they sing the upper register pianissimo in private, they will find that the forte effects will readily respond when public performances demand it. On the days when I sing in opera or concert I run through a few scales in full voice during the morning, and if I cannot sing top D perfectly I consider myself out of form.[3] Just before going on I try my voice again for a few seconds to warm it.

Apart from the scientific necessity for proper economy of vocal means, I wish to point out that the general muscles of the body become slack in the case of students who spend half the day or more sitting or standing by a piano, wearing out their vocal and physical resources in a mistaken endeavour at advancement. A beautiful voice, beautifully used, can only continue to come from a healthy body, and their cause would be far better served if they gave much of their wasted time to indulgence in open-air exercise.

An excess of diligence might easily become a hindrance rather than a help, and as robust health is an essential to any large measure of success, anything that impairs the physical vigour should be rigidly avoided. Happily, there is a great deal in a singer's life conducive to bodily strength, the most important being the strong and consistent use of the breathing apparatus, which in itself is almost sufficient to counteract such degenerating influences as late hours, night travelling, concentrated efforts, and the disappointments which, owing to the caprice of the public, the singer, the weather, or from other causes, must be reckoned with in every career. Many students, in their eagerness for musical headway, entirely neglect their physical welfare, and forget that plenty of fresh air, simple, nourishing food, and eight or nine hours' sleep are all necessary to the young singer, whose larynx invariably reflects her bodily condition. Common-sense regard for the individual requirements is almost the only dictum needed in this particular, and the student who has based her studies on physiological principles will have early learned the delicacy of her vocal organs and the course necessary for their protection. I personally greatly favour fruit and vegetables as an important item in the regular régime. For breakfast I take only toast and tea; at luncheon a cutlet, or a little chicken, with a light salad and fruit, but no rich dishes. My chief meal is dinner, which I have rather late—7:45 or 8 o'clock—and there is nothing to distinguish it from the same meal in the average household. When I am singing in the evening, I do not dine, but have a very light repast consisting of either fish, chicken, or sweetbread, with a baked apple and a glass of water at 5 o'clock, and I always find myself very hungry for supper when I get home from the opera or concert. On the evenings when I am not singing or entertaining, I am always in bed by half-past 10 o'clock, sometimes earlier.

My views on the value of individual training are well known, and carry with them a consequent opposition to class tuition. It is impossible for a singing student to give out her best as one of a group directed by a supervision which must in its very essence partake of the perfunctory. The singers who have succeeded after class training have been those whose personality and endowments have made them independent of circumstances.

Reliance on choir or chorus singing as a helpful factor in the early period of vocal study I hold to be a most unwise course, as an unplaced voice may easily be permanently injured by its free employment in any such body. The following of any trade or profession during the early years of study is a very questionable economy, giving, as it does, to some extraneous interest the vitality which should be the treasure-house of the vocal organs.

Every grade of student may safely follow all phases of tuition where the voice is not called into use in the classes of the admirable colleges and conservatoires now existent in every large community. I think all singers should make a thorough study of the piano, harmony, and counterpoint, which are as important in the expression of music as is grammar to the spoken or written language. The most serious study begins when the student comes before the public, a study which must be endless; but if a young singer is not able to make a promising public début after eighteen months' legitimate work, then, in my opinion, she will never make any great success in her profession. Many British and American students are inclined to regard a fairly successful public appearance as an indication that future research is unnecessary, and so find themselves unable to escape from the chains of mediocrity.

The drama should be carefully cultivated by the vocal novice, and as a collateral aid, both to the science and art of singing, nothing counts for more than intimacy with the work of the great artists of the day. No opportunity should be missed of hearing and seeing famous singers and actors in their most important rôles. What an inspiration, too, comes to all who have a soul for music when they hear some famous conductor lead a fine body of musicians through a great masterpiece by Beethoven, Bach, Mozart, Brahms, or Wagner! No matter what branch of music a student may aim at mastering, every chance of hearing the best in opera, orchestra, recital, or oratorio should be eagerly seized on and seriously considered. Speaking for myself, I am always inspired and helped by every noble interpretation I hear, and into my own succeeding work I seem able to put something I had not so perfectly understood before.

The technique of singing is incalculably helped by everything that improves the intellectual calibre, so the ambitious student should read not only all that is authoritative and informative on music, but become familiar with the beauties of general literature and art, and the wonders of natural science. The power of interpretation is immensely helped by a fine imagination, which comes easiest from a mind illuminated and beautified by wide culture. The singer who can appreciate great pictures, poetry, and statuary, who can reasonably apprehend the glories of the mountains, the forest, and the ocean, can more surely fathom the joys and sorrows of the human heart than the one who is merely well informed on affairs of music.

And now I feel myself drifting from the surer ground of science towards the indefinable sphere of art, the elusive qualities of which are beyond the

pale of this article. I am convinced that the art of song lies outside the possibility of human generation, and that only those who are born to this subtle
heritage can ever reach the topmost heights. It is impossible for any teacher
to impart temperament or an unerring musical ear, but even these God-
given gifts, and the minor endowments of mind and body, can be developed
and enhanced to a remarkable degree by the intelligent and consistent
application of those who seek to make themselves and others happier and
better through the profession of music.

Neither do the entire powers of the artist come to anyone as a completed
gift; the ideal balance of the mental and physical faculties must be a matter
of slow development fostered by manifold influences. This attainment
should, therefore, be the aim of everyone who seriously enters on the study
of singing, for in its pursuit may be revealed, even where not suspected, that
soulful spark which illumines with a mystic torch the work of the truly
great. Perfection of technique is but the stepping-stone to the high plane of
repose, where, after many vicissitudes, the student is transformed into the
artist; but then, in that day of self-determining realities, the artist must still
remain the servant, as well as the master, of technique.

NOTES

1. During the trial of the Horspool versus Cumming musical libel suit heard at the
Royal Courts of Justice, London, in February, 1908, Dr. Milson Rees, the famous
throat specialist, whose patients include all the greatest contemporary singers of
Europe and America, was called as a witness. In reply to a question from the exam-
ining counsel as to the unusual retention of an unimpaired singing voice by some of
these artists, Dr. Rees said: "It is the result of elasticity in the ligamentous portion of
their vocal cords. The most elastic vocal cord to-day is Madame Melba's. She makes
use of the anterior portion of the cord, and that accounts for the lasting quality of
her voice. She knowingly uses head notes instead of chest notes. It is an automatic
process. A scale can be sung by putting the full tension on the reeds, or varying from
the long reed to the short. . . . In the case of Madame Melba, there is no singer with
more resonance and less nasal quality."

2. The late Sir Morell Mackenzie, the eminent throat specialist, thought that
Melba used the same register throughout the voice.

3. The range of Melba's voice is three octaves, terminating on the high F sharp.

LECTURE ON DICTION

NELLIE MELBA

This lecture was delivered to the students of the Guildhall School of Music in London.

The opinion is held largely that English is not a musical language, or at least not a language which lends itself felicitously to expression in music. I rather think that, for a time, I held that opinion myself. My maturer judgment and experience tell me that I was wrong, and, although the English language lends itself to expression in music less readily than the Italian, it is, in that respect at least equal to the French, and certainly superior to the German— [cheers]—and that the reason why I held that opinion for a time—and why others hold it still—is that the art of English diction, whatever it may have been in other days, of which we have no direct knowledge, has been during our own time in a very uncultivated condition. It is true that there are exceptional instances to the contrary, and that occasionally we hear our native language spoken in song with distinction and clearness; but it is, alas! equally true that our ears are tortured too frequently by mispronunciations and verbal obscurities, and at times to such an extent that it is difficult to decide in which particular language the singer is delivering his message. [Cheers and laughter].

After all, what are we singers but the silver-voiced messengers of the poet and the musician? That is our call, that is our mission; and it would be well for us to keep it constantly and earnestly in our minds. What we should

From: *The Argus* (Melbourne), June 27, 1911.

strive for is to attain as nearly to perfection as possible in the delivery of that message—[cheers]—sacrificing neither the musician for the poet nor the poet for the musician. If we sing a false tone or mispronounce one word we are apt to awaken the critical faculty which, consciously or unconsciously, exists in every audience; to create a spirit of unrest, and destroy the burden of our message. A similar disastrous effect, of course, may be made by a miscalculation of breathing power, an inappropriate facial expression, or by many another unartistic happening on the singer's part. As, however, these reflections would lead us into wider considerations than those we are prepared for today, let us return to the subject of English diction.

I think it will be generally admitted as an ideal that the English language should be sung as it should be spoken, with just sufficient added distinctness, or one might even use the word "exaggeration", to counteract the obscuring effect of the singer's voice and the piano or other musical accompaniment. [Hear, hear]. You have observed that I have said "as the English language should be spoken"—[hear, hear]—and I am sure that the thought has occurred to you that the majority of people, singers and non-singers, do not habitually speak the language with justice, distinction and grace. [Cheers]. How many persons do you know who could read aloud a verse of poetry, or of fine prose, in a manner to include the qualities mentioned? Not many, I fear. And yet I have a strong feeling that that is what the singer should be able to do before he or she enters seriously into the training of the singing voice. [Cheers]. In a word, if verbal diction were early acquired, vocal diction would not be so serious a stumbling block to our singers. [Cheers].

> She dwelt among the untrodden ways
>   Beside the springs of Dove,
> A maid whom there were none to praise
>   And very few to love.

These words of Wordsworth are very simple, very beautiful, surely very singable; and yet, I suppose, I am not the only person present today who has heard them sadly mutilated in song. [Hear, hear]. I have heard the word "Dove" given as "Doive"—[laughter]—the word "whom" as "oom", and the word "love"—a particularly long-suffering word in song, by the way —[laughter]—given as "loive". [Laughter]. Suppose that a man (I am particularly addressing the lady students at the moment)—suppose that a man, anxious to communicate to you the condition of his sentiments, were to say to you, "I loive you" [laughter] he would surely excite either your ridicule or your distrust. [Laughter]. In any case the exhilarating message would be dreadfully discounted by the preposterous delivery. [Laughter]. Perhaps, if singers knew that audiences unconsciously made that discount every time the beautiful old Saxon word is mishandled in song, they would make some effort to sing the word as it is spoken.

For another example: Would any man, with the possible exception of an Irishman, address you as "darrling", or draw your fugitive attention to the emotions of his "hearrt", as do singers in your concert rooms daily? [Laughter]. In speaking "darling" or "heart" your tongue never curls up to touch the "r"; then why should it in song? Consider for a moment the word "garden". Speak it aloud to yourself. It is a simple word of two syllables, in the pronunciation of which the tongue is practically unemployed. It is too simple a word, apparently, for a great many singers—a determined attack must be made on the unoffending "r", and the result is a word of three syllables, which sounds anything but English. [Laughter]. The "r" in garden is the third letter in a six-lettered word. It occupies the same position in the word "forest"; but if you will speak the word "forest" to yourself, you will find that your tongue comes into active employment. I think, then, that it logically follows that when you sing "garden" the "r" should be passive, and when you sing "forest" the "r" should be active; and I feel sure that in this, and in all that is implied in the passing examples I have ventured to give you, I shall have the approval of the eminent professors of elocution and singing who add so much lustre and efficiency to this splendid school of music. [Cheers].

If you wish to sing beautifully—and you all do—you must love music, and the nearer you get to music the more you will love it. If you wish to sing your native language beautifully—and you all should—you must love your native language; and the nearer you get to it the more you will love it. [Hear, hear].

Aim high. Let your ambition be ever on tip-toe. [Hear, hear]. Fill your minds with Shakespeare's sonnets, Keats' "Ode to a Grecian Urn", Shelley's "Ode to a Skylark", Matthew Arnold's "Forsaken Merman", Swinburne's "Spring Song", "In Atalanta", and many other of the poetic ecstasies with which your beautiful language is so rich. [Hear, hear]. Let them become the delightful companions of what might otherwise be sometimes lonely hours; learn to speak them aloud with distinction and understanding, and so enable yourselves to bring to your singing the added glory of a perfect diction. [Loud cheers].

DAME NELLIE MELBA: HER METHODS EXPLAINED

NELLIE MELBA

Valuable Help for Singers (Dame Nellie Melba's First Article)

For 30 years Australians have been proud of Nellie Melba as the only Australian who has taken one of the arts for a kingdom, and attained in it unchallenged sovereignty. But even now few suspect how much they have to be proud of. That hers is the most wonderful voice of modern times, that the critics of all nations have hailed her as the Queen of Song—so much they know. What they do not know is that this remarkable Australian is something more than a singer of unique charm.

Entranced by her golden voice, they have been content to attribute it to some form of magic—some freak of nature which cannot be accounted for or explained. And to the extent that Melba's triumphs would have been impossible without an extraordinary throat, this attitude is perhaps justifiable. But what the world does not generally realise is that her God-given voice is only one part of her equipment. Equally important has been the brain which evolved a new scientific method, and carried it to a degree of perfection that had hitherto not been dreamed of.

From: *The Advertiser* (Adelaide, South Australia), 1922.

NEW METHOD EVOLVED

To have a wonderful throat and conventional training—that, Melba soon discovered, was not sufficient to carry her to the greatest heights. On the contrary, her early tuition was so faulty that even the most beautiful of voices would speedily have been ruined. Though the world never suspected it, the system with which she began was so unscientific—she was attacking with the glottis instead of further forward on the hard palate—that she began to develop a growth which must soon have wrought havoc. Faced with this impending calamity, she rejected the conventional teaching, and with characteristic independence decided to solve the problem for herself. The result is the Melba method, scientific and artistically incomparable.

To help Australia and the Australians whom she loves—that has always been Dame Nellie's ambition. For years she has given advice and tuition to pupils at the Melbourne Conservatorium of Music without any reward, except the knowledge that she is giving the singers of today and tomorrow the benefit of her genius and experience.

Now, she has decided to do far more. In order to help as many students as possible up the road to success, she has consented to explain her method in a series of articles in *The Advertiser*, the first of which we publish today.

That they will be of great interest and importance to every student and lover of music goes without saying. Everyone who hears Melba sing today, after a reign of 30 years as the world's foremost soprano, is struck by the purity and extraordinary freshness of her voice, and it is obvious that a detailed exposition of a system which has given such miraculous results in her case must vitally concern every student and immediately take a place among the permanent literature of music.

MELBA'S COMING TOUR

For personal reasons, also, these articles will be of great interest, for they will be amongst the last public activities undertaken by Dame Nellie before she leaves for Europe. Discussing her plans with a special representative, she stated that she was leaving for Europe in September. She is to sing in London in November and December, will give a season in Monte Carlo, and will probably return to Paris in the spring. "After that," she said, "I have no plans, but it is fairly certain that I will not return to Australia until the following year—that is, about eighteen months after my departure. I have gladly undertaken to write a series of articles for *The Advertiser* before I go, because I believe that I can do more in this way than in any other to help young students along.

"And certainly they need advice," she added emphatically. "Many of them are taught wrong; others ruin their voices by practising for absurdly long periods—sometimes as much as two hours at a time. The very maximum for a beginner should be ten minutes at a time, and at no period should it extend over more than half an hour. To the young singer I would offer the Italian motto, 'Chi va piano va sano, chi va sano va lontano'— 'Who goes slowly goes healthily; who goes healthily goes for a long time.' "

The best proof of the truth of the proverb is Dame Nellie herself, for in the whole history of music there is probably no one whose voice has worn as well as hers. That is why we take the greatest pleasure in publishing a series of articles which will explain the method by which such extraordinary results have been accomplished.

NO. 1—SINGING

It is easy to sing well and very difficult to sing badly! How many students of singing are really prepared to accept that statement? Few, if any. They smile and say, "It may be easy for you, but it is not for me," and seem to consider that ends the matter. Or they sigh and say, "I wish it were," and they also dismiss the subject. But if they only knew it, on their understanding and acceptance of that saying depends much of their success as singers.

Let me say the same thing in other words: "In order to sing well, it is necessary to sing easily."

For some unknown reason, practically all teachers and students accept this statement with enthusiasm. But though they accept it, comparatively few achieve the ease, which is one reason why there are never at any time many singers who can be called great vocalists as well as artists. For, undoubtedly, more than one famous singer has become famous in spite of the way they sang, rather than because of it.

If, as I have said, teachers agree that in order to sing well it is necessary to sing easily, how is it that there are so many methods of teaching singing, each of which contradicts all others and condemns them as utterly bad?

If we look into these conflicting methods we generally find that they are built up round an idea which has proved helpful in some cases. The reason of this help not being properly understood, the idea is seized upon and acclaimed as a panacea for all ills.

When we give ourselves time to think, we realise that this is absurd, for no one exercise, vowel, or position of mouth or tongue (as the case may be) can cure all difficulties. The only method that can be helpful must be built up on commonsense and a close observation of Nature's laws. The only way to get over a difficulty is to find its root cause. And one very general cause of trouble is that so few people have any real idea of what "ease" means.

The beginner at any game watches the champion and groans "it looks so easy." It is easy, or the player would not be a champion.

Or you hear Heifetz play, and every budding violinist despairingly says, "Everything seems easy to him." It is, or he would not play in the entrancing way he does.

Indeed, so little is the necessity for ease understood, that many people feel they are not getting their money's worth unless the performer seems to be working a little to get his effects, even though that effort may defeat his aim. Therefore, we sometimes see a performer, who is not entirely free from the spirit of the showman—if he be a pianist, throw up his hands much higher than is necessary to get weight into his big chords; or, if he be a violinist, sway from side to side and make great play with his bow; or, if a singer, get red in the face, almost to the point of bursting a blood vessel, over a top note. Then the audience feels someone is really working for their entertainment, and go away exclaiming how wonderful it has been!

What, then, is ease? I take it that it is doing anything without any unnecessary muscular action.

That sounds very simple; but is it? How many of us know when we are making unnecessary movements? Not one person in a hundred knows.

For nearly everyone is self-conscious instead of being conscious of self. The former is fatal to success; the latter entirely necessary.

What is self-consciousness, and how can it be cured? For it should really be treated as a disease that must be cured. So-called self-consciousness arises from a state of divided consciousness, and that state is nearly always caused by fear. As fear is paralysing, there can be no freedom or ease in singing while the mind entertains such a dangerous guest. We fear we may be laughed at if we try to sing as the teacher suggests, we fear we may make unpleasant sounds; we fear we cannot reach a high note or sustain our breath for a long one; and many other things do we fear.

In every case, fear takes our attention away from what we should be doing in order to sing well, and causes us to stiffen muscles that should be free to work, or to be at rest.

Therefore, we must strive to banish fear, and the best way is by being conscious of ourselves.

Consciousness of self means that we keep our minds quiet and free from disturbing influences so that we may concentrate on the particular part of the body that needs to be active at the moment, and thus realise not only what we ought to do, but also what we are doing. When we come to know that certain actions produce certain results, and when we can, at will, perform those actions, uncertainty is removed, and uncertainty is at the root of most of our fears. In singing, as in all else, the precept "Know thyself" is of the utmost importance.

When we know what we want to do, and how to do it, we find ourselves at the point from which I started, and realise that it is easy to sing well.

The Art of Easy Singing (Dame Nellie Melba's Second Article)

If there is one thing more than another that is of interest to students of singing, it is the study of the means whereby great vocalists have reached the pinnacle of their chosen art. While there is a certain element called "luck" which enters into the matter, it is by far the least important factor in a great singer's career. Luck, or whatever other term one may use, is merely being in a position to take advantage of such opportunities for advancement as may unexpectedly present themselves. The foundation of all true success is proper training, so that when the fateful moment arrives, and the young student finds himself or herself confronted by opportunity with a big O, he or she is adequately equipped to seize the advantage. This is the view which Dame Nellie Melba will be found to take in the series of articles which are being published in *The Advertiser*. Having devised a method peculiarly her own, by which her voice has been wonderfully preserved, Dame Nellie is now passing on the fruits of her years of study and experience for the benefit of young Australians. It is a generous bequest, and every hint from the great singer should be taken to heart by students. An English musician remarked not very long ago, "Australia is a land of voices; one doesn't have to look for them; one can find them anywhere. But one does wish good teachers were correspondingly as plentiful." It is because she is a "good teacher" that Dame Nellie Melba's advice should not be lightly disregarded.

The second article, published below, is on breathing. This, perhaps, is the most important part of the student's work, because it is the foundation on which the remainder of the vocal structure will be built. It scarcely needs emphasising that finished singing is impossible unless the breathing is correct. It is the first essential of that apparent lack of effort which every great singer displays on the platform, and which conveys to an audience a pleasing sense of ease. The uninitiated may regard what is really a difficult piece of music as quite simple because the skill of the artist, a master in breath-control, has made it appear so. Dame Nellie Melba, of all vocalists, is the mistress of this art, and for that reason her views claim respect.

NO. 2—BREATHING

Voice is vibrating air.

When the air leaves the lungs it passes into the windpipe. There, if we have willed to sing, it finds an obstruction in the shape of the vocal cords. The thin, flexible edges of the vocal cords are set in vibration by the air pushing its way between them, and they, in turn, set the air above and below them in vibration. The vibrations (not the breath itself) travel at an extraordinary rate like waves, and if the sound waves are well shaped and have room to develop the tone of a voice is full and pleasing. It is poor and thin when the sound waves are cramped and mis-shapen.

Many methods of breathing for singing seem to concern themselves only with the manner of taking air into the lungs; but, as sound is caused by its outflow, it would seem better to concentrate on how we are going to let air out of the lungs and take air into the lungs in such a manner as will give us the most certain and easy control of the outflow. Everyone knows they have lungs and whereabouts they are situated, but very few have any definite knowledge about them or realise how very important it is to the general health, as well as to production of voice, that all parts of the lungs should be well developed and kept elastic. The heart and lungs are in the thorax, which has for its walls the breastbone, the ribs, and the backbone. Since there is nothing the body needs so much as oxygen, it will be readily understood that the more oxygen we can get into the lungs, the better the health. Also, that the more air we can expel out of the lungs, the more waste matter do we get rid of in this manner.

Full, rhythmical breathing in good air will do wonders to relieve tiredness and overstrain, and is the best aid to conquering nervousness.

Of the ways in which we can breathe, abdominal breathing should not be used by women unless they are lying down; then it helps the digestion and is very useful in cases of sleeplessness from overstimulated nerves, if the breathing be steady and rhythmical, and the muscles of the body not employed in the act of breathing relaxed.

It must always be remembered in breathing both for health and for singing, that no effort is required to get the air into the body.

It is the natural function of the lungs to expand and contract, and unless we close or half-close the passages the air will rush into them when they expand, without our having to draw it in, or, indeed, without our taking any active part. That is where many teachers of physical culture err so grievously; they teach their pupils to take breath by a muscular effort, and though there may be considerable expansion, owing to the fact that the throat muscles are tightened, very little air is getting into the lungs, and so very little oxygen is being supplied to the blood.

That method is like trying to fill a toy balloon by pulling its sides apart, instead of by blowing air into the tube. Whenever you can hear the breath being drawn in, or see the throat muscles tightened, you may know the method of breathing is wrong.

In breathing to sing, it should be remembered that the less breath used the better the tone. Too strong a blast of air will force the vocal cords too far apart for them to set all the air in vibration as it passes between them, and we get what is called breathy tone; or the throat muscles try and control the breath stream by tightening, and we get throaty tone; and in either case there is a very severe strain put on the delicate organ situated in the larynx.

If we fill the lungs to their fullest extent with air, they at once try to expel it, and it is very difficult to control the stream so as to allow only enough to reach the vocal cords to produce good tone. One is liable to have the feeling that one must let go or burst!

Therefore, for singing we must take in no more air than we feel we can comfortably control.

The method which gives most control with least effort may be described as that in which all the parts of the body that we can see or feel are in the same relationship to one another when a full breath has been taken as they are when they have exhaled. Test your breathing by this in front of a mirror.

The muscles which control the lower ribs are capable of great development, and it is there that we should have consciousness of control.

The chest should not be moved at all; it should be kept expanded, when it acts as a sounding-board, greatly reinforcing the tone.

Remember: —

Not to take too much breath.

Not to draw it in, but to allow it to go into the lungs.

Not to use too much breath.

That upon control of the breath depends, not only the beauty of your voice, but its very life.

Correcting an Evil (Dame Nellie Melba's Third Article)

Mr. Paul Dufault, the French Canadian tenor, was, perhaps, the most artistic vocalist who ever sang in Adelaide. Not only was he a master of voice production, but he never sang until he had got his song as near perfection as it was humanly possible to do. His vocal work was as studied and as polished as the writings of a master in literature. Asked how he reached such perfection, he explained that he never sang in public any song that he had not studied for two years. Every note, every phrase, every word was analysed, and its meaning grasped, and attention in particular was paid to diction. It is surprising how few vocalists, even among those who have gained eminence in their profession, pay regard to enunciation and pronunciation—the subjects of the third article by Dame Nellie Melba. It is a common complaint amongst concert audiences that they do not understand the words the artist is singing. Words carry meaning, and if a clear conception of the composer's intentions is to be conveyed to the listeners they must understand the words. We all know the story of the lady, who, talking of her brother's "hay bake," failed to make it understood that she referred to a "high bike." The concert platform is crowded with such offenders against commonsense and artistic decency, and it is towards the correction of such errors that the present article is directed. One could, if it were desirable, give numerous illustrations of offences against the ear by faulty diction; but it is sufficient to say that often an otherwise splendidly rendered song has been seriously marred by the vocalist's failure to grip the importance of enunciation and pronunciation. If one heard a reciter talk of the "spoyder and the floy" one would laugh; yet such monstrosities of diction are as common in singing as the average man's grievances against the Government. If Dame Nellie's advice can reduce this evil she will earn the gratitude of all lovers of music.

NO. 3—ENUNCIATION AND PRONUNCIATION

Nine out of every ten persons enjoy a song far more if the words are clearly enunciated so that they can readily understand them.

As the words have inspired the composer to write the song, it seems only fair that the singer should try to give the audience the words as well as the music.

This depends on clear enunciation. The words must not be swallowed, neither must they be mouthed or forcibly "spat out" (to use a vulgar but expressive phrase). They must be easily and naturally spoken on the notes to which they belong.

There are a few people who have the gift of good enunciation, but most of us have to give time and thought to the acquirement of it.

But clear enunciation may give pain rather than pleasure, if the pronunciation is faulty.

French as sung is very different from spoken French, but this is not the case with English. We should sing as we speak, always provided that what we speak will pass as educated speech. Any brand of accent, whether Australian, Lancashire, Glasgow, or what you will, becomes more marked in singing than in speech through the sustaining of the vowels, so those who wish to sing would do well to listen to their own speech and compare it with that of someone English, or with that of an Australian who has travelled.

Our difficulties are increased by the fact that the experts in phonetics still disagree as to what should be regarded as standard English. But neither they nor anyone else who had thought about the matter would uphold the use of "oy" for "I," or "ah-ee" for "ay," distortions which may be heard wherever Australians congregate!

As it is with the Australian accent that we have to concern ourselves out here, a little consideration of why the vowels are twisted in this way may be helpful.

Australians can move quickly and briskly enough when they wish to, but if they have no particular reason for doing so their general tendency is to dawdle and slouch along, and this tendency lies at the root of the Australian accent.

Every movement of the tongue or jaw, no matter how slight, makes an alteration in the vowel sound. There are certain vowels which are called "tense." The movement to form them must be quick and decided, and then the position must be held, but the Australian way is to approach the vowels through one or more other vowel positions because the movement of the jaw is slow and lazy. Take "ay," for example: This is a tense vowel, and the mouth should only be half open for it, but too often the jaw is dropped as for "ah," then the mouth is gradually closed to the "ee" position, and instead of "day" you get "die."

"Aw" requires a less decided movement of the jaw than "ah," and when the mouth closes to the "ee" position, the result is "Oi" instead of "I." The vowel "oo" is formed by pouting the lips and raising the back of the tongue while the tip is drawn back from the teeth. In the word "to" the tongue touches the upper teeth and hard palate to form the consonant, and should then spring sharply back for the vowel. If, as is too often the case, the tongue remains lazily near the teeth, you get "ee" and "oo" said together, a sound not to be found in the English language. It is, however, the sound in the French words "tu" which English people find so difficult, and Australians, too, when you ask them to do it in speaking or singing French.

There are other vowels which receive bad treatment here, but enough has been said, I think, to prove that slackness lies at the root of the trouble.

So far we have been considering pronunciation in connection with singing, but there is another reason why it is important. Any singer who aspires to a career must learn not only to sing, but to speak in what is, to cultivated ears, an educated manner.

Unfortunately in Australia, too many well-educated people have given no thought to their speech, and have found that it prejudices people on the other side against them, and is a serious handicap. In no walk of life is it so important as in the case of a singer where success depends much on the singer's power to interest and charm. A girl may have a beautiful voice and sing well, a pretty face and dress well, but if she speaks badly people will say with a shrug, "very charming till she opens her mouth," and take no further interest in her.

A serious study of foreign languages helps a singer to improve in her own, because if she learns them with the help of phonetics she learns to listen to herself, which is all that is necessary with many people. We take the way we speak English for granted, and do not listen to ourselves. For another reason the study of foreign languages is necessary. The student who is in earnest and means to succeed must not be content with success in one country; she must look upon the world as her kingdom. To conquer the people in France she must sing to them in French, and it must be in good French. The same applies to Italy and Germany, for in these countries the people are far less complaisant than are the English, who will listen to English being murdered without a murmur.

Never say to yourself about the Australian accent, "What does it matter?" for in addition to what has already been said there is this to be remembered, that as a result of the lazy movements the soft palate hangs flabbily, which makes the tone nasal, in some cases painfully so. This flabbiness of the soft palate causes difficulties in producing the voice, and until it is overcome there can be no resonant tone. There are some mispronunciations which are reserved for singing, such as "harpy" for "happy," "arnd" for "and," and so on. This is by no means only an Australian fault; many English singers of reputation are guilty of this, but it is very ugly. A slight raising of the back of the tongue is almost the only difference between the two vowels. "Heel" for "hill" is another irritating mistake.

English is often said to be a difficult language to sing because it has so many diphthongs, but once it is understood that except in the case of the sounds in "fear" and "few" the first part of the diphthong should be sustained for nine-tenths of the duration of the note, difficulties tend to disappear. If the second vowel sound is thought of as belonging to the following consonant, it will be found helpful. Many people do not realise that "night" is "nah-eeght" and try to sing both sounds at once and get something like "nayte" as a result.

In the case of "fear" and "few" the singer should glide very smoothly over the first vowel sound and sustain the second, but these are the exceptions that prove the rule.

In singing, the vowels carry the tone, but the consonants convey the meaning and the dramatic interest of the words, so that they must receive their share of attention.

Some consonants are sung, but others are not, and cannot be, for they have no vocal sound in them. Among the latter are p, t, and s.

These consonants must be treated in the same way in singing as they are in speaking. In order to pronounce them without voice we must leave off singing even in the middle of a word. This may sound strange, and as though it must break up the musical phrase, but the cessation of voice is for so short a time that it is imperceptible. The result is that the consonant comes out clearly and does not interfere with the vowel that follows it, as is the case when the attempt is made to sing an unvoiced consonant. Special care must be taken to enunciate final consonants distinctly. When they are slurred over, or (as is often the case) left to the imagination, the listener feels as though the unfinished word were still hanging in the air! And in trying to decide what the word must have been, the next word or two are lost, and probably the drift of the whole sentence.

Learn to speak well and to speak the words on the notes of the musical phrase.

The Soul of Song (Dame Nellie Melba's Fourth Article)

There are two ways of singing—the right way and the wrong way. This is so obviously a truism that it sounds silly. But is it? Take an average concert season, and critically review the manner in which songs were sung. Put in one column the songs which approximated to correctness, and in the other those which did not. The latter column will probably be found much the longer. If this be so, it will follow that it is still necessary to say there is a right way and a wrong way of singing. Students know this, but they forget it. Now, interpretation is the soul of song. But its practice is difficult, and involves the employment of every known art of technique and sentiment in the vocalist's equipment. For this reason Dame Nellie Melba's fourth article will be found extremely useful. It contains many hints by one who has had vast experience. After reading Dame Nellie Melba's comments one feels that she has covered a very comprehensive field. She puts her finger on a great many of the points which constitute the common weaknesses of aspiring vocalists. It may possibly be argued—it so often is—that all this technique has the very opposite effect to what is aimed at—that is, that it tends to destroy the natural imagination, leaving the vocalist a kind of perfect human machine. That point, Dame Nellie answers herself, but we may add that, while it might, for a certain time have such an effect, the phase will pass, and the student will find himself or herself the better for the technical equipment which he or she has acquired at such pains.

NO. 4—INTERPRETATION

What may be said to come under this heading?

Is it not everything that tends to make the poet's and composer's purpose clear, and that helps to convey their message to the audience?

In order to convey this message we must study:

Vocal technique.

The value of notes and rests.

Rhythm.

Enunciation.

We must also have a sympathetic understanding of the text and the power to visualise what is described in it, and we must cultivate the feeling for phrasing.

There are those connected with every art who consider that the study of technique deadens the natural artistic feeling, and that this study must be avoided as much as possible, or their temperament will be stifled and their art become lifeless.

To speak of singing only, what is the study of vocal technique but the means by which we exercise and discipline the physical part of our equipment so that it may serve the temperament. Untrained muscles can only hinder the fulfillment of what the temperament desires, and as they soon become overtired and strained, loss of voice results.

But the greatest care must be taken that the training is on right and natural lines. In practice the second requirement is even more generally disregarded than the first.

Every singer should study harmony and counterpoint, but every singer must study the rudiments of music. It is extraordinary how seldom even the simplest song is sung in correct time. Singing in time does not seem to matter! But surely if the composer wrote a crotchet he wants the note to have the value of a crotchet!

If a dot is added to a note the word belonging to that note is given more importance than was intended; if a crotchet is shortened to a quaver the word is given too little importance. Further, if the value of the notes be altered, the melody is no longer the same and the rhythm is destroyed.

There are many people who have the knowledge, but fail through carelessness or through singing by ear only instead of using their eyes to verify and correct; this is unpardonable.

To sing rhythmically does not mean to sing like a metronome; it includes the employment of Rubato, which may be described as the power to vary the rate of performance without disturbing the rhythm.

The pulse must always beat (it may be more or less quickly) and vary with the intensity of emotion, but just as in the body an irregular pulse is a sign of ill-health, so it is in music. Music that is vital always has the strong pulse of rhythm, and unless we can make others feel it we are not interpreting the music aright.

So much has been written about enunciation in a former article that it is only necessary to say that unless the audience can easily understand the words of a song, they are only getting half of it—the composer's half.

Sympathetic understanding of the text will be found to have important bearing on enunciation, which means more than clearly pronounced words. The way in which words are enunciated must be modified by the emotion they are intended to convey. The emotions affect the muscles, which in turn affect the voice, and in this way we get varying tone color. A voice, no matter how beautiful, that never changes in color, soon becomes monotonous. But this color cannot be applied from within, from real feeling for and understanding of what is being sung.

How many students read the words of a song they are to study before they even play it through? The words come first, and to realise what the composer felt, it is necessary first to consider them as a poem rather than as part of a song. It is not enough to understand them with the brain, for the emotion expressed in the words must be felt also.

It will be found helpful to say the words of a song aloud, with natural emotion and dramatic stress. This practice will be found useful in the avoidance of a very common fault of accenting an unaccented syllable. This wrong accent is caused by using a different vowel on the weak syllable in singing from that used in speaking. To sing "garden" as "gar-den" gives an equal accent to both syllables, which is incorrect. The second should not be pronounced "en," it should be a sound that is not represented by any letter in the English alphabet. The best way to arrive at the correct sound is to say the word aloud a few times, listening carefully to the vowel sound of the second syllable and then to sing it in the same way.

Even a sympathetic understanding does not end one's duty to the text. It is necessary to be able to visualise what is being described. How much more vividly we feel a thing if we picture it as happening to ourselves! And that is what we must try to do.

For example, we may be called on to describe something in nature which has an effect on the emotions of the persons in the poem. If we can SEE heavy banks of clouds with our mind's eye, portending we know not what, it will color the voice, and we will pass the picture on to the audience. But we must first have seen it and have seen it vividly.

Lastly we come to phrasing, the final test of an artist.

A beautiful range of mountains seen against the sky-line does not consist of a straight row of neat peaks all joined together at the same height. Very often there are peaks which, when seen close at hand, seem isolated, but which are joined to the main range by distance, so that they form part of the beautiful flowing line. What distance does to a range of mountains, phrasing does to a composition.

Each phrase must, of course, be studied separately and made as perfect as possible, so that each may be like a polished gem. But a number of gems, no matter how beautiful, are useless as adornment unless they are first set together. A dull or badly cut stone may spoil a necklace, so a song may be spoilt by a phrase in which the quality of tone is lost, by one in which the stress is put in the wrong place, or one which is too loud or too soft to balance with the phrase on either side of it.

In making a necklace, a jeweller works out his design first, and then suitable stones are chosen, so in a song we should study the shape and line of the whole first, and then polish the phrases until they all fit in and give us that perfect thing—beauty of line. Without a deep appreciation of this beauty, fine interpretation is impossible.

In conclusion, there are a number of words or phrases used in music which most singers ignore or do not understand. For instance, Ritardando means a gradual slowing of the tempo. When it is observed at all, we generally hear one bar at the original tempo and the next bar half that rate. Crescendo means gradually becoming louder, and Diminuendo, gradually becoming softer. But the qualifying word is almost always forgotten. Also, "poco" means "a little," but written in a composition "poco più animate" will nearly always cause the singer to bolt, when it only means "a little quicker."

Two other things that interfere with fine interpretation are the introduction of high notes at the end of a song and of long pauses where the composer has not asked for them. To treat a song in this way is to use it for the purpose of self-aggrandisement, which is both inartistic and in bad taste. Real art is always simple, and must be approached in a spirit of humility and sincerity. When it is approached thus it gives a greater happiness than almost anything else one can think of and one that is well worth striving after.

Voice Production and Control (Dame Nellie Melba's Fifth Article)

From the first article published in *The Advertiser* to this, Dame Nellie Melba has preached the doctrines of "easy singing," "good singing," and "good taste in singing." The great value of these articles lies in their lucidity and the fact that Dame Nellie knows in the highest degree just how to explain and what needs explanation in the art of vocal culture. In these printed addresses she has discussed most of the faults which manifest themselves on the concert platform, and, further, a strong plea has been put forward for stringent correction. Technique and notation, rhythm and phrasing, enunciation and pronunciation, breath control and resonance, as well as interpretation, have all been concisely and skilfully dealt with in not too technical language.

Every student, and many teachers, will welcome the following illustrative description of the resonance cavities, their uses, and how to control them. Too often has it happened that a fine natural voice has been ruined by pitiless forcing, wrongly applied physical effort, and wilful disregard of "right thinking" and "right doing." Dame Nellie Melba has given of her very best and widest experience in the cause which is so dear to her heart—that of helping young singers to appreciate the wonderful art of song, the high influences of music, and its advancement in her native country.

NO. 5—VOICE AND RESONANCE

Voice (or the sound waves to which we give that name) is caused by the pressure of the outflowing breath against the flexible edges of the two vocal cords. The vocal cords run from the front to the back of the larynx (known as the Adam's apple when prominent).

They are far apart in the act of inspiration, but the will to sing brings them toward each other with the thin edges almost touching. They are as delicate as two little bits of cotton if badly used, but as strong and flexible as two elastic bands if they are not strained or jerked.

As we have no conscious control over the vocal cords or any part of the larynx, it is not necessary for a singer to know the names and functions of the various cartilages and muscles employed. In fact, the less we think about that part of the throat the better. If anyone is conscious of sensations in the throat muscles when singing, it means there must be some unnecessary tension, which will inevitably injure the voice.

Many students are so occupied with the diverse activities that go to the singing of the song or aria that they are unconscious of any strain while singing. Afterwards many are conscious of aching throats or hoarseness. Both are signs of wrong use of the throat, and should be taken as Nature's warning that if the method of singing is not altered the voice will deteriorate and finally fail.

Voice, as produced by the vocal cords, is small and thin compared to what it may become if the resonance cavities are properly used. As it is possible to get direct control over some of these cavities and indirect control over others, it is well to know something about them.

Above the larynx is the pharynx, which divides into two outlets, the lower being the mouth and the upper the nose. Between them lies the soft palate ending in the uvula. The soft palate is, or should be, very flexible, and its position and movements have very great influence on the quality of tone.

The mouth is the largest of the resonance cavities. The lips, by their flexibility or rigidity, help or hinder the tone more than is understood by most English-speaking people. The hard palate lies behind the upper jaw and forms the greater part of what is called the roof of the mouth, but the mucous membrane covering it is extended still further back, forming the soft palate with the uvula hanging from the centre. Down each side run two folds of membrane connecting the tongue with the soft palate. Above the soft palate are the nasal cavities. They are not very large, and the space is broken up by the tarbinated bones.

There are also cavities in the cheekbones and forehead which undoubtedly add to the color and resonance of the tone. This can best be proved by noticing the loss of tone caused by inflammation in any of these cavities in the bones of the face.

Over these cavities we have no conscious control, but they will play their part if those we can control are in the right position to give the sound waves a clear passage.

The soft palate and tongue do not themselves add to the resonance of a tone, but they have great power to alter the shape of the resonance cavities. These cavities determine the shape of the sound waves, and only well shaped and regular sound waves can give beautiful tone.

From this it will be seen how important is the control of the tongue and soft palate.

Control does not mean rigidity or holding in any one position. If we have at some time had real consciousness of the movements of tone and soft palate, we will be able to detect and correct anything unnatural or strained in their position. This is what is meant by controlling them.

A very common fault in the use of the tongue is to stiffen the muscles at its root. This enlarges the back of the tongue so that it almost closes the passage above the larynx. As a result of this closing the tone is thin and poor, for the sound waves are forced through a narrow passage at a point where they should have had room to expand. They are also deflected and strike the non-resonant soft palate, instead of the resonant hard palate—as they should.

This fault can readily be detected by the enlargement and hardening of the muscles just below the chin, and if persisted it leads to ugliness, in the shape of a double chin, and eventually the loss of voice.

The stiffening of any part of the tongue causes loss of quality in the tone.

If the soft palate is allowed to hang loosely, the sound waves are divided by it, and some pass into the nose and some into the mouth, and the soft palate acts as a damper on both parts. The singer feels the lack of resonance and tries to remedy it by physical effort. For a time this may seem successful, but sooner or later Nature will demand payment (for to use force in singing is to break one of her laws), and the payment will be loss of voice.

In place of effort, all that was necessary was to allow the velvet curtain of the soft palate to spring up out of the way of the sound waves. If at first the soft palate does not seem flexible or capable of much movement, the following exercise will be found very useful. Hold a handmirror so as to reflect the light right to the back of the mouth without having to open the mouth unnaturally wide. With the mouth open breathe in through the nose. This will bring the tongue and soft palate together. Next breathe sharply out through the mouth, whispering the vowel "ah." When breathing out through the mouth the tongue and soft palate should spring apart. This exercise will soon increase flexibility and give conscious control. No effort must be used, and the soft palate must not be drawn up into a point; it must be allowed to go up, making the back of the throat like a wide archway.

When the tongue has learnt that it must not try to help in the production of tone, when it knows just how much it has to do in the production of vowels and consonants, when the soft palate has learnt to spring out of the way of the sound waves, then the other resonance cavities will be free to do their part and will do it if they are healthy.

Does it begin to be clear that it is easy to sing well if we do not interfere? That is one of the chief lessons we have to learn, and to nearly everyone it is one of the most difficult.

The Soul of Song (Dame Nellie Melba's Final Article)

In this sixth and final article Dame Nellie Melba has dwelt at length upon the subject of musicianship for singers. She asks—"Why should a singer, having a poor knowledge of music, expect to succeed merely because she has a beautiful voice?" On this theme the famous musician—Dame Nellie is singer, organist, pianist, teacher, and theorist—has written an article which is full of sound advice, based on personal knowledge and showing how to avoid the wasting of early opportunities. Concentration is the ideal for those who aim at recognition in the world of song. With this are bracketed relaxation, healthy environment, knowledge of every branch of musical art, and a live interest in literature and painting.

Dame Nellie also recommends the singer to share in social affairs, to guard against the sin of narrow-mindedness, and to acquire mental poise, a happy demeanor, and certainty of deportment. Speaking of the never-ending sacrifices which are necessary before success can be attained, she makes light of them and says progress in art more than compensates for them.

NO. 6—IDEAS AND IDEALS

Too often in the past the name of singer has been deemed synonymous with poor musicianship, but happily this deplorable state of things is rapidly becoming ancient history.

Why should a singer, having a very poor knowledge of music, expect to succeed merely because she has a beautiful voice? A violinist may have a very beautiful instrument, but he does not, on that account, consider the study of harmony and counterpoint unnecessary.

The connection between counterpoint and singing may not at first seem obvious, but everything that quickens the ear and develops the musical intelligence must be useful. It is in these ways that the study of harmony and counterpoint proves so beneficial. Everything we study earnestly and intelligently adds to our powers, though its immediate use may not be perceived by the student. When we are listening to a fine musician are we not conscious of a feeling of authority and mastery? Authoritative interpretation is only acquired through knowledge, and the gaining of knowledge entails much study of what may at first seem to be dry subjects. As we give our minds to any subject, however, we find that it becomes interesting—quite apart from the value it may prove to us in the future.

Except in very exceptional cases, girls should not study singing until they are 17. But, any girl who, at 15 or 16, shows promise of a good voice should work very hard at piano, theory, and languages. A girl who has had good musical training while at school will make more rapid progress than one who has to begin everything at once. To be able to play the piano and to read well at sight is necessary for anyone who hopes to be regarded as an artist.

A good general education is of great advantage to a singer, for the habit of orderly work cannot be formed too early. In fact, it must be formed early or not at all with the average person.

Many students who are anxious and eager to get on, do not know how to work. They work by fits and starts, doing too much to-day and nothing to-morrow! They are "in the mood" or "not in the mood" to work, and they wonder why they don't get on very fast.

Steady, regular work, with the mind concentrated on what is being done, is absolutely necessary.

No work of any value can be done without concentration. Concentration does not mean knitting the brows and tensing every nerve and muscle. On the contrary, there can be no concentration without relaxation. We must be still and quiet, with the mind in a receptive state. When we are able, at will, to put away all disturbing thoughts, we can give our minds to that which we wish to do. (In other words, concentrate upon it.) Then we find that the difficulties which had seemed insuperable melt away. Nearly all difficulties are of our own making, and are the result of wrong or confused thinking. In other words, we try to do, or think of several things at once, fearing all the time that no one of them is possible!

I have said that there can be no concentration without relaxation. The power of relaxing any part of the body at will shows complete control over the muscles, and the nerves which convey the impulses to the muscles. It is only when we have acquired this control that we have the power to concentrate, and it is only when we concentrate that we can work quickly and easily.

The power of relaxing is one of the most important things in the study of singing, as it is in the preservation of health and in the art of living! It is so simple a matter that it is difficult to make people understand how to relax. They will try instead of just letting the muscles remain quiet until they are needed for some action. It is one of the greatest stumbling blocks in singing; everyone will try to sing instead of just singing. How many people can drop the lower jaw really loosely when they want to sing? Not one in a hundred,

I should say. Yet this is necessary if we are to sing easily, and it is one of the first things a student must learn to do.

A singer should not be satisfied to have a knowledge of vocal music only. She should be really interested in the other branches of her art. Every possible opportunity should be taken of hearing orchestral and instrumental music, especially the work of fine violinists, for much may be learnt about phrasing from a violinist.

Interest in the other arts is also necessary to a singer. Such interest develops the mind and broadens the sympathies. If we think our own art is the only one our outlook will be very narrow and our work must suffer, just as our bodies would suffer if we only took one sort of food. A singer should read fine books, both poetry and prose, and above all learn to love pictures. Painting and music are the most nearly related arts, for both give us form and color. A real and vivid love of the beautiful in all its manifestations will add life and color to all that we do in our own art.

To do good work we must be happy, and to be happy we must be in good health. Reasonable care of the health is of very great importance. By this I do not mean that a singer should coddle herself and not do this or that for fear of catching cold or of making herself tired. Every singer should try to make herself so strong that she can resist colds and work with enjoyment. Not to do anything to excess, whether it be to eat, drink, work, or play, is an exellent rule. Abundance of fresh air is necessary to health, and regular exercise. Walking is good exercise, but it alone will not keep all the nerves and muscles of the body completely fit. For that the specialised exercises of physical training must be studied and practised quite regularly. Ten to fifteen minutes spent in physical exercises every day will make the difference between feeling fairly well and feeling very well.

A certain amount of pleasure and enjoyment is necessary for a singer. The mind which is always fixed on one thing becomes dull and one-sided. If we work with enthusiasm, then put our work aside and play with enthusiasm, we return to work refreshed and keener than ever. A singer must also come into contact with other people, trying to see life through their eyes and to sympathise with their views. In this way social intercourse helps in our development. Not that we should meet people with the object of getting as much from them as we can. If we give of ourselves to others, we unconsciously gain much from them. It is not possible, however, to dance nearly every night and do good work during the day. There must be moderation in all things.

When we are physically fit (and only such as are fit can hope to have careers as singers) we feel glad to be at work and enjoy all that we have to do, and it is only happy work that counts for anything. When we are dull and depressed we see nothing but difficulties ahead of us, and we become a discouraged and go back instead of forward. If we are happy our difficulties seem to vanish and we are left wondering why we worried about them.

To be happy in our art we must believe in ourselves and in our power of doing fine work. If we do not believe in ourselves we will accomplish very little.

This is not conceit. Conceit is so satisfied with what it can do at present that there is no incentive to a striving after anything better. Those who really believe in themselves are usually very humble about their present attainments, for they see clearly how much they have to do before they can realise their ideal.

The life of a singer is in many ways a very hard one, and we must be prepared to make many sacrifices if we wish to succeed. Most of us are quite ready to let our friends make sacrifices for us, but that is not what is necessary. We must make the sacrifices ourselves. When they are made we will generally find what we have given up was of no moment, and that what we have gained in progress in our art more than compensates us.

Let no one think they know all there is to know about singing when they have studied for a year or so. The wonderful thing about all the arts is that we can never come to the end of them. If we retain our voices by obeying Nature's laws, we can go on studying and singing and enjoying when we have reached what most people consider "old age." Old age is a condition of mind rather than a set number of years. Some people are old at forty and some are young at eighty. We reach old age when we cannot assimilate new ideas and act upon them. If we keep our minds elastic and retentive by study we keep old age at bay in a perfectly natural manner, without the aid of drugs or injections.

In conclusion. We must learn to let the mind be calm and quiet so that it may control all parts of the body. Through this control we learn to relax and to concentrate on whatever we are asked to do at the moment. Then we shall do everything in the most simple and direct manner possible, and find that it is easy to sing well.

THE MELBA METHOD

NELLIE MELBA

DO YOU WISH TO SING WELL?

Then sing easily, for it is one of the paradoxes of song that easy singing is good singing, and difficult singing is bad singing.

Does that surprise you? It should not do so, if you think. When the voice is badly used you are making complicated movements of the throat muscles, and many difficulties of your own making have to be surmounted before the voice can be produced out at all. Nature does not ask for that. She asks you to sing, not to *try* to sing. To sing happily like the birds, as naturally as you speak.

To do that, before all things you must have control of the breath. Not taking too much, not struggling to hold it. It is not the air in the lungs which causes voice, but that which has left them, setting the vocal cords vibrating as it passes between them. It is the control of this outflowing air which is so vital. We *must* learn to control our muscles in such a way that the supply may be adequate and even.

The floating ribs should be trained to act as bellows, the diaphragm descending as they expand. I cannot better describe it than to say that your ribs should feel so firm and steady that they seem actually to support the tone. Too often the throat muscles rather than the ribs are employed in this tone process, so that the throat swells and reddens with the strain. This, sooner or later, will ruin the voice.

From: Nellie Melba, *The Melba Method* (1926).

Try to realise—

1. That it takes very little "breath" to set the vocal cords vibrating, and that this is all that the breath is called upon to do.
2. That the less "breath" you use, the better will be the tone.
3. That if only a little breath is necessary, it is obviously wise not to take too much air into the lungs.
4. That it is always wrong to lift the chest and shoulders. Why? Because real control is impossible if we breathe in that way. Moreover, we are sure to tighten the throat muscles and cramp the voice.

There are three registers in a woman's voice.

The chest register should, except in exceptional cases, end on the E above middle C. I myself occasionally sing F in chest. But that is not usually right, and for heavy voices it is very dangerous.

The medium (or middle) register consists of the octave from F above middle C.

The head register must begin on F sharp, above the C on the third space. All tones above this are sung in head register. It is most unwise to carry the chest register too high. This practice may well cause a break in the voice, which is often very hard to mend.

On the other hand, if the low tones are not sung in chest register, they will be weak and uncertain, and the medium tones will not show the strength and fullness of tone which they might otherwise have possessed. Exercises are given for curing a break caused by carrying the chest register too high, as well as directions for singing head notes.

Do not attack with a jerk, nor with an escape of breath. The attack must be neat, and precisely on the note. To begin the note too low, and then to slur up to the right note, is an unforgiveable fault. There can be no real singing without a good attack.

To sing well you must sing happily, for happiness relaxes the muscles and gives a feeling of confidence. Fear, on the other hand, contracts the muscles and, by creating a vicious circle, helps to bring about the very thing you fear.

Remember that when you sing, the act of singing is not complete until it has carried its message to the listeners. Think of them. Speak to them, telling them the story contained in the song or aria you are singing. If the singer really thinks of what she has to say, and of the person to whom she is saying it, she will have very little time in which to think of herself, or of whether she can get this or that note! Consequently she will be much less troubled with nervousness.

When anyone asks you to give them something, there are three couses to be taken: you can refuse to give it and clutch it to yourself; you can fling it at the other with force and rudeness; you can give it graciously and willingly. In these three ways may the voice be used. It may be held in, it may be forced out, it may be given to the audience easily and graciously.

Which do you do? And which would you prefer to do? Sing for love, not merely because you have a voice which someone says will make your fortune.

Always treat the words and music with respect, for they are not yours. You are merely the vehicle for presenting them to the audience.

Show respect to the *Poet* in the following ways: (1) By studying the words till the very heart of them is yours; (2) by enunciating the words clearly so that the audience may understand them easily; (3) by pronouncing the words correctly, so that educated ears may not be irritated; (4) by giving to the words the natural inflection and accent, so that the emotion they express is conveyed to the audience.

Show respect to the *Composer* by singing what he has written, down to the last double dotted demi-semiquaver; (2) by paying attention to, and carrying out, all marks of expression; (3) by studying the *shape* of each phrase and by handling your voice so as to bring out that shape; (4) by studying the relation of each phrase to the whole.

The eternal task of song can never be finished in a single lifetime. That is the beauty and fascination of the art. Once you begin to phrase finely, you will feel more joy in the beautiful finish of a beautiful phrase than that caused by the loudest applause of an immense audience. The latter excites for a moment; the former endures for ever.

In order to *sing* well you must *be* well. No one should dream of the career of a singer who is not naturally robust. Given, at the outset, good health, it must be your aim to keep fit. That can only be done by taking regular exercise. Walking is good, but walking does not fulfil all requirements. Your exercises must be regulated, and should take the form of physical exercises carried out under the direction of a good teacher. They must be practised daily, for, as in all the arts and practices of life, regularity is the thing that counts.

Food should be plain but nourishing. Every type of rich food and sweet should be avoided, for every singer must be careful not to get stout. Cocktails and cigarettes must not be even in a singer's vocabulary. The watchword for a singer must be "Moderation in everything," whether it be work, play, eating, or drinking (especially the last named). But whether it is work or play, put your whole heart into it. Half-hearted, dull work is worse than useless: it tires and discourages without accomplishing anything.

Learn from the very beginning to depend upon yourself. Your teacher can do no more than point out the way. You must walk along it yourself. Use your own ears and do not depend on anyone else's opinion. Train yourself to listen with concentration. When you hear others, listen for their good points; when you sing yourself, listen for your faults. This is a reversal of the usual process of human nature, but is necessary for all who wish to become artists. Above all, try to hear your own voice, not as you imagine it to sound, but as it actually sounds to others. Until that is done, no singer can stand on her own feet, or claim to be an artist.

Use your own voice. It may be said that of course one must do that. But it does not follow at all. If you try to imitate someone else's voice because it is beautiful, you are trying to use their voice, not your own. A parrot is often a wonderful mimic, but it is not an artist. Listen to your own voice, and when you hear a good tone try to produce the rest so as to match that. No two voices are exactly alike, nor would we have them so, for it is that which is individual to each voice that is its chief charm. Listen, by all means, to the way in which a great artist obtains her effects, but never try to copy her tone. Use your own brain. Do not depend on your teacher. Before an audience can visualise a song the singer must have seen it herself. No one can do that for you. When studying, do not ask yourself how the teacher would treat such and such a phrase. Delve deep down into your own self until your own feelings are reached.

Above all, never practise without concentrating. I do not mean that the muscles must be rigid or the brows drawn together, nor do I mean that you must force yourself to think of the work. To concentrate one must be very still and quiet, letting thoughts about the work take possession of one. When you wish to sing a note, do not think *about* that note, whether it can or cannot be produced, or whether this or that thing should be done with your throat. No, you must quietly and calmly make your preparations by taking your breath and opening your mouth. Finally, if I may coin a phrase, simply *think the note* and allow it to come. In a very short time you will be astonished at the ease with which certain notes you have always considered difficult can be sung. When singing, you will be greatly helped by keeping the mind on the words. The emotion contained in them will cause many difficulties to disappear.

POSITION

Have you ever thought how important it is that you should stand well when you sing?

It is important for at least three reasons:

(1) For the sake of appearance.
(2) For breath control.
(3) For control of the nerves.

(1) Everybody knows that it is necessary to look well on the platform. The singer takes extra pains in doing her hair when she is going to sing, and wears the prettiest dress she can afford. But the matter does not end there. Unless she knows how to walk well as she makes her entrance, how to stand

well when she is there, all her trouble over her dressing will have been wasted. A graceful carriage wins the interest of the audience before the singer has opened her mouth, while awkwardness kills it.

In order to test for yourself, stand in front of a long mirror. First stand as I expect you generally do, on one foot with head inclined forward. You will probably exclaim: "Oh, I can't bear to look at myself in a mirror when I sing." And if you always stand in that way, I am not surprised at your distaste.

But why look like that? As you watch yourself, lift the head and look yourself straight in the eye, put the shoulders back and stand with the weight on both feet—on the ball of the foot, not on the heels, Now, do you not see something much more worth looking at? To be successful you must sing with authority, but how is that possible if your attitude is awkward or apologetic? Train yourself to use the mirror constantly, for it can be your best friend if it is properly used.

The position I have described is that which should be assumed on the platform, with the slight difference that on the platform it is better that one foot should be a little in advance of the other.

I have not mentioned the position of the hands. The hands should not be clenched, nor held out at arms' length first to one side and then to the other, or held in any position that is unnatural or strained. It is often a help to hold something, either a small fan or a folded programme. It should not be held too tightly, for that will probably cause the throat muscles to be stiffened, and the hands should not be higher than the level of the waist: that is to say, the natural waist, as opposed to the waist of fashion. The beginner should allow the hands to hang loosely, keeping the shoulders back.

(2) If you stand with the weight on one foot, one side of the body will be contracted, and one lung will be called upon to do almost all the work. If you stand erect, with the shoulders back, the breathing apparatus is placed in the best position for filling the lungs without effort, and for controlling the outflow of air. As that control is of the utmost importance, anything that will help towards gaining it should be practised from the very beginning of the studies.

(3) Nervousness is far more likely to attack a singer who stands first on one foot and then on the other, than a singer who stands quietly and easily. Fidgeting with the hands or feet, or pushing the head forward, are sure signs of a lack of self-control. To take and hold a certain position is in itself a useful discipline in the all-important matter of self-control. Many students seem to consider that to be "so nervous" is sufficient excuse for singing badly when they have to face an audience. They also seem rather to pride themselves upon it. But they should be ashamed. It does not matter if you are nervous beforehand so long as you can control yourself when the time comes to do the actual work. Remember that nervousness is really the result of self-consciousness. If you are thinking of yourself and your difficulties,

the nervousness increases. But if you make yourself stand still, you will be able to give your mind to what you have to sing, and nervousness will cease to trouble you.

NOTE FOR TEACHER OR ACCOMPANIST

In the following exercises the accompaniments must not be played too loudly. It is a mistake to attempt to help a student by playing loud chords on the piano, with the idea of supporting the voice or of giving confidence. The young singer must learn to depend on herself, and to listen to her own voice. She can do neither if her voice is drowned by the piano. Nor should the teacher allow the student to sing with her when she wishes to correct or illustrate anything. When both are singing, neither can properly hear the other, and a mere waste of time ensues.

PRACTICE

Regularity in practising is of very great importance, not merely in the amount done, but in the time of day at which it is done. If practice is left for any odd minutes when you do not particularly want to do anything else, you will never get very far. Unless the work is the thing to be considered first, you will never be more than an amateur. And the public does not wish to hear amateurs—at least, it does not wish to *pay* to hear them. Have a regular time table and keep to it, unless of course you have a cold or are not feeling well.

Your practice should be divided into periods of actual singing. At first they should be very short, not more than five minutes at a time, gradually working up to twenty minutes. Three periods of twenty minutes each are enough for any student.

But the time of study, *apart from actual singing*, should extend over several hours daily. How are you to find the real meaning of the words of a song unless they are read over many times, both silently and aloud? Should they be in a foreign language which you do not speak, much time must be spent in translating them, so that you know the exact meaning of every word you sing.

The accompaniment also should be studied, and each phrase of the voice part played over time and again before you attempt to sing it once. So many people learn everything by singing it over and over again. That is yet another waste of time, and very trying to the voice. The voice must be used so that you may hear that it is reflecting the meaning of the words. It should not be used merely to learn the notes of a song.

Never memorise anything by singing it repeatedly. Memorise silently, looking at the music and then repeat the phrase in your mind without looking at it. Silent singing is very useful. A breath should be taken as though you were going to sing, and without making any sound, the notes should be thought, and all the words formed with your mouth, while your mind rests on the meaning of what you are singing. You can do this no matter how bad a cold you may have.

When you have a cold that has at all affected the throat, the voice should not be used at all, as singing brings blood to the throat, which naturally increases any inflammation that may be there.

Above all, watch yourself in a mirror as you practise, so that you may at once correct any tendency to mouth your words. This is a very ugly trick and does not really make for clear enunciation, for you are making a fuss about something that should be done without any waste of energy, without any exaggerated or unnecessary movements. Practise breathing exercises every day, and remember that you must continue to do so as long as you sing. Many students think they need not practise them once they have got the idea of how to take the breath, but many forget that the muscles must be kept in good condition, and that to do that they must concentrate on exercising them every day.

BREATHING EXERCISES

Since the method of breathing which gives most control does not exercise the upper part of the lungs, it seems to me wise to begin the exercises with one which will do so. It is important to exercise and aerate the whole of the lungs, for reasons of health. The following exercise also helps the student to gain control of the chest, which acts as a sounding board when it is expanded, and adds greatly to the resonance of the voice.

(1) Stand erect before a mirror. Expel as much air as possible from the lungs, letting the head fall forward, while the chest sinks in and the shoulders come forward. Then inhale, raising the head and expanding the chest, at the same time putting the shoulders well back without raising them at all. Keep the chest and shoulders in that position while you expel the breath by allowing the ribs to sink in. This serves to show that the ribs can work quite independently of the chest and throat muscles. Still keeping the chest and shoulders in the expanded position, breathe in and out quickly by expanding and contracting the ribs. Repeat five or six times.

(2) Stand erect, with chest expanded and shoulders back, and inhale by expanding the ribs, allowing the front of the body to expand at the same time. Remember that the tension must be on the rib muscles. Having taken a breath, keep the ribs quite still while you silently count six. Then let the breath go while letting the ribs sink as slowly as possible. Repeat five or six times. (This exercise is very useful in helping to cultivate a clean attack. When we attack a note, we should not let the ribs move at all. The diaphragm will supply enough air for the attack without any consciousness on our part of having used any breath.)

(3) Stand as in the last exercise, expand the ribs and then count aloud as many as you can while you let the ribs sink in as slowly as possible. The movement must be quite steady, not in a series of jerks, and the voice in counting must be quite conversational, with no feeling of its being held in. While saying "one" do not allow the ribs to move at all. Repeat five or six times. All three exercises should be practised several times a day. Even when good control has been obtained the exercises must be continued at least once a day.

In singing it is not necessary to expand the ribs to their full extent. That is only tiring and it becomes an effort to control the outflow of breath. It is necessary in the exercises, but in singing you should never take more breath than you feel you can easily control.

SUSTAINED NOTES

Take a breath . . . , and consciously steady the ribs as you attack the note. As soon as you have inhaled, allow the mouth to open by dropping the jaw as far as it will go of its own weight. Do not pout the lips nor draw the corners back. The vowel which results from this position of the mouth is the vowel sound in the word "Of." This vowel will be found very useful in the early stages of voice production. As soon as you have allowed the mouth to assume the vowel shape, you must "think" the note you wish to sing, and allow it to fill the vowel shape prepared for it.

There must be no breathiness in the attack. Nor will there be, if the ribs have been held still until after the attack. There must be no jerk or click in the attack. This is known as the "Coup de glotte," and it has ruined many voices. It is usually caused by allowing too much breath to collect behind the vocal chords, before releasing them to begin to sing. If you begin to sing immediately you have thought the note, there will be little danger of this form of attack.

EXERCISES FOR DEVELOPING RESONANCE

Close the lips lightly, and hum, feeling the resonance in the nose. Do not increase the pressure immediately before opening the mouth for the vowel.

The vowel used . . . lies between "ah" and "aw" and was described before the last exercise.

When you hum, the sound waves must pass through the nose. Do not try to put them there, or you will make some unnecessary movement which will block the sound waves, instead of helping them. There must be no feeling of tightness or strain in the throat. If there is, you are humming incorrectly. You are probably tightening the muscle at the root of the tongue.

If . . . exercises are sung with any tightening of the throat they will do more harm than good. Stiffening of the tongue can easily be detected by the hardening and enlargement of the muscle under the chin. While you hum, try to realise how little breath it takes to cause and sustain sound. . . .

EXERCISE FOR TEACHING THE STUDENT TO LISTEN TO HER OWN VOICE

I have said several times that every student must learn to be able to hear her own voice. The following exercise will be found very helpful.

Sing the five simple vowels, oo, oh, ah, ay, ee, (Italian vowels u, o, a, e, i) on one note and in one breath. Begin on the G above middle C and repeat the exercise on each note up to C on the third space. Allow the mouth to move easily in order to form the different vowels, but make no break between the different sounds. Keep them all of the same quality, with the same amount of resonance. At first you will probably find it difficult to keep the ah of the same quality as oh, and the ay and ee will probably be even more different.

Do not stiffen the throat and endeavour to make them all the same. There must be ease and a clean and natural shaping of each vowel.

You will only learn to sing this exercise correctly if you use your ears and keep the soft palate in the same high position for all the five vowels, that it quite naturally takes for oo.

When you can hear your voice in this exercise you will find it much easier to hear your voice when you sing songs, and you will more readily detect the changes of quality which so often spoil a phrase.

EXERCISES FOR DEVELOPING CHEST NOTES

Sing the . . . exercises with a moderate tone on the "middle" notes, and with as full a tone as possible on the "chest" notes. The first of these exercises will be found valuable for the correction of certain grave vocal defects which invariably result when the lower middle notes have been sung in the chest register.

Begin the exercise well above the highest note to which the "chest" register has been carried, and work downwards only. Sing each repetition of the exercise in a key successively one semi-tone lower. Listen carefully to the notes in the middle register and endeavour to keep that quality intact as you work down to the F above middle C. Sing very easily without using too much tone. You will then be able to detect more readily any drop into chest tone before the proper place has been reached. If this exercise is persisted in patiently and intelligently, the break in a voice will be healed, and the lower middle notes will gradually gain in tone and quality.

The vowel should be the same as in the sustained notes, but it is often helpful to use the "M" before the vowel on each note.

EXERCISES ON INTERVALS

In these exercises the voice must move from one note to the next without slur, or portamento. The latter is an ornament that must at all times be used very sparingly. *It must not be used at all by beginners.*

Each note must be held for its full length, without any increase or decrease of tone. The student must then *think* and immediately *sing* the next note, alighting on it clearly and certainly, without anxiety or any elaborate preparation.

The student must never anticipate. The mind must concern itself with the note that is being sung, until that instant when it is necessary to sing the next note.

EXERCISES ON SCALE PASSAGES

These exercises should be sung in full voice until the head notes are reached. Otherwise the voice will not develop. The head notes must be sung pianissimo—not by closing the throat, or by holding back the tone, but by using less breath.

In rapid scale passages the middle notes that lead up to the head notes should be sung more softly, so that there may be no break in the even tone of the scale.

All scales must be divided into rhythmic groups of notes; —the first note of each group being accented very lightly. This accent must not be a jerk; neither must it be caused by an increased expenditure of breath. It should be a *mental*, rather than a *physical*, accent.

Do not change the vowel, either in ascending or descending the scale, and do not allow the mouth to open more widely when you reach the head notes. This is very important.

STACCATO

In singing . . . exercises for the development of Staccato, it should be remembered that a staccato note is one that is cut off quickly. Too many people think that it should be attacked differently from a sustained note, but that is a mistake which leads to heaviness instead of lightness, and often causes the Coup de Glotte to appear. Concentrate on cutting off the tone quickly and neatly, by stopping the breath supply. Remember also, that the less breath used the more brilliant will be the staccato passage.

THE TRILL

Some few fortunate people have a natural trill, but even they are wise to practise it regularly and systematically.

Almost everyone can acquire a serviceable trill if they study it in the right way, and are patient enough to go on working at it for a long time.

In trilling, nearly everyone sinks from the upper note of the trill. In order to correct this tendency, a slow exercise must first be practised, with the mind concentrated on the upper note of the trill, and with a slight accent on the first note of each group. Let the voice drop easily to the second (lower) note taking care that the interval is a whole tone.

The trill on two notes a semitone apart is much easier, and does not require so much practice, but it should be studied too.

THE RECORDINGS
OF NELLIE MELBA

Although Thomas Alva Edison's "favorite invention" spoke its first uncertain words in 1877, as far as recording material for posterity was concerned, the phonograph may be said to have had an ill-spent youth. It came at a time when its inventor was preoccupied with his electric light and other projects, and even though the new product of "the wizard of Menlo Park" brought forth profound predictions for its future, the tinfoil cylinder phonograph remained a curious toy for several years. It was a strictly commercial aspect which inspired Chichester A. Bell, a cousin of Alexander Graham Bell, and Charles Sumner Tainter to work on refinements of Edison's invention between 1880 and 1885. They thought they saw possibilities in a machine to replace the court reporter in transcribing testimony, and for use in office dictating. Their experimentation led to the engraving of wax cylinders, and the year 1887 saw the foundation of the American Graphophone Company, the grandparent of today's Columbia Company, for the manufacturing of dictating machines. The same year, 1887, the first disc Gramophone was patented by Emile Berliner, a German-born inventor from Washington, D.C. He recorded his lateral-cut groove in a coating of grease spread over a zinc disc.

Edison became alarmed that others were about to capitalize on his invention, and began work in earnest on the perfection of the phonograph. His "improved machine," which closely followed the changes made by Bell and Tainter, was demonstrated in 1888 and went into production at the Edison Laboratories.

For various reasons, the phonograph as a dictating machine had little appeal, but by 1894 the cylinder machine had been perfected to the point where it was practical for home use, and this same year the greatly improved Berliner disc Gramophone was also

---

A portion of the historical discussion presented here is from: William R. Moran, "Recordings and Lillian Nordica" (1963).

placed on the market. The phonograph was still a novelty toy which was directed at the masses. Very little thought had been given to it as a serious musical instrument: Its first tottering commercial steps in this direction were taken in Europe, but not until 1901.

At the time of the first excitement over the invention of the phonograph in 1877, much was said about the potentialities of the instrument for the preservation for all time of the voices of the great artists of the day. During the period of the rapid expansion of the cylinder business in the 1890s, these predictions seem to have been forgotten by the commercial interests. One individual, however, did try to remedy the situation. This was a young and wealthy Italian by the name of Gianni Bettini who was married to New York socialite Daisy Abbott. In 1888 Bettini purchased one of the early Edison cylinder machines and immediately set to work to improve it. Bettini was an opera lover, and his social status threw him into contact with the operatic stars of the day, who became frequent visitors to his New York home. It was perfectly natural for him to try out his new improvements on the phonograph on his guests. Eventually, Bettini set up recording studios on Fifth Avenue, and in time he offered copies of some of his cylinder recordings for public sale. A detailed study of all known Bettini material (Moran, 1965) shows that his recording activities are clearly divided into two periods: During the earlier period he was obviously experimenting with recording as a hobby, and during this time he recorded the voices of many great singers of the day, including Nellie Melba. No documentation has survived indicating systemmatic recording activities, although there exist in print several accounts by people who visited Bettini's establishment and report hearing the voices of many specific singers. By May 1897 he had apparently decided to "go commercial," for he issued the first (?) of a series of lavishly printed catalogs, featuring recordings he had for public sale. Notably absent from his earliest catalogs are many of the names of artists mentioned in earlier articles as "heard" in the Bettini Laboratories, among them Nellie Melba. He did secure recordings by some famous artists, for instance, Adams, Ancona, Arnoldson, Bernhardt, Calvé, and others, but his published catalogs are filled with listings of lesser artists. By 1965, only sixty-six Bettini records were actually reported as having been found, the most important being one by Marcella Sembrich, which was probably recorded in 1900. No Bettini recordings by Melba have ever been located.

If Bettini may be looked upon as possibly the only dilettante in the phonograph industry of his times, there were undoubtedly many amateurs who played with the hobby of making cylinder records. One of these, Lionel Mapleson (1865-1937), was particularly fortunate in that he gained his livelihood as librarian of the Metropolitan Opera House in New York. In March 1900 he purchased a "home model" Edison phonograph which could record as well as reproduce wax cylinders. From January 16, 1901, through at least March 14, 1903, Mapleson recorded an unknown number of excerpts, usually under two minutes in length, of actual Metropolitan Opera performances. In 1937, at the suggestion of Olive Fremstad and with the help of Geraldine Farrar, William H. Seltsam, founder and "secretary" of the International Record Collectors' Club of Bridgeport, Conn., contacted Mr. Mapleson and persuaded him to lend him two cylinders to see if he could be successful in re-recording them to 78 rpm discs. One of these was identified at the time as by Nellie Melba: The music was the second part of the Queen's air from *Les Huguenots*, at first thought to be from the Metropolitan performance of March 11, 1901, but later (since it was discovered that the performance that date was sung in Italian, and the recording was in French) ascribed to the performance of January 28, 1901. The cylinder was successfully re-recorded in 1938, and Seltsam was able to arrange with Mapleson's son Albert to borrow 120 more cylinders still in the father's collection. The first detailed review of this important historical find was reported by Ira Glackens (1938) in *The Gramophone*. Seltsam announced the Melba recording (IRCC No. 5002) in his Bulletin 83 in May 1939 with the statement, "Never would we have thought of issuing this record unless it had not first been submitted to the aural scrutiny of a large number of critical collectors."

The release caused a minor sensation and was reviewed by many critics who were familiar with the Melba voice and technique, both in person and from commercial recordings. Many singers who had known Melba intimately, or who had heard her in the flesh, were alive at the time, among them Geraldine Farrar, Olive Fremstad, Emma Eames, and Emilio de Gogorza. De Gogorza had been in charge of contracting artists for Victor's Red Seal series from 1903 until 1908. He had noted that commercial recordings of the acoustical era had poorly conveyed the voice quality of many singers, including Melba. When he heard the Mapleson *Les Huguenots* recording, he stated: "*That* is the true Melba quality." Present at some of the Mapleson re-recording sessions were Edyth Walker, Eva Gauthier, Mrs. Henry Hadley, and Oscar Thompson. Knowledgeable critics, such as Max de Schauensee and Desmond Shawe-Taylor, were extravagant in their remarks about the recording. The late Francis Robinson, long an assistant manager at the Metropolitan and an authority on singers and their recordings, wrote in the American edition of *MELBA* by John Hetherington (1967) (after quoting Henderson's New York *Sun* article of February 28, 1931, on the quality of the musical tone of Melba's voice):

There is one record which bears all this out, a record made a good three years before her first commercial recording. . . . The ungodly wheeze and thump of Mapleson's prehistoric machine are still there, but so are Melba's octave jumps leaping through the murk and fog like a shower of meteors in a winter sky. There is a roar of applause at the end, and more than ever you know why the toast, the rich dessert, a cigar, a lipstick, theaters in Dallas, Texas, and a number of other cities, and quite a few little girls born around 1910 were named Melba. It is the thrill, the lump in the throat, that a champion, and only a champion can give you.

The Canadian collector John Stratton (1962) produced an excellent review article for *The Record Collector* titled "The Mapleson Cylinders" in which he tells the story of the Mapleson cylinders, comments on the singers whose voices are preserved on them, reports on a thorough review of the existing cylinders themselves, and lists in alphabetical order eighty titles with the details of those that had been released to the date of publication. Among his comments are: "It seems that Melba would tolerate him [Mapleson] in the prompter's box, hence we have the wonderfully vivid fragment of her rendition of the cabaletta to the Queen's aria from *Les Huguenots*." To this he adds:

There is no more striking indication of what a remarkable era it was in those years when Mapleson was busy, than that even while Sembrich was earning praise from every quarter, there was another light soprano there who could bowl her audiences over. This was Nellie Melba. In fact her voice and style were quite different, tending to the lyric rather than the soubrette. If Sembrich was bright and scintillating, Melba was, in those days, dazzling and even electrifying. Her full-throated singing of a portion of "Un di felice" from *La Traviata* is breathtaking, especially the remarkable echo effects. The bits from *Le Cid* and the cadenza from the *Lucia* mad scene are not very good recordings, but her highly individual quality of voice is unmistakable, and in the latter, particularly, her vocal command is in evidence. Of course the fragment "A ce mot" from *Les Huguenots* has become something of a legend, for there is little doubt that a more spectacular piece of singing has never been recorded. The facility of her scale work, the full-voiced brilliance of her attacks even up to the D-flat, the wonderfully light upward skips, and finally the marvellous full trill held to what seems to be the end of her breath before ascending undaunted to the D-flat again—such singing is not often heard! By extreme good fortune this cylinder is both forward and clean in sound. . . . Melba fared a good

deal better than Sembrich at the hands of the recording companies. . . .
Only her earliest commercial discs, however, particularly the 1904 operatics
display anything like the dazzling brilliance of the Maplesons.

It is hard to accept the fact that the author of the above words, just
six years later (Stratton, 1968), was to write of the same *Les
Huguenots* recording:

. . . there's not a note anywhere, scarcely a single inflection, that really
sounds like Melba. Indeed, except perhaps for the sheer brilliancy of the
trills, many of the sounds the singer produces—particularly the high Ds
with the very open placement—seem to me quite uncharacteristic of Melba.
More recently, on having had an opportunity to make a detailed examination of the entire Mapleson collection [which no one since Mapleson's death
had been in a position to do], I came to the conclusion that it is *extremely
unlikely* that it was Melba's voice that inscribed this remarkable cylinder.

He based this assertion on the unlikeness of the recording to
Melba's voice, as quoted above, on the fact that the other known
1901 Maplesons are fainter, and that Mapleson had made only one
"in-house" recording prior to January 28, 1901 (Melba in an excerpt
from *Le Cid* on January 19).

Recently, David Hall (1981, 1982, 1983), curator of the Rodgers
and Hammerstein Archives of Recorded Sound in New York, which
now owns all the original Mapleson cylinders that have survived,
has written three excellent articles describing a current project of re-
recording, by modern methods, all of the accessible material. In
these articles he gives the complete history of the collection,
together with "A Provisional Mapleson Cylinder Chronology" in
his 1981 paper. Hall reports that in an inventory listing made in
1938 when Seltsam first received 120 cylinders from Alfred
Mapleson is found a crossed-out notation apparently made from
a cylinder box that contained an orchestral selection, "Adams:
Queen Act II (Mar. 1, 1902)." Hall reasons that the *à ce mot*
recording had become separated from its box prior to the time the
cylinder was given to Seltsam for experimentation. No such box
can now be found. Hall concludes, "So it seems that we may have
solid proof here for Stratton's argument." Moreover, in a new
(1983) and detailed inventory of the Mapleson cylinders, Hall now
credits the recording in question to Adams, without the use of an
interrogation mark! In a letter dated March 4, 1983, Hall wrote the
author: "Being neither a *bel canto* opera buff nor an authority on
THE voice, I feel that I have been able to take a more dispassionate

view than most on the subject of (mis)attributions. Until verifiable evidence to the contrary turns up, such as a conclusive voice print analysis, I fear that the weight of evidence favors (however inconclusively) the Adams attribution to *à ce mot*." On my part, I have left the listing in the Melba discography but have inserted what I consider to be a required question mark in recognition of the existing controversy. In 1981, when the tapes were being prepared for the Australian RCA Lp edition of Melba's American recordings, space had been left on the final disc to accommodate a newly discovered unpublished disc that had turned up in England (Burleigh's *Jean*, Discography entry #87A). When the promised tape did not materialize, it was decided to include a dubbing from Seltsam's original disc transcription of the *Huguenots* cabaletta. The 1962 Stratton opinion was discussed, but Australian authorities, as well as the present author, agreed with the long-established opinion that the recording was indeed Melba. A discussion of the authenticity of this recording was promised (Moran, 1982); the foregoing is that promised discussion.

While Mapleson was experimenting with his amateur recording efforts in the Metropolitan Opera House, important events were taking place in the world of commercial recordings. The improvements in the Berliner method of disc recording were so pronounced that the Columbia Company realized that it too must get into the disc business. The story of how it did, and the ensuing injunctions and legal battles over patents, is too long and complicated to recite here. (For a very readable account of these events, see Gelatt [1955] and Aldridge [1964]). It is enough to say that by the end of 1901, Columbia and Victor were the major contenders for the disc market in the United States, while Edison stuck to his cylinders.

Meanwhile, disc-recording "laboratories" had been established in the principal musical cities of the world, and arrangements were in force whereby affiliated companies could exchange matrices made at any foreign studio for use in the local pressing of records. The disc phonograph was especially successful in Russia, where recordings were made of some of the stars of the Imperial Opera in St. Petersburg in 1901. The young Feodor Chaliapin was one of those to record. The records sold well, and the Gramophone Company (then and for the next fifty years to be Victor's European affiliate) followed up the idea by sending a team of recording experts to various European capitals to line up talent and obtain recordings. One of the stops was Milan where, in March 1902, the "talent scouts" attended the second performance of Franchetti's new opera, *Germania*, at La Scala. A young singer named Enrico Caruso had created the principal tenor role. Fred Gaisberg, the American recording technician, tells in his autobiography (1942) of his excitement at hearing Caruso's perfect recording voice for the first time, and how a recording session was arranged a few days later in a Milan hotel room at which the young tenor made his first ten discs for the Gramophone-Victor combine. They were an immediate sensation. One of the first to hear one of these records was Heinrich Conried, manager of the Metropolitan Opera Company of New York, who was then in Paris. He took the record to New York, where he played it for the Metropolitan directors. The result was the cabled Metropolitan contract that brought Caruso to America in 1903.

The success of the Caruso records did much to establish the phonograph as an instrument to be taken seriously. The Gramophone Company hired a musical director, Landon Ronald, who immediately set to work to sign up many world-famous singers then appearing at Covent Garden. Back in the United States, Victor was greatly impressed with the idea of establishing an expensive "carriage trade" in the record business and began to publicize the release of pressings of European celebrity recordings. Victor hired the well-known baritone Emilio de Gogorza as artistic director to sign up Metropolitan Opera artists for Victor's own Red Seal series. Columbia made a brief attempt to get into the field, but unfortunately produced some rather unsatisfactory records which did not sell well enough to pay the high fees asked by the singers. The directors of the company made one of their greatest mistakes in deciding that making records for wealthy patrons was not in their line and by returning to the coon song and the brass band for their principal offerings. By the time they decided, in 1906, to get back into the classical music business, many of the great artists were already contracted to the Victor-Gramophone combine on an exclusive basis.

It has often been said in print that Melba was the first famous singer to make commercial recordings. This is not true: Her first recordings were made at her London home in Great Cumberland Place in March 1904. By that time, such artists as Plançon, Calvé, Scotti, and Santley had recorded in London; Caruso, Bellincioni, Tamagno, and Fabbri in Milan; Ackté, Garden (with Debussy at the piano), Maurel, Renaud, and Rousseliere in Paris; Sembrich, Edouard de Reszke, Schumann-Heink, Scotti, Homer, Gadski, Plançon, and Caruso in New York; Slezak in Vienna; Battistini in Warsaw; Chaliapin, Sobinov, and Figner in Moscow—all had made phonograph recordings. Melba was actually a holdout, and great effort was expended on the part of Landon Ronald and the Gramophone Company to add the prestige of her name to their growing list of "exclusive" artists. Actually, her first recordings were supposedly made for the singer to send to her father in Australia, and it was some time after she had approved test pressings that she was persuaded to allow them to be sold to the public—at a price, it may be noted, set by contract at one shilling more than the prestigious Tamagno recordings made the previous year. Also, like Tamagno, she demanded a royalty on each copy sold, instead of the then prevalent fixed fee for a recording session. There is little doubt that Melba's acceptance of the Gramophone (and the financial awards attached thereto) had a great deal to do with the acceptance of the media by other famous artists, including the real prize, Adelina Patti, who finally capitulated and allowed her voice to be recorded late in 1905.

Viola Tait (1971) tells us that Nevin Tait brought back the first Melba recordings to Australia, and on August 17, 1904, the Tait brothers gave their first Melba Gramophone Concert, "for which the demand was so great that Allan's box office had to remain open until midnight. People flocked to hear Melba's voice recorded on this new invention and the concerts proved so popular a total of fourteen were given." Melba was a perfectionist, as can be shown by her willingness to re-record many titles as the recording process improved, but, unfortunately, also as her vocal powers began to diminish. Her first recordings for Victor in the United States were made in 1907, at which time she repeated some titles previously made in England. After a series of disappointing sessions in London in May 1910, she again remade many titles in the United States in August of the same year. Four titles she made in London for the Gramophone Company in May 1913 were again attempted by Victor in October of the same year in the United States, even though the two companies exchanged matrices, allowing mutual publication on both sides of the Atlantic and in many countries around the world.

MELBA'S LONDON RECORDINGS

ANDREW PORTER

In 1976, EMI Records Ltd. of London, the successor to the Gramophone Company, issued a ten-sided long-playing album (RLS 719) presenting all but two of the existing recordings that Melba had made in Europe from March 1904 to December 1926, including many recordings never before publicly released. Included with the set is an informative booklet which is recommended reading for those who are interested in Melba's art as preserved on recordings. Here is the review of the EMI collection, as written by Andrew Porter for *High Fidelity* magazine.

Nellie Melba was the greatest soprano of her day—a "day" that lasted for some forty years.

As Helen Porter Mitchell she was born in Melbourne, Australia, in 1861. In 1886 she studied with Mathilde Marchesi, the teacher of Emma Eames and many another famous soprano. In 1887, as Melba, she made her debut, in Brussels, in *Rigoletto*. She was at Covent Garden in 1888, sang there every season but two until 1914, reopened the house after the 1914-18 war, and gave her Covent Garden farewell in 1926. She made her Met debut in 1893. The New York critic W. J. Henderson, who heard her regularly during her prime, once wrote:

Excerpted from: Andrew Porter, "Melba: The London Recordings," *High Fidelity* (January 1978). All Rights Reserved.

The quality of musical tone cannot be adequately described. No words can convey to a music lover who did not hear Melba any idea of the sounds with which she ravished all ears. . . . Maurel used to say of the voice of Tamagno, *"C'est la voix unique du monde."* One could equally well have said of Melba's: "It is the unique voice of the world." Its beauty, its power, its clarion quality differed from the fluty notes of Patti. . . . It has been called silvery, but what does that signify? There is one quality which it had which may be comprehended even by those who did not hear her: it had splendor. The tones glowed with a star-like brilliance. They flamed with a white flame.

Happily, music lovers can still listen to Melba singing. She made her first records in 1904, when she was forty-two, and her last in 1926, when she was sixty-five; and there are many of them that, when well reproduced, still reveal the "star-like brilliance," the beauty of timbre, the complete command of vocal technique, and the scrupulous interpretative finish that made her unrivaled.

There were, and are, singers more piquantly charming and singers with more intensely passionate vocal personalities, but in recorded vocal history there is perhaps only Pol Plançon, the bass, on a comparable level of technical accomplishment (insofar as such voices can be compared at all), while singing like Melba's is simply not to be heard today. It belongs to a different, and vanished, world of vocal achievement; and even in that world Melba was unique: As Henderson said, "The full, flowing, and facile emission of the tones has never been surpassed, if matched, by any other singer of our time."

Now EMI has issued a set that collects in chronological sequence, on ten LP sides, all the surviving material from Melba's London recording sessions, the first of them held in March 1904 in her drawing room in Great Cumberland Place, the last in December 1926 in the Small Queen's Hall. As an appendix there is *"On m'appelle Mimi,"* a solitary Paris recording, dated June 1908 in most discographies but here moved back to early May.

Many of the items are described as "previously unpublished," but this means unapproved and unpublished in her lifetime. Collectors discovered that, by ordering from HMV, "blind," individual pressings of the matrix numbers that were gaps in Melba sequences, they could obtain valuable unpublished material; some of this was then published for W. H. Seltsam's International Record Collectors' Club and has appeared since in various Melba LP anthologies. One of the most familiar of these "unpublished" sides is the "distance test" of 1910: two phrases of Ophelia's mad scene (from Thomas's *Hamlet*)—the trill on F sharp followed by a downward arpeggio, and *"Pâle et blonde dort sous l'eau profonde"*—each of them sung first close to the recording horn, vivid and immediate in sound, and then repeated at increasing distances from it.

In themselves, these two phrases provide a microcosm of much of Melba's art. Let me quote Henderson again:

The Melba attack was little short of marvelous. The term attack is not a good one. Melba indeed had no attack; she opened her mouth and a tone was in existence. It began without ictus, when she wished it to, and without betrayal of breathing. It was simply there. . . . Her staccati were as firm, as well placed, and as musical as if they had been played on a piano. Her cantilena was flawless in smoothness and purity. She phrased with elegance and sound musicianship as well as with consideration for the import of the text.

And then, on two sides recorded in 1904, we can hear these two phrases of Ophelia in context, and discover that Melba's "technique was such as to bring out completely the whole beauty of her voice and to enhance her delivery with all the graces of vocal art."

Often she is described as "cold," and certainly her singing does not have the vibrant emotional quality to be found in the voice and style of such a contemporary as Gemma Bellincioni or of, say, Claudia Muzio. But it seems to me that only a coldhearted, unmusical listener can remain unmoved by the beauty of timbre and of phrasing to be heard in her Ophelia, her Desdemona, her Violetta, her Mimì. As Arthur Sullivan put it, "So perfect is Melba's vocal utterance that by the mere emission of tone, independent of all collateral aid, she can express the whole gamut of human feeling."

She was a champion of contemporary music. *Otello* and *La Bohème* were modern operas when she sang them; *Pagliacci* was less than a year old when she introduced it to London; she studied her roles with Gounod, Massenet, Delibes, Saint-Saëns, Thomas, Verdi, Puccini. Her repertory ranged from Rossini's Semiramide, Donizetti's Lucia di Lammermoor, and Gounod's Marguerite and Juliette to Verdi's Aïda and Wagner's Elisabeth and Elsa. She contemplated Tosca (and recorded "*Vissi d'arte*") but never sang the part. The *Siegfried* Brünnhilde she essayed once, at the Met in 1896, with Jean de Reszke; it was not a success. (At a private performance she once sang the Woodbird's music; that is something one would like to have on record.) But in the years covered by the recordings she restricted her operatic repertory to the roles that suited and did not strain the marvelous instrument. In an essay accompanying the present album, Michael Aspinall remarks that "at one time critics only too glibly supposed that since she did not sing Isolde she must be 'unmusical.' All they had to do was to listen to her record of Tosti's 'Goodbye' to recognize one of the most musical of all singers."

Almost all of what made Melba unique can be heard in the results of the 1904 sessions in her drawing room (which must have been very large; were the three orchestrally accompanied arias really made there?). There are seventeen surviving sides, collected on the first disc of the album. The very first word, "Mary," of Tosti's "*Mattinata*" is a miracle of limpid sound shaped by consonant and vowel. The next song, Bemberg's "*Nymphes et sylvains*," brings one of her star-bright notes on "*dansez*," matchless mordents on *"et vous naïades, faunes, dryades,"* and, in the cadenza and coda, her brilliantly incisive, clean-cut, but never *hard* coloratura and a chain of her perfect trills. (To appreciate the perfection of a Melba trill, play one of her records at half-speed, and the absolute precision of the vocal mechanism is revealed; apply the test to modern singers, and the result is usually a sloppy smear.)

Then comes Violetta's first aria. The album quotes a London *Times* review of 1908: "Madame Melba is perhaps the only singer who can delude her hearers into believing for a moment that *Traviata* is a work of beauty. . . . How this most tedious of operas reaches in her hands almost the level of real music drama can hardly be guessed, for it is certainly not in any appreciable degree due to great or even convincing acting. The secret would seem to be in the singer's marvelous power of giving expression to the voice itself without altering the purity of its quality or the exquisite finish of its style."

This was the season when Melba and Tetrazzini were alternating in the role and when the younger singer's apparently carefree, spontaneous virtuosity was electrifying London: the critic notes that, while Melba's coloratura had all its wonted ease, certainty, and delicacy, her "eloquently expressive phrasing" of *"Ah! fors'è lui"* and "the magical power of her cantilena and her musical phrasing" set her apart. Other things to remark are Melba's stylish use of portamento and rubato (as well as some decoration of the vocal line such as Bellincioni, a Violetta whom Verdi admired, also practiced). Portamento and rubato are even more striking in the *"Dite alla giovine"* of the final, 1926 session, with John Brownlee as Germont; what modern conductor would allow his soprano to sing the phrase *"unico raggio di bene"* so eloquently?

As originally recorded, *"Ah! fors'è lui"* continued with the recitative *"Follie! follie!"* and an almost recklessly brilliant, high-speed *"Sempre libera,"* but when the disc was published these were blocked out. A little later, with orchestra, Melba recorded a new *"Sempre libera"* in a performance equally brilliant but less hurried. However, the "buried" section of the earlier disc was not lost forever. In a Melba anthology in HMV's Great Recordings of the Century series, of 1904-6 recordings (COLH 125, published in 1961, now deleted), the piano-accompanied recitative was retrieved, to lead into the orchestral *"Sempre libera"*; and in the present issue we have both sides complete. Aspinall calls the downward runs "a jumble"; in fact, Melba sings the once fairly standard smoother variant, in roulades, by which sopranos avoided the yapping effect so often produced by Verdi's repeated-note downward scales grouped in pairs.

Some of these early sides begin with a background voice giving the signal to start and end with a faint jumble of voices, presumably in congratulation, after the song or aria is done. In the first of two versions of Handel's "Sweet Bird" a slip occurs, and Melba says: "We'll have to do it all over again." When it was done all over again, she started at a much later point in the song; in this reissue, as on COLH 125, the two versions are ingeniously conflated to give us a "Sweet Bird" in full. The earlier, interrupted side then reappears, unedited, as an appendix.

It is tempting to continue with a title-by-title commentary, for in every Melba disc—even in "God Save the King," accompanied by the Band of His Majesty's Coldstream Guards, her least interesting record—there is something worth remarking. A few points must suffice: the utterance of the word "bada," in Mimì's farewell, especially in the earliest (from March 1904) of the three versions here gathered; the ineffable combination of power, purity, and sweetness that flowers in the coda of Tosti's "La Serenata" without ever breaking the scale of the song; the beauty of the move from note to note on the word "lark" in Bishop's "Lo! here the gentle lark"; the verve and vivacity in the "Sevillana" from Massenet's Don César de Bazan, which can make even a solitary listener feel like breaking into applause. (Three unpublished "Sevillana"s of 1910 are here; I like the first best, though Aspinall does not; the "Sevillana" eventually released was a Victor recording.)

But all listeners will find their own favorites, in a repertoire that ranges from a very grand "Porgi amor" and an Elsa's Dream (in Italian) of uncommon purity and sweetness to the high spirits of Alfred Scott-Gatty's "Goodnight" ("Darkies, let us sing a song, in de old plantation") and—Melba's last record—"Swing low, sweet chariot," where one "home," in particular, is spun out to a note of almost unearthly beauty. John Pitts Sanborn Jr. wrote in 1907 that Melba "can lay a note out on the air as a painter lays his color on the canvas." At the age of sixty-five she could still do so.

The last discs, of course, were electrically recorded. So, earlier that year, was the Covent Garden farewell, comprising Act III of Roméo et Juliette, the Willow Song and "Ave Maria" from Otello, and Acts III and IV of La Bohème. Charles Hackett, the Roméo, was not an HMV artist, and so Roméo went unrecorded, but Otello and six Bohème excerpts, sometimes beginning or ending abruptly, were taken down over land line from the theater. Only the first part of the Willow Song, Mimì's farewell, and Melba's farewell speech were found suitable for release at the time; but all ten sides—together with a dull address by Lord Stanley—are here, and they form a precious document of Melba on the stage. There are some uncomfortable, as well as some very beautiful, moments in Otello. As Mimì, at the close of what must have been an emotionally as well as technically exhausting evening, the voice seems to take on new freshness and ease.

Yet, on the whole, it is perhaps the first (1904-5) and the very last records that are the best of all. The early records were probably hard to play on early equipment; and first takes are often more brilliant—closer to the horn?—than the subsequently published versions, or than later remakes of the same titles more cautiously recorded. But the closer, the better, when it's a question of modern tracking from unworn copies; the "distance test" makes that clear. (The 1904 orchestral sound is also surprisingly good.) Later engineers were more circumspect when incising what Sanborn described as "the large voluptuous body of her voice," for grooves containing loud high notes soon wore out and began to blast under the pressure of steel needles in heavy acoustic tone arms. In the final 1926 recordings the "presence" is back again, though the repertoire—*"Dite alla giovine"* and a Bemberg duet with Brownlee, Szulc's *"Clair de lune,"* and "Swing low"—does not call for the large, brilliant, fearless manner of Melba's prime.

There are a few things to be said against Melba. Sometimes the final note of a song seems to be just a shade below pitch. Aspinall remarks that "poor recording robs the higher notes of some harmonics, and may make them sound slightly flat when in fact she was singing in tune"—but that does not explain why the same note elsewhere in the same song should be unaffected and remain perfectly in tune. As a rule, Melba's pitch is impeccable. Her pronunciation is sometimes ugly: Marguerite's *"Il me trouverait belle"* rhymes with Norman Mailer. (But when it was suggested to Delibes that the singer's French was not good enough for *Lakmé*, he is said to have replied: *"Qu'elle chante en chinois, si elle veut, mais qu'elle chante mon opèra!"*— "Let her sing in Chinese, if she likes, so long as she sings my opera!")

Her performance of Lotti's *"Pur dicesti,"* for all the marvelous trills, is less winning than Patti's, and her "Comin' thro' the rye" less vivid and personal. In the course of his long, interesting essay, Aspinall raises other issues, concerned with register change and with "backward" florid technique; listeners may well find themselves agreeing with his factual observations while not agreeing that they demonstrate "two alarming flaws" in that superlative technique. And when he describes "Home, sweet home" as "wobbly," eyebrows will surely rise.

EMI's earlier Patti album (EMI Odeon 1C 147 01500/1, distributed by Peters International) enshrines the art and at any rate the later voice, miraculously well preserved, of the prima donna who reigned in the second half of the nineteenth century. This album presents her great successor with vivid power and beauty. The transfers, edited by Bryan Crimp, have a full-bodied, immediate sound that is often difficult to draw from worn, treasured copies of the original 78s. Many of the shells survive at Hayes, EMI's headquarters, and collectors were generous in providing the best possible copies of other items. The album should dispel the myth that Melba's voice was "white" or "cold"; listen to it ring out triumphantly in the final trio of *Faust*, with McCormack and Sammarco. The discographical information is ample but stops short of giving Victor, later HMV, or IRCC numbers. The Aspinall essay includes several interesting contemporary reviews (some of which I have quoted above). The serious omission is of the texts; these are needed for a full enjoyment of the singing, and could easily have been compiled.

Now it is up to RCA to publish a complementary volume of Melba's fifty-odd American recordings, made between 1907 and 1916. Among other wonderful things, they include *"Soave fanciulla"* with Caruso, *"Depuis le jour,"* a Willow Song and *"Ave Maria"* more exquisitely sung than in the 1926 Covent Garden live recording, and a melting "Songs my mother taught me."

MELBA AND I

JOHN BROWNLEE

By 1976, EMI (successors in England to the Gramophone Company) and RCA (successors in the United States to the Victor Talking Machine Company) were no longer affiliated, even though each company retained the rights to the famous "His Master's Voice" trademark in its respective areas. Thus it was that the EMI collection of Melba's European recordings could not include over sixty recordings that Melba had made in the United States for Victor. Fortunately, this situation has been resolved, appropriately by the Australian branch of RCA, with the publication in the spring of 1982 of a five-disc "long-playing" album containing all of the existing Victor Melba recordings.

It also seems fitting that this discussion of Nellie Melba's recordings be concluded by an article written in 1954 by the late Australian baritone, John Brownlee, who took part in the famous Australian soprano's final recording session in December 1926.

As a young man in Australia, having won a gold medal as "Champion Vocalist," I was singing the *Messiah* with the Melbourne Philharmonic Society when Madame Nellie Melba attended a performance with friends, and was interested enough to come backstage and talk to me. "I should go to Europe to study for opera. Did I have enough money! Was I interested

From: John Brownlee, "Melba and I," *Saturday Review* (December 25, 1954). © 1954 Saturday Review Magazine Co. Reprinted by permission.

enough to work hard, study languages, learn repertoire, and climb the hard road to success!" At the end of this rapid-fire inquiry from the great *diva* I managed to blurt out some sort of breathless thanks, meanwhile squeezing her hand so hard that I hurt her because of the rings she was wearing. Melba cried out and spanked me soundly. As an afterthought she said, however, that she loved a firm grip. Well, two years later I arrived in London, called on Melba, got some sound advice, and packed myself off to Paris, where my intensive studies began in 1923.

"The word Melba has come to mean more than an artist possessed of perhaps the most perfect organ of her day. It has come to mean crowded audiences, doubled prices, long packed lines of motor cars and carriages, rows upon rows of waiting footmen, flowers, emotions, a golden superfluity of money, and that touch of solemnity with which we crown our enthusiasm."

The above was written by Filson Young in 1908, and I quote it because I had a first-hand taste of this wonderful adoration when Melba invited me to sing with her at her farewell to grand opera at her beloved theatre, The Royal Opera House, Covent Garden, in London, June 1926. What a night on which to make a debut! Melba's last Mimi, and my first Marcello, a role that has remained one of my favorites through the years. How can one describe such a night, when the whole of England, from the Royal family down, had come to pay homage to another kind of queen! One will hardly ever see such a galaxy of notables and so many diamond tiaras in an opera house again. The atmosphere was charged almost beyond endurance, and at the end of it all the ovation with all its overtones of love, affection, and adoration, as only the cold English can bestow upon those whom they worship.

This, too, was the closing of an era, long called the Golden Age of Opera, which it was in more ways than one. Looking back, I realize how very fortunate I was to be able to peep into that world, for although only just beginning my career I heard and mingled with many of the great ones, at Melba's fabulous parties in Paris and London—Battistini, Chaliapin, Jean de Reszke, Tetrazzini, Mary Garden, Titta Ruffo, and Maurice Renaud, who gave me several of his costumes, and coached me in the roles of Marcello and Scarpia. How things have changed since these great names reigned supreme in the field of opera and concert! One could devote pages to that question alone, but . . .

My association with Melba, from that early beginning in Australia, brought about a curious situation in connection with recording. At the time of the farewell electrical recording had just appeared on the scene, and the Gramophone Co. (HMV) put microphones in Covent Garden for experimental purposes, and unknown to any of us at the time got some remarkable recordings of the actual performance. Spurred on by this success, HMV was most anxious to have Melba record something under the new conditions, but, hating her old recordings as much as she did at the time, she stoutly refused. This is where I was brought into the picture, almost as a decoy—would I try and persuade the great lady, just as a souvenir for myself, to record a couple of the duets we so often sang together at parties in London and Paris! I persuaded, and to my great surprise and joy Melba consented.

How vividly I can still remember that day. When Melba was asked to stand up to this new instrument of torture, the microphone, the great prima donna was true to form; "How can anything good come out of that obnoxious looking box?" she exclaimed, as she stalked around the helpless microphone, while I stood by petrified, lest at the last minute she might refuse. She finally calmed down enough to agree to a test, and the result, when played back, so amazed her that she would not believe it, so we had to make another. By this time she was really excited. "For the first time I hear something of what I think my voice really sounds like. Why wasn't this thing invented before?" she exclaimed. As the excitement grew intense Melba, impulsive and always quick to make a decision, suddenly said, "John, we'll record the duets, and I'll also do a couple of songs." I felt quite sure that the Gramophone people there, who had been in on this from the start, would explode at this moment, but the good English calm prevailed. This is one Britisher, however, who almost lost it completely. As we stood there awaiting the signal to begin the duet from *La Traviata*, the impact of this great event suddenly hit and almost bowled me over. There was I, a mere youngster of twenty-five, about to make a recording with the Queen of Song—my fairy godmother, the one person who, through her interest and guidance, had helped me more than anyone else to get where I was; do you wonder I was scared, and almost frozen to the spot! How it ever came out as well as it did, I'll never know, but I'm eternally grateful.

I well remember how much Melba was criticized for singing so many popular songs and cheap ballads, which she always included in her concert programs along with the operatic fare. The operatic arias provided the fireworks for the glorious voice and singer, and by that time, having the audience in the palm of her hands, she would caress them with the songs they loved to hear. She did not have to plumb the depths of *lieder*. Her public paid, and paid well, to hear what they wanted, and Melba gave it to them. Don't forget that she was a great showman who could make the simplest song seem like a big event, "Comin' thru the Rye," Tosti's "Goodbye," etc. When she sat at the piano and sang "Home Sweet Home," thousands of people went home happy, feeling THAT was the gem of the evening. Can one blame John McCormack for singing so many Irish songs, when his public clamored for more and more? Let us not forget the great singers of that era were all on very high pedestals with their audiences, and stout indeed would be the heart of one who set about loosening those pedestals. There was the occasion when Clara Butt was leaving for a concert tour of Australia and she asked Melba what she should prepare, lest the public taste had changed! "No," said Melba, "just sing 'em muck!" When this friendly advice unfortunately got into the press there was a terrific hullabaloo, and Melba was furious, but to the end, I'm sure, she never felt that she had to elevate the public taste.

In opera, I truly believe Melba strove hard for perfection. She studied many of her roles with the composers themselves: Marguerite and Juliette with Gounod, Manon with Massenet, Mimi with Puccini, and Desdemona with the grand old man himself. The story of how Verdi went to hear her sing in *Rigoletto*, and went backstage to pay his respects, inviting her to his home where the day was spent, he playing and she singing through the whole of *Otello*, is typical of that amazing era. I well remember many a lecture, during the preparation of the farewell for Covent Garden, as to how Puccini wished *Bohème* performed. That went for conductor as well as the rest of us.

Amongst the tremendous collection of photographs Melba possessed I recall one in particular, autographed: "To the greatest of the great, Arthur Nikisch." Melba had built herself a reputation with the way she sang certain phrases, and the first time she sang *Faust* with Nikisch at Covent Garden the famed conductor went backstage after the first act, kissed her hand, and said, "Now I know madame, why you are such a great artist." He had only heard her sing the phrase, *"Non, monsieur, je ne suis demoiselle ni belle, et je n'ai pas besoin qu'on me donne la main."* Many an oldtimer at the opera in Paris and London told me that they would not miss hearing Melba sing that opening phrase for anything, she had a way of molding it with that incredible floating tone of hers, and it would leave them in heaven for the rest of the evening. Another phrase I would like to mention is the one *"Dite alla giovane si bella e pura"* from *La Traviata*. How many times I stood beside her as we sang this duet, just spellbound by the way this phrase would pour out!—the perfect diction, the beautiful blending of each note to the other in the ascending passage (heavenly *legato* in other words), then on the words, "un unico coraggio"—the way she would drop down to the "D" with such fullness of tone, such smoothness of scale, the like of which I have never heard anyone else do. Fortunately, you can hear this in the recording of the duet we made together in 1926.

To return to the subject of the early Melba recordings, I would like if I may to quote again from that article of Filson Young written in 1908.

I fear that the gramophone, like the motor car, has come to stay. There is hardly a country house in England, in which, straying unsuspectingly into some tapestried gallery, or some vaulted hall, you are not liable to be confronted by the sight of a monstrous trumpet, sitting on a table and emitting, after initial rasp and buzz, the loud nasal travesty of Melba's heavenly voice. It is true, however, that there are few singers or performers of any great eminence who have not sung or played into the gramophone, and in doing so have not committed the sin of blasphemy, but I think that no one has done so much to make that deadly instrument popular as Melba has done, and therefore she is the greatest sinner.

I have been fortunate enough, lately, to be able to listen to a great collection of Melba records belonging to a good friend. Played with the equipment of today, there is undoubtedly a lot more fidelity in those old recordings than was suspected years ago, and they at least give to the present generation some idea of what the Melba voice sounded like. I have chosen a few, in chronological order of recording, which I think are good examples of the great art that was Melba's:

"Se saran Rose" (1904): Shows off the wonderful coloratura.

"Jewel Song": "FAUST" (1905): A good example of the perfection of her scale, always likened to a string of pearls, the brilliance of her roulads, and the famous trill.

"Aubade": "ROI D'YS" (1906): This is the tenor aria in the opera, but Melba sings it with great *élan* and a different ending, probably arranged for her by the composer.

"Mi chiamano Mimi" (1906): A very good recording of the true Melba quality, with the luscious tone.

"Voi che sapete" (1907): Here is the perfect Mozart style, the clean attack, the smooth legato, the shaping of phrases, all so natural and easy to her.

"Salce, Ave Maria": "OTELLO" (1910): These are also good records of the Melba voice in one of her favorite roles. I could not help comparing these with the ones made at the farewell.

"Vissi d'arte": "TOSCA" (1910): Shows well her dramatic quality as well as that glorious legato.

"Depuis le jour": "LOUISE" (1913): I particularly liked an unpublished one which shows so well the perfection of her voice control and production.

"John Anderson, My Jo" (1913): This simple little song is a good example of her enunciation and projection of words.

Melba made a great number of records, recording certain items over and over again. One must remember of course, that recording was in its infancy and that the quality of the sound reproduction varies through the years, no doubt due to experimentation. There are also some startling blemishes, giving the impression that Melba "hooted," a thing I can assure everyone she was never guilty of doing, any more than the variance of pitch—these must be due to technical difficulties of the time. No, the great singer who was called "Madame Stradivarius" by Jules Massenet could never have committed such atrocities.

Melba was a lyric soprano, but her technique was such that she sang all the famous coloratura roles as well, and the voice had a certain fulness, so that she ventured into other fields, not usually associated with the lyric, per se. She sang Aïda at Covent Garden, numerous performances of Elsa in *Lohengrin* throughout the world, including the exciting days of the Imperial Opera in St. Petersburg. I remember the story of how she learned the role of Elizabeth in *Tannhäuser* in three days. One morning at breakfast she read an announcement in the *New York Herald* that she was to sing Elizabeth the following Friday, but instead of calling the Opera House and refusing, as she did not know the rôle, she sent for a repetiteur and learned it. Incidentally, the point of the story was by way of advice to young singers— what you learn quickly you easily forget. While she got through the first performance very well, at a repetition three days later in Philadelphia she had a dreadful time remembering it all. Melba also had a burning desire to sing Brünnhilde in *Siegfried*, and in spite of all Marchesi's warnings not to do it she went ahead and sang it at the Metropolitan—once. That, she used to say, was her worst mistake.

Melba's career began in Brussels in 1887, after a year of intensive study with Madame Marchesi in Paris, and ended in London in 1926, at the age of sixty-seven. It was simply amazing how little toll the years had taken of that glorious voice, so much of the old beauty and steadiness of tone was still there. The proof of all this is in the unpublished recordings actually taken during the performance. Very few will be fortunate enough to be able to hear these records, I know, but the same qualities are in the two duets we recorded together, and which were published, along with the two songs done at the same time, "Clair de Lune" and "Swing Low, Sweet Chariot."

DISCOGRAPHY: THE MELBA RECORDINGS

WILLIAM R. MORAN

I. BETTINI PHONOGRAPH LABORATORY
(110 5th Ave., New York)

The activities of Gianni Bettini and his Phonograph Laboratory have been previously mentioned. A reporter for *The Phonoscope* in an 1896 article tells of visiting the Bettini Laboratory and some of the recordings he heard there: "The next cylinder was one labeled 'Melba' which was truly wonderful; the phonograph reproducing her wonderful voice in a marvelous manner, especially the high notes which soared away above the staff and were rich and clear. Mark Twain interrupted the singer with a few remarks on the experience he had in trying to make practical use of the instrument. The humorist is now on his lecturing tour around the world, and the record he made in the phonograph was taken in December, 1893. . . ." In several Bettini catalogs, a quotation is given from an article in an 1896 issue of the *New York Evening Telegram*, in which the author mentions hearing in the Bettini Laboratory the voices of Melba, Calvé, Nordica, Tamagno, Plançon, Bernhardt, Réjane, Salvini, and many others.

In spite of the foregoing evidence that Bettini had Melba recordings in his possession, when he began to produce recordings on a commercial scale and issue catalogs, Melba recordings were never listed. Presumably her recordings for Bettini were not intended for commercial sale; none have ever been found.

II. THE MAPLESON CYLINDERS

The history of the Mapleson Cylinders, and the controversy with respect to the authenticity of No. 2 (*Les Huguenots*) are found in the previous section, "The Recordings of Nellie Melba." The "R&H No." listed in the tabulation below is that assigned to the original cylinders as they now exist in the Rodgers and Hammerstein Archives of Recorded Sound in New York (Hall, 1983). Those recordings with no reissue information shown had not been made available in transcribed form as of July 1984.

Dis- cog. No.	R&H No.	Date	Transcribed Releases "78" rpm Catalog Numbers	LP Issues	Speed of Original Issue
1. LE CID: Allez en paix . . . Alleluia! (Massenet) (F) (Conductor: Luigi Mancinelli)					
	23	16 Jan. '01	—	IRCC L-7004	33.33
*(?)2. LES HUGUENOTS: (a) A ce mot tout s'anime . . . (b) Le ruisseau le répète (Meyerbeer) (F) (Conductor: Philippe Flon)					
	49	(?)28 Jan. '01	(a) IRCC 5002	RCAust	87.80
			(b) IRCC 3034	—	78.26
				(b) IRCC L-7006; L-7032	33.33
3a. LUCIA DI LAMMERMOOR: (Verrano a te . . .) . . . sospiri ardenti . . . su questo pegno (Donizetti) (I) (w. A. Saléza (Conductor: L. Mancinelli)					
	73	2 Mar. '01	—	—	
3b. LUCIA DI LAMMERMOOR: Spargi d'amaro pianto (Mad Scene) (Donizetti) (I) (Conductor: L. Mancinelli)					
	75	2 Mar. '01	—	—	
4. FAUST: (Anges purs . . .) . . . Le vous-tu? . . . au sein des cieux (Gounod) (w. Albert Saléza & Ed. de Reszke) (Conductor: L. Mancinelli)					
	36	4 Mar. '01	—	—	
5. ROMEO ET JULIETTE: Je veux vivre . . . avant de l'effeuiller! (Gounod) (F) (Conductor: L. Mancinelli)					
	84	9 Mar. '01	—	—	
6. LA TRAVIATA: (Un di felice . . .) . . . Ah, se ciò . . . e delizia al cor (Verdi) (I) (w. Andres Dippel) (Conductor: P. Flon)					
	100	16 Mar. '01	—	IRCC L-7006	33.33

*preceding discography number indicates note at end of listings.

7. LUCIA DI LAMMERMOOR: Spargi d'amaro pianto (Mad Scene) (Donizetti) (I) (Conductor: L. Mancinelli)

| 74 | 18 Mar. '01 | — | IRCC L-7004 | 33.33 |

8a. FAUST: (Comment n'être pas coquette? . . . le bracelet et le collier! (Jewel Song) (Gounod (F) (Conductor: L. Mancinelli)

| 30 | 28 Mar. '01 | IRCC L-7004 | 33.33 |

8b. FAUST: Anges purs (Complete) (Gounod) (F) (w. Albert Saléza & Pol Plançon)

| 37 | (?)28 Mar. '01 | — |

III. THE GRAMOPHONE & TYPEWRITER CO (London)

Discog. No.	Matrix No.	Date	Single fc. Cat. No.	Double fc. Cat. No.	Victor Cat. No.	"78" rpm reissues	Re-recordings on Long-Playing Discs	Speed of Original Issue
*9. Mattinata (Enrico Panzacchi—F. Paolo Tosti) (I) (pf. Landon Ronald)								
1.		Mar. '04	03015	—	95022	—	RLS-719; COLH-125; NP-4; 60113; Rococo 5	71.00
10. Nymphes et sylvains (O. Ocampo—Hermann Bemberg) (F) (pf. L. Ronald)								
2.		Mar. '04	03016	—	95023	IRCC-123	RLS-719; COLH-125; TDQ-3005; Rococo 5	71.00
*11. LA TRAVIATA: (a) Ah! fors' è lui . . . (b) Follie! . . . (c) Sempre libera (Verdi) (I) (pf. L. Ronald)								
6.		Mar. '04	(a) 03017	—	(a) 95014	—	(a) Rococo 5; TAP 310; ORL 208	71.00
			—		—	—	(a + b) COLH-125; Seraphim 60274	
			—		—	—	(a + b + c) EMI RLS-719	
*12. Comin' thro' the Rye (Robert Burns—Old Scottish Air) (E) (pf. L. Ronald)								
7.		Mar. '04	(03018)	—	—	—	RLS-719; BC-233; Rococo 5	71.00
13. Se saran rose (P. Mazzoni—Luigi Arditi) (I) (pf. L. Ronald)								
9.		Mar. '04	03019	—	95019	—	RLS-719; COLH-125; Rococo 5	71.00
*14. LUCIA DI LAMMERMOOR: Del ciel demente un riso (from Mad Scene) (Donizetti) (I) (pf. L. Ronald; flute Philippe Gaubert)								
12.		Mar. '04	03020	—	95013	—	RLS-719; COLH-125; ORL-208; BC-233; Rococo 5; TAP-306	75.00

Discog. No.	Matrix No.	Date	Single fc. Cat. No.	Double fc. Cat. No.	Victor Cat. No.	"78" rpm reissues	Re-recordings on Long-Playing Discs	Speed of Original Issue
*15. IL PENSIEROSO: (a) Sweet Bird That Shunn'st the Noie of Folly (b) Error & Melba comment (Milton-Handel) (E) (pf. L. Ronald; flute P. Gaubert)								
	(?)13	Mar. '04	—		—		(a) RLS-719; COLH-125 (a + b) RLS-719; EJS 142	75.00
*16. IL PENSIEROSO: Thee, Chauntress, Oft the Woods among I Woo (Milton-Handel) (E) (pf. L. Ronald; flute P. Gaubert)								
	15.	Mar. '04	03021	—	95016		RLS-719; COLH-125; Rococo 5	75.00
17. Good-bye (George John Whyte-Melville—F. Paolo Tosti) (E) (pf. L. Ronald) (Two verses only)								
	16.	Mar. '04	03022	—	95012		RLS-719; COLH-125; Rococo 5	75.00
*18. HAMLET: À vos jeux, mes amis, permettez-moi de grâce (Thomas) (F) (or. L. Ronald) (Mad Scene, Part 1)								
	20.	Mar. '04	03023	—	95020	IRCC-47	RLS-719; COLH-125; ORL-208; GVC-3; Rococo 17; Scala 846; Saga 7029	76.00
*19. HAMLET: Et maintenant, écoutez ma chanson! (Thomas) (F) (or. L. Ronald) (Mad Scene, Part 2)								
	21.	Mar. '04	03024	—	95021	IRCC-47	RLS-719; COLH-125; ORL-208; GVC-3; Rococo 17; Scala 846; Saga 7029	76.00
20. RIGOLETTO: Caro nome che il mio cor (Verdi) (I) (or. L. Ronald)								
	22.	Mar. '04	03025	—	95018	IRCC-2	RLS-719; COLH-125; ORL-208; Rococo 5	76.00
21. LA TRAVIATA: Sempre libera (Verdi) (I) (or. L. Ronald)								
	23.	Mar. '04	03026	—	95015	—	RLS-719; COLH-125; Seraphim 60274; ORL-208; Rococo 5	76.00
22. Three Green Bonnets (A. L. Harris—Guy d'Hardelot) (E) (pf. L. Ronald)								
	25.	Mar. '04	03027	—	95017	IRCC-181	RLS-719; Rococo 5	76.00
23. LE NOZZE DI FIGARO: Porgi amor (Mozart) (I) (pf. L. Ronald)								
	26.	Mar. '04	03028	—	95025	IRCC-34; VB-40	RLS-719; OXLP-7534; BC-233; TAP 323; Rococo 5	76.00

No. & Title	Matrix	Cat. A	Date	Cat. B	78 issue	Reissues	Value
24. Si mes vers avaient des ailes (Victor Hugo—Reynaldo Hahn) (F) (pf. L. Ronald)	27.	95024	Mar. '04	03029	—	RLS-719; ORL-208; Rococo 5	76.00
*25. LA BOHÈME: Donde lieta usci al tuo grido d'amore (Addio) (Puccini) (I) (pf. L. Ronald)	28.	—	Mar. '04	(03030)	—	RLS-719; COLH-125; XIG-8002; Rococo 17	76.00
26. Chant Vénitien (Georges Roussel—Hermann Bemberg) (F) (pf. Hermann Bemberg)	6149b	—	20 Oct. '04	—	—	—	—
27. Chant Vénitien (Georges Roussel—Hermann Bemberg) (F) (pf. H. Bemberg)	6150b	94002	20 Oct. '04	3575	—	RLS-719; TQD-3005	77.43
28. Les anges pleurent (G. Audigier—Hermann Bemberg) (F) (pf. H. Bemberg)	6151b	94001	20 Oct. '04	3576	IRCC-54	RLS-719; TQD-3005; GVC-3; Rococo 17; Scala 846	77.43
*29. Ave Maria (Meditation on Bach's Prelude, WTC 1—Ch. F. Gounod) (Latin) (vln. Jan Kubelik; pf. L. Ronald)	400c	—	20 Oct. '04	—	—	—	77.43
30. Ave Maria (Meditation on Bach's Prelude, WTC 1—Ch. F. Gounod) (Latin) (vln. J. Kubelik; pf. L. Ronald)	401c	03033	20 Oct. '04	—	—	RLS-719; GVC-3; Scala 846	77.43
31. La Serenata (G. A. Cesareo—F. Paolo Tosti) (I) (pf. L. Ronald)	402c	03034	20 Oct. '04	—	—	RLS-719; COLH-125	77.43
32. ROMEO ET JULIETTE: Je veux vivre dans ce rêve (Waltz) (Gounod) (F) (pf. L. Ronald)	404c	03035	20 Oct. '04	—	DB 367	RLS-719; COLH-125; GVC-3; ORL-208; Rococo 17; Scala 846	77.43
33. Chant Hindou (O. Ocampo—Hermann Bemberg) (F) (pf. H. Bemberg)	405c	03036	20 Oct. '04	—	IRCC-34	RLS-719; TQD-3005	77.43
*34. LA BOHÈME: Donde lieta usci al tuo grido d'amore (Addio) (Puccini) (I) (pf. L. Ronald)	406c	03037	20 Oct. '04	—	—	RLS-719; ORL-208; GVC-3; Scala 846	77.43
*35. God Save the King (Traditional) (E) (w. H. M. Coldstream Guards Band, cond. Lieut. Mackenzie Rogan)	7200b	3625	4 Sept. '05	—	—	RLS-719; Cantilena 6207	72.00
*36. Auld Lang Syne (Robert Burns—Old Scottish Air) (E) (w. H. M. Coldstream Guards Band, cond. M. Rogan)	7201½b	3615	4 Sep. '05	—	—	RLS-719; Rococo 17; Cantilena 6207	72.00

Discog. No.	Matrix No.	Date	Single fc. Cat. No.	Double fc. Cat. No.	Victor Cat. No.	"78" rpm reissues	Re-recordings on Long-Playing Discs	Speed of Original Issue
*37. Come Back to Erin (Mrs. Charles Barnard, "Claribel") (E) (w. H. M. Coldstream Guards Band, cond. M. Rogan)								
	7202½b	4 Sep. '05	3616	—	94003	IRCC-150	RLS-719; Cantilena 6207	72.00
38. Old Folks at Home (Stephen C. Foster) (E) (w. Gwladys Roberts, Ernest Pike & Peter Dawson; pf. L. Ronald)								
	7203b	4 Sep. '05	3617	DA 337	94005	—	RLS-719; Cantilena 6207	75.00
39. Good Night (Sir Alfred Scott-Gatty) (E) (w. Gwladys Roberts, Ernest Pike & Peter Dawson; pf. L. Ronald)								
	7204b	4 Sep. '05	3618	DA 337	94006	IRCC-150	RLS-719	75.00
40. Away on the Hill There Runs a Stream (from "Four Songs of the Hill") (Landon Ronald) (pf. L. Ronald)								
	7205b	4 Sep. '05	3619	—	94007	—	RLS-719; GVC-3; Scala 846	75.00
41. Sur le lac (Hermann Bemberg) (F) (pf. H. Bemberg)								
	520c	5 Sep. '05	03046	—	95028	IRCC-123	RLS-719; TQD-3005; GVC-3	74.23
42. Lo, Here the Gentle Lark! (Wm. Shakespeare—Sir Henry Bishop) (E) (flute Albert Fransella; pf. L. Ronald)								
	521c	5 Sep. '05	03047	DB-347	95027	—	RLS-719; COLH-125; BC-233; GVC-3; Scala 846	74.23
43. FAUST: Ah! je ris de me voir (Air des bijoux) (Gounod) (F) (pf. L. Ronald)								
	522c	5 Sep. '05	03048	—	—	—	RLS-719; COLH-125; GVC-3; ORL-208; Scala 846	74.23
44. Home, Sweet Home (from CLARI, THE MAID OF MILAN) (John Howard Paine—Sir Henry Bishop) (E) (pf. L. Ronald)								
	523c	5 Sep. '05	03049	—	95026	—	RLS-719; BC-233; GVC-3; Rococo 17; Scala 846	74.23
45. Goodbye (George John Whyte-Melville—F. Paolo Tosti) (E) (pf. L. Ronald) (Three verses)								
	524c	5 Sep. '05	03050	—	—	—	RLS-719	74.23
*46. Ave Maria (Meditation on Bach's Prelude, WTC 1—Ch. F. Gounod) (Latin) ('cello W. H. Squire; pf. L. Ronald)								
	689c	7 Jul. '06	03069	—	—	—	RLS-719; Saga 7029	81.00
47. ELAINE: L'amour est pur comme la flamme (P. Ferrier—Hermann Bemberg) (F) (w. ladies' chorus; pf. H. Bemberg) (CR)								
	690c	7 Jul. '06	—	—	—	IRCC-17	RLS-719; TDQ-3005; Rococo 17	77.43
48. Pastorale (Régnard-Bizet) (F) (pf. L. Ronald)								
	691c	7 Jul. '06	03070	—	—	IRCC-35	RLS-719; TQD-3005; GVC-3; Rococo 17; Saga 7029; Scala 846	77.43

*49. LA BOHEME: Mi chiamano Mimì (Puccini) (I) (pf. L. Ronald)

| 692c | 7 Jul. '06 | 03071 | — | — | | | RLS-719; ORL-208; XIG—8002 | 77.43 |

50. LE ROI DYS: Puisqu'on ne peut fléchir ces jalouses gardiennes . . . Vainement, ma bien aimée (Aubade) (Lalo) (F) (pf. L. Ronald)

| 693c | 7 Jul. '06 | 03072 | — | — | VB-13rr | | RLS—719; COLH—125 | 77.43 |

51. The White Sea Mist (No. 5 from "In Sunshine and Shadow") (Harold Simpson—Landon Ronald) (E)

| 8473b | 11 Jul. '06 | — | — | — | — | |

IV. VICTOR TALKING MACHINE COMPANY (New York)[1]

Matrix No.	Date	G&T/HMV Single Fce.	G&T/HMV Double Fce.	Victor Sgl. Fce.	Victor Dbl. Fce.	"78" rpm reissues	Re-recordings on Long-Playing Discs	Speed of Original Issue
52. LA BOHÈME: Sì, mi chiamano Mimì (Puccini) (I) (or. Walter B. Rogers)								
C-4281-1	5 Mar. '07	—	—	—	—	—	—	
-2	24 Mar'07	053106	—	88074	—	—	RCAust	77.43
53. TOSCA: Vissi d'arte, vissi d'amore Puccini) (I) (or. W. Rogers)								
C-4282-1	5 Mar. '07	—	—	—	—	—	—	
-2	24 Mar. '07	053115	—	88075	—	—	RCAust.	77.43
54. RIGOLETTO: Caro nome che il mio cor (Verdi) (I) (or. W. Rogers)								
C-4283-1,-2	5 Mar. '07	053110	DB-346	88078	6213	—	RCAust.; OXLP 7534; BC-233; Saga 7029	78.26
55. LA BOHÈME: O soave fanciulla (Puccini) (I) (w. Enrico Caruso) (or. W. Rogers)								
C-4326-1,-2	24 Mar. '07	054129	—	95200	—	—	RCAust.; ORL-208; R-17; XIG-8002; MH920328; LCT-6701	76.60
56. LE NOZZE DI FIGARO: Voi che sapete (Mozart) (I) (pf. acc.?)								
C-4337-1	27 Mar. '07	—	—	—	—	—	—	

1. The matrix number for a Victor record consists of a letter prefix, a serial number, and a suffix number called a "take." Where more than one take is shown on one line, the underlined number indicates the take that was published.

Matrix No.	Date	G&T/HMV Single Fce.	G&T/HMV Double Fce.	Victor Sgl. Fce.	Victor Dbl. Fce.	"78" rpm reissues	Re-recordings on Long-Playing Discs	Speed of Original Issue
57. FAUST: Ah! je ris de me voir (Air des bijoux) (Gounod) (F) (or. W. Rogers)								
C-4338-1,-2	27 Mar. '07	033029	—	88066	—	—	RCAust.; LM-6171	77.43
*58. LA TRAVIATA: Ah! fors' è lui . . . Sempre libera (Verdi) (I) (or. W. Rogers)								
C-4339-1	27 Mar. '07	053108	DB-346	88064	6213	—	RCAust.; OXLP-7534; BC-233	77.43
59. Goodbye (George John Whyte-Melville—F. Paolo Tosti) (E) (or. W. Rogers)								
C-4340-1	27 Mar. '07	03091	—	88065	—	—	RCAust.	77.43
*60. LA BOHÈME: Donde lieta uscì al tuo grido d'amore (Addio) (Puccini) (I) (or. W. Rogers)								
C-4341-1	27 Mar. '07	053111	—	88072	—	—	RCAust.	77.43
61. La Serenata (G. A. Cesareo—F. Paolo Tosti) (I) (harp Ada Sassoli)								
C-4342-1,-2	27 Mar. '07	053114	DB-349	88079	6221	—	RCAust.; Scala 875	77.43
62. Per valli, per boschi (Giuseppe M. Blangini) (I) (w. Charles Gilibert) (or. W. Rogers)								
C-4347-1	28 Mar. '07	054128	DM-117	89011	—	—	RCAust.; Saga 7029; Rococo 17	77.43
63. Un ange est venu (Paul Mariéton—Hermann Bemberg) (F) (w. Charles Gilibert) (or. W. Rogers)								
C-4348-1	28 Mar. '07	034014	DM-117	89012	—	—	RCAust.; TQD-3005	77.43
*64. LUCIA DI LAMMERMOOR: Alfin son tua, alfin sei mio (Mad Scene) (Donizetti) (I) (flute Charles K. North; or. W. Rogers)								
C-4349-1	29 Mar. '07	—	—	—	—	—	—	
-2	30 Mar. '07	053112	—	88071	—	—	RCAust.; Saga 7029	77.43
65. Lo, Here the Gentle Lark! (Wm. Shakespeare—Sir Henry Bishop) (E) (flute C. North; or. W. Rogers)								
C-4350-1	27 Mar. '07	—	—	—	—	—	—	
-2	28 Mar. '07	03090	—	88073	—	—	RCAust.	77.43
66. Si mes vers avaient des ailes (Victor Hugo—Reynaldo Hahn) (F) (harp acc. Ada Sassoli)								
C-4352-1	29 Mar. '07	033026	DB-361	88080	—	—	RCAust.; TQD-3005	77.43
67. LE NOZZE DI FIGARO: Voi che sapete (Mozart) (I) (or. W. Rogers)								
C-4353-1	29 Mar. '07	053113	—	88067	—	—	RCAust.	77.43
*68. HAMLET: À vos jeux, mes amis, permettez-moi de grâce (Thomas) (F) (or. W. Rogers) (Mad Scene, Part 1)								
C-4354-1	29 Mar. '07	033028	DB-710	88069	—	AGSB-7	RCAust.	77.43

454

*69. HAMLET: Pâle et blonde dort sous l'eau profonde (Thomas) (F) (or. W. Rogers) (Mad Scene, Part 2)
C-4355-1 29 Mar. '07 033027 DB-710 88070 — AGSB-7 RCAust. 77.43

70. Se saran rose (P. Mazzoni—Luigi Arditi) (I) (or. W. Rogers)
C-4356-1 29 Mar. '07 053109 — 88076 — — RCAust. 77.43

71. ROMEO ET JULIETTE: Je veux vivre dans ce rêve (Waltz) (Gounod) (F) (or. W. Rogers)
C-4357-1 29 Mar. '07 — — — — — —

72. IL PENSIEROSO: Sweet Bird That Shunn'st the Noise of Folly (John Milton—G. F. Handel) (E) (flute Charles K. North; or. W. Rogers)
C-4358-1 30 Mar. '07 03089 — 88068 — — RCAust. 77.43

73. Ave Maria (Meditation on Bach's Prelude, WTC 1—Ch. F. Gounod) (Latin) (harp A. Sassoli; violin & organ)
C-4359-1,-2 30 Mar. '07 — — — — — —

74. Mattinata (Enrico Panzacchi—F. Paolo Tosti) (I) (pf. Nellie Melba)
C-4360-1 30 Mar. '07 053107 — 88077 6221 — RCAust.; OXLP-7534 77.43

*75. LA BOHÈME: O soave fanciulla (Puccini) (I) (w. Enrico Caruso) (or. W. Rogers)
C-4326-3,-4 1 Apr. '07 — — — — — —

76. RIGOLETTO: Tutte le feste al tempio (Verdi) (I) (w. Giuseppe Campanari) (or. W. Rogers)
C-4361-1 1 Apr. '07 — — — — — —

V. THE GRAMOPHONE COMPANY (Paris)

*77. LA VIE DE BOHÈME: On m'appelle Mimi (Mi chiamano Mimi) (Puccini) (F) (w. orch.)
602-i (?)9 May '08 033062 DB-702rr — — — RLS-719; GBC-3; Scala 846 73.47

VI. VICTOR TALKING MACHINE CO. (New York)

78. En sourdine (Fêtes Galantes, Series I, No. 1) (Paul Verlaine—Claude Debussy) (F) (pf. Nellie Melba)
C6697-1 1 Jan. '09 (033076) — — IRCC-35 RCAust.; TQD-3005 75.00

79. Down in the Forest (No. 2 from "A Cycle of Life") (Harold Simpson—Landon Ronald) (E) (pf. N. Melba)
C-6698-1 1 Jan. '09 (03130) — — IRCC-52 RCAust. 75.00
AGSB-67

80. The White Sea Mist (No. 5 from "In Sunshine and Shadow") (Harold Simpson—Landon Ronald) (E) (pf. N. Melba)
C-6699-1,-2 1 Jan. '09 (03134) — — IRCC-52 RCAust.; Cantilena 6207; B&B-3 75.00
AGSB-53

| | | | | Victor | "78" rpm | Re-recordings on | Speed of Original |
Matrix No. Date	G&T/HMV Single Fce.	G&T/HMV Double Fce.	Victor Sgl. Fce.	Dble. Fce.	reissues	Long-Playing Discs	Issue
81. D'une prison (Paul Verlaine-Reynaldo Hahn) (F) (pf. N. Melba)							
C-6700-1 1 Jan. '09	(033077)	—	88151	—	—	RCAust.; TQD-3005	75.00
82. Believe Me, If All Those Endearing Young Charms (Thomas Moore—Old Irish Air)(E) (pf. N. Melba)							
C-6701-1,2 1 Jan. '09	03131	DB-357	88156	—	—	RCAust.; OXLP-7534	75.00
	03694						
*83. OTELLO: Piangea cantando . . . O Salce! Salce- (Willow song) (Verdi) (I) (or. W. Rogers)							
C-6704-1 6 Jan. '09	053211	—	88148	—	—	RCAust.	75.00
*84. OTELLO: Ave Maria (Verdi) (I) (or. W. Rogers)							
C-6705-1 6 Jan. '09	053212	—	88149	—	—	RCAust.	75.00
*85. LA BOHÈME: Donde lieta uscì al tuo grido d'amore (Addio) (Puccini) (I) (or. W. Rogers)							
C-4341-2 6 Jan. '09	053111	—	—	—	—	RCAust.	75.00
*86. O Lovely Night (from "Summertime") (Edward Teschemacher—Landon Ronald) (E) (or. W. Rogers)							
C-6706-1 6 Jan. '09	03133	—	(88157)	—	—	RCAust.	75.00
			88182				
87. Ye Banks and Braes o' Bonnie Doon (Robert Burns—Tune: Miller's "Caledonian Hunt's Delight") (E) (pf. N. Melba)							
C-6707-1,-2 6 Jan. '09	03132	DB-362	88150	6218	—	RCAust.	75.00
	03696						

VII. THE GRAMOPHONE COMPANY, LTD. (London)

*87A. Jean (Frank Lebby Stanton—Harry Thacker Burleigh) (E) (pf. Landon Ronald)							
11689e 11 May '10	—	—	—	—	—	—	78.26
88. TOSCA: Vissi d'arte, vissi d'amore (Puccini) (I) (w. New Symphony Orchestra, cond. L. Ronald)							
4183f 11 May '10	2-053020	DB-702	—	—	—	RLS-719	77.43
*89. DON CÉSAR DE BAZAN: A Séville, belles Señoras (Jules Ruelle—Jules Massenet) (F) (w. New Symphony Orchestra, cond. L. Ronald)							
4184f 11 May '10	—	—	—	—	—	RLS-719	77.43

90. LOHENGRIN: Sola ne' miei prim' anni (Elsa's dream) (Wagner) (I) (w. New Symphony Orchestra, cond. L. Ronald)
4185f   11 May '10   2-053019   DB-366   —   —   VB-53   RLS-719; TAP-322; Saga 7029; Can. 6207   77.43

91. TOSCA: Vissi d'arte, vissi d'amore (Puccini) (I) (w. New Symphony Orchestra, cond. L. Ronald)
4186f   11 May '10   —   —   —   —   RLS-719   77.43

*92. LA TRAVIATA: Parigi, o cara (?) (Verdi) (I) (w. John McCormack) (w. New Symphony Orchestra, cond. L. Ronald)
4187f   (?)12 May '10   —   —   —   —   —

93. FAUST: All'erta! All'erta! o tempo più non è! (Gounod) (I) (w. John McCormack & G. Mario Sammarco) (w. New Symphony Orchestra, cond. L. Ronald)
4188f   (?)12 May '10   —   —   —   RLS-719; Cantilena 6207   76.00

94. RIGOLETTO: Bella figlia dell'amore (Verdi) (I) (w. Edna Thornton, John McCormack & G. Mario Sammarco) (or. L. Ronald)
4189f   (?)12 May '10   2-054025   DM-118   —   —   RLS-719; BC-233; Saga 7029; A-110   77.43

95. FAUST: All'erta! All'erta! o tempo più non è! (Gounod) (I) (w. John McCormack & G. Mario Sammarco) (w. New Symphony Orchestra, cond. L. Ronald)
4190f   (?)12 May '10   —   —   IRCC-7 15-1019   RLS-719; BC-233; Asco A-110   76.00

96. Bid Me Discourse (Wm. Shakespeare—Sir Henry Bishop) (E) (pf. L. Ronald)
4193f   (?)12 May '10   03188   DB-347   —   —   RLS-719; Cantilena 6207   77.43

97. The Sounds of Earth Grow Faint (No. 4 from "Four Impressions") (Mrs. Norman Grosvenor—Landon Ronald) (pf. L. Ronald)
4194f   (?)12 May '10   —   —   —   —   RLS-719   77.43

*98. Distance Test (Vocalises on phrases from Hamlet Mad Scene) (pf. L. Ronald)
4195f   (?)12 May '10   —   —   —   —   RLS-719; TQD-305; MLG-54; EJS-127   77.43

*99. DON CÉSAR DE BAZAN: A Séville, belles Señoras (Jules Ruelle—Jules Massenet) (F) (w. New Symphony Orchestra, cond. L.Ronald)
4206f   19 May '10   —   —   —   —   RLS-719   77.43

*100. DON CÉSAR DE BAZAN: A Séville, belles Señoras (Jules Ruelle—Jules Massenet) (F) (w. New Symphony Orchestra, cond. L. Ronald)
4207f   19 May '10   —   —   —   —   RLS-719   77.43

101. LE CID: Pleurez, pleurez, mes yeux (Massenet) (F) (w. New Symphony Orchestra, cond. L. Ronald)
4208f   19 May '10   2-033020   DB-711   —   —   RLS-719; Saga 7029; Rococo 17   77.43

102. Soir païen (Georges Hue) (F) (flute John Lemmoné; pf. L. Ronald)
4209f   19 May '10   —   —   —   —   RLS-719; TQD-3005; Rococo 17   77.43

Matrix No. / Date	G&T/HMV Single Fce.	G&T/HMV Double Fce.	Victor Sgl. Fce.	Victor Dbl. Fce.	"78" rpm reissues	Re-recordings on Long-Playing Discs	Speed of Original Issue
103. Spring (Thomas Nash—Sir George Henschel) (E) (pf. L. Ronald)							
4210f 19 May '10	—	—	—	—	—		
104. Hear My Prayer: Oh! for the Wings of a Dove (Psalm 55—Felix Mendelssohn) (E) (pf. L. Ronald)							
4211f 19 May '10	—	—	—	—	—		
105. Hear My Prayer: Oh! for the Wings of a Dove (Psalm 55—Felix Mendelssohn) (E) (pf. L. Ronald)							
4212f 19 May '10	03199	DB-351	—	—	—	RLS-719	77.43
106. Spring (Thomas Nash—Sir George Henschel) (E) (pf. L. Ronald)							
4213f 19 May '10	03328	—	—	—	IRCC-181	RLS-719	77.43
107. Pur dicesti, o bocca, bocca bella (from ARMINIO) (Antonio Lotti) (I) (pf. L. Ronald)							
4214f 19 May '10	—	—	—	—	—	RLS-719; GVC-3; EJS-127; R-17; Scala 846	77.43

VIII. VICTOR TALKING MACHINE COMPANY (Camden, N.J.)

Matrix No. / Date	G&T/HMV Single Fce.	G&T/HMV Double Fce.	Victor Sgl. Fce.	Victor Dbl. Fce.	"78" rpm reissues	Re-recordings on Long-Playing Discs	Speed of Original Issue
108. LA BOHÈME: Mi chiamano Mimì (Puccini) (I) (or. Walter B. Rogers)							
C-4281-3,-4 22 Aug. '10	2-053025	DB-356	88074	6210	—	RCAust.; OXLP-7534	76.00
109. FAUST: Ah! je ris de me voir (Air des bijoux) (Gounod) (F) (or. W. Rogers)							
C-4338-2 22 Aug. '10	—	—	88066	6215	—	—	
-3 24 Aug. '10	2-033022	DB-361	—	—	—	RCAust.; Saga 7029	76.00
*110. LA TRAVIATA: Ah! fors' è lui . . . Follie! Follie! . . . Sempre libera (Verdi) (I) (or. W. Rogers)							
C-4339-2 22 Aug. '10	—	—	88064	—	—	—	
-3 23 Aug. '10	2-053029 (?)053108	—	—	—	—	RCAust.; Saga 7029; Scala 875	76.00
111. Good-bye (George John Whyte-Melville—F. Paolo Tosti) (E) (or. W. Rogers)							
C-4340-2 22 Aug. '10	—	—	88065	6222	—	—	
-3 26 Aug. '10	03206	DB-358	—	—	—	RCAust.; OXLP-7534; Scala 875	76.00

No.	Title / Recording	Matrix	Date						Issues	Price
*112.	LA BOHÈME: Donde lieta usci al tuo grido d'amore (Puccini) (I) (or. W. Rogers)	C-4341-3,-4	23 Aug. '10	2-053028	DB-356	88072	6210	—	RCAust.	76.00
113.	Lo, Here the Gentle Lark! (Wm. Shakespeare—Sir Henry Bishop) (E) (flute John Lemmoné; or. W. Rogers)	C-4350-3	23 Aug. '10	03203	DB-348	88073	6214	—	RCAust.; OXLP-7534; Cantilena 6207	76.00
114.	LE NOZZE DI FIGARO: Voi che sapete (Mozart) (I) (or. W. Rogers)	C-4353-2	23 Aug. '10	2-053027	DB-367	88067	6219	—	RCAust.; OXLP-7534; BC-233; LCT-1039	76.00
115.	Se saran rose (P. Mazzoni—Luigi Arditi) (I) (or. W. Rogers)	C-4356-2	23 Aug. '10	2-053023	DB-349	88076	6220	—	RCAust.; Scala 875	76.00
116.	TOSCA: Vissi d'arte, vissi d'amore (Puccini)(I) (or. W. Rogers)	C-4282-3	24 Aug. '10	—	—	—	—	—		76.00
		-4	25 Aug. '10	2-053024	—	88075	6220	—	RCAust.; Scala 875	
117.	IL PENSIEROSO: Sweet Bird That Shunn'st the Noise of Folly (John Milton—G. F. Handel) (E) (flute J. Lemmoné; or. W. Rogers)	C-4358-2	24 Aug. '10	03089	DB-350	88068	6214	—	RCAust.; Scala 875	76.00
*118.	LUCIA DI LAMMERMOOR: Ardon g l'incensi (Mad Scene) (Donizetti) (I) (flute J. Lemmoné; or. W. Rogers)	C-4349-3	24 Aug. '10	2-053026	DB-364	88071	6219 18143	—	RCAust.; OXLP-7534; Scala 875	76.00
*119.	DON CÉSAR DE BAZAN: A Séville, belles Señoras (Jules Ruelle—Jules Massenet) (F) (or. W. Rogers)	C-9370-1	24 Aug. '10	2-033023	DB-711	88252 88662	6216	—	RCAust.; Saga 7029	76.00
*120.	HAMLET: Des larmes de la nuit (Mad Scene) (Thomas) (F) (or. W. Rogers)	C-9371-1	25 Aug. '10	2-033024	DB-364	88251	6215	—	RCAust.; LCT-6704; TQD-3005; TAP-325	76.00
121.	LE ROI D'YS: Puisqu'on ne peut fléchir ces jalouses gardiennes . . . Vainement, ma bien aimée (Aubade) (Lalo) (F) (or. W. Rogers)	C-9372-1, -2	25 Aug. '10	2-033025	DB-354	88250	—	—	RCAust.; TQD-3005	76.00
*122.	OTELLO: Piangea cantando . . . O Salce! Salce! (Willow song) (Verdi) (I) (or. W. Rogers)	C-6704-2	25 Aug. '10	2-053022	DB-366	88148	6211	—	RCAust.; XIG-8015	76.00
*123.	OTELLO: Ave Maria (Verdi) (I) (or. W. Rogers)	C-6705-2	25 Aug. '10	2-053021	DM-118	88149	6211	—	RCAust.; OXLP-7534; XIG-8015; Rococo 17	76.00

Matrix No. Date	G&T/HMV Single Fce.	G&T/HMV Double Fce.	Victor Sgl. Fce.	Victor Dble. Fce.	"78" rpm reissues	Re-recordings on Long-Playing Discs	Speed of Original Issue
*124. O Lovely Night (from "Summertime") (Edward Teschemacher—Landon Ronald) (E) (or. W. Rogers)							
C-6706-2 26 Aug. '10	03204	DB-350	88182	6222	AGSB-67	RCAust.; Scala 875	76.00
125. STABAT MATER: Inflammatus (Giacomo Rossini) (Latin) (or. W. Rogers)							
C-9373-1 26 Aug. '10	—		—	—	—	—	
126. Bid Me Discourse (Wm. Shakespeare—Sir Henry Bishop) (E) (Pf. C.H.H. Booth)							
C-9374-1 26 Aug. '10	—		—	—	—	—	
*127. By the Brook (Idyll) (Paul Wetzger) (Flute solo by John Lemmoné, pf. Nellie Melba)							
C-9375-1,-2 26 Aug. '10	—		—	—	—	—	
-3,-4 7 Nov. '10	09151	D-477	70023	55111	—	RCAust.	76.00

IX. THE GRAMOPHONE COMPANY, LTD. (London)

Matrix No. Date	G&T/HMV Single Fce.	G&T/HMV Double Fce.	Victor Sgl. Fce.	Victor Dble. Fce.	"78" rpm reissues	Re-recordings on Long-Playing Discs	Speed of Original Issue
128. Chanson triste (J. Lahor—H. Duparc) (F) (pf. Gabriel Lapierre)							
Y-16572e 6 May '13	7-33004	DA-334	—	—	—	RLS-719	78.26
*129. Ave Maria (Bach—Gounod) (Latin) (Vln. Jan Kubelik; pf. Gabriel Lapierre; organ Stanley Roper)							
Z-7321f 6 May '13	—	—	—	—	—	—	
Z-7323f 6 May '13	03333	—	—	—	—	RLS-719	78.26
130. IL RE PASTORE: L'amerò, sarò costante (Mozart) (I) (Vln. J. Kubelik; pf. G. Lapierre)							
Z-7322f 6 May '13	2-053083	DK-112	—	—	—	RLS-719; Cantilena 6207	78.26
131. Le temps des lilas (from Poème de l'amour et de la mer) (M. Bouchor—E. Chausson, Op. 19) (pf. G. Lapierre)							
Z-7324f 6 May '13	—	—	—	—	—	—	
Z-7325f 6 May '13	2-033037	—	—	—	IRCC-7	RLS-719; Cantilena 6207	78.26

X. VICTOR TALKING MACHINE COMPANY (Camden, N.J.)

Matrix No. Date	G&T/HMV Single Fce.	G&T/HMV Double Fce.	Victor Sgl. Fce.	Victor Dble. Fce.	"78" rpm reissues	Re-recordings on Long-Playing Discs	Speed of Original Issue
*132. IL RE PASTORE: L'amerò, sarò costante (Mozart) (I) (Vln. Jan Kubelik; pf. Gabriel Lapierre)							
C-13896-1,-2 2 Oct. '13	2-033044	—	89074	—	—	RCAust.	76.00

*133. Ave Maria (Meditation on Bach's Prelude, WTC 1—Ch. F (Gounod) (Latin) (Vln. J. Kubelik; pf. G. Lapierre)

Matrix	Date						Label	Price
C-13897-1,-2	2 Oct. '13	03333 / 03364	DK-112	89073	—	—	RCAust.	76.00

134. Magdalen at Michael's Gate (Henry Kingsley—Liza Lehmann) (E) (pf. G. Lapierre)

C-13898-1	2 Oct. '13	03370	DB-709	88452	—	—	RCAust.	76.00

135. (a) Romance (L'âme évaporée et souffrante) (from "Deux Romances": P. Bourget—C. Debussy) (F) (pf. G. Lapierre)
(b) Mandoline (Paul Verlaine—Claude Debussy) (pf. G. Lapierre)

C-13899-1	2 Oct. '13	—	—	—	—	—	—	
-2	3 Oct. '13	2-033042	DB-709	88456	—	—	RCAust.; Cantilena 6207	76.00

136. LOUISE: Depuis le jour (Charpentier) (F) (or. Walter B. Rogers)

C-13900-1	3 Oct. '13	2-033076	DB-354	88477	6216	—	RCAust.	75.00
-2	3 Oct. '13							

137. LOUISE: Depuis le jour (Charpentier) (F) (pf. G. Lapierre)

C-13903-1	3 Oct. '13	—	—	—	—	—	RCAust.; Cantilena 6207	76.00

138. Old Folks at Home (Stephen C. Foster) (or. W. Rogers)

C-13904-1,-2	3 Oct. '13	03363	DB-348	88454	6217	—	RCAust.	75.00

139. John Anderson, My Jo (Robert Burns—Maud Valérie White) (E) (pf. G. Lapierre)

C-13905-1	3 Oct. '13	03371	DB-363	88455	—	—	RCAust.; Cantilena 6207	76.00

140. Chanson triste (J. Lahor—H. Duparc) (F) (pf. G. Lapierre)

C-13906-1	3 Oct. '13	—	—	—	—	—	—	

*141. Phidylé (L. de Lisle—H. Duparc) (F) (pf. G. Lapierre)

C-.......	3 Oct. '13	—	—	—	—	—	—	

142. Comin' thro' the Rye (Robert Burns—Old Scottish Air) (E) (pf. G. Lapierre)

C-13907-1	4 Oct. '13	03369	DB-362	88449	6218	—	RCAust.	76.00

143. (a) Les Anges pleurent (G. Audigier—H. Bemberg); (b) Chant Vénitien (G. Roussel—H. Bemberg) (F) (pf. G. Lapierre)

C-13908-1	4 Oct. '13	(2-033043)	—	(88457)	—	AGSB-53	RCAust.; Cantilena 6207	76.00

*144. Le temps des lilas (from Poème de l'amour et de la mer) (M. Bouchor—E. Chausson, Op. 19) (pf. G. Lapierre)

C-.......	4 Oct. '13	—	—	—	—	—	—	

145. Vocal Lesson No. 1 (pf. Nellie Melba)

C-13909-1	4 Oct. '13	—	—	—	—	—	—	

Matrix No. / Date	G&T/HMV Single Fce.	G&T/HMV Double Fce.	Victor Sgl. Fce.	Victor Dble. Fce.	"78" rpm reissues	Re-recordings on Long-Playing Discs	Speed of Original Issue
146. Annie Laurie (William Douglass—Lady John Scott) (E) (or. W. Rogers)							
C-17001-1 12 Jan. '16	03523	DB-357	88551	6217	—	RCAust.; Cantilena 6207	76.00
147. Songs My Mother Taught Me (No. 4 from "Gypsy Songs," Heyduk—Dvořák, Op. 55) (E) (or. W. Rogers)							
C-17002-1,-2 12 Jan. '16	03695	DB-363	88485	—	—	RCAust.	76.00
148. Annie Laurie (William Douglass—Lady John Scott) (E) (pf. Frank St. Leger)							
C-17003-1 12 Jan. '16	—	—	—	—	—	—	
*149. Songs My Mother Taught Me (No. 4 from "Gypsy Songs," Heyduk—Dvořák, Op. 55) (E) (pf. F. St. Leger)							
C-17004-1 12 Jan. '16	—	—	(88553)	—	—	RCAust.; StARS 1000	76.00

XI. THE GRAMOPHONE COMPANY, LTD. (Hayes, Middlesex)

Matrix No. / Date	G&T/HMV Single Fce.	G&T/HMV Double Fce.	Victor Sgl. Fce.	Victor Dble. Fce.	"78" rpm reissues	Re-recordings on Long-Playing Discs	Speed of Original Issue
150. SADKO: Les diamants chez nous sont innombrables (Chanson indoue) (Rimsky-Korsakov) (F) (or. Landon Ronald)							
Cc-147-1,-2 12 May '21	03759	DB-358	—	—	—	RLS-719; OASI-562	76.60
151. (a) Away on the Hill There Runs a Stream (from "Four Songs of the Hill") (Landon Ronald) (E) (pf. L. Ronald)							
(b) Down in the Forest (No. 2 from "A Cycle of Life") (Harold Simpson—Landon Ronald) (E) (pf. L. Ronald)							
Cc-148-1 12 May '21	—	—	—	—	—	RLS-719; EJS-532	76.60
152. By the Waters of Minnetonka (J. M. Cavanass—Thurlow Lieurance) (E) (pf. L. Ronald)							
Bb-149-1 12 May '21	2-3568	DA-334	—	—	—	RLS-719; OASI-562	76.60
153. Annie Laurie (William Douglass—Lady John Scott) (E) (pf. Nellie Melba)							
Bb-150-1 12 May '21	—	—	—	—	—	RLS-719	76.60
*154. Home, Sweet Home (from CLARI, THE MAID OF MILAN) (John Howard Paine—Sir Henry Bishop) (E) (pf. N. Melba)							
Cc-151-1 12 May '21	03049	DB-351	—	—	—	RLS-719	76.60

XII. THE GRAMOPHONE COMPANY (Royal Opera House, Covent Garden)

Recorded during actual performance during Melba's Farewell, 8 June 1926. (w. Royal Opera House Orchestra, conducted by Vincenzo Bellezza. Speeds of originals all 78.26 rpm)

No.	Matrix No.	Title (Beginning words . . .)	Ricordi Score Pg. Ref.	Artists	78 rpm Cat. Nos.	Dubbings on Lp.
155.	CR-417	OTELLO: Piangea cantando (Willow song, pt. 1)	328-332	Melba	IRCC-2 DB-1500	7ER-5201; RLS-719; RLS-742; RLS-751; EJS-127; EJS-144; OASI-562; MLG-84
156.	CR-418	OTELLO:Scendean gli augelli (Willow song, pt. 2)	332-337	Melba	—	RLS-719; RLS-751; EJS-127; EJS-144; MLG-84
157.	CR-419	OTELLO: Ave Maria	338-341	Melba	—	RLS-719; RLS-742; EJS-127; EJS-144; MLG-84
158.	CR-411	LA BOHÈME: Entrate. . . C'è Rodolfo?	181-191	Melba, John Brownlee	—	RLS-719; RLS-742; EJS-127; EJS-144; MLG-84
159.	CR-412	LA BOHÈME: Donde lieta uscì (Addio)	206-209	Melba	DB-943 DB-1500 ND-973	7-ER-5201; RLS-719; RLS-707; RLS-742; OASI-562; MLG-84; EJS-127
160.	CR-413	LA BOHÈME: Addio, dolce svegliare	210-222	Melba, Brownlee, Aurora Rettore, Browning Mummery	—	7ER-5201; RLS-719; EJS-127; MLG-84
161.	CR-414	LA BOHÈME: Gavotta. Minuetto	242-251	Melba, Brownlee, Rettore, Mummery, Frederic Collier, Edouard Cotreuil	—	RLS-719; EJS-127; MLG-84
162.	CR-415	LA BOHÈME: Sono andati?	261-269	Melba, Mummery	—	RLS-719; EJS-127; MLG-84
163.	CR-416	LA BOHÈME: Oh come è bello	271-277	Melba, Mummery, Brownlee, Rettore, Collier, Cotreuil	—	RLS-719; EJS-127; MLG-84; OASI-562
	(CR-420 Address by Lord Stanley of Alderley, Ex-Governor-General of Victoria)					RLS-719; EJS-127; MLG-84
164.	CR-421	Farewell Speech		Melba	DB-943 ND-973	7-ER-5201; RLS-719; RLS-742; MLG-84; EJS-127; OASI-562

XIII. THE GRAMOPHONE COMPANY (Small Queens Hall, London)

Matrix No. Date	G&T/HMV Single Fce.	G&T/HMV Double Fce.	Victor Sgl. Fce.	Victor Dbl. Fce.	"78" rpm reissues	Re-recordings on Long-Playing Discs	Speed of Original Issue
165. LA TRAVIATA: Dite alla giovine (Verdi) (I) (w. John Brownlee) (pf. Harold Craxton)							
Cc-9550-1 17 Dec. '26	2-054171	DB-987	—	—	VB-64	RLS-719; OASI-562	78.26
166. Un ange est venu (Paul Mariéton—Hermann Bemberg) (F) (w. John Brownlee) (pf. H. Craxton)							
Cc-9551-1A 17 Dec. '26	2-034041	DB-987	—	—	VB-64	RLS-719; OASI-562	78.26
167. Clair de lune (Paul Verlaine—Joseph Szulc, Op. 83 No. 1) (F) (pf. H. Craxton)							
Cc-9552-1,-2 17 Dec. '26	2-033115	DB-989	—	6733	—	RLS-719; OASI-562	78.26
*168. Swing Low, Sweet Chariot (Traditional, arr. H. T. Burleigh) (E) (pf. H. Craxton)							
Cc-9553-1A 17 Dec. '26	03894	DB-989	—	6733	—	RLS-719; EJS-564; OASI-562	78.26

KEY TO RECORD LABELS: LONG PLAYING REISSUES

AGSB: American Gramophone Society (78s)

Asco: American Stereophonic Corp.

B&B: B & B Records

BC: Bel Canto Disc

Can: Cantilena Records

COLH: EMI Ltd.

EJS: Golden Age of Opera

GVC: Ember

IRCC: International Record Collectors' Club (78s and Lps.)

LCT; LM: RCA Victor (USA)

MH: Murray Hill

MLG: Opus

OSAI: Violi

ORL: Olympus

OXLP: EMI Ltd.

R (or Rococo): Ross, Court & Co.

RCAust: RCA Records Australia

StARS: Stanford Archive of Recorded Sound

TAP: Top Artists Platters

TQD: Delta

VB: The Gramophone Co. (78s)

XIG: Heritage

NOTES ON THE RECORDINGS

2. As noted, there are four presentations of the Mapleson Melba *Les Huguenots* recording. The first, issued as a single-faced disc (5002) in May 1939, is the only one of the four that contains the dubbing of the complete cylinder, beginning with the words "A ce mot tout s'anime" (page 128 of the Benoit score) and is by far the best transcription from a technical sense, being much more forward and having less objectionable filtering. Unfortunately, the cylinder was turning at the wrong speed, and to reproduce this first disc edition in the correct key, it must be played at 87.80 rpm. The performance date on the label of this edition is given as March 11, 1901. A second dubbing, which is reproduced in the correct key at 78.26 rpm, is found on IRCC 3034, issued in August 1943. Because of some damage which occurred to the opening grooves of the original cylinder after the first transcription was made, this recording begins with the words "Le ruisseau le répète" (p. 129 of the Benoit score), some ten bars later than the initial release. The date is given as 1901 on this edition. The third IRCC edition was on a 10" Lp (L-7006), published in May 1955. The selection is reproduced in pitch at 33⅓ rpm, but the shortened version is used (but still titled with the opening words of the initial release) and the date is still given as March 11, 1901. On the 12" Lp disc (L-7032) (January 1967) the dubbing is reproduced slightly below pitch and is by far the poorest of the four transfers. It too is the abbreviated version, but the date has been corrected to January 28, 1901.

9 through 25. The date for these recordings has always been given as "March 1904." It would appear that at least three recording sessions are involved, each producing recordings of slightly different speeds. It is known that the first Melba sessions (thus perhaps all those for March 1904(?)) were made at the singer's home at 30 Great Cumberland Place, Mayfair. It is said that Melba made these recordings to send to her father in Australia and was later persuaded to release them for public sale. Matrix numbers not listed (Nos. 3, 4, 5, 10, 11, 14, 17, 18, 19, and 24) are missing, and there is no information about them in the EMI files today. We can speculate that Nos. 10 and 11 were probably the beginning of the *Lucia* Mad Scene, since No. 12 is the conclusion of this scene. The owner of the unique copy of the *Il Pensieroso* (Discography No. 15) has told the author that the test copy bears no numbers whatsoever; it is shown as No. 14 in the EMI booklet to accompany set RLS-719, and since this copy was used, the assignment of No. 14 must have been speculation on the part of the producer. How much more logical would be the surmise that the selection was originally intended to be made in two parts: that Matrix 13 was the version with the error, which was then remade as No. 14, with the second part following as No. 15(?).

11. The original Matrix No. 6 contained the complete aria, recitative, and cabaletta (that is, the parts designated a, b, and c). The "Sempre libera," however, was rushed, and the end of the recording was cut too close to the center of the disc. In pressing copies of 03017 (and Victor 95014), a plate was placed over the inner grooves, so that the published record ended just before the piano introduction to the "Follie! Follie!" Special pressings of Matrix 6, however, disclosed that even though scratched by six radial lines, the inner portion of the record could still be played. Long-playing editions dubbed from the original issue, therefore, contain only the first part of the aria; later dubbings made use of the marked-out "Follie" portion, joined to the later separate recording of the "Sempre libera" (Discography No. 21), even though the latter was recorded at a different speed and was with orchestra. Finally, the EMI set RLS-719 contains the first public release of the entire recording of Matrix 6.

12. Unpublished except as long play, although a catalog number was assigned. The selection is very short, and the recording machine was allowed to run for about 40 seconds after the final note. Sounds of a conversation can be heard faintly, presumably between Melba and Ronald, and perhaps the technicians, but no specific words can be distinguished.

14. There are three published commercial recordings of portions of the Mad Scene: Discography Nos. 14, 64, and 118. Each begins at a slightly different point. As noted above, the March 1904 recording (No. 14) was probably the second or third of a multipart recording, as it opens with the last two lines of the first part of the aria, just before the cadenza. The 1910 recording (No. 118) begins with "Ardon gl'incensi," some forty-five seconds before the "Alfin son tua," which opens the 1907 recording (No. 64).

15 (and 16). The master for this recording was destroyed, but it exists in one unnumbered test pressing. At a point just before the beginning of the cadenza, Melba makes a false start and can be heard to exclaim, "No, no . . . oh bother (?) it. . . . We'll have to begin it all over again." Apparently, the remake (Matrix 14(?)) was for some reason not acceptable and was destroyed, but the cadenza portion (Matrix 15) received publication. Two long-playing dubbings overlapped Part 1, cutting off just before the error, and matching the cadenza portion of Matrix 15. EMI set RLS-719 first gives the matched version and, as an "appendix," presents a dubbing of the complete first side with the error and Melba's comments. These are also heard on EJS-142.

18. The 1904 and the 1907 (Discography Nos. 18 and 68) versions of the *Hamlet* Mad Scene, Part 1, cover exactly the same music, both ending with the words "Et moi je suis Ophélie" (page 289 of the Heugel score). The 1904 Part 2 (No. 19) begins with the recitative for the Ballade ("Et maintenant écoutez . . . ," p. 293), while the 1907 Part 2 (No. 69) begins three bars later ("Pâle et blonde . . ."). Both versions have the same cut from the bottom of page 295 to the top of page 298 to the descending staccato phrase (marked "pleurant") and continue to the bottom of the page through "Bonheur suprême!" Here the 1904 version has a reprise of 10 bars and continues to the end of the aria, while the 1907 version drops one bar before concluding. The shortened 1910 version (No. 120) compresses the whole scene onto one record side. It begins on page 286, with "Des larmes de la nuit," cuts after ten bars to "Pâle et blonde," and has additional cuts to the end of the scene.

19. See note 18.

25. Unpublished except on Lp, although a catalog number was assigned. There is a piano chord after the first "addio" and before "senza rancor"; also piano chords with final "senza rancor," concluding with two piano chords, as in the score. See also note 34.

26 through 34. Recorded at 21 City Road, London.

29. A test pressing of this recording is known to be in a private collection; unfortunately, it was not made available for the MI RLS-719 Lp release.

34. No piano chord after first "addio"; final "addio, senza rancor" is unaccompanied, and there are no concluding piano chords. See note 25.

35. The original issue of this recording bore a special mauve label reading "Special Gramophone Record made for Madame Melba. The profits on the sale of this record are devoted to the fund for the unemployed inaugurated by H. M. Queen Alexandra," as well as the date, November 1905. The December 1905 issue of *The Phono Trader and Recorder* carried a full-page advertisement headed QUEEN ALEXANDRA'S UNEMPLOYED FUND over a photograph of Mme. Melba. This is followed by the statement that "Madame Melba approached us as soon as H. M. The Queen inaugurated the above fund. With the help of H. M. Band of the Coldstream Guards, conducted by Lieut. Mackenzie Rogan, a Record was made by Madame Melba of GOD SAVE THE KING. Madame Melba gave her services for nothing and the profit on the sale of this record will be credited to the above Fund." The price was given as 12/6, and the advertisement carried the name of The Gramophone & Typewriter, Ltd., 21 City Road, London. The same publication had a companion article stating that the directors of the Gramophone Company "have already sent a contribution of £500 to the fund on account of sales" and urging dealers to support the cause. "Send your orders in at once and let them be large."

36 and 37. The one-half after a matrix number usually indicated a second take; so presumably there were unpublished and destroyed first takes of these two selections.

46. The standard soprano key is "G," which Melba used in the October 1904 recordings; in addition, the label for 03069 specifies key of G. This requires that the record be played at 81.00 rpm, which is at variance with the speeds of the other recordings made at this session.

49. The label for this recording gives the key as "F Natural," which is obviously a printer's error, as it is certainly sung in the published key of D. The record opens with "Mi chiamano . . ." (the "Si" is omitted), and there is a lengthy cut of sixteen bars following ". . . mio svago gar gigli e rose" to "Sola mi fo il pranzo." However, Melba sings the final bars, beginning "Altro di mi non le saprei . . ." which is omitted from subsequent recordings.

58. The recitative "Follie! Follie!" before the "Sempre libera" is cut in this recording but was included in the August 23 remake (No. 110). Normally, the 1910 series was used when double-faced records were pressed beginning in 1923. However, in this case, the 1907 version was used for the double-faced pressings in both the United States and England.

60. See note **112**.

64. See note **14**.

68 and 69. See note **18**.

75. The duet, first recorded on March 24 (No. 55), was apparently considered not entirely satisfactory for some reason, so an attempt was made to remake it on April 1, but both takes made that day were destroyed, and the first take was finally released.

77. This single recording from the Paris branch of the Gramophone Company has been something of a mystery. Surely Melba would not have gone to the "laboratories" to make a single disc! The recording books cannot now be located, and no other parts are on hand from this session at the EMI factory. Late copies of this recording were pressed from a new master made by mechanical dubbing and are marked 602i-2 (or 602j-2).

83. The second word Melba sings on this recording does not seem to be "contando" as in the score: it sounds something like "te mano." In the 1910 replacement (No. 122) she clearly sings "cantando." In the 1909 version there is very little emotion shown in the final "Emilia, addio, Emilia addio," whereas these phrases are sung with exaggerated emotion in the 1910 version.

84. The 1909 version begins with a single chord in the orchestra; the 1910 version (No. 123) with the six orchestral bars that open the scene.

85. This, Melba's fourth recording of the *Bohème* "Addio," is almost unknown. Although made in the United States, it was published for a short time only in Europe, probably only in countries served from the Hanover factory of the Gramophone Company. The master no longer exists at RCA or in any of the European plants. Melba holds the "addio" in "addio, senza rancor" some ten seconds; in both the 1907 and the 1910 versions she holds the "addio" about five seconds.

86. C-6706-1 (1909 recording). After Melba's final note there is a rest before final chord for the orchestra. Playing time 4'00" @ 75.00 rpm. In take 2 (Discography #124), there is no rest. Playing time 3'59" @ 76.00 rpm.

87A. During a search for Melba recordings at the Hayes factory some years ago, this Matrix number was reported to the author as a "Melba recording, title unknown," but the master could not be found. Recently, just as this discography was going to press, a copy turned up in a search for recordings by Edna Thornton. The author of the lyrics is Frank L. Stanton (1857-1927), better known for his "Jest a-wearyin' fer You" and "Mighty Lak' a Rose." The composer, H. T. Burleigh (1866-1949), was a negro baritone, composer, and arranger. As a young man he copied manuscripts for Antonín Dvořák and is credited with influencing the Czech composer in his use of American Negro spirituals in the *New World* Symphony. Burleigh published over 200 songs, including many arrangements of negro spirituals still in use today. "Jean" was also recorded by Paul Althouse, Claudia Muzio, and Evan Williams.

89. This is a vocal arrangement of the instrumental entr'acte preceding Act III of Massenet's second opera, which was first performed in 1872. This vocal arrangement was first published in 1895.

92. The title suggested for this recording is pure speculation. The original entry in the recording books merely notes a duet from *Traviata*; it could even have been by Melba and Sammarco. The entry further reads "broken," which usually meant that the wax had been broken in processing, so no copies could have been made. The booklet with EMI RLS-719 gives dates for this and subsequent titles through No. 98 as 11 May, but there is reason to believe they were made on the twelfth. In spite of much speculation with respect to the titles for matrix numbers 4191f, 4192f, and 4196f, there are no entries opposite these numbers in the recording ledgers, meaning that whatever the proposed selections may have been, they were not made.

98. Melba vocalizes on some phrases from the *Hamlet* Mad Scene, first close to the recording horn and then repeating the same phrases in successive moves away from the horn. Those tests close to the horn are full-voiced and brilliant, with the quality decreasing with more distance. Unfortunately, most of Melba's recordings were obviously made from the more distant positions, as the technicians were no doubt afraid of "blasting" in the closer positions.

99 and 100. See Note 89.

110. See Note 58.

112. Differences in three Victor versions of this selection may be summarized as follows.

C-4341-1: The final "Addio, senza rancor" accompanied by chord in orchestra; "Addio, senza" held for 5 seconds. Playing time 3'00" @ 77.43 rpm.

C-4341-2: No U.S. release. Final "Addio" held for 10 seconds. Playing time 3'08" @ 75.00 rpm.

C-4341-3: The final "Addio, senza rancor" accompanied by harp arpeggio. "Addio, senza" held for 5 seconds. Playing time 3'16" @ 76.00 rpm.

118. See Note 14.

119. See Note 89.

120. See Note 18.

122. See Note 83.

123. See Note 84.

124. See Note 86.

127. It was Melba's custom to play the piano for her old friend John Lemmoné for a flute solo encore. Both Melba and Lemmoné were in the recording laboratory on August 26, 1910, and it was natural for the two artists to recreate the familiar concert scene. However, neither of the first two takes made in August was satisfactory for some reason, so the flute solo was remade on November 7. Melba made no recordings this day, and one wonders if she would pay a visit to the recording studio merely to play this one accompaniment. Could the published take be accompanied by some other pianist, even though the catalogs and labels always listed Melba as the accompanist? Unfortunately, the master no longer exists, so the metal part cannot be checked.

129. This recording was not satisfactory; it was quickly withdrawn and the American recording of the same selection (No. 133) was substituted, using the same British catalog number. Some British pressings of the American matrix reached the market with the original British label, showing organ by Roper.

132. The cadenza is by Saint-Saëns. This recording was never published in the United Kingdom, but a number was apparently assigned by the French branch of the Gramophone Company, so the recording may have been available in France.

133. See Note 129.

141 and 144. These were personal records made for the singer and were never assigned matrix numbers. The matrices cannot now be located, and no copies were found in Melba's personal collection at Coombe Cottage in 1960.

149. The master for this recording was approved by Melba for release but was destroyed in 1916 on technical grounds. A single test pressing was found at Coombe Cottage by the author in 1960, from which the indicated releases have been made.

154. The label on this recording states that the accompaniment is by Landon Ronald, but this is in error.

168. This is the last commercial recording Melba made. There is a persistent story which is revived every few years in the Australian press, each time with more fanciful improvements, that Melba made recordings in Australia, that these records were to be sealed for fifty years, and that these records have now been lost. The original story was innocent enough when it appeared in 1932: "As a tribute to the memory of the late Dame Nellie Melba, who died on February 23 last year, the Gramophone Co. (H.M.V.) has decided to present the Music Teachers' Association two records of the diva's voice and the metal matrices from which the disks are made. . . . The records are to be sealed and not opened for at least 50 years. Thus Dame Melba's voice will be preserved for future generations." The article went on to say that the records were Melba's "addio" from *La Bohème* and her farewell speech at Covent Garden in 1926. There was nothing said about the recordings' having been made in Australia. In 1958, the press carried a story which said in part: "Only a few technicians of His Master's Voice . . . and the singer herself have heard [the records]. After she sang in the record-cutting studio at Homebush, Sydney, about 1920, Dame Nellie ordered 'They are not to be played for 50 years.' "

An inquiry directed to the Sydney branch of the Gramophone Company brought a reply from the then (1958) Director of the Recording Division which said, among other things, that the Homebush factory had not been built in the 1920s, that if anyone would have recorded Melba he would have been in charge of operations, and, finally, that "we can assure you that no recordings have been made by our companies of Dame Nellie in this country. . . ."

A NOTE ON SUGGESTED PLAYING SPEEDS OF THE ORIGINAL RECORDINGS

For some reason, no written record was ever made in the early recording studios of the turntable speeds used when recordings were made. A deviation in speed of 4 revolutions per minute (rpm) changes the pitch (and thus the key) by one-half tone. Not only is the pitch incorrect when a record is not played at the speed at which it was recorded, but, even more important, the tone and quality of the voice is distorted. Thus it is extremely important to play these old recordings at a turntable speed that is as close as possible to that used when they were originally recorded. Since there is no historical record of the speeds used, these must be determined by adjusting the playback speed to an instrument that is correctly tuned. An organ is best for this purpose. All of the speeds given in this discography have been so determined. A variation of one rpm can be detected by the trained ear. The fact that playing speeds are given to two decimal points is not intended to suggest an accuracy to that degree. The most convenient method of ascertaining the speed of a revolving turntable is by use of a stroboscopic card placed on the turning record while it is playing. Such cards are designed with different bands of patterns or lines for certain specific speeds. These lines will appear to stand still when the table is revolving at the speed indicated for each band. The numbers shown for suggested playing speeds are equivalent to those on certain standard stroboscopes or are an arithmetical average of speeds falling between two named bands which appear to be revolving in opposite directions at the same rate. If the listener, using whatever method at his or her disposal, will attempt to adjust the turntable speed as closely as possible to those indicated, the records should be reproduced at very close to the original recording speeds.

TITLE INDEX OF RECORDINGS

Note: Numbers in this index refer to the discography numbers.

SELECTED BIBLIOGRAPHY

Aldrich, Richard (1903). "Mme. Melba's Concert: The Briliant Soprano Sings at Carnegie Hall with the Philadelphia Orchestra." N.Y.: *The New York Times* (13 December).

Aldrich, Richard (1908). "La Bohème at the Manhattan Opera House." N.Y.: *The New York Times* (16 December).

Aldrich, Richard (1913). "Mme. Melba Sings: A Great Audience Hears Her Concert at Carnegie Hall." N.Y.: *The New York Times* (22 October).

Aldridge, B. L. (1964) "The Victor Talking Machine Company." In Fagan, Ted, and Moran, William R. (1983). *The Encyclopedic Discography of Victor Records*, Vol. 1. Westport, Ct.: Greenwood Press.

Alfonte, James M. (1962). "Battles for *Bohème*." N.Y.: *Opera News*, Vol. 26, No. 10 (20 January).

Armstrong, William (1922). *The Romantic World of Music*. N.Y.: E. P. Dutton & Co.

Best, Ailwyn (1970). "How I Sang with Melba." London: *Opera*, Vol. 21, No. 12 (December).

Briggs, John (1969). *Requiem for a Yellow Brick Brewery: A History of the Metropolitan Opera*. Boston: Little, Brown and Company.

Brownlee, John (1954). "Melba and I." N.Y.: Saturday Review (25 December).

Burgess, Harry (1911). *My Musical Pilgrimage: An Unconventional Survey of Music and Musicians*. London: Simpkin, Marshall, Hamilton, Kent & Co.

Casey, Maie (1975). *Melba Re-visited*. Melbourne: Privately printed.

Chamier, J. Daniel (1938). *Percy Pitt of Covent Garden and the B.B.C.* London: Edward Arnold & Co.

Colson, Percy (1930). *I Hope They Won't Mind*. London: Eveleigh Nash & Grayson, Ltd.

Colson, Percy (1932). *Melba: An Unconventional Biography*. London: Grayson & Grayson.

Cone, John Frederick (1966). *Oscar Hammerstein's Manhattan Opera Company*. Norman: University of Oklahoma Press.

Cooke, James Francis (1921). *Great Singers on the Art of Singing: Educational Conferences with Foremost Artists*. Philadelphia: Theo. Presser Co. (Includes chapter entitled "Common Sense in Training and Preserving the Voice" by Nellie Melba. This material originally appeared in *The Etude* for January 1914, under the title "A Talk with a Girl Who Would be a Prima Donna.")

Danieli, Elena (1961). "What Melba Did to Help Me." London: *Music and Musicians* (May).

Davis, Ronald L. (1966). *Opera in Chicago*. N.Y.: Appleton-Century.

Dawson, Peter (1951). *Fifty Years of Song*. London: Hutchinson & Co.

deGogorza, Emilio (1937). "Emilio deGogorza Tells of Prima Donnas in the Early Days of Recording." N.Y.: *Opera News*, Vol. 2, No. 2 (22 November).

deWeerth, Ernest (1961). "Melba at Windsor Castle." N.Y.: *Opera News*, Vol. 25, No. 16 (25 February).

Dicker, Jan G. (1974). *J.C.W.: A Short Biography of James Cassius Williamson*. Rose Bay, N.S.W.: The Elizabeth Tudor Press.

Downes, Olin (1931). "Melba's Art of Song; Her Career in Perspective; The Age of Voices Gives Way to the Age of Machines." N.Y.: *The New York Times* (1 March 1931).

Duval, J. H. (1958). *Svengali's Secrets and Memoirs of the Golden Age*. N.Y.: Robert Speller & Sons, Publishers.

Eames, Emma (1927). *Some Memories and Reflections*. N.Y.: D. Appleton and Company (Reprint: 1977 Arno Press, with discography).

Eaton, Quaintance (1957). *Opera Caravan: Adventures of the Metropolitan on Tour (1883-1956)*. N.Y.: Farrar, Straus and Cudahy. (Contains detailed casts.)

Eaton, Quaintance (1965). *The Boston Opera Company*. N.Y.: Appleton-Century. (Contains detailed casts.)

Eaton, Quaintance (1968). *The Miracle of the Met: An Informal History of the Metropolitan Opera, 1883-1967*. N.Y.: Meredith Press.

Eulass, Elizabeth (1943). "Melba's Debut Fifty Years Ago." N.Y.: *Opera News*, Vol. 8, No. 6 (29 November).

Finck, Henry T. (1909). *Success in Music and How It Is Won*. N.Y.: Charles Scribner's Sons.

Foster, Roland (1949). *Come Listen to My Song*. Sydney: Collins.

Fraser, R. (1926). "Sound Photography: Scientist Photographs Melba's Voice." London: *The Sound Wave* (April).

Garden, Mary (and Biancolli, Louis) (1951). *Mary Garden's Story*. N.Y.: Simon and Schuster.

Gaisberg, Fred W. (1942). *The Music Goes Round*. N.Y.: The Macmillan Co. (Reprint: 1977 Arno Press). London: Robert Hale (1946) (as *Music on Record*).

Gelatt, Roland (1955). *The Fabulous Phonograph*. Philadelphia: J. B. Lippincott Company. London: Cassell & Company (1956).

Glackens, Ira (1963). *Yankee Diva: Lillian Nordica and the Golden Days of Opera*. N.Y.: Coleridge Press.

Goldin, Milton (1969). *The Music Merchants*. N.Y.: The Macmillan Company.

Hackett, Arthur (1956). "No Mad Scenes for Melba." N.Y.: *Opera News*, Vol. 21, No. 4 (3 December).

Hall, David (1981). "The Mapleson Cylinder Project at the Rodgers and Hammerstein Archives of Recorded Sound, New York Public Library: A Preliminary Report. Hyattsville, Md.: *Journal Association for Recorded Sound Collections*, Vol. 13, No. 3.

Hall, David (1982). "The Mapleson Cylinder Project (At Rodgers and Hammerstein Archives of Recorded Sound—Performing Arts Research Center, New York Public Library at Lincoln Center." London: *Recorded Sound—Journal of the British Institute of Recorded Sound*, No. 82 (July).

Hall, David (1983). "The Mapleson Cylinder Project, Part II." London: *Recorded Sound—Journal of the British Institute of Recorded Sound*, No. 83 (January).

Haughton, John Alan (1931). "Melba's Career a Long Succession of Triumphs." N.Y.: *Musical America* (March 10).

Henderson, William James (1938). *The Art of Singing*. N.Y.: The Dial Press.

Hetherington, John (1967). *Melba: A Biography*. Melbourne: F. W. Cheshire, Pty.; London: Faber & Faber. N.Y.: Farrar, Straus and Giroux, Inc. (1968) (with introduction by Francis Robinson).

Hurst, P. G. (1958). *The Age of Jean de Reszke: Forty Years of Opera, 1874-1914*. London: Christopher Johnson.

Kingston, Claude (1971). *It Don't Seem a Day Too Much*. Adelaide: Rigby Publishers, Ltd.

Klein, Hermann (1903). *Thirty Years of Musical Life in London, 1870-1900*. London: William Heinemann; N.Y.: The Century Co.

Klein, Hermann (1910). *Unmusical New York: A Brief Criticism of Triumphs, Failures and Abuses*. London & N.Y.: John Lane.

Klein, Herman* (1931a). "Melba: An Appreciation." London: *The Musical Times* (1 April).

Klein, Herman (1931b). *Great Woman-Singers of My Time*. London: George Routledge & Sons.

Klein, Herman (1933). *The Golden Age of Opera*. London: George Routledge & Sons.

Kolodin, Irving (1940). *The Metropolitan Opera, 1883-1939*. N.Y.: Oxford University Press.

Kolodin, Irving (1953). *The Story of the Metropolitan Opera, 1883-1950: A Candid History*. N.Y.: Alfred A. Knopf.

Krehbiel, Henry Edward (1908). *Chapters of Opera, Being Historical and Critical Observations and Records concerning the Lyric Drama in New York from Its Earliest Days Down to the Present Time*. N.Y.: Henry Holt & Co.

Krehbiel, Henry Edward (1919). *More Chapters of Opera, Being Historical and Critical Observations and Records concerning the Lyric Drama in New York from 1908 to 1918*. N.Y.: Henry Holt & Co.

Lahee, Henry C. (1898). *Famous Singers of To-Day and Yesterday*. Boston: L. C. Page & Co.

Lahee, Henry C. (1912). *The Grand Opera Singers of To-Day*. Boston: L. C. Page & Co.

---

*Hermann became Herman after World War I.

Lawton, Mary (1928). *Schumann-Heink: The Last of the Titans*. N.Y.: The Macmillan Company.

Ledbetter, Gordon T. (1977). *The Great Irish Tenor (John McCormack)*. N.Y.: Charles Scribner's Sons.

Legge, Robin H. (1931). "Melba." London: *Saturday Review* (28 February).

Leiser, Clara (1933). *Jean de Reszke and the Great Days of Opera*. London: Gerald Howe; N.Y.: Minton, Balch & Company (1934).

Lemmoné, John (1924). "The Merry Pipes of Pan." Melbourne: *The Herald* (7 June).

Lindsey, Joan (1962). *Time without Clocks*. Melbourne: F. W. Cheshire, Pty.

Mackenzie, Barbara, and Mackenzie, Findlay (1967). *Singers of Australia, from Melba to Sutherland*. Melbourne: Lansowne Press, Pty.

Maine, Basil (1931). "Melba." London: *The Spectator* (28 February).

Marchesi, Blanche (1923). *Singer's Pilgrimage*. London: Grant Richards.

Marchesi, Blanche (1936) (as interviewed by Constance Vaughan). "Melba, Dictator of Song, Suffered No Rivals." London: *Sunday Referee* (19 January).

Marchesi, Mathilde (1897). *Marchesi and Music: Passages from the Life of a Famous Singing Teacher*. N.Y.: Harper and Brothers.

McCormack, John (1918) (as transcribed by Pierre V. R. Key). *John McCormack: His Own Life Story*. Boston: Small, Maynard & Co. (Reprinted with added photographs and index, N.Y.: Vienna House, 1973).

McKay, Claude (1961). *This Is the Life: An Autobiography of a Newspaperman*. Sydney: Angus and Robertson.

Melba, Nellie (1895a). "The Care of the Voice." In *The Music of the Modern World*, edited by Anton Seidl. N.Y.: D. Appleton & Co.

Melba, Nellie (1895b). "Grand Opera." Philadelphia: *Lippincott's Monthly Magazine* (April).

Melba, Nellie (1898). "History of My Life." N.Y.: *The Musical Age* (25 August).

Melba, Nellie (1907). "The Gift of Song." N.Y.: *Century Magazine* (June).

Melba, Nellie (1909a). "Music as a Profession: Some Personal Advice." Sydney: *Lone Hand* (magazine) (1 February).

Melba, Nellie (1909b). "On the Science of Singing." In *Melba: A Biography* by Agnes G. Murphy. London: Chatto & Windus; N.Y.: Doubleday Page & Co. (Reprinted, 1974, N.Y.: AMS Press).

Melba, Nellie (1911). "Lecture on Diction to the Students of the Guildhall School of Music, London." Melbourne: *The Argus* (27 June) (reprinted in Mackenzie & Mackenzie (1967), *Singers of Australia*).

Melba, Nellie (1914). "A Talk with a Girl Who Would Be a Prima Donna." Philadelphia: *The Etude* (January). (Later included under the title "Common Sense in Training and Preserving the Voice," in James Francis Cooke (1921).

Melba, Nellie (no date, but 1915). *Melba's Gift Book of Australian Art and Literature*. Melbourne: George Robertson and Co.; London: Hodder & Stoughton. "The Entire Profits from the Sale of this Book Will be Devoted by Madam Melba to the Belgian Relief Fund."

Melba, Nellie (1921). "Common Sense in Training and Preserving the Voice." (Same text as originally appeared in *The Etude* for January 1914 under the title "A Talk with a Girl Who Would Be a Prima Donna," in James Francis Cooke (1921).

Melba, Nellie (1922). "Dame Nellie Melba: Her Methods Explained—Valuable Help for Singers." Adelaide: *The Advertiser*. (A series of newspaper articles in six parts which appeared during the month of April. The first of these articles became the first part of Melba's *Melba Method*.)

Melba, Nellie (1925a). "Melba on Life after Death: 'The True, Eternal Me.' " Melbourne: *The Herald* (26 October).

Melba, Nellie (1925b). *Melodies and Memories*. London: Thornton Butterworth, Ltd.; N.Y.: George H. Doran Company (1926) (Reprinted, N.Y. Books for Libraries Press (1970), and N.Y.: A.M.S. Press (1971). Reset with new introduction and notes by John Cargher, Melbourne (1980); Thomas Nelson, Australia and London: Hamish Hamilton (1981). In Swedish as *Mitt Liv Som Sångerska: En Divas Minnen och Upplevelser* (Stockholm: Wahuström & Widstrand, 1927). (Ghost-written by Beverley Nichols, this work first appeared in serial form in the United States in *Liberty Magazine* in 1925 and 1926.)

Melba, Nellie (1926). *Melba Method*. London & Sydney: Chappel & Co. (The first chapter in this work first appeared in *The Advertiser* (1922) *q.v.* In a letter dated April 18, 1983, Mr. Nichols stated to the author that he had also ghost-written this work. However, the material in *The Advertiser* had appeared prior to Nichols' association with Melba.)

Melba, Nellie (1927a). "Melba's Indictment: 'Our Musical Reputation a Myth.' " Melbourne: *The Herald* (5 September).

Melba, Nellie (1927b). "Where Is Happiness? Is It in Fame?" Melbourne: *The Herald* (10 September).

"Melba's Voice" (1931). (Editorial.) N.Y.: *New York Times* (1 March).

Moore, Edward C. (1930). *Forty Years of Opera in Chicago*. N.Y.: Horace Liveright. (Reprinted, N.Y.: Arno Press, 1977).

Moore, Jerrold Northrop (1976). *A Voice in Time: The Gramophone of Fred Gaisberg (1873-1951)*. London: Hamish Hamilton.

Moran, William R. (1963). "Recordings and Lillian Nordica." In Glackens, Ira, *Yankee Diva: Lillian Nordica and the Golden Days of Opera*. N.Y.: Coleridge Press.

Moran, William R. (1965). "The Legacy of Gianni Bettini." Ipswich: *The Record Collector*, Vol. 16, Nos. 7 & 8.

Moran, William R. (1977). "Melba's Farewell to Covent Garden." N.Y.: *High Fidelity* (July).

Moran, William R. (1982). "The Musical Triumphs of Nellie Melba." In *Melba: The American Recordings, 1907-1916*. Sydney: The Australian Broadcasting Commission and RCA (Australia), booklet to accompany RCA Record Album VRL5 0365.

Murdoch, William (1931). "Melba, 1861-1931." London: *Monthly Musical Record* (1 April).

Murphy, Agnes G. (1909). *Melba: A Biography*. London: Chatto & Windus; N.Y.: Doubleday, Page & Co. (Reprinted, N.Y.: AMS Press (1974).

Newton, Ivor (1966). *At the Piano: Ivor Newton: The World of an Accompanist*. London: Hamish Hamilton.

Nichols, Beverley (1926). *25; Being a Young Man's Candid Recollections of His Elders and Betters*. London: Jonathan Cape.

Nichols, Beverley (1927). *Are They the Same at Home?* London: Jonathan Cape.

Nichols, Beverley (1932). *Evensong. A Novel.* London: Jonathan Cape.; N.Y.: Doubleday, Doran & Company.

Nichols, Beverley (1949). *All I Could Never Be.* London: Jonathan Cape.

Nichols, Beverley (1958). *The Sweet and the Twenties.* London: Weidenfeld & Nicolson.

Nichols, Beverley (1972). *Father Figure.* London: William Heinemann.

Norton, John (1903). "An Open Letter to Mme. Melba." Melbourne: *Truth* (28 March).

O'Donnell, Josephine (1936). *Among the Covent Garden Stars.* London: Stanley Paul & Co.

Orchard, W. Arundel (1943). *The Distant View.* Sydney: The Currawong Publishing Company.

Pearl, Cyril (1958). *Wild Men of Sydney.* London: W. H. Allen & Co.

Pleasants, Henry (1966). *The Great Singers from the Dawn of Opera to Our Own Time.* N.Y.: Simon and Schuster.

Ponder, Winifred (1928). *Clara Butt: Her Life-Story.* London: George C. Harrap & Co. (The original edition was recalled, and pages 138 & 139, with the "Sing 'em muck!" story were replaced.)

Porter, Andrew (1978). "Melba: The "Star-like Brilliance" of Dame Nellie Melba Is Vividly Preserved in EMI's Five Disc Collection of the Soprano's London Recordings." N.Y.: *High Fidelity* (January).

Ronald, Landon (1922). *Variations on a Personal Theme.* London: Hodder and Stoughton.

Ronald, Landon (No date, but 1931). *Myself and Others: Written Lest I Forget.* London: Samson Low, Marston & Co.

Rosenthal, Harold (1958). *Two Centuries of Opera at Covent Garden.* London: Putnam.

Russell, Donna Shinn (1964). "The Meanest Woman in the World." N.Y.: *Opera News,* Vol. 28, No. 24 (11 January).

Russell, Frank A. (1924). "Melba Looks Back on Magic Moments in Her Great Career." Melbourne: *The Herald* (13 October).

Russell, Henry (1926). *The Passing Show.* London: Thornton Butterworth.

Salès, Jules (1971). *Théâtre Royal de la Monnaie, 1856-1970.* Nivelles: Editions Havaux.

Scholes, Percy A. (1947). "The Mirror of Music, 1844-1944." London: Novello & Co. and Oxford University Press. (Extract from the pages of *The Musical Times* for September 1928.)

Seltsam, William H. (1947). *Metropolitan Opera Annals: A Chronicle of Artists and Performances.* N.Y.: The H. W. Wilson Company.

Shaw, Bernard (1932). *Music in London, 1890-94.* London: Constable and Co. (Vols. 2 and 3).

Shawe-Taylor, Desmond (1955). "Nellie Melba (No. 2 in "A Gallery of Great Singers")." London: *Opera,* Vol. 6, No. 2 (February).

Sheean, Vincent (1956). *Oscar Hammerstein I: The Life and Exploits of an Impresario.* N.Y.: Simon and Schuster.

Sherman, Paul (1976). *Melba.* (Contemporary Australian Plays: 6). St. Lucia, Queensland: University of Queensland Press. (A play with four brief sequences from Melba's early life, followed by scenes set at Melba's home,

Coombe Cottage, Lilydale, Victoria in 1928, and in Melba's dressing room at His Majesty's Theater, Melbourne, during Melba's last performance. Characters, aside from Melba, are Beverley Nichols, Helen Daniel [Elena Danieli] and Stella Power, two of Melba's protégées. While not intended as "history," the work is generally accurate.)

"Signor Pietro Cecchi" (1889). Melbourne: *Table Talk*, 6 December.

Standing, Percy Cross (1899). "Madame Melba." London: *Strand Magazine* (January).

Stratton, John (1962). "The Mapleson Cylinders." Ipswich: *The Record Collector*, Vol. 14, Nos. 3 & 4.

Stratton, John (1968). "The Mapleson Cylinder of 'A ce mot' from Les Huguenots." London: *Recorded Sound*, No. 31 (July).

Strong, L.A.G. (1941). *John McCormack: The Story of a Singer*. London & N.Y.: The Macmillan Co.

Tait, Viola (1971). *A Family of Brothers: The Taits and J. C. Williamson; A Theater History*. Melbourne: William Heinemann Australia Pty.

Thompson, John (1962). *On the Lips of Living Men*. Melbourne: Lansdowne Press.

Wagnalls, Mabel (1924). *Opera and Its Stars*. N.Y.: Funk & Wagnalls Inc.

Wagner, Charles L. (1940). *Seeing Stars*. N.Y.: G. P. Putnam's Sons. (Reprint edition, N.Y.: Arno Press, 1977.)

Walsh, T. J. (1975). *Monte Carlo Opera, 1879-1909*. Dublin: Gill and Macmillan.

Waters, Thorold (1951). *Much besides Music*. Melbourne: Georgian House, Pty.

Wayner, Robert (1981). *What Did They Sing at the Met?* N.Y.: Wayner Publications (3d edition).

Wechsberg, Joseph (1961). *Red Plush and Black Velvet: The Story of Dame Nellie Melba and Her Times*. Boston: Little, Brown & Co.; London: Weidenfeld and Nicholson (1962).

Wolff, Stéphane (1962). "L'Opéra au Palais Garnier (1875-1962): Les Oeuvres; Les Interprètes." Paris: *L'Entr'acte*.

Wood, Henry J. (1938). *My Life of Music*. London: Victor Gollancz.

INDEX

About the Compiler

William R. Moran is Vice President of Exploration for Molycorp, a subsidiary of the Union Oil Company of California, and founder and Honorary Curator of the Stanford Archive of Recorded Sound. He has written *Geraldine Farrar, The Recordings of Lillian Nordica*, and many articles, which have appeared in *The Record Collector, Recorded Sound, Record News, High Fidelity*, and other journals. He is the co-compiler with Ted Fagan of *The Encyclopedic Discography of Victor Recordings* (Greenwood Press, 1983).